Unfailing Patience and Sound Teaching

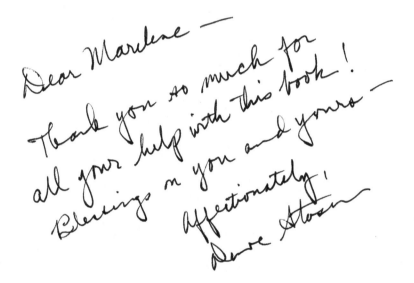

Dear Marlene —
Thank you so much for
all your help with this book!
Blessings on you and yours —
Affectionately!
Dave Stosur

Unfailing Patience and Sound Teaching

Reflections on Episcopal Ministry

In honor of Rembert G. Weakland, O.S.B.

Edited by David A. Stosur

LITURGICAL PRESS
Collegeville, Minnesota

www.litpress.org

Cover design by David Manahan, O.S.B. Photo by James D. Pearson of bronze sculpture of Rembert Weakland, O.S.B., by the Koh-Varilla Guild.

1	2	3	4	5	6	7	8	9

Library of Congress Cataloging-in-Publication Data

Unfailing patience and sound teaching : reflections on episcopal ministry in honor of Rembert G. Weakland, O.S.B. / edited by David A. Stosur.
    p. cm.
  Includes bibliographical references.
  ISBN 0-8146-2798-6 (pbk. : alk. paper)
  1. Catholic Church—Bishops. 2. Episcopacy. I. Weakland, Rembert. II. Stosur, David A., 1960– II. Title.
BX1905.U54 2003
262'.122—dc21
                           2003011684

Contents

Part Two

THE BISHOP AS SUBJECT AND AGENT OF DIALOGUE

Part Three

EPISCOPACY AND CONTEMPORARY CULTURE

Foreword

First of all, the bigger picture.

It was the glory of the Council of Trent (1545–1563 C.E.) to have finally addressed the serious need for reform in the medieval Church, head and members, by first courageously reforming their own lives and ministries as bishops. The more familiar one becomes with the patient determination that the Fathers of that council brought to their task at a moment of disastrous schism in the life of the Church, the more clearly their success shines forth across the pages of history and the centuries of time. Charles Borromeo of Milan and Francis de Sales of Geneva are stellar examples of that reform in action.

Personal residence of the bishop in his own diocese and tireless dedication to the work of preaching the gospel, celebrating the sacraments, and catechizing became the marks of that postconciliar Church for three hundred years. Moreover, those who gathered in the little diocesan see of Trent in the Italian Dolomites, and then in the city of Bologna when threat of the plague forced the council's relocation, were remarkably wise. They refused to resolve theological issues which had been debated throughout the Middle Ages by eminent and saintly theologians across the entire spectrum of knowledge and which were viewed as not "Church dividing" at any level.[1]

The deliberations of the First Vatican Council (1869 C.E.) addressed the role and responsibilities of the papacy in an age of absolute statism. It was a time when bishops throughout all parts of Europe were faced with serious interference in their pastoral work by strong national

1. Recent studies of great insight and value would include such works as Robert Birely, *The Refashioning of Catholicism 1450–1700* (Washington: Catholic University of America Press, 1999).

efforts toward civil unification and Enlightenment autonomy. Invoking the authority of the bishop of Rome gave local bishops the support needed to pursue their ministry amid the shambles of countless regional revolts and anti-monarchical upheavals.[2]

That council's consideration of pastoral authority remained unfinished, as we know, because of the outbreak of the Franco-Prussian War and the subsequent invasion of Rome by the troops of Garibaldi. Thus it was a reflection and a teaching left incomplete, because the intended corresponding statement on the role of the bishop never had the opportunity to reach the floor of the council in the Basilica of St. Peter.

For a century, then, the Church was forced to limp along, as it were, without the needed support and assistance for the bishop's work in a very different kind of world from that of Trent. The exercise of the papacy grew in power and strength, and Catholic bishops, ever loyal to both Church and their civil homeland, particularly in the dioceses of the United States, invoked the piety and image of a common Holy Father in an effort to unify the vastly different ethnic populations that flooded Catholic parishes and dioceses everywhere during the latter nineteenth and early twentieth centuries.

It was the teachings of the Second Vatican Council (1962–1965 C.E.) that were finally able to articulate the fuller picture and to produce a vast vision of the role of the Church, again liturgically reformed and reinvigorated, sent to serve and transform the modern world. Central to that vision were the council's variously repeated teachings regarding the ministry of the local bishop, vicar of Christ, teacher of faith, and sign and means of communion with Peter and all other members of the episcopal college scattered across the world. It was truly a global Church come into being, at least in hope, united through the ministry of bishops.

Although deeply involved in my own graduate studies in Scripture during the first three sessions of the Second Vatican Council in Rome, I managed to exercise a bit of devious creativity, and thus found myself inside the Basilica of St. Peter on that historic opening day of the council. In that way I became a personal witness to the famous "aggiornamento" speech of Pope John XXIII and took the solemn oath administered that morning by the Holy Father to be faithful to all the decrees of the council, whatever they might be as the work unfolded.

---

2. Jeffrey von Arx, ed., *Varieties of Ultramontanism* (Washington: Catholic University of America Press, 1998).

Though I never attended another session, the memory has remained unbelievably vivid over all these years.

Twelve years after returning to the Archdiocese of Milwaukee to teach Scripture in the local Seminary of Saint Francis (de Sales), I joined my fellow priests and laity of southeastern Wisconsin in welcoming the then abbot primate Rembert G. Weakland, O.S.B., as the ninth archbishop of Milwaukee. On November 8, 1977, he began his service of leadership to a vital local church with a long and distinguished reputation for ethnic diversity, a clear sense of support for Catholic parochial education, and a history of outstanding individual proponents for the Church's social teaching.

To this local church Archbishop Weakland brought his monastic commitment to liturgy and learning, as well as his vast experience of the worldwide Church as a result of his ten years of abbatial visitations to every corner of every continent of the world—wherever Benedictine communities flourished or struggled to implant the faith in a hundred different languages and cultures.

Most of all, Archbishop Weakland brought a clear and refined sense of the gospel's call to be a bishop for the Church in this concrete world called "modern." Embodying the vision of the Second Vatican Council's *Gaudium et Spes* in a remarkable way, he attempted to open church doors to the larger civic community and to forge strong ecumenical and interfaith bonds of faith and action with other religious traditions, and thus both to serve and to transform the larger community. He did so without compromising the deepest beliefs of the Catholic tradition.

For almost a quarter of a century Archbishop Weakland has been a keen analyst of contemporary American culture, engaging that reality with the regard born of respect for human dignity and the courage of his convictions rooted in a solid Catholic faith. Confreres and critics alike have found him to be clear in his thinking and persevering in his commitment to be a wise and courageous priest of his time. He has always been a voice to be listened to, a person to be respected and a mind to be reckoned with. Ever attempting to embody his abbatial and episcopal motto, "Aequalis omnibus caritas," which he borrowed from the Rule of St. Benedict, he was confronted at times with some harsh and bitter foes who saw the world differently. Coming to terms with his own human limitations enabled him to respect the limitations of others.

The divisions within the Church at the beginning of the twenty-first century may well be those generated by diverse conciliar loyalties, namely, between those committed to the image of the Church as inwardly united and transformed by grace into the Church of *Lumen Gentium* and those with a strong sense of the Church's call to embrace the joys and sorrows of the larger world as described in *Gaudium et Spes*. When the Church is viewed as "either/or," conflicts and tensions inevitably arise. Perhaps only someone with a strong sense of the ancient Benedictine tradition, with its commitment to the glory of the Catholic liturgy and the transformation of society, will be able finally to reunite these two strands in the life of the Church today.

Even though the perspective may be perhaps too close for objectivity, there have been well-known Catholic historians in recent years who have opined that the name of Weakland of Milwaukee will come to have the same resonance, impact, and historical significance in the Catholic Church's dialogue with American culture at the end of the twentieth century as did that of Archbishop John Ireland of St. Paul a century earlier. We leave that judgment to a further age and greater wisdom. We do salute Archbishop Weakland and his ministry for his desire to engage today's world with the full vision and hope of the Second Vatican Council.

The following essays, each written by a significant bishop or theologian of our Church, attempt to explore what it means to be a bishop implementing that council at the beginning of the twenty-first century.

Those of us who have worked closely with Archbishop Weakland over the past twenty-five years have come to respect, treasure, and love him greatly. We are profoundly grateful to the Church's leaders and scholars who have contributed the fruits of their study to this volume. Inspired by his own love of learning, we pay him tribute, and on this, his seventy-fifth birthday, we dedicate this festschrift to him as the person and figure he has become for us, truly a teacher of faith and a herald of hope.

Richard J. Sklba

Auxiliary Bishop of Milwaukee

April 2, 2002

Preface

Unfailing Patience and Sound Teaching is the main title of this festschrift in honor of Rembert G. Weakland, O.S.B., commemorating in the year 2002 his seventy-fifth birthday (on April 2) and the twenty-fifth anniversary as Archbishop of Milwaukee (appointed September 17, 1977, and installed November 8, 1977). The title is taken from the injunction given to the newly ordained bishop by the principal consecrator-bishop during the rite of episcopal ordination, at the presentation of the Book of the Gospels: "Receive the Gospel and preach the word of God with unfailing patience and sound teaching."[1] By all accounts, from organizing listening sessions for women to being a leading voice among bishops on issues such as economic justice and liturgical reform, from consulting with theologians to representing the Roman Catholic Church in ecumenical and interfaith dialogue, from asserting the canonical rights of the local ordinary to delivering a public apology that modeled true penitence, Rembert Weakland has lived up to this injunction.

The initial idea to honor Archbishop Weakland with a festschrift emerged during the 2000–2001 academic year from discussions among Richard J. Sklba, Auxiliary Bishop of Milwaukee; Michael G. Witczak, currently rector, at the time vice rector of Saint Francis Seminary, and other members of the seminary faculty; and the "transition team," led by Barbara Anne Cusack, J.C.D., chancellor of the Archdiocese of Milwaukee, which prepared for Archbishop Weakland's retirement and the arrival of his eventual successor, Archbishop Timothy M. Dolan. Bishop

---

1. "Ordination of a Bishop," no. 29, in *The Rites of the Catholic Church as Revised by the Second Vatican Ecumenical Council*, vol. 2, Study ed. (Collegeville, Minn.: The Liturgical Press, 1991).

Sklba first proposed the theme of the contemporary episcopate, an idea that proved all the more timely when the same topic was soon after announced for the Synod of Bishops to be held in Rome in October 2001. Contributors to this festschrift were asked to respond, from the perspective of their particular theological expertise and experience, to the following question: *What does episcopal ministry that embraces the tenets of the Second Vatican Council look like at the beginning of the twenty-first century?*

In Part One of this collection, "Episcopal Office: Sanctifying, Teaching, Governing," five essays investigate the nature of the episcopacy from the standpoint of one (or more) of the threefold functions named in LG 20. David M. Coffey explores what he calls the "unities" of the episcopal office. He argues that the ministry of unity belonging to the bishop—a ministry that serves the unity of the Church—entails a relational understanding of the episcopal functions not only among themselves but also with other ecclesial elements or "unities," namely, the college of bishops, the presbyterium, and the priesthood of the Church. Susan Wood develops a theology of the episcopacy by mining the Church's liturgical texts and symbols. She finds that the mutuality of relationship between bishop and local church reflected in the liturgical assembly provides a model and vision for the Church's extra-liturgical life. Walter Burghardt's "The Bishop as Preacher" examines how the official Church's perception of the preaching role of the bishop has been realized in the preaching of Archbishop Weakland, and offers from his critique of both some characteristics of effective preaching. Francis Sullivan addresses questions about the episcopal teaching office: What is the nature of this teaching authority, and how can a person be understood to receive it through ordination? The first part concludes with a short reflection by Archbishop Daniel Kucera on an aspect of episcopal governing not often considered, but apropos to the honoree of this volume, namely, how the role of monastic abbot can speak to the role of bishop.

Part Two, "The Bishop as Subject and Agent of Dialogue," treats the concept of episcopacy as an issue in ecumenical understanding and the bishop's role in advancing mutual understanding between various groups. John Erickson presents an Orthodox perspective on the generally positive place of episcopacy within the current Orthodox-Catholic dialogical quest for unity, noting that the real sticking point is the issue of one particular bishop—the bishop of Rome. Lutheran scholar Michael Root examines the ecumenically ambiguous concept of the

Roman Catholic episcopate that has emerged since the Second Vatican Council. Rabbi Michael Signer pays tribute to episcopal models of dialogue with the Jewish community, such as Archbishop Weakland, the late Joseph Cardinal Bernardin, and Pope John Paul II. Oscar Lipscomb, Archbishop of Mobile, discusses the bishop's ministry of unifying from within the Roman Catholic community through a reflection on his experience with the Catholic Common Ground Initiative.

The third and final part of this collection offers several perspectives on "Episcopacy and Contemporary Culture." Bradford Hinze looks at some recent efforts of bishops to consult more widely with various groups as an emerging model of teaching with authority. Dianne Bergant reflects more specifically on the ever expanding and increasingly significant role of women in influencing episcopal leadership. Kenneth Himes looks back on the U.S. bishops' pastoral letters—one on the economy (developed by a committee headed by Archbishop Weakland) and the other on peace and justice—for the wisdom offered by this episcopal body as a contribution to the Church's social teaching in the contemporary national and global context.[2] The bishop's role in proclaiming the specifically biblical concept of justice is examined by John Donahue. And Edward Foley argues that aesthetic sensitivity, while not typically considered high on the list of qualities associated with episcopal leadership, is actually a sine qua non of theologically authentic episcopacy in the current cultural context.

To say that the world and the Roman Catholic Church have changed significantly since this particular collection of essays was conceived early in the year 2001 and the contributions to it were first received in the waning months of 2001 would qualify as a serious understatement. Only by way of late revision of original contributions could the authors even consider making reference to the earth-shattering events of September 11, 2001, or to the Church-shattering crisis of clergy sexual abuse of minors that broke into the public spotlight in the early part of 2002. A few contributors chose to make some slight revisions to the chapters they had initially submitted; substantial incorporation of these "current events," however, would have demanded the kind of reflection and revision that in truth would have required delaying for some time the publication of these already

2. Himes's essay is a slightly modified version of his presidential address delivered to the fifty-sixth annual convention of the Catholic Theological Society of America on June 10, 2001, in Milwaukee. Coincidentally, Archbishop Weakland was inducted into the CTSA at that convention.

well-wrought essays on the episcopate. The task of suggesting some lines of thought for ongoing reflection on the episcopate in light of these issues is taken up briefly in my Epilogue.

A number of individuals, in addition to the contributors to this volume, deserve special acknowledgment for the part they have played in making this festschrift a reality. Rev. Andrew Nelson, then rector of Saint Francis Seminary, was most generous in granting the sabbatical for the last half of 2001 that allowed me to undertake the role of editor. The editorial duties were made all the easier thanks to the other members of the "Festschrift Committee"—Bishop Sklba, Dr. Cusack, and Rev. Richard Schlenker—who have enlivened and sustained the project throughout, from initial discussions about possible contributors to assistance in proofreading manuscripts. Mark Twomey, editorial director at Liturgical Press, offered assistance and guidance on a variety of issues as the concept became a manuscript. I wish to thank Rev. Richard Sparks, editor of the *Proceedings of the Catholic Theological Society of America,* for permission to reprint Kenneth Himes's presidential address to the CTSA as Chapter Twelve of this collection. I am deeply grateful to Ms. Mary Carian, public services librarian at Saint Francis Seminary's Salzmann Library, who provided invaluable resource assistance to me as well as to those contributors who referenced Archbishop Weakland's writings and speeches in their essays. Finally, a word of thanks to Ms. Marelene Groff of Office Services at the seminary, who performed so many of the copying and mailing duties for this project.

David A. Stosur

November 8, 2002, Twenty-fifth anniversary of
the installation of Rembert G. Weakland
as Archbishop of Milwaukee

Contributors

Dianne Bergant, C.S.A., Ph.D., is Professor of Old Testament Studies at Catholic Theological Union, Chicago. Her publications include *Israel's Wisdom Literature: A Liberation-Critical Reading* (1997) and *Preaching the New Lectionary* (Years B, C, and A; 3 vols., 1999–2001). She authors "The Word" column in *America* magazine.

Walter J. Burghardt, S.J., S.T.D., is founder and director of Preaching the Just Word, a national program sponsored by the Woodstock Theological Center to assist priests and other ministers of the gospel to be more effective in preaching social justice. He is Professor Emeritus of Theology at The Catholic University of America, former editor-in-chief of *Theological Studies,* and former president of the Catholic Theological Society of America, the Mariological Society of America, the American Theological Society, and the North American Academy of Ecumenists. He is co-editor of *Ancient Christian Writers* and *The Living Pulpit* and author of nineteen books, including *Let Justice Roll Down Like Waters: Biblical Justice Homilies Throughout the Year* (1998) and *Long Have I Loved You: A Theologian Reflects on His Church* (2000).

David Michael Coffey, S.T.D., a priest of the Archdiocese of Sydney, holds the William J. Kelly Chair in Catholic Theology at Marquette University. He has written extensively on grace, Christology, pneumatology, and the Trinity. His latest book is *The Sacrament of Reconciliation* in the *Lex Orandi* series (2001). The present essay complements his 1997 article in *Theological Studies* on the common and the ordained priesthood.

John R. Donahue, S.J., is the Raymond E. Brown Distinguished Professor of New Testament Studies at St. Mary's Seminary and University,

Baltimore. Among his recent publications are *The Gospel of Mark* (with Daniel Harrington) in the *Sacra Pagina* series (2002) and *Hearing the Word of God: Reflections on the Sunday Readings, Year B* (2002).

John H. Erickson is Peter N. Gramowich Professor of Church History and Associate Dean for Academic Affairs at St. Vladimir's Orthodox Theological Seminary, Crestwood, New York. In addition to publishing many articles in the fields of canon law, Church history, and ecumenics, he is the author of *The Challenge of Our Past: Studies in Orthodox Canon Law and Church History* (1991) and *Orthodox Christians in America* (1999), and co-editor (with John Borelli) of *The Quest For Unity: Orthodox and Catholics in Dialogue, 1965–1995* (1996). He has had the privilege of serving on the U.S. Orthodox-Catholic Theological Consultation for nearly twenty-five years, thirteen of them under the inspired leadership of Archbishop Weakland.

Edward Foley, Capuchin, M.M., PH.D., is Professor of Liturgy and Music and Chair of the Department of Word and Worship at Catholic Theological Union, Chicago. His numerous publications include *Preaching Basics* (1998), *Mighty Stories, Dangerous Rituals,* co-authored with Herbert Anderson (1997), *Ritual Music* (1995), *Developmental Disabilities and Sacramental Access* (1994), and the well-known *From Age to Age* (1991). *Worship Music: A Concise Dictionary,* for which he serves as general editor, is his most recent book (2000). He is past president of the North American Academy of Liturgy and a founder and originating member of the executive committee of the Catholic Academy of Liturgy.

Bradford E. Hinze, PH.D., is Associate Professor of Theology at Marquette University, specializing in fundamental and systematic theology with a concentration in revelation, ecclesiology, and theological hermeneutics. He is the author of *Narrating History, Developing Doctrine: Friedrich Schleiermacher and Johann Sebastian Drey* (1993), has co-edited *Advents of the Spirit: An Introduction to the Current Study of Pneumatology* (2001), and is the editor of *Spirit, Church, and World* (College Theology Society Annual Volume 2003). He is currently writing on the promise and perils of dialogue in the Church.

Kenneth R. Himes, O.F.M., PH.D., is Professor of Moral Theology at Washington Theological Union. A regular contributor to both general and academic periodicals, he co-edited a popular textbook, *Introduction to Christian Ethics* (1989), and co-authored *Fullness of Faith: The*

Public Significance of Theology (1993), which won first prize among theology books from the Catholic Press Association. His most recent book is *Responses to 101 Questions on Catholic Social Teaching* (2001). Formerly president of the Catholic Theological Society of America and editor of *New Theology Review,* he serves as a consultant to the Office of Social Development and World Peace at the United States Conference of Catholic Bishops.

Most Reverend Daniel W. Kucera, O.S.B., PH.D., is Archbishop Emeritus of Dubuque, Iowa.

Most Reverend Oscar H. Lipscomb, PH.D., is Archbishop of Mobile, Alabama, and Chair of the Catholic Common Ground Initiative.

Michael Root, PH.D., is Edward C. Fendt Professor of Systematic Theology at Trinity Lutheran Seminary in Columbus, Ohio. Formerly the Director of the Institute for Ecumenical Research in Strasbourg, France, he serves as consultant to the Lutheran-Catholic Coordinating Committee (USA), Faith and Order Commission Observer of the Anglican-Roman Catholic International Commission, ecumenical member of the Inter-Anglican Theological and Doctrinal Commission, consultant to the Anglican-Lutheran International Commission, and member of the editorial council for *Dialogue: A Journal of Theology.*

Michael A. Signer, PH.D., is Abrams Professor of Jewish Thought and Culture in the Department of Theology and a Senior Fellow of the Medieval Institute at the University of Notre Dame. He is Director of the Notre Dame Holocaust Project and co-chair of the Joint Commission on Interreligious Affairs of the Reform movement. Rabbi Signer is the author and editor of five books on topics that range from medieval Latin biblical commentaries to contemporary Jewish-Christian relations, such as *Humanity at the Limit: The Impact of the Holocaust Experience on Jews and Christians* (2000), *Memory and History in Judaism and Christianity* (2000), and *Jews and Christians in Twelfth-Century Europe* (2001). He has written articles for the *Oxford Dictionary of Judaism,* the *Encyclopedia of Medieval France,* and the *Encyclopedia of St. Augustine.* He is one of the four authors of *Daberu Emet: A Jewish Statement on Christians and Christianity.*

David A. Stosur, PH.D., is Academic Dean and Associate Professor of Liturgical Studies at Saint Francis Seminary, Milwaukee. His recent publications include articles in *Worship, Liturgical Ministry,* and *TLC:*

Today's Liturgy with Children. He is currently writing on liturgy and liturgical theology from the perspective of contemporary narrative theory.

Francis A. Sullivan, S.J., S.T.D., is Professor Emeritus of Theology at the Pontifical Gregorian University and is currently Adjunct Professor of Ecclesiology at Boston College. His recent publications are *Creative Fidelity: Weighing and Interpreting Documents of the Magisterium* (1996) and *From Apostles to Bishops: The Development of the Episcopacy in the Early Church* (2001).

Susan K. Wood, S.C.L., Ph.D., is Professor of Theology at Saint John's University, Collegeville, Minnesota. She is the author of *Spiritual Exegesis and the Church in the Theology of Henri de Lubac* (1988) and *Sacramental Orders* in the *Lex Orandi* series (2000).

Abbreviations

AAS   *Acta Apostolicae Sedis*

CD   *Christus Dominus:* Decree on the Pastoral Office of Bishops in the Church

CDF   Congregation for the Doctrine of the Faith

CP   *The Challenge of Peace: God's Promise and Our Response*

CTSA   Catholic Theological Society of America

DS   H. Denzinger and A. Schönmetzer, *Enchiridion Symbolorum, definitionum et declarationum de rebus fidei et morum*

DV   *Dei Verbum:* Dogmatic Constitution on Divine Revelation

EJA   *Economic Justice for All: Pastoral Letter on Catholic Social Teaching and the U.S. Economy*

GS   *Gaudium et Spes:* Pastoral Constitution on the Church in the Modern World

IGMR   *Institutio Generalis Missalis Romani:* General Instruction of the Roman Missal

LG   *Lumen Gentium:* Dogmatic Constitution on the Church

NAB   New American Bible

NCCB   National Conference of Catholic Bishops

NRSV   The Holy Bible: New Revised Standard Version

OT   *Optatam Totius:* Decree on the Training of Priests

PO   *Presbyterorum Ordinis:* Decree on the Life and Ministry of Priests

RSV   The Holy Bible: Revised Standard Version

SC   *Sacrosanctum Concilium:* Constitution on the Sacred Liturgy

SPCK   Society for the Promotion of Christian Knowledge

UR   *Unitatis Redintegratio:* Decree on Ecumenism

USCC   United States Catholic Conference

WCC   World Council of Churches

Part One

EPISCOPAL OFFICE: SANCTIFYING, TEACHING, GOVERNING

Chapter One

The "Unities" of the Episcopal Office

David M. Coffey

It is highly fitting that the twenty-five-year episcopate of the Most Reverend Rembert G. Weakland, O.S.B., be celebrated by a festschrift devoted to the many pastoral initiatives with which he has become associated over the years. I feel greatly honored at being invited to reflect, in the light of the Second Vatican Council, on that which unifies these initiatives, namely, the episcopal office itself. Throughout his ministry Archbishop Weakland has striven to realize the council's vision of this office as outlined in its Decree on the Pastoral Office of Bishops in the Church *(Christus Dominus)*. Though the closing days of his ministry were somewhat darkened by controversy and recrimination, they by no means extinguished the splendor of the preceding quarter century. On the contrary, they gave him the opportunity to provide for his people "an example of sanctity in charity, humility and simplicity of life," as enjoined by that decree (no. 15). These pages are offered to him in deep appreciation and gratitude for his long and outstanding service to both Milwaukee and the wider Church.

My essay has, I admit, a rather strange-sounding title. Normally the word "unity" is used in the singular. Unity expresses intelligibility: a thing is understood only when its diverse elements are grasped in terms of a deeper and organizing unity. An example from the patristic Church would be the efforts undertaken to understand Christ after Chalcedon. The theologians of that era strove to grasp him in terms of their own philosophical and religious culture. Instinctively they knew that while confessing the two natures, they needed to go beyond them and find that which unified them, namely, the relationship existing between them, and thus there emerged the theology of enhypostasia, the "in-being" of the human nature in the divine nature personified in the Word. Similarly, when we turn to the office of bishop and try to understand exactly what it is, we immediately encounter diversity. Vatican II's Dogmatic Constitution on the Church *(Lumen Gentium)* speaks of it, in no. 20, in terms of the three functions by means of which it presents itself: sanctification (here called ministry of worship), teaching, and governing. To understand episcopal office, we need to comprehend these functions in terms of what unifies and organizes them. However, when we have done this, we will still not have fully understood episcopal office, for over and above being unified in itself, it has relations to "other" entities that enter into its very constitution (and for that reason cannot be said to lie entirely outside its essence or to be truly "other" than it).

The reason for this remarkable state of affairs is that the episcopate is an element within an organism, namely, the Church. In its own way, therefore, it helps build up the unity of the Church. *Lumen Gentium* 23 presents it precisely as a ministry of unity. "Individual bishops," it says, "are the visible principle and foundation of unity in their particular churches," and it goes on to detail ways in which, as members of the college of bishops, they can foster the unity of the Church as a whole. This essay will show that the episcopate does this by contributing to unities (note the plural) with other ecclesial elements, unities that then feed directly into the unity of the Church. Hence the title of this essay. Its thesis is that episcopal office, unified to some extent already in terms of its functions, enters by its nature into certain higher ecclesial unities contributing to the overall unity of the Church. Only in the light of all these unities is episcopal office itself adequately understood. What are the intermediate unities referred to here? There are, I submit, three: the college of bishops, the presbyterium (the body of the priests of the local church), and what I have called elsewhere "the priesthood of the Church."[1]

Our principal source for this study will be *Lumen Gentium* (hereafter LG), and our task will be twofold: first, to unify the three particular functions of the bishop, namely, sanctifying, teaching, and governing; and second, to investigate the other ecclesial unities named above, in which he participates by his office. All are comprehended within the episcopal office conferred by the sacrament of episcopal consecration.[2]

1. See David Coffey, "The Common and the Ordained Priesthood," *Theological Studies* 58 (1997) 209–236, at 230–234.

2. In this essay I shall speak of the "consecration" of a bishop rather than his "ordination," partly because "consecration" is the term used by both the Second Vatican

The Unity of the Three Episcopal Functions

In LG 20, Vatican II presents the office of bishop as one in itself and threefold in its characteristic functions. The unity of the role is expressed formally as a "ministry" *(ministerium)* and "office" *(munus)*, and is given material content by use of the word "shepherd" *(pastor)*. It must have been felt, however, that even "shepherd" was too vague, for it is immediately "explained" in terms of the three functions. Thus it is said that bishops are "shepherds in that they are teachers of doctrine, priests of sacred worship, and ministers of government"[3] in their respective churches. These functions, otherwise known as teaching, sanctifying, and governing, reflect and participate in the three functions of Christ as prophet, priest, and king. However, in regard to the bishop, the last named of these is accommodated to his ecclesiastical situation by being rendered "shepherd."[4] Evidently, then, "shepherd" bears at least two meanings—one at the level of unity (office) and another at the level of diversity (function). We will have more to say about this later.

What emerges as problematic in this is the unity of the bishop's office—not the *fact* of this unity, for that we can accept on the authority of the dogmatic constitution, but rather *how this unity is to be understood.* What we have in the reported statements above is not so much an explanation of the unity as a description of it. It remains in no way clear how the role of shepherd is explained in terms of such apparently disparate categories as teaching and sanctifying; and if the category of governing is more congenial to it, it is of no help that the term "shepherd" is repeated at the second level, that of diversity. What is needed is an exploration of the meaning of "shepherd" at the level of unity.

The issue of diversity is complicated by the fact that before the council it was customary to make a twofold distinction of episcopal office into the powers of orders and jurisdiction rather than the threefold distinction of sanctifying, governing, and teaching. And indeed, as Peter Drilling observes, at the council the introduction of the threefold

---

Council and the Code of Canon Law, and partly because by this it will be clear that I am referring to episcopal rather than presbyteral ordination.

3. My own literal translation of the words "pastores, ut doctrinae magistri, sacri cultus sacerdotes, gubernationis ministri." The translations from *Lumen Gentium* throughout this essay are my own unless I have stipulated otherwise. For the Latin text, see *Sacrosanctum Oecumenicum Concilium Vaticanum II: Constitutiones, Decreta, Declarationes* (Vatican City: Typis Polyglottis Vaticanis, 1966).

4. See LG 21.

distinction was initially resisted by the Dutch episcopate on precisely this ground.[5] In their submission they wrote:

> The threefold distinction of the office of Christ is a Protestant invention from the 19th century. It would be better if this distinction were reduced to a twofold distinction, namely, of prophet and priest, which is more traditional from a Catholic point of view and better suited to the classical distinction between the power of jurisdiction and the power of orders.[6]

Drilling further records that the nineteenth-century Roman school dealt with this problem by assigning teaching to either orders or jurisdiction or both, and was thus able to speak of two powers with three functions.[7] In essence this is still done today in some quarters. Thus Jean Marie Aubert maintains that jurisdiction consists of two powers: the power to teach revealed truth authoritatively and the pastoral power, derived from this, to govern the Church.[8] But, we may ask, is this an acceptable solution? In what follows we offer not only a critique of the adequacy of the twofold distinction of powers but our suggested solution to the problem of the unity of the episcopal office. The remainder of this section will then be devoted to establishing this solution and exploring its content.

In the concluding verses of St. Matthew's Gospel, Jesus says to the eleven disciples:

> All authority in heaven and on earth has been given to me. Go therefore and make disciples of all nations, baptizing them in the name of the Father and of the Son and of the Holy Spirit, teaching them to observe all that I have commanded you; and lo, I am with you always, to the close of the age (Matt 28:18-20, RSV).

The tasks that Jesus lays upon the disciples are: (1) to make further disciples, that is, to win people to faith in him through preaching; (2) to baptize the newly acquired disciples, thus admitting them to the Church and the blessings of the kingdom; and (3) to enjoin on them the obligation to observe his precepts, that is, to adopt a Christian way of life subject to their (the Eleven's) supervision. In theological terms,

---

5. See Peter Drilling, "The Priest, Prophet and King Trilogy: Elements of Its Meaning in *Lumen Gentium* and for Today," *Église et théologie* 19 (1998) 179–206, at 182.

6. *Acta Synodalia Sacrosancti Concilii Oecumenici Vaticani Secundi*, vol. 2, part 1 (Vatican City: Typis Polyglottis Vaticanis, 1971) 591 (my translation).

7. See Drilling, "The Priest, Prophet and King Trilogy," 194, note 42.

8. See J. M. Aubert, "Pouvoir," in *Catholicisme: hier, aujourd'hui, demain* 11 (Paris: Letouzey et Ané, 1988) 696–718, at 710.

he gives them the charge of exercising the threefold office of teaching, sanctifying, and governing. But note that the ground of this charge is Jesus' own supreme and single authority. This he delegates to them, and in this act it passes into the threefold form.

Two things follow immediately from this. First, in the Church not just teaching and governing but sanctifying as well is exercised with authority, authority communicated by Christ. Do not Catholics recognize this with the claim that the sacraments are celebrated *ex opere operato*, that is, not just by force of the recipient's faith but by the authority of Christ? Herein lies our criticism of the adequacy of the twofold distinction of orders and jurisdiction: in its framework the purview of jurisdiction, in the sense of authority, does not embrace orders.

The second point is that authority exists at three levels. The first is that of Christ, where even though it may be exercised in the forms of priest, prophet, and king, it exists prior to these as a property of his incarnate divine Person. The categories of priest, prophet, and king, then, are secondary and consequent, derived from an ontological reality that in Christ must be identified as the theandric authority of the incarnate Son of God, and in the case of the Eleven and of bishops, as the apostolic or episcopal charisms, respectively.[9] (In the interests of brevity, we need not dwell on the apostolic charism, as it suffices to stress that the bishops are the successors of the apostles. This said, we may pass directly from Christ to the bishops.) The second level at which authority exists, then, is that of the bishop, where it is a property of the episcopal charism received at his consecration. The third level is that of episcopal government as a reality distinct from teaching and sanctifying (though connected with them).

The necessity of this third level as a distinct category arises from the social nature of the human beings to whom the bishop preaches, a quality carried over into their life in the society that is the Church. Although Christianity, unlike ancient Israel and some Islamic states even today, does not require a way of life prescribed in every respect (which will inevitably merge religion and politics), it does constitute a distinct society or community in which it is necessary for the service of teaching and sanctifying to support these by certain rules and laws,

9. For the episcopal charism, see the 1971 Synod of Bishops, *The Ministerial Priesthood: Justice in the World* (Washington: USCC, 1972) 13. See also Coffey, "The Common and the Ordained Priesthood," 227–228, and Georges Chantraine, "Synodalité, expression du sacerdoce commun et du sacerdoce ministeriel?" *Nouvelle revue théologique* 113 (1991) 340–362, at 342.

the responsibility for the creation and supervision of which rests on the legitimate authority, the bishops or the episcopal college (of which we shall speak later). Hence the authority of level two is not simply duplicated at level three. At the second level it is a property of the undifferentiated episcopal charism; at the third it has to do with matters which are not directly covered by teaching and sanctifying but which are necessary for their service, and it comes to expression in canon law, its local derivatives, and the particular directives of bishops. At this level it is, to use Rahner's term, a *Restbegriff,* a "remainder concept," for dealing with those necessary matters left over from the other categories.[10]

What has been expounded here is confirmed by the statement of the 1971 Synod of Bishops that "when we speak of the priesthood of Christ, we should have before our eyes a unique, incomparable reality, which includes the prophetic and royal office of the Incarnate Word of God."[11] This may be regarded as an attempt to express the basic unity of Christ's threefold office that resides in the dignity and authority of the Word incarnate. Here it is called priesthood. More properly, it is authority. *Mutatis mutandis,* the same may be said of the single office and the three functions of the bishop. What the synod said in relation to priesthood—and note that I am now speaking of the bishop—can also be said in regard to prophethood and kingship. In other words, while the three are distinct at the level of function, any one of them can be selected for investment with a deeper, unifying meaning at the level of office. It seems to me that there is nothing absolute about this; it may be done equally with any of the three to give the desired emphasis. Each is simply redefined (somewhat) at the level of office. Thus in LG 25 the council said that "among the more important duties of bishops, that of preaching the gospel has pride of place [*eminet,* 'stands out']." Here prophethood is selected for particular elevation, and in the light of its newly conferred unitive power, administering the sacraments and rightly governing the community appear as other ways of preaching the gospel. The same exercise could be done with kingship. But, as I shall now argue, the authority of kingship—not kingship itself—is different. The difference resides in the fact that while priesthood, prophethood, and kingship are functions, the authority of

10. See Karl Rahner, "Concerning the Relationship Between Nature and Grace," *Theological Investigations,* vol. 1, trans. Cornelius Ernst (Baltimore: Helicon Press, 1961) 297–317, at 313.

11. *The Ministerial Priesthood,* 12.

kingship, in both Christ and, by participation, the bishop, is something more. In Christ it is a corollary of his dignity by virtue of the hypostatic union, and in the bishop it is a corollary of his sacramental participation in the authority of Christ. Hence, unlike the three functions, authority does not need to be redefined when transferred from function to office; it requires only a broadening of scope.

One thing that is clear from all this is that it is futile to seek the unity of the episcopal office at the level of function, as though some one of the three can be seen in an absolute way as the organizing principle of the other two.[12] Rather, when one is selected for this purpose—as it may—it is invested with a further, deeper meaning at the level of office, person, being. It is at this deeper level, not that of function, that unity is to be sought and found.

In an earlier publication I made the point that the priestly office, which is dependent on the episcopal office, is understood in terms of three points of reference, namely, christological, ecclesiological, and sociological.[13] (In this context, by "christological" is meant, not what pertains to Christ directly, but what pertains to the Church understood in relation to Christ. "Ecclesiological" means what pertains to the Church understood in terms proper to itself, terms of themselves expressive of its faith. And by "sociological" is meant what pertains to the Church but is expressed in secular terms, without thereby intending to reduce the Church to the secular level.) What is said here about the priesthood is not just true in regard to the episcopate also; it is true of the episcopate in the first instance, and is true of the priesthood only in the second instance and by derivation. According to these ways of understanding, episcopacy can then be said to be, respectively, the office of headship in the Church (that is, a participation in the headship of Christ), the office of official witness to Christ, and the

---

12. Which is precisely what Drilling does in "The Priest, Prophet and King Trilogy," 194, note 42, in interpreting the statement of LG 21: "But episcopal consecration, together with the office of sanctifying, also confers the offices of teaching and governing." To me it seems that the council, far from interpreting teaching and governing in terms of sanctifying, here awards pride of place to the latter only because it provides the statement's context, which is the conferral of a sacrament, episcopal consecration. But we have already seen that elsewhere, namely, in LG 25, where the context is that of teaching, it is to it that the constitution attributes preeminence. There is another reason as well. The constitution wants to isolate teaching and ruling from sanctifying because it is just of the first two that it wants to say that they "can be exercised only in hierarchical communion with the head and members of the college." I submit, however, that this is true of sanctifying, too, at least insofar as lawfulness is concerned, and perhaps even validity.

13. See Coffey, "The Common and the Ordained Priesthood," 223–225.

office of leadership in the community. These are different ways of saying the same thing viewed from different perspectives. We shall here concentrate on the ecclesiological understanding of episcopacy, because that is its direct and proper reference. We shall now compare the concept of authority, derived from St. Matthew's Gospel, with that of official witness, which is found in St. Luke's Gospel and the Acts of the Apostles.

The theme of apostolic witness is quite prominent in the Lukan writings (see Luke 24:46-49; Acts 1:8, 21-22; 3:15; 10:39-41; 13:31). The apostles were the close chosen companions of Jesus during his ministry and hearers of his preaching and teaching, and were commissioned by the risen Lord to be his Spirit-filled witnesses to the ends of the earth. This idea is echoed by *Christus Dominus* 11: "Bishops should devote themselves to their apostolic office as witnesses of Christ to all." They carry out this mandate in the power of the Holy Spirit by sanctifying, teaching, and shepherding the community. They are the office-bearers, on whom rests the responsibility for the community's welfare and increase.

In the article referred to, I pointed out that the designation "official witness" belongs to the ordained person as such, irrespective of whether he be a bishop, priest, or deacon.[14] This is because the commission of the Twelve took place prior to these differentiations. While supremely true of the bishop, "official witness" needs to be further specified in his regard so that he can be distinguished from the priest and the deacon. But it does not easily lend itself to such specification. However, the Matthean notion of authority does so lend itself. All three office-bearers have authority, but bishops, as "transmitters of the apostolic line,"[15] represent its highest concentration and source (for the others, whom they ordain and who function under them). Priests share their authority, but to a lesser degree. Deacons, too, have authority, but it is of a different order. *Lumen Gentium* tells us that the ordained priesthood is shared by the bishop and the priest, but not by deacons, since the latter are ordained "not unto the priesthood but unto the ministry."[16] This means that the authority they have as office-bearers is of a different kind, and not just of degree, from that of bishops and priests. Finally, laypersons do not have authority over others in the Church, except insofar as it is delegated to them by the

14. Ibid., 226.
15. LG 20, quoting Tertullian.
16. LG 29, quoting the *Constitutions of the Egyptian Church*.

bishop. This is so even though they share after their own manner in the kingship of Christ, as *Lumen Gentium* teaches.[17]

Thus the word "shepherd," which expresses authority, has three different applications, all of them found in *Lumen Gentium*. The first is that by which Christ is said to be the Good Shepherd, in nos. 27 and 28. Here, to be Good Shepherd means to have charge of the flock that is the Church, a charge received directly from the Father. It is an aspect of the dignity of Christ's divine Person as redeemer and savior. The second application is that by which the bishops (and the apostles before them) are the inheritors of this charge. The Incarnation is not repeated in their persons; they are sons (lowercase) of God, "sons in the Son" as is any baptized person, but by the episcopal charism they participate in the unique authority of the only-begotten Son incarnate over the Church. By virtue of this, they are empowered to teach, sanctify, and govern their respective churches. The third is that by which the bishop is said to govern his church, as distinct from teaching and sanctifying it.

Each of these meanings represents a different instantiation of the authority of Christ. None of them is to be thought of simply juridically. They are more adequately characterized as sacramental (though the juridical dimension becomes prominent in the third). In the person of the bishop, Christ the Good Shepherd is made sacramentally present and active. Hence the Eastern Orthodox practice of honoring the bishop as "the living icon of Christ" (though all the baptized are awarded this title also and possess it in their own way). LG 21 teaches that "in the bishops, assisted by the priests, the Lord Jesus Christ, supreme high priest, is present in the midst of believers." The 1971 Synod of Bishops expressed a similar idea, though it was speaking directly of the priest rather than the bishop. However, the idea applies more properly to the bishop. In its activity, they said, the priestly charism "makes Christ, the head of the community, present in the exercise of his work of redeeming mankind and glorifying God perfectly."[18] This statement, then, better characterizes the bishop; and we are fully justified in substituting for the christological reference of "head" (of the body) the ecclesiological one of "shepherd" (of the flock).

17. See LG 36, which speaks of the "royal liberty" of laypersons and goes on to say that by serving Christ in others they bring them to that king "to serve whom is to reign" (*cui servire regnare est*), thus quoting the postcommunion prayer of the *Missa pro pace* of the preconciliar Missal, the *Missale Romanum* of Pius V.

18. See *The Ministerial Priesthood*, 13–14.

Why does the saving presence of Christ come to expression in the bishop's ministry in precisely the functions of sanctifying, teaching, and governing? The communication of Christ's saving presence through the episcopal ministry can take place only in a sacramental way, that is, in the manner of an effective sign, where "effective" denotes the authority, the power, of Christ and God, and "sign" denotes the words and acts by whose means this power touches the hearts of believers. These words and acts, therefore, will affect the whole person in both his or her individual and communitarian dimensions: they will lay claim to the intellect, and in so doing will assume the form of teaching; they will lay claim to the will, and in so doing will assume the form of laws and directives, in other words governing; and they will lay claim to the imagination, and in so doing will assume the form of sacramental rites, in other words the ministry (priesthood) of worship. The saving presence of Christ, which might appear to be "out there" in the ministry of the bishop, in fact is actualized in the depths of the human heart, and in the only ways theologically and anthropologically open to it: the teaching, governing, and sanctifying[19] constitutive of the episcopal ministry.

At this point we need to correct two false impressions given by the Dutch submission quoted earlier. The first is that the twofold distinction of the office of Christ into priest and prophet is more traditionally Catholic than the threefold one of priest, prophet, and king. First, it is surprising that the Dutch prelates did not recognize that Christ's office of king was no less traditional than those of priest and prophet and that it belongs with them. In the New Testament the very title "Christ" indicated the eschatological king, and the feast of Christ the King had been celebrated in the universal Church since its institution by Pius XI in 1925. And Pius XII had used the threefold distinction in his encyclical letter *Mystici Corporis:*

> Moreover he imparted a threefold power to his apostles and their successors, namely, of teaching, ruling and leading people to holiness, and

---

19. This reflection shows that "priesthood of worship" may well express the essence of this function more accurately than "sanctifying" does. Since sanctification is the ultimate purpose of both teaching and governing, the term "sanctifying" seems to award this third function an absolute superiority over the other two, a position against which I have argued in this essay. For *Lumen Gentium's* apparent concurrence (in speaking of bishops as "teachers of doctrine, priests of sacred worship, and ministers of government"), see note 3 and the accompanying text.

indeed he established this power, determined by appropriate precepts, rights and duties, as the first law of the whole Church.[20]

Secondly, as has been well documented by Drilling, the threefold distinction goes back to patristic times,[21] and hence is considerably older and more traditional than the twofold distinction of orders and jurisdiction.

The second false impression is that the threefold distinction is a recent Protestant innovation. Obviously it cannot be this if it is already found in the Church Fathers. But there is a grain of truth in the statement, and it is recognized by Drilling: in dependence on the doctoral dissertation of Josef Fuchs,[22] he argues that though the threefold distinction was available in the deposit of faith, *in fact* it made its way into modern Catholic theology through the influence of rationalist Protestant theologians.[23] This, of course, is no argument against it.

In the earlier article to which reference has been made, I stressed with other recent writers that the ordained priesthood is not above the Church but is squarely within it. I pointed out that the idea that the priesthood is above the Church can be traced back to its exclusively christological reference, which allowed (without encouraging) this misconception, even though the New Testament consistently presented Jesus himself as fulfilling a function within the kingdom. The same is true, of course, of the episcopate, and indeed in the first instance. In itself, the christological reference was not only correct but basic; but it remained open to this misunderstanding as long as it was not balanced with ecclesiological and sociological references (the former being by far the more important). The ecclesiological reference that I singled out was the Lukan one of "official witness." In the present essay I have complemented the Lukan idea with the Matthean one of authority, which better lends itself to differentiating the bishop from the priest and the deacon.

20. Pius XII, encyclical letter *Mystici Corporis*, in AAS 35 (1943) 193–248, at 209 (my translation). In the same document an earlier reference to the threefold power, as bestowed on the whole Church, is found on p. 207.

21. See Drilling, "The Priest, Prophet and King Trilogy," 188–189.

22. Josef Fuchs, *Vom Wesen der kirchlichen Lehrgewalt: Eine Kontroverse des 19. Jahrhunderts; historische Beitrag und systematischer Versuch* (Valkenburg, Germany: doct. diss., 1940; in the possession of J. Fuchs). After the war it was published in a limited edition that is available at the Gregorian University, Rome, the Universities of Münster and Munich, and the Theological Faculty of Erfurt. This information is from Drilling, "The Priest, Prophet and King Trilogy," 192, note 39.

23. See Drilling, "The Priest, Prophet and King Trilogy," 192–196.

Ecclesial Unities in Which the Episcopal Office Participates

1. *The College of Bishops*

We now move on to consider the ecclesial unity that is constituted by the individual bishops as they form a single body, the college of bishops (see LG 22). To this college individuals are aggregated through episcopal consecration (see LG 21). This becomes permanently evident in the practice, by bishops, of hierarchical (collegial) communion in the various ways open to them, which range from ecumenical councils to regional assemblies and episcopal consecrations, which require—for lawfulness, not validity[24]—the participation of at least three bishops. What it shows forth is that each bishop shares in the single office of episcopacy. Of course, they participate in different ways. The head of the college, the pope, without whom there can be no college,[25] clearly participates in a different way from the others. (Rahner has even speculated—unconvincingly in my opinion—that the papal office might constitute a higher grade of the sacrament of orders than that of other bishops.[26]) Not all are local bishops, some being auxiliaries

24. See can. 1014 and the comment thereon in John P. Beal, James A. Coriden, and Thomas J. Green, eds., *New Commentary on the Code of Canon Law* (New York: Paulist Press, 2000) 1196.

25. See LG 22: "The college or body of bishops has for all that no authority unless united with the Roman Pontiff, Peter's successor, at its head . . . ."

26. See Karl Rahner, "The Episcopal Office," *Theological Investigations*, vol. 6, trans. Karl-H. and Boniface Kruger (Baltimore: Helicon Press, 1969) 313–360, at 347–348, note 16. Here Rahner advances a number of positive arguments and deals with some possible objections. He argues that the conferring of the papacy with its special powers constitutes an *opus operatum* that is indistinguishable from a sacrament. However, he overlooks the fact that a sacrament is a social institution necessarily shared by many in the community. It makes no sense to speak of a sacrament for one. The claim about the *opus operatum* is to be conceded, but it is better, and more traditional, to see it as the supreme, unifying concentration of episcopacy rather than an isolating "modification" (his word) of it. We shall argue later—with Rahner—that the collegial aspect of episcopacy takes precedence over its local aspect. This granted, it is clear that primacy is of the very nature of episcopacy, and not something above it, for the college must have a head. Rahner was closer to the truth when he wrote a few years earlier: ". . . in the sense and to the extent that the whole Church is completely present in the local Church, the Church's powers of jurisdiction and order are completely present in the local bishop. The papal authority is not more comprehensive in this respect, but in the sense that the pope alone, by divine right of course, represents the unity of the whole Church as the totality of the local Churches" (*The Episcopate and the Primacy*, 29; see note 33 below for the reference). Peter was not a super-apostle among the apostles; he was one of them, like them in every way. His special authority came purely from his appointment by the Lord as their leader. So it is, then, with the

and others officials of the Roman Curia. Even those whose participation appears on this criterion to be the same differ in practice, in that each has to adapt the episcopal office (without compromising it) to a unique context—unique, that is, in terms of culture and contingent historical conditions.

Collegiality is not just a juridical entity, something into which individual bishops are called by the pope after their consecration. *Lumen Gentium* links it so closely with sacramentality that we may conclude that it is sacramental of its nature. The constitution treats sacramentality and collegiality in successive articles (nos. 21 and 22). In no. 21 it relates them in a sacramental way, though there, of course, its references to collegiality are anticipatory. It begins with the words "In the bishops, then, assisted by the priests, the Lord Jesus Christ, supreme high priest, is present in the midst of believers. Though sitting at the right hand of God the Father, he is not absent from the assembly of his pontiffs." These two sentences contain essentially the same message. The council is speaking here not of individual bishops as such but of all the bishops of the Church, whether assembled or dispersed; in other words, it speaks of the episcopal college. And of this college it says that it contains the presence of Christ the high priest, a presence that can only be sacramental. The same article ends with the statement: "It is the right of bishops to admit newly elected members into the episcopal body by means of the sacrament of Orders."

We conclude from all this that the college itself is constituted by the sacrament of episcopal consecration. Episcopal consecration is a sacrament, indeed *the* sacrament, constitutive of both individual bishops and the episcopal college as such. Collegiality, then, is sacramental of its nature. It is not a mere juridical feature supervening upon episcopal consecration. This conclusion contains important implications for the way the pope as head of the college, acting either directly or through the Roman Curia, should relate to the rest of the college.

Seamus Ryan writes that the November 1962 draft of *Lumen Gentium* contained propositions regarding the sacramentality and the

---

pope and the bishops. The pope is not a super-bishop with a sacrament all his own; his authority derives from the fact that he is the head of the episcopal college. Finally, the opinion that the papacy constitutes a distinct sacrament is hard to square with the doctrine of LG 21 that "the fullness of the sacrament of Orders is conferred by episcopal consecration . . . ." (And not only was *Lumen Gentium* already published when Rahner wrote "The Episcopal Office," but he refers to it in the very section we are considering.)

collegiality of episcopal consecration but in no way attempted to relate them. He continues, however:

> The subsequent debate in St. Peter's and the discussions of the Theological Commission eventually led to the fusion of the sacramental and collegial aspects of the episcopal office; this was, without doubt, the most significant single contribution of the council towards the working out of an integral theology of the episcopate.[27]

The fact of this fusion is supported by the following reflection. What is communicated in the sacrament of episcopal consecration is the priesthood of Christ in the broad sense of the term as inclusive of his prophethood and kingship. This reality is essentially one, both in Christ and in the receiving bishop. But this priesthood is a mandate to minister effectively to the entire world (see Matt 28:19-20), something that can be accomplished only through a zeal that adapts it—of course without compromise—to the manifold conditions of all times and places of human history. This cannot be accomplished by any single individual. It would be idle to speculate on how it might be accomplished. A better methodology is to consider how it was done in fact and to discern the suitability of this means in view of its divinely given end. It was done initially by a college organized by Christ himself under a single individual, a college whose members were thus facilitated to cooperate in its achievement. I refer, of course, to the apostolic college under Peter. But even it could not achieve the task unless authorized to continually co-opt new members in order to perpetuate itself throughout history.

The symbolic number twelve, which initially indicated the twelve tribes of Israel, the original People of God, was expanded into the total number of bishops required to reach the entirety of humankind awaiting salvation in Christ and destined to become the new People of God. The co-option of new members could not continue to take place in the way in which the apostles were first constituted, that is, by a direct commission from the risen Lord. It now took place only through an equivalent commission that was sacramental (for the biblical ground of this, see 1 Tim 4:14 and 2 Tim 1:6). Hence there emerged the episcopal college, headed by the pope, in succession to the apostolic college led by Peter. The achievement of the object of the college takes

---

27. Seamus Ryan, "The Hierarchical Structure of the Church," in *The Church: A Theological and Pastoral Commentary on the Constitution on the Church*, ed. Kevin McNamara (Dublin: Veritas Publications, 1983) 163–234, at 179.

place through the ministry of each bishop in his diocese (or other appointed place) and the hierarchical cooperation (communion) of all. By this presentation I hope to have succeeded in presenting the intrinsic link between the sacramentality and the collegiality of the episcopate in a sufficiently clear light.

This raises the question of which element of the episcopate is primary—its orientation to a particular church or its relation to the college. With Rahner, it is important to stress at the outset that each element is essential and that therefore it is impossible that there be one without the other.[28] But this observation does not dispose of the question, which has been answered differently by different theologians. Rahner opts for the priority of membership of the college on the grounds that, strictly speaking, episcopal succession takes place in terms not of person to person, but of college to college.[29] With the exception of the pope, who is the successor of Peter, no particular bishop succeeds to any particular apostle; but the episcopal college as such succeeds to the apostolic college as such. In addition to the dissimilarity noted, however, there exists a similarity between episcopal and papal succession, one that Rahner exploits as a subsidiary argument for his thesis. Just as the appointment of Peter as chief apostle was prior to any determination of the place in which he would render the ultimate witness (of martyrdom), and the appointment of the other apostles contained no specification of their ministry to particular places, so in subsequent history did collegiality remain the primary element of episcopacy, with specification of place secondary.[30] Note that I have deliberately used words like "orientation" and "specification" in preference to "restriction," because the bishops, as members of the supreme governing body of the Church (see LG 22), have, even individually, responsibilities toward the Church as a whole. These are elaborated in LG 23.[31]

Seamus Ryan takes the opposite view, claiming that "many others" are with him in this, and that it is the view of the Church Fathers.[32] This view, he says, enables us to see how the two elements of episcopacy coincide, for the local church is not just part of the universal

28. See Karl Rahner, *Bishops: Their Status and Function,* trans. Edward Quinn (Baltimore: Helicon Press, 1964) 18–19.

29. Ibid., 19–20.

30. Ibid., 20–22.

31. See the quoted comments of Rahner in note 26 above.

32. See Ryan, "The Hierarchical Structure of the Church," 216–217.

Church but *is* the total mystery of the Church realized in a particular place. It is difficult to show that the early Church conceived the bishop primarily as a member of the college; rather, the liturgical prayers presented him as destined for a local church, a commission that he fulfilled in communion with his fellow bishops.

In response to Ryan, it must first be pointed out that Rahner espoused the same "sacramental" theology of the local church as he himself does. Indeed, he was advocating this theology even before the council.[33] Secondly, be it remembered that Rahner insisted on a necessary link between the two elements of episcopacy. These things being said, we should not be surprised to find ancient liturgies concentrating on the new bishop's ministry in his local church. After all, he was appointed to fill a particular position, namely, a vacancy in a local church. However, in deed if not in word, the element of collegiality was also to be discerned in the rite, being expressed by the plurality of consecrating bishops. The present rite of consecration, as evidenced in both its official homily and prayer of consecration, expressly embraces both elements, awarding primacy to membership of the college.[34] And, as mentioned earlier, at least three consecrators are required, though it is appropriate that all the bishops present participate.

Ryan's argument does not establish any absolute priority of ministry in the local church over membership of the episcopal college, but only that these, the elements of episcopacy, necessarily coexist, a point figuring prominently in Rahner himself. In this matter it is not helpful to insist on an ontological priority of one element over the other, since "ontological priority" denotes priority in the order of being, and being, or rather finite being, is composed of essence and existence. It is possible that one element be primary in the order of essence and another primary in the order of existence, in which case there is no absolute priority in the order of finite being as such.

This I claim to be the case here. I argue that essential priority belongs to membership of the college, and existential priority to ministry in the local church. The reason for the latter part of this affirmation is that the college pertains immediately to the universal Church, and the latter exists only "in and out of" the local churches (see LG 23). On the

---

33. See Karl Rahner and Joseph Ratzinger, *The Episcopate and the Primacy,* trans. Kenneth Barker, Patrick Kerans, Robert Ochs, and Richard Strachan (Montreal: Palm, 1962) 25–26. The German original appeared in 1961, the year before the council.

34. See International Commission on English in the Liturgy, *The Rites of the Catholic Church,* vol. 2 (Collegeville, Minn.: The Liturgical Press, 1991) 68–70, 73–74.

other hand, the essence of episcopacy is expressed in the apostolic mandate of Christ in Matthew 28:19-20 and the various Lukan texts quoted, in each of which the commission is given to the group as such, though with the implication that it be executed by individuals in particular places. As mentioned earlier, the current liturgy contains this emphasis. Rahner's concern is only with the essential priority of membership of the college over ministry in the place of appointment.

2. *The Presbyterium of the Local Church*

The bishop shares his priesthood (in the broad as well as the narrow sense) with the priests of and in his diocese. LG 28, which is devoted to the priesthood or presbyterate, clearly states that the priesthood of the presbyter is dependent on that of the bishop in both its being and its exercise: "presbyters do not possess the fullness of the pontifical office, and they depend on the bishops in the exercise of their power." These facts notwithstanding, "they [presbyters] are united to them [bishops] in the sacerdotal dignity," so much so that "they constitute one presbyterium with their bishop [note the use of the singular]."[35] In this last quotation we see a second ecclesial unity to which the bishop contributes and in which he participates as its head: the one presbyterium of the local church consisting of the bishop together with the presbyters of his diocese, both secular and religious.

In this section, which is necessarily brief (though it merits an essay of its own), I shall discuss just two questions, the first of which asks about the more exact nature of the sharing-in-being in the priesthood of bishops on the part of presbyters. This is an abstract question; it has to do with the way the priesthood of presbyters shares in the being of the priesthood of bishops. The answer will affect the response given to the concrete question, In what way does a particular bishop share his priesthood with the presbyters whom he ordains? but the two questions are not identical.

35. In these examples the Flannery version (for the reference see note 38) unwittingly prejudices the two theological questions that I shall pursue here. The first problem is the translation of the Latin word "apex" (which means the same in English as it does in Latin) by "supreme degree." I have rendered it by "fullness" and wish to argue that there are no degrees in the priesthood as communicated from bishop to presbyter. The second is the translation of "presbyterium" by "sacerdotal college" (in the text Flannery supplies the Latin word in parenthesis). I have left it untranslated. The constitution never calls the body of priests with their bishop a college, a point that is theologically significant, given that the body of bishops with the pope is called precisely that.

We begin by pointing out once again that *Lumen Gentium* teaches a dependence in the being, and not just in the exercise, of the presbyteral office on the episcopal office. But this teaching has to be understood in the light of the constitution's further statement that the bishop and the presbyters constitute one presbyterium, that is, one body sharing a single priesthood. This I take to mean that the priesthood itself is indivisible. It cannot be communicated in varying degrees, but if it is communicated at all, it is communicated whole and entire. How can these two parts of the teaching be affirmed together without contradiction? The answer, I suggest, is that the one priesthood is communicated to the presbyter but does not exist fully actualized in him. The degree to which it is actualized—and now, granted that the whole priestly office is communicated, it is permissible to speak of degrees of its actualization—will depend not on the will of the ordaining bishop but on the needs of the Church as determined in that age by the supreme authority, namely, the college of bishops or the pope as head of the college.

This solution corresponds better to the actual history of the presbyterate, in which, in the words of Susan Wood, "over an extended period of time presbyters took over the sacramental functions of bishops out of necessity."[36] Presbyters were not reordained each time a crisis occurred but were ordained only once. What happened was that to meet the increased needs of the Church, the presbyterate was actualized to ever higher degrees according to the will of the authorities. This cannot be explained merely by an increase in jurisdiction in the canonical sense; the only satisfactory explanation, I submit, is a growing actualization of the authority possessed by virtue of the sacrament of ordination, where authority itself is understood in a fully sacramental sense.

The presbyter, therefore, relates to the bishop differently from the way in which the bishop relates to the pope. In the latter case the pope is not, as we saw, a super-bishop but a bishop like his colleagues, except that he holds a unique position as successor to Peter. The pontifical office is fully actualized in the bishop, and not in the pope alone, as we earlier saw Rahner pointing out. (There is an orthodox sense of *primus inter pares* [the pope as the "first among equals"] as well as an unorthodox one.) But the sacerdotal office is not fully actualized in the presbyter, as it is in the bishop. The presbyter is in no way the equal

---

36. Susan K. Wood, *Sacramental Orders* (Collegeville, Minn.: The Liturgical Press, 2000) 118.

of the bishop, as the bishop is of the pope. This, I suggest, is how we can best uphold the ontological dependence of the presbyterate on the episcopate and at the same time assert the one priesthood in both.

This brings us to the second question: What kind of community do the presbyters of the diocese, secular and religious, form with the bishop? Negatively, from the knowledge we already have, we can answer that it is not a college. In a true college all members are "colleagues," in the sense that there is a genuine equality among them. This is the case with the pope and the bishops, all of whom are equally bishops. Though the bishop exercises his episcopate in hierarchical communion with the pope, head of the college, he does not exercise it in dependence on the pope. He exercises it in dependence on Christ, via the sacrament of episcopal consecration. Between the presbyters and the bishop, however, this kind of equality is lacking. True, the presbyters share the one priesthood of and with the bishop, and they too receive it from Christ, that is, in the sacrament of ordination, but both ontologically and operationally their priesthood depends on the fullness of actualization given only in the case of the bishop. Nevertheless, the community that they co-constitute with the bishop is a true and important ecclesial unity. What should we call it? I can suggest no better name than that given it by Vatican II, that is, the single "presbyterium." From all this there emerges a definition of the presbyter. He should not be defined in terms of what he can or cannot do, as this can change in the course of history; rather, he should be defined as the priest whose priesthood depends in its very being on that of the bishop. It then follows that he can exercise his priesthood only in dependence on the bishop.

3. The Priesthood of the Church

In my article referred to earlier I also presented the "priesthood of the Church" as the integration of the common priesthood of the baptized with the ordained priesthood.[37] The priesthood of the Church is the property not of persons as such but rather of the social reality of the Church in union with Christ the High Priest. The ordained priesthood is a special charism within the Church, that is, in the community of those who possess the common priesthood, which not only enables the latter to function in its full reality but also functions itself only when thus acting in concert. This total reality constitutes the

37. Reference the same as for note 1.

priesthood of the Church. One can readily understand how the misconception that the ordained priesthood was somehow above the Church led to the further misconception that the priesthood of the Church was simply the common priesthood of the baptized. For if the ordained priesthood was above the Church, then the priesthood of the Church could only be the common priesthood.

The relation of the ordained and the common priesthood spelled out above disposes of the idea that the ordained priesthood alone is active, while the laity are passive under its ministry. Certainly it is true that the priest as the minister of Christ gives and that the laity receive, but this is only one aspect of the common priesthood. For the laity are also active in their priesthood. Priest and people act in their own respective ways, thus constituting acts of the priesthood of the Church. Speaking of the participation of all in the Eucharist, the high point of priestly action in the Church, LG 11 says:

> Taking part in the Eucharistic sacrifice, the source and summit of the Christian life, they offer the divine victim to God and themselves along with him. Thus both by offering and by Holy Communion, all play, not in an undifferentiated way but in different ways, their proper part in the liturgical action.[38]

The "different ways" mentioned here are in fact only two: that of the ordained priest and that of the baptized but not ordained. The active nature of the priestly participation of both clergy and laity in the priesthood of the Church could hardly be more clearly stated.

Note that what is said above of the priest (presbyter) applies first and foremost to the bishop. The conclusion from this is that the episcopal office is likewise not above the Church but is a ministry within it. And the "high priesthood" of the bishop is realized in act only when exercised in concert with the common priesthood. Only when so acting does it constitute, or rather co-constitute, the priesthood of the Church.

---

38. The first sentence of this quotation is taken from Austin Flannery, ed., *Vatican Council II: The Basic Sixteen Documents: Constitutions, Decrees, Declarations: A Completely Revised Translation in Inclusive Language* (Northport, N.Y.: Costello, 1996) 15. The second sentence is my own translation of the Latin, "*ita tum oblatione tum sacra communione, non promiscue sed alii aliter, omnes in liturgica actione partem propriam agunt.*" The interpretation given above is supported by the commentary of Aloys Grillmeier in *Commentary on the Documents of Vatican II*, vol. 1, ed. Herbert Vorgrimler, trans. Lalit Adolphus, Kevin Smyth, and Richard Strachan (New York: Herder and Herder, 1967) 160–161.

If this is so with the priestly function of the bishop, it must be so also with his prophetic and pastoral functions. Hence it may, and must, be said both that the bishop teaches and governs only when his teaching and governing are met by the acceptance and obedience of his church, and that the laity are not passive but active in their engagement with his exercise of these functions. Thus ecclesial events of teaching and governing occur only in the interplay of episcopal and lay acts.

Another point to be mentioned is the caution added by LG 21 that teaching and governing "of their very nature can be exercised only in hierarchical communion with the head and members of the [episcopal] college," that is, with the pope and the bishop's episcopal colleagues. A further caution is that mentioned by LG 25 in regard to solemn papal definitions and applied here, *mutatis mutandis,* to the teaching and governing of bishops. Echoing the anti-Gallican clause of the definition of Vatican I, this text states that papal definitions "are rightly said to be irreformable by their very nature and not by reason of the consent of the Church."[39] Similarly, the teaching and governing of bishops does not become authoritative through the reception and compliance of their local churches; though these factors are essential elements of episcopal teaching and governing, the latter draw their authority from the office itself, which, being the fullness of the sacrament of orders, has its authority directly from Christ (see LG 21).

We now consider the prophetic and pastoral functions of the bishop separately in the context of our present discussion, and we take the prophetic function first. If the laity are to "receive" the teaching of bishops, this receiving certainly appears to be a passive function, which, if verified, would give the lie to the claims made above. Whilst affirming a certain passivity in its regard, however, we stress that the lay role here is primarily active. LG 12 speaks of a *sensus fidei,* an instinct for the true faith, which is possessed by the People of God as a whole and which is infallible.[40] This *sensus* resides also in each of the faithful individually (though in this case, of course, it is not infallible). When bishops in hierarchical communion with the episcopal college exercise their teaching function, they engage the *sensus fidei* of the faithful. This engagement is clearly active on both sides, and it explains why in the end the people "receive" the teaching of their bishops. But to explain this fully, we need to invoke the theology of "recognition"

39. DS 3074 (my translation).
40. See Ormond Rush, "*Sensus Fidei:* Faith 'Making Sense' of Revelation," *Theological Studies* 62 (2001) 231–261.

developed by Gerard Kelly from the documents of the Faith and Order Commission of the World Council of Churches.[41]

Encountering an item of authentic Church teaching for the first time, laypeople will "recognize" it as an expression of the Christian faith they already have. This will lead them to receive it. This insight allows us to see that recognition is the essential step between the *sensus fidei* and reception. Where Christian faith is lived authentically, there will always be the *sensus fidei*, spiritual readiness for its authentic articulation. When this is actually done, the layperson will first recognize the accomplishment intellectually and then receive it intellectually. The *sensus fidei* is an "instinct," an active power, in itself lacking intellectual content, while recognition is an active intellectual act, and reception a passive intellectual act (if I may speak thus). There can be no proper reception without a prior *sensus fidei* and recognition. This analysis enables us to grasp the active elements pertaining to reception despite its initial wholly passive appearance.

Just as a bishop teaches authentically only in hierarchical communion with the rest of the episcopal college, so the local church authentically receives his teaching only in communion with the rest of the faithful throughout the world. If a teaching is not received by the universal Church, there must have been something wrong with it from the start: it must have fallen short of authentic teaching. The divine authority spoken of above as attaching to the authentic teaching of bishops is not granted to defective teaching. Failure to receive episcopal teaching cannot occur in regard to infallible (or "definitive") doctrine,[42] for reception is based on the universal *sensus fidei*, which is also infallible, and the Spirit's gift of infallibility cannot be brought into contradiction with itself. But it can occur in the case of the next level of teaching, which elicits not the assent of faith but, to use the language of LG 25, a "*religiosum voluntatis et intellectus obsequium*," a religious submission of will and intellect, for teaching at this level is not guaranteed by the gift of infallibility. If it appears doubtful whether

41. See Gerard Kelly, *Recognition: Advancing Ecumenical Thinking*, American University Studies, Series VII, Theology and Religion, vol. 186 (New York: Peter Lang, 1996).

42. It is not meant here that infallibility is ever attached to the *person* of an individual local bishop when teaching (that is contradicted by LG 25), but it may well be attached to the *teaching*, that is, when it is something that has been solemnly defined by either the pope or an ecumenical council or when taught as infallible in the "ordinary" manner, that is, by the pope and the episcopate dispersed throughout the world (see LG 25).

a teaching on this level is actually received, only time will tell; in the end the situation will be clarified and become definitive, as the teaching will be either received or rejected by the Church as a whole. (Of course, in the meantime it could also be repudiated or modified by the teaching authority.)

In the case of sanctifying and teaching, we have been able to point to realities already established in tradition and theology, namely, the common priesthood and the *sensus fidei*, to show that the laity are active contributors to the exercise of these functions, and that the priestly and prophetic functions of the Church as such are not constituted by the hierarchy alone but by the synergy of hierarchy and laity. However, in the case of governing, the task is more difficult, for there is nothing universally recognized in tradition or theology that we can invoke for this purpose. The assumption is readily made that the laity are simply passive under the ruling power of the hierarchy. LG 36 recognizes the existence of the royal dignity of the laity and expresses its content in terms of overcoming the reign of sin in themselves and playing their part in the spread of the kingdom. These two activities, however, can perhaps more properly be seen as pertaining to their priestly and prophetic functions, respectively, than to their royal function. Another factor is that *Lumen Gentium*, in chapter 2, "The People of God," deals successively with the priestly (nos. 10 and 11) and the prophetic function (no. 12) of the Church as a whole, but in no. 13 turns to the question of the catholicity of the Church, which only indirectly involves its royal function of "establishing" (*inducens*) the kingdom of Christ. LG 36 occurs in chapter 3, "The Laity," and is preceded, in nos. 34 and 35, by a treatment of their priestly and prophetic functions, respectively. In no. 36 there is no hint of an active role for them in concert with the hierarchy in regard to the exercise of the royal function. The conclusion seems inevitable: while *Lumen Gentium* regarded the priestly and prophetic functions of the Church as such as synergies of the hierarchy and the laity, it did not so regard the royal function. While the laity had a royal function of its own, this did not combine with that of the hierarchy to constitute the royal function of the Church as such. Under the governing authority of the bishops the laity were simply passive.

It cannot be concluded from this, however, that *Lumen Gentium* excludes an active role for the laity in respect of the royal function of the Church as such. It is possible that theological thinking at the time of the council was not sufficiently advanced to justify a positive teaching about an active role. I would now like to suggest that this was the case and to present my reason for so thinking. In his commentary on canon 7 of the 1983 Code of Canon Law,[43] Ladislas Orsy distinguishes between two approaches to law, the first of which he calls "essentialist," while the second he leaves unnamed. The first approach, typified by St. Thomas Aquinas, is worked out in "the abstract world of essences," while the second is formed "within the context of the existing order, in the order of *esse* [being, existence]." I therefore propose to call it "existentialist." Question 90 of St. Thomas's *Summa Theologiae*, I-II, at the end of which he offers his definition of law, actually carries the title *"De essentia legis"* ("Concerning the Essence of Law"). In the fourth and last article of this question, he is in a position to define law, according to its essence, as "an ordinance of reason, for the common good, from the person in charge of the community, [and] promulgated." Orsy asks, "'What is law?'—that is, 'What is the normative element in the mind and heart of people which actually, *actu*, moves them to act?'" In answering his own question, Orsy provides an existentialist definition of law. "The law," he says, "is a norm of action in the existing world, adopted and used by a community of free and intelligent persons in order to build well-balanced social structures." Here is his comment on this approach:

> *To live*, the norm must become a vital force in the community, informing the minds and hearts of the people, directing their operations. They must come to the appreciation of the value the law intends to promote. Then they must freely decide to act on the norm proposed and thus implement the law. When this happens there is a new fact: the norm is a force moving the group; it has been received by the community.

Notice that the essentialist approach says nothing about the role of the subjects of the law, while the existentialist approach, which equally calls for obedience, in stressing the intelligence and freedom of the subjects presumes that they make a mature and committed judgment about the law. In other words, the existentialist approach prescribes an active role for the subjects, while the essentialist one presumes for them a passive role. Notice, too, that in the existential-

---

43. In *The Code of Canon Law: A Text and Commentary*, ed. James A. Coriden, Thomas J. Green, and Donald E. Heintschel (New York: Paulist Press, 1985) 29–30. No further references are provided for Orsy in the text above, as all citations can be found in the section referred to. The quotation from St. Thomas is my own translation from the Latin.

ist approach the concept of reception enters the process of governing in a way analogous to that of teaching. Orsy leaves us in no doubt as to which he regards as the more adequate understanding. "Canon law, in particular," he says, "has suffered and is still suffering from this essentialist approach." Hence my suggestion is that the reason for Vatican II's failure to assess the royal function of the Church along lines similar to its priestly and prophetic functions is most likely that as a product of its times it was laboring under the essentialist approach to Church law, and hence to the governing function of bishops. I stress that in the existentialist approach the element of reception is analogous to, and not identical with, reception in regard to teaching. Just as teaching and governing are distinct functions, there will be differences as well as similarities in the nature of the reception of each. Here we shall pursue, briefly, just two of the questions that could be asked.

First, given that recognition is an essential element of the reception of Church law, what is it that the faithful recognize as they take their first step in the appropriation of a law? I suggest that they recognize both the harmony between the law and some gospel value and the necessity, or at least the utility, of the law as a means of promoting it. This will move them to receive the law not as a resented burden but as a welcome guide for living out the gospel in the conditions of daily life. It goes without saying that it is prudent for a bishop at the time of the promulgation of a law (or some analogous decision) to take pains clearly to point out these two objects of recognition. If he does so, he will be truly shepherding his people to an appropriate attitude to the particular law and to Church law in general, and disposing them to the desired obedience.

Secondly, we may ask: What is it in the recognition and reception of Church law that corresponds to the *sensus fidei,* the "instinct for the true faith," that obtains in the case of Church teaching? If the manner of life appropriate to the Christian community can fittingly be referred to simply as the "Way," as it is in Acts 9:2, 18:25-26; 19:9, 23, 22:4, and 24:14, 22, then this element can be called the *sensus viae,* the "instinct for the right way," which the faithful also have. (I suggest *via* rather than *mores* ["morals"] because the latter pertain to teaching rather than governing in the strict sense employed here; and I suggest lowercase rather than uppercase because in the biblical expression the uppercase denotes the total life of the Christian in his/her community and not just its legal dimension as implied in the strict sense of governing.)

Thus is explained the limited life that Church laws, unlike Church teaching, have. This is a factor recognized by Orsy in his observations on the existential approach to law. He writes, "Finally, human laws are mortal, as people are. Once they have fulfilled their purpose, they should *die.*" If teaching is true at one time, it is true at all times. But laws that are appropriate for a particular time and place may become inappropriate—either irrelevant or harmful—in other times and places. When this happens, the bishop can repeal them or quietly let them fade away; in either case, the faithful will already have ceased to recognize and receive them. When the bishop insists on maintaining a law in the face of non-reception on the part of a minority or even a majority of his local church, the presumption must remain on the side of the bishop rather than on that of the recusants until such time as Rome has ruled on the matter. Bishops, be it remembered, govern in hierarchical communion with the episcopal college and its head, who alone are the official teachers in the Church.

We have now shown that each of the three episcopal functions—sanctifying, teaching, governing—is exercised only in concert with the corresponding active function of the laity. Hence what I said in my earlier article about the integration of the ordained and the common priesthood into the one priesthood of the Church, applies, *mutatis mutandis,* to the other two functions as well. That is to say, episcopal teaching combined with lay reception based on the *sensus fidei* constitutes the prophetic function, and episcopal governing combined with lay reception based on what I have called the *sensus viae* constitutes the royal function of the Church. And these three ecclesial functions participate in their own way in the priestly, prophetic, and royal functions, respectively, of Christ himself. And finally, just as in Christ the three functions unite in the single office of the incarnate divine Word and Son, so do they unite in the Church in its single mission, in the persons of bishops in their single episcopal office, and in the persons of the laity in their own single mission, based on baptism and confirmation.

Conclusion

In the introduction I stated that the episcopate is an element within the organism that is the Church. That is to say, it is an organ within an organism. The rather complex account of its unity (its being) given in this essay will appear not so strange once it is pointed out that its unity is not unlike that of any organ of an organism. What, for example, is the human heart? We can describe it in terms of its inner components, its ventricles, atria, etc., but we must not stop there. To do so would be to simplify to the point of falsification. We must proceed to tell of its relations to the other organs with which it cooperates to maintain the life of the human person.

So it is with the episcopate. Merely to speak of the union of the three sacred functions comprising the ministry of the bishop in his local church would actually be to mislead as to the true nature of the episcopacy, for its most important feature, namely, membership of the college of bishops, as well as other important features, would have been omitted. Hence the approach I have taken in this essay. Whatever we say of the episcopal office must be directed to the life of the Church, universal as well as local, and ultimately to its "communion" or fellowship, which is celebrated principally in the Eucharist and which participates in the perichoresis of the Persons of the Holy Trinity, Father, Son, and Holy Spirit, who constitute the one true God.

Chapter Two

A Liturgical Theology of the Episcopacy

Susan K. Wood, S.C.L.

A theology of the episcopacy lies embedded in the liturgy, both in the rite of episcopal ordination and in the eucharistic liturgy at which the bishop presides, and is communicated through the language of the liturgy, that is, through symbol. These symbolic actions not only inform us about the pastoral role of a bishop; they reveal a theology of the Church as a dynamic, ordered community under the pastoral leadership of a bishop. In this essay I extract a theology of the episcopacy from liturgical texts and symbols in order to uncover the rich mutual relationship between a bishop and his flock. I argue that the mutual relationship between a bishop and his local church is analogous to their relationship within a liturgical assembly.

The Bishop and the Liturgical Assembly

The chief manifestation of the Church is liturgical. The liturgical assembly reflects the diversity of the People of God as an ordered community according to the various charisms and offices of that people. The Constitution on the Sacred Liturgy *(Sacrosanctum Concilium)* states: ". . . the principal manifestation of the church consists in the full, active participation of all God's holy people in the same liturgical celebrations, especially in the same Eucharist, in one prayer, at one altar, at which the bishop presides, surrounded by his college of priests and by his ministers" (SC 41). In the liturgy the diversity within the Church is manifested in a variety of roles. The paradigm of the Eucharist is one at which a bishop presides. Historically, since the bishop was unable to be present at all the gatherings of the faithful, he set up assemblies of believers, particularly parishes, under the care of the pastor, who acted in his place.[1] Thus what is said of the role of the priest within the liturgy applies above all to the bishop. Conversely, the bishop's role in the Eucharist dictates why his name is mentioned in the anaphora and why presbyters who preside at the Eucharist must be in communion with him.

The irony of this text is that very few Roman Catholics experience the bishop in a liturgical setting apart from his appearance in their parishes at confirmations. Even though *Lumen Gentium* describes a particular church, the basic unit of the Church in Roman Catholicism, as a "community of the altar, under the sacred ministry of the bishop,"[2] the "church" for most Catholics remains the parish and the face-to-face eucharistic assembly experienced there. Their most frequent contact with the bishop is probably not in the liturgy but through his regular column in the local diocesan paper. Although too often perceived as an ecclesiastical CEO, the bishop has an important role in connecting the Church to its apostolic past and in linking a particular church with other particular churches within the communion of churches that is the universal Church. He is primarily a pastor before he is an administrator. Identifying him and his relationship to his church in terms of his liturgical role and liturgical symbols gives priority to his spiritual leadership.

There is a relationship of mutual interiority between the head and the body, the priest and the assembly. A bishop exists not apart from the Church or above the Church, but within the Church. As Cyprian noted, "The bishop is in the Church and the Church is in the bishop." John Chrysostom said that "the body is the fullness of the head, and the head, the fullness of the body."[3] The ordained minister is in the Church, not above the Church or apart from the Church.

Nothing is more clearly insisted upon in the 1990 rite of ordination than the bishop's relation to his church.[4] Thus a bishop is to be ordained in the Christian community he is going to serve rather than at home or in another location. The rite stipulates that since the bishop

1. SC 42.
2. LG 26.
3. Cyprian: *Epist.* 66, 8. Chrysostom: *In Eph.,* c. 1. Hom. 3, 2 (PG 52, 26). Cited by Yves Congar, "L'Ecclesia ou communauté chrétienne, sujet intégral de l'action liturgique," in *La Liturgie après Vatican II,* Unam Sanctam 66, ed. J. P. Jossua and Y. Congar (Paris: Éditions de Cerf, 1967) 281.
4. Frederick R. McManus, "The New Rite for Ordination of Bishops," *American Ecclesiastical Review* 159 (1968) 413.

is ordained for the sake of the local church, it is appropriate that great numbers of clergy and faithful attend the ordination.[5] Two presbyters of the diocese for which the bishop-elect is being ordained assist him in the celebration of his ordination. One, in the name of the local church, requests the ordaining bishop to confer ordination on the bishop-elect.[6] After his ordination the bishop assumes his role as pastor of the local church. The new bishop takes his place in the bishop's chair of his church and presides over the Eucharist, because he presides over the communion of this local church. Presbyters from the local diocese concelebrate with him.

The bishop is a member of the Church even as he has a distinctive role within it. The mutual relationship of church and bishop is analogous to the nature of the liturgical assembly, which includes all those present at liturgy—bishop, presbyters, deacons, and lay faithful. In other words, the liturgical assembly is not simply those folks who sit in the nave of the church. It is not the people vis-à-vis the priest or bishop-celebrant, but rather the entire People of God gathered by word and sacrament in liturgical prayer, inclusive of the ordained presider. Everyone present at the liturgy is a member of the assembly.

Likewise, all Christians are the *Christifideles* before they are identified by distinctive subsets as laity, clerics, or religious. Unity exists before distinction within that unity, similarity before difference. Thus *Lumen Gentium* describes the People of God as a whole in chapter 2 before addressing the hierarchy, the laity, and religious in subsequent chapters. Title I in the Code of Canon Law (1983) outlines the obligations and rights of all the Christian faithful before Title II addresses the obligations and rights of the lay Christian faithful, and Title III does the same regarding sacred ministers or clerics. Nevertheless, there are a variety of offices and charisms which order the Church.

The interplay between the bishop and the community is reflected in the diversity of liturgical ministries. The revised *Institutio Generalis Missalis Romani* (November 2002) teaches that the eucharistic celebration belongs to the whole Body of the Church, which is "a holy people united and ordered under the Bishop." The Church is an ordered community reflected in the ordered eucharistic assembly:

---

5. *De Ordinatione Episcopi, Presbyterorum et Diaconorum,* editio typica altera (Rome: Typis Polyglottis Vaticanis, 1990) 5, 22.

6. Ibid., 17, 24.

The Eucharistic celebration is an action of Christ and the Church, namely, the holy people united to and ordered under the Bishop. For this reason, the Eucharistic celebration pertains to the whole Body of the Church, manifests it, and has effects on it. It also touches the individual members of the Church in different ways, according to their different orders, offices, and actual participation in the Eucharist. In this way, the Christian people, "a chosen race, a royal priesthood, a holy nation, a people set apart," expresses its cohesion and its hierarchical ordering.[7]

The liturgical assembly is paradigmatic of the Church, exercises the priesthood of the faithful, and consequently reflects the characteristics of the priestly People of God.

The *Institutio Generalis Missalis Romani* notes not only the organic unity of the assembly but also its hierarchical structure and diversity "expressed by different ministries and a different action for each part of the celebration."[8] It stipulates that "the general plan of the sacred building should be such that in some way it conveys the image of the gathered assembly" and that it should "allow all the participants to take the place most appropriate to them and should encourage the proper carrying out of each one's function."[9] The presider's chair stands as a symbol of his function of presiding over the assembly and of directing prayer. The places for the faithful should facilitate their active participation. The purpose of the introductory rites is that "the faithful who are assembling should become a community and dispose themselves to listen properly to God's word and to celebrate the Eucharist worthily."[10] The purpose of the opening liturgical song is not only to open the celebration but to "intensify the unity of those who have assembled."[11]

Priesthood of the Bishop and the Priesthood of the Baptized

The bishop is ordained as "high priest." The prayer for the ordination of a bishop says:

Grant that this, your servant,
whom you have chosen for the office of bishop,
may shepherd your holy flock

7. *Institutio Generalis Missalis Romani*, editio typica tertia: General Instruction of the Roman Missal, including adaptations for the Dioceses of the United States of America (November 2002) 91. Hereafter this is the edition cited as IGMR.

8. Ibid., no. 294.

9. Ibid.

10. Ibid., no. 46.

11. Ibid., no. 47.

and, serving you night and day,
fulfill before you without reproach
the ministry of high priest.
So may he intercede always with you
to look kindly upon us
and may he offer the gifts of your holy Church.[12]

As high priest, the bishop not only offers gifts and intercedes on behalf of the Church, but he also engages the priesthood of the baptized.
The faithful are active subjects of the Eucharist by reason of their baptism.[13] The baptized have the right to join the community in common
prayer, have a part in the general intercessions, bring gifts to the altar,
exchange the sign of peace, share in the offering of the sacrifice, express the spirit of adoption as God's children, which they have received in baptism through the recitation of the Lord's Prayer, and
commune in the Eucharist.[14] Beyond this, they actively engage with
the presider. The bishop, as presider-president of the assembly and
pastoral leader of the local church, greets the faithful, carries on a dialogue between himself and the assembly, invites the people to pray
with him, and leads the people in the eucharistic prayer. They join
their voices to the Eucharistic Prayer at four points: in the introductory dialogue, where there is a reciprocal recognition of the Lord's
presence in both the assembly and the minister, the Sanctus, the
memorial acclamation, and the Great Amen. The priest prays the Eucharistic Prayer in the name of the rest of the assembly. With the exception of the words of institution, the anaphora is in the first person
plural, even though the presbyter or bishop recites it by himself. Hervé
Legrand's analysis of the liturgical vocabulary of the first millennium
shows that in the Roman sacramentaries the subject of the verb "celebrate" is always the "we" of the assembly, never the "I" of the
presider.[15] The liturgical "we" made Lombard say that a priest cut off

12. *Rites of Ordination of a Bishop, of Priests, and of Deacons*, second typical edition, prepared by the International Commission on English in the Liturgy (Washington:
March 2000) no. 47. Hereafter *Rites of Ordination*.

13. IGMR, no. 18.

14. *Rite of Christian Initiation of Adults* (Washington: USCC, 1988), no. 217.

15. Hervé Legrand, "The Presidency of the Eucharist According to the Ancient Tradition," in *Living Bread, Saving Cup*, ed. R. Kevin Seasoltz (Collegeville, Minn.: The
Liturgical Press, 1982) 216; Benedicta Droste, *"Celebrare" in der römischen
Liturgiesprache* (Munich: Max Hueber, 1963) 3–80. Note the exception in the rubrics of
the Gelasian Sacramentary, 80. Cited by Thomas P. Rausch, "Priest, Community, and
Eucharist," in Michael J. Himes and Stephen J. Pope, eds., *Finding God in All Things: Essays in Honor of Michael J. Buckley* (New York: Crossroad, 1996) 262–275, at 265–266.

from the Church could not validly celebrate Mass, since he could not say *offerimus quasi ex persona Ecclesiae* in the anamnesis.[16] Furthermore, in the revised Communion rite, the preparation of the priest and the people for Communion occur together in the one recitation of the "Lord, I am not worthy." Since the bishop is also a representative of Christ, he both engages the priesthood of the faithful and represents the priesthood of Christ to that priesthood.

The Fathers of the Church emphasized the dialogue between priest and people in the liturgy. For example, in the exchange "The Lord be with you" and the response "And also with you," there is a reciprocal recognition of the Lord's presence in both the assembly and the minister who is the primary celebrant of the sacred mysteries.[17] John Chrysostom commented that the Eucharistic Prayer is a common prayer because the priest does not give thanks (which is to say that he does not celebrate the Eucharist, which means "to give thanks") alone, but only with the people. He does not begin the Eucharistic Prayer without first gathering the faithful and assuring their agreement to enter into this action through the dialogue: "Lift up your hearts." "We lift them up to the Lord." "Let us give thanks to the Lord our God." "It is right to give him thanks and praise."[18] In our own time the *Institutio Generalis Missalis Romani* states that both the dialogues between the celebrant and the faithful and the acclamations "are not simply outward signs of celebrating in common, but they encourage and achieve the communion between priest and people."[19]

The *Institutio Generalis Missalis Romani* regards the entire assembly as the primary agent of the liturgical action, for the celebration of the Eucharist is the action of Christ and the Church.[20] The *Catechism of the Catholic Church* also emphasizes that "it is the whole *commu-*

16. Peter Lombard, *Sent.* IV, d. 13. See B. D. Marliangeas, *Clés pour une théologie du ministère. 'In persona Christi, in persona Ecclesiae'* (Paris: Beauchesne, 1978) 55–60. Cited by Louis-Marie Chauvet, "Ritualité et Théologie," *Recherches de Science Religieuse* 78, no. 4 (1990) 537.

17. Congar, "L'Ecclesia ou communauté chrétienne," 277.

18. "The eucharistic prayer is common; the priest does not give thanks alone, but the people with him, for he begins it only having received the accord of the faithful. . . . If I say that, it is so that we learn that we are all a single body. Therefore let us not rely on the priests for everything, but let us, too, care for the Church." *Com. in 1 Cor.*, Hom. 8, 3 (PG 61, 527); cited by Congar, "L'Ecclesia ou communauté chrétienne," 277–278. Also cited by Legrand, "Presidency," 218.

19. IGMR, no. 34.

20. IGMR, no. 19.

nity, the Body of Christ united with its Head, that celebrates."[21] *Sacrosanctum Concilium* says of the assembled: "Offering the immaculate victim, not only through the hands of the priest but also together with him, they should learn to offer themselves."[22]

There is a fear on the part of some that making the assembly the subject of the liturgical action makes the priest a delegate of the assembly, thus obliterating the distinction in essence between the priesthood of the baptized and the ordained priesthood. Here it is important to differentiate between delegation and authorization. Delegation would consist in arranging for a member of a congregation to preside at the congregation's assembly without empowering that person with a presbyteral relationship to the assembly. This constricts liturgical presidency to a liturgical function rather than relating it to a larger pastoral role. Authorization to ministry, however, always occurs in the context of prayer to the Holy Spirit accompanied by the laying on of hands. Authorization does not proceed only from the community but requires an anointing by the Spirit.

Furthermore, a priest can never be seen as a delegate of the People of God if we envision the priest and the people within a head/body relationship. The priest, in speaking the Eucharistic Prayer in the name of the people *in persona ecclesiae,* speaks as the head of that community that is the Body of Christ. He also speaks *in persona Christi* as head of the community, for the community in union with Christ, its Head, is the Mystical Body of Christ.[23] In this role there is a relationship of over/againstness of the priest to the community: at the same time that the priest is within the community as a head he is also a member of the body. This is not a relationship of democratic representation. Nor does it represent a horizontal relationship between priest and assembly. The over/againstness of the bishop acting *in persona Christi* as head of the community enables him to challenge the community prophetically, to exercise a pastoral ministry of oversight,

21. *Catechism of the Catholic Church,* 2nd ed. (Washington: United States Catholic Conference, 2000) no. 1140.

22. SC 48.

23. The encyclical *Mediator Dei* defined the liturgy as "the public worship which our Redeemer gives to the Father as Head of the Church; it is also the worship given by the society of the faithful to its head, and through him, to the eternal Father: it is, in a word, the integral worship of the mystical body of Jesus Christ, that is, of the head and its members." Cited by Congar, "L'Ecclesia ou communauté chrétienne," 269.

to direct the charisms of the community, and to preside sacramentally as the instrument of Christ's action in the sacraments.

If the liturgy is a manifestation of the Church, as *Sacrosanctum Concilium* indicates, this full, active participation of the baptized in the liturgy, their role as active agents of the liturgical action, and their dialogic interplay with the presider should reflect the relationship between the bishop and the people in the pastoral life of the Church outside the liturgy. Just as the nature of the liturgy is ecclesial, not clerical, so is the nature of the Church. The relationship between the bishop and the rest of his local church is one of mutual recognition of the presence of the Spirit in the other, mutual listening, and mutual dialogue. Just as the high priesthood of the bishop engages the common priesthood of the faithful in the liturgy, so he also draws forth their full, active participation in the life of the Church.

The *sensus fidelium* is given to the whole Church, hierarchy and laity included. The whole body of the faithful, anointed by the Spirit, cannot err in matters of belief: "It shows this characteristic through the entire people's supernatural sense of the faith [*sensus fidei*], when 'from the bishops to the last of the faithful,' it manifests a universal consensus in matters of faith and morals."[24] The Church teaching and learning includes both bishops and the rest of the people. Both learn and both teach.[25] When the bishops, gathered in ecumenical council or dispersed throughout the world, teach infallibly, they articulate the faith of the Church, for the charism of infallibility is given to the Church as a whole. Thus, for example, when Pope Pius XII proclaimed the doctrine of the Assumption in 1950, he had previously polled the bishops to ascertain that this doctrine was, in fact, the faith of the Church.

Episcopal Authority

In the rite of ordination the epicletic prayer specifies a particular gift of the Spirit for the person being ordained, appropriate for the particular order to which he is being ordained. The request for the bishop is a "governing Spirit":[26]

---

24. LG 12.

25. Ladislas Orsy, *The Church: Learning and Teaching* (Wilmington, Del.: Michael Glazier, 1987).

26. The expression *spiritus principalis* in this prayer of ordination from the *Apostolic Tradition* attributed to Hippolytus raises certain difficulties and has been variously translated. Bernard Botte comments, ". . . [the *spiritus principalis*] is the gift of the spirit ap-

So now, pour out upon this chosen one
that power which is from you,
the governing Spirit,
whom you gave to your beloved Son, Jesus Christ,
the Spirit whom he gave to the holy apostles,
who founded the Church in every place to be your temple
for the unceasing praise and glory of your name.[27]

Episcopal teaching authority is often misunderstood, either because this theology of the infallibility of the Church is confused with a democratic political process or because episcopal authority is viewed as an extension of papal authority. In the first instance, episcopal teaching is reduced to an opinion poll; in the second, the episcopacy is seen as a branch office of the Vatican. Neither respects the sacramental basis of episcopal authority in episcopal ordination whereby episcopal authority is "proper, ordinary and immediate."[28] This means that bishops possess authority in their own right and not by delegation from the pope. Conversely, papal teaching is not dependent upon the agreement of the bishops, since the First Vatican Council ruled that papal definitions are "irreformable of themselves and not from the consent of the Church," the Church in this context referring to the episcopacy.[29] The Second Vatican Council extended this same principle to the episcopacy. The official relation on LG 25 comments: ". . . definitions of a Council are also irreformable of themselves and do not need the approbation of the people, as some of the East mistakenly hold, but rather they carry with them and express the consent of the whole community."[30]

The Church, the bishops, and the pope each possess an authority that could be properly called "proper, ordinary, and immediate." Hence this authority does not depend on the approval of the whole—the Church for a bishop or the episcopacy for the pope—for its proper

---

propriate for a leader. The best translation would perhaps be 'Spirit of authority.'" "'Spiritus Principalis' (Formule de l'Ordination Episcopale)," *Notitiae* 10 (1974) 410–411.

27. *Rites of Ordination*, no. 47.

28. LG 27.

29. "ex sese, non autem ex consensu Ecclesiae," DS 3074. Francis Sullivan, in *Magisterium: Teaching Authority in the Catholic Church* (New York: Paulist Press, 1983) 103, comments: "It is historically certain that what the majority of Vatican I intended by this phrase was the definitive repudiation of the fourth of the 'Articles of the Gallican Clergy' of 1682, which said that a doctrinal decision made by the pope would be irreformable only if it obtained the consent of the Church (DS 2284)."

30. *Acta Synodalia Concilii Vaticani II*, III/1, 253. Cited by Sullivan, 225, n. 37.

exercise. However, these are not separate authorities because of the mutual interiority that obtains among them. The bishop does not exercise authority over and against the Church because he is part of the Church, just as the presider is part of the assembly, although he exercises a specific role with respect to the rest of the assembly. Likewise, the pope, by sacramental ordination and as bishop of Rome, is a member of the episcopal college. Even though there is personal, individual authority exercised, it is an authority from within rather than over. Ideally, bishop, pope, and presider recapitulate the faith and prayer of the body of which they are a part. "Reception" occurs when the Church recognizes its faith and prayer in what is articulated, and this passes into the life of the community.

Instructions for a bishop in *Christus Dominus* emphasize this dialogical approach to the pastoral duties of a bishop. He is to seek out people and promote dialogue with them, presenting his positions clearly, unaggressively, and diplomatically. These discussions should promote sincere friendship as conducive to a union of minds.[31] Similarly, he is to guide the faithful according to the circumstances of each, while striving to acquire an accurate knowledge of their needs in the social conditions in which they live. He is to show concern for all and to respect the place proper to the faithful in the affairs of the Church, acknowledging also their duty and right to work actively for the building up of the Mystical Body of Christ.[32] In the pastoral life of the local church, this dialogical relationship is accomplished through diocesan listening sessions, diocesan councils, and synods, as well as in less structured ways.

The Bishop and the Word of God

The primary responsibility of the bishop is to preach faithfully the gospel.[33] In the rite for the ordination of a bishop, the principal ordaining bishop receives the Book of the Gospels from one of the deacons and places it, open, over the head of the bishop-elect. Two deacons hold it above his head until the end of the prayer of ordination. In the explanatory rites after the prayer of ordination, the book is presented to him, with the injunction "Receive the Gospel and

31. CD 13.
32. CD 16.
33. LG 25.

preach the word of God with all patience and sound teaching."[34] This powerful symbol indicates that the bishop is subject to a higher authority, the law of the gospel. Bishops are heralds of the faith, authentic teachers who are endowed with the authority of Christ and given the duty to preach the faith to the people assigned to them.

Among the ritual changes in the revised *Institutio Generalis Missalis Romani* (2002) is the option for the bishop to bless the people with the Book of the Gospels after its proclamation.[35] This symbolic gesture shows that the Church venerates the Scriptures as it venerates the Lord's body and blesses with both.[36] There is one table of God's Word and Christ's Body.[37] Both the bishop and the people are under the authority of the gospel, even though the interpretation of Scripture is subject to the judgment of the Church.[38] This is sometimes misunderstood as meaning that the truth or authority of the gospel rests on the authority of a particular church or human institution.[39] The liturgical use of the Book of the Gospels, however, makes clear that it is an object of reverence in the Church and that the authority of the Church in the person of the bishop is in service to the gospel.

Although a number of different people are authorized to proclaim the Word of God in the eucharistic liturgy, the proclamation of the gospel is ordinarily reserved to an ordained bishop, presbyter, or deacon. The official proclamation of the gospel in liturgical prayer belongs to an ordained minister because it is not just a matter of reading a text from a book, a function that any literate person can perform, but an act of official witnessing on behalf of the community and in the name of the apostolic tradition. Through election by the community, prayer to the Holy Spirit, and the laying on of hands, the ordained person is graced by the Spirit and recognized by the community as an official witness to the community's apostolicity. This is most directly evident in the case of bishops as successors to the apostolic college. By fact of ordination, the bishop exercises the symbolic function of guaranteeing the exemplarity of the proclaimed text for the assembly.[40] He symbolically links the assembly and the church to its apostolic roots.

34. *Rites of Ordination,* no. 50.
35. IGMR, no. 175.
36. *Catechism of the Catholic Church,* no. 103.
37. Ibid.
38. Ibid., no. 112.
39. "A Call to Evangelical Unity," *Christianity Today* (June 14, 1999) 54.
40. Louis-Marie Chauvet, *Symbol and Sacrament* (Collegeville, Minn.: The Liturgical Press, 1995) 210.

In a second level of representation, the bishop, as a member of the assembly and one of the People of God, witnesses to the exemplarity of the text, because he stands within the assembly and testifies that this text reflects the present life and faith of the community. The assembly recognizes the proclamation of a past experience of the People of God as the living Word of God in its present circumstances. Just as in the Eucharist the priest functions both *in persona Christi* and *in persona ecclesiae,* representing Christ to the community and the community to Christ, so in the liturgical proclamation of the word the ordained minister connects the community to the faith proclaimed in the text and represents the canonicity and apostolicity of the text to the community.

The Bishop and the Communion of Churches

The Introduction to the rite for the ordination of a bishop begins with the statement: "By virtue of episcopal ordination and in hierarchic communion with the head of the college and its members, a person is constituted a member of the body of Bishops."[41] This is ritualized by the ancient practice of requiring that at least three bishops celebrate the ordination. The primary purpose of this requirement is not to legitimize the ordination, but to indicate that a local church cannot survive in and of itself and is incapable of perpetuating itself apart from other churches. The ordaining bishops minister the gift of the Spirit through the imposition of their hands and accept the new bishop into their episcopal college through ordination. This act not only creates an episcopal communion of bishops but also establishes a relationship among particular churches.

In the Roman Catholic Church, authorization to ministry also links the present assembly to other assemblies in the recognition that no particular church can be Church apart from communion with the other particular churches or apart from the apostolic Church with which it is in continuity and communion. The communion of churches is personalized in the college of bishops to which each bishop is admitted upon ordination and in communion with the bishop of Rome. The bishop in his person represents his church within the communion of particular churches. Consequently, the communion of churches is mediated by the communion of bishops. Parishes are united within this communion through the relationship between priests and their bishop. Thus there

41. *Rites of Ordination,* no. 12.

is both a synchronic communion of churches within the universal Church, sacramentalized in the communion of bishops, and a diachronic communion in history with the apostolic faith, sacramentalized in episcopal apostolic succession. Episcopal ordination—what it signifies and what it effects in the person of the bishop and his relationship with other bishops—is that which lends a sacramental character to synchronic and diachronic communion.

The "fullness of orders" within episcopal consecration represents not a fullness of power, but a fullness of ecclesial relationship. Sacraments reserved to a bishop have varied historically. For example, the bishop at one time was the ordinary minister not only of what we now call confirmation but also of baptism and the Eucharist. There is evidence of presbyteral ordinations authorized by the pope.[42] Ultimately, what a bishop can do that a presbyter cannot is to represent his church within the communion of churches by virtue of his membership in the episcopal college. The "fullness" in episcopal ordination consists in a fullness of ecclesial representation, that is, fullness in signifying the communion of his church within the communion of churches.[43] The implication is that the sacrament of order orders the Church.

Conclusion

Liturgy mirrors the life of the Church, and so the liturgical role of the bishop reflects his pastoral role. As the principle presider at the sacrament of unity, he presides over the unity of the church. Together the bishop and the rest of the people comprise both the liturgical assembly and the Church. Since both the bishop and the church are identified eucharistically, the Eucharist implies a communion not only between the bishop and the rest of the People of God but also his role in assuring the community's communion with its apostolic origins and its communion with other eucharistic communities.

When viewed liturgically, the relationship between bishop and people is rich and interactive. The bishop not only ministers to his church; he also receives from the Church. He receives from the Church the same word of apostolic faith that he transmits to it as a

42. See the documentation provided by Arthur Carl Piepkorn, "A Lutheran View of the Validity of Lutheran Orders," in *Lutherans and Catholics in Dialogue IV: Eucharist and Ministry,* Bishops' Committee for Ecumenical and Interreligious Affairs (1970) 220–225.

43. See Susan K. Wood, "The Sacramentality of Episcopal Consecration," in *Sacramental Orders* (Collegeville, Minn.: The Liturgical Press, 2000) 64–85.

word of salvation. He receives the gifts of bread and wine from the Church in the preparation of the gifts and returns them in eucharistic communion. His prayer of intercession to the Father is the prayer of the Church praying with him.[44] His offering is the offering of the entire community. The relationship between the liturgical action of the bishop and that of the community is so integral that "by consecrating the gifts so that they become the body and blood the community offers, he celebrates not only for it, nor only with it and in it, but through it."[45] In short, there is a great gift exchange[46] between the bishop and the rest of his church, the gift being one and the same.

That which is celebrated in the language of symbol in liturgical time often awaits full realization in the historical time of everyday life. The unity we celebrate eucharistically is sometimes torn asunder by ideological factions within the Church. Bishops and their flocks are not exempt. The unity of apostolic faith and communion among communities may seem to be a goal ahead of us rather than a reality achieved. Unless we can enact and envision that goal liturgically, however, we have little hope of achieving it pastorally.

44. Joint Commission for Theological Dialogue Between the Roman Catholic Church and the Orthodox Church, Second Plenary Meeting, Munich, June 30–July 2, 1982, "The Mystery of the Church and of the Eucharist in the Light of the Mystery of the Holy Trinity," in *One in Christ* 19, no. 2 (1983) 193.

45. Ibid.

46. I borrow this phrase from Margaret O'Gara's *The Ecumenical Gift Exchange* (Collegeville, Minn.: The Liturgical Press, 1998).

Chapter Three

The Bishop as Preacher

Walter J. Burghardt, S.J.

Three questions sum up my approach to the bishop as preacher. (1) How does the official Church see the bishop as preacher? (2) How is this ecclesial perception realized in the preaching of Archbishop Rembert Weakland? (3) From his experience, what conclusions might we draw for effective preaching?

Official Directives on Bishop as Preacher

It might be helpful here to link two ecclesial movements: canon law and the theology that the canons reflect. Canonist Ladislas Orsy has expressed the relationship in an engaging paragraph:

> The relationship between theology and canon law can be best summarized by saying that in theology the Church contemplative is speaking to the people, and in canon law the Church active is guiding the faithful. There are not, however, two churches; one and the same Church is contemplative and active. There is a season for reflection and there is a season for action. The two operations blend into one but without losing their distinctive characters: they mutually support each other. They together reveal something of the internal life of God's covenanted community.[1]

With that relationship in mind, let us look at four pertinent canons and suggest their relationship to the Church's theology.

---

1. Ladislas M. Orsy, S.J., "Theology and Canon Law," in *New Commentary on the Code of Canon Law*, ed. John P. Beal, James A. Coriden, and Thomas J. Green (New York/Mahway, N.J.: Paulist Press, 2000) 1–9, at 8–9. Hereafter *New Commentary*.

CANON 386, NO. 1

> A diocesan bishop, frequently preaching in person, is bound to propose and explain to the faithful the truths of the faith which are to be believed and applied to morals. He is also to take care that the prescripts of the canons on the ministry of the word, especially those on the homily and catechetical instruction, are carefully observed so that the whole Christian doctrine is handed on to all.[2]

Of high significance here is a statement almost hidden in a subordinate clause. The bishop of a diocese does not fulfill his function by simply assuring that the canonical prescriptions on preaching are carefully observed by others, e.g., priests and deacons. It is assumed that the bishop himself preaches frequently. Here the law reflects not only the reforms of the Council of Trent but a strong statement of the Second Vatican Council: "Among the more important duties of bishops, that of preaching the Gospel has pride of place. For the bishops are heralds of the faith, who draw new disciples to Christ."[3] This emphasis reminds me of the remarkable bishops of the golden age of the Church Fathers—fourth- and fifth-century prelates like Gregory of Nazianzus, Basil the Great, and John Chrysostom in the East, Hilary of Poitiers, Augustine, and Pope St. Leo I in the West—all of whom preached not only frequently but with singular style.

CANON 756, NOS. 1 AND 2

> With respect to the universal Church, the function of proclaiming the gospel has been entrusted principally to the Roman Pontiff and the college of bishops.
>
> With respect to the particular church entrusted to him, an individual bishop, who is the moderator of the entire ministry of the word within it, exercises that function; sometimes several bishops fulfill this function jointly with respect to different churches at once, according to the norm of law.[4]

For our purposes, the significant sentence is the declaration that *preaching* the gospel (not simply seeing to it that the gospel is preached) has been committed *principally* to the pope and the college of bishops.

---

2. *New Commentary,* 523. The translations of the canons in this volume are taken from *Code of Canon Law, Latin-English Edition* (Washington: The Canon Law Society of America, 1998).

3. LG 25.

4. *New Commentary,* 920–921.

CANON 762

Sacred ministers, among whose principal duties is the proclamation of the gospel of God to all, are to hold the function of preaching in esteem, since the people of God are first brought together by the word of the living God, which it is certainly right to require from the mouth of priests.[5]

"Sacred ministers" embrace, of course, bishops, priests, and deacons. Vatican II stressed the high priority of preaching: ". . . it is the first task *(primum officium)* of priests *as co-workers of the bishops* to preach the gospel of God to all."[6] As the council recognized, the proof thereof is clear from Paul's letter to the Christians of Rome:

Everyone who calls on the name of the Lord will be saved. But how can they call on him in whom they have not believed? And how can they believe in him of whom they have not heard? And how can they hear without someone to preach? And how can people preach unless they are sent? . . . Thus faith comes from what is heard, and what is heard comes through the word of Christ (Rom 10:13-15, 17, NAB).

CANON 763

Bishops have the right to preach the word of God everywhere, including in churches and oratories of religious institutes of pontifical right, unless the local bishop has explicitly forbidden it in particular cases.[7]

In recognizing a bishop's right to preach anywhere in the world, the Code recognizes that in Catholic doctrine and theology a bishop's right and duty to preach are based on sacramental ordination, not on his jurisdiction or canonical mission. As a member of the college of bishops, each individual bishop shares a responsibility for proclaiming the gospel in the Church universal.[8]

Archbishop Weakland as Preacher

Before delving into Archbishop Weakland's actual homilies, I think it instructive to recall his understanding of the preacher's function. I draw this from an address to the National Conference of Priests of England and Wales, delivered at Newman College/Bartley Green in

---

5. Ibid., 924.
6. PO 4. Emphasis added.
7. *New Commentary*, 925.
8. See LG 21, 24-25 and CD 3-4.

Birmingham on September 5, 1995. Though the talk was addressed specifically to *priests* as part of "A Renewed Priesthood in a Renewed Church," and granting that an address to *bishops* might have expanded his reflections somewhat, I believe that the ideas here summarized express basically how the archbishop understood his own role as preacher.

The preacher's primary task is "to sustain the faith of the people" and give them hope, especially in troubling times. This was more difficult in 1995 than in earlier generations, when "God could be introduced as the answer to, or the cause of, many of the blessings and catastrophes of this world." How to respond to Christians' need to experience God in their lives? It is the preacher's task "to help them understand the sacramental principle so that they can believe that God is with us in those signs and symbols, even though they might seem so ordinary."

An advantage since Vatican II is the people's hunger for Scripture. The preacher must make Scripture come alive, relate God's Word to today's world and today's problems. He bridges the gap between the Church's mission as *koinonia* (inward-looking) and *diakonia* (outward-looking). He tries to bring God's point of view and the historical events of the mission of Jesus Christ to the inner life of the Church, as well as to the Church's mission to the world. Not easy in a world that does not have windows open to the transcendent, a scientific world that needs to put everything under a microscope. Unfortunately, the social teaching of the Church "has not been interiorized by most of our faithful." That became evident to the archbishop when he was chairing the drafting committee of the American bishops that fashioned the 1986 pastoral letter *Economic Justice for All.*

Through his preaching the priest "must help the faithful in their quest for holiness." He brings God's revelation to the practical needs of his people "so that they can find God in their lives and in their duties and work."

So much for principles; turn now to homilies actually delivered. While aware that each of the canons reproduced earlier is pertinent for Archbishop Weakland's involvement in the ministry of preaching,[9] I

---

9. For example, the legislation on the bishop's function as moderator of the entire ministry of the word in his diocese and his obligation to see to it that the canonical prescriptions on preaching are carefully observed in his diocese; here I recommend Archbishop Weakland's "Norms for Preaching in Archdiocese of Milwaukee," published in the July 29, 1993, issue of the archdiocesan newspaper, the *Catholic Herald.*

shall focus on his own experience of "frequently preaching in person." In the course of a quarter century as archbishop, his homilies ranged widely in content, style, and length. He often preached for four or five minutes to half a hundred people at the 7:45 a.m. weekday Mass in his cathedral. "Often the theme dealt with the vicissitudes of belonging to a changing Church and the need for faith in the midst of it all."[10] But, with space at a premium, I shall select for lengthier treatment homilies drawn from special occasions, where Weakland's homiletic concerns touched not only his Catholic archdiocese but the wider world of humanity that is a bishop's (and every priest's) parish.[11]

The Vision

Rembert Weakland offered a glimpse into his worldwide homiletic vision at the beginning of the homily he preached on November 8, 1977, in the Cathedral of St. John the Evangelist, on the occasion of his episcopal ordination and installation as ninth archbishop of Milwaukee:

> On becoming a bishop in 1977, my first thought was: Could any moment of history seem more challenging than this one? So many and such rapid cultural changes, lying outside our control, affect profoundly our lives. Yes, even the Church cannot remain outside the sphere of such changes, for she continues Christ's work of redemption in this world and no other. Christ came to redeem this world; the Church cannot wait till it becomes better of itself. She must give to changing, and often confusing, times a sense of hope, an assurance that it all has meaning, and a conviction that that hope and meaning are derived—not from earthly causes—but from that Spirit of the Risen Lord which the Father has sent among us.
>
> For these reasons the role of the bishop in such a time of change takes on new importance and significance. He knows that sociological and cultural traditions alone will not sustain the faith of his people and [will not] provide answers to the many new problems facing them.

Almost three years later, September 6, 1980, Weakland preached in his cathedral at a memorial Mass celebrating the fortieth anniversary of the Katyn Forest massacre. Remembered specifically were the fifteen

10. Paul Wilkes, "The Education of an Archbishop—I," *The New Yorker* (July 15, 1991) 38–59, at 42.

11. Quotations from these homilies are drawn, unless otherwise specified, from manuscript copies graciously supplied to me by Mary E. Carian of the Salzmann Library at Saint Francis Seminary in Milwaukee.

thousand or more Polish officers and soldiers slaughtered by Soviet military in a wooded area around Katyn in 1940. Here the archbishop insisted that "our heroic sacrifices, our renunciations—even if they be of life itself—are not without hope." We are all "a part of [Jesus'] mission of bringing God's kingdom to all nations, to all peoples—a kingdom of justice and peace," striving "to make this world a place where such massacres and such tragedies cannot be repeated, . . . where the rights and freedoms of all are honored and respected." The critical issue is "being with Jesus," following Jesus; for then "we are bearers of His love and goodness, His care for all, especially the weak, the hungry, the sick, the defenseless. We cry out against evil and the shedding of innocent blood."

Obvious occasions for the expression of Christian hope linked with Christlike suffering were the archbishop's funeral homilies. In his homily of September 24, 1988, for his predecessor William E. Cousins ("Uncle Bill"), he rang the changes on a Christian archbishop who walked for eighty-six years with Christ and now shares his glory before the Father. It was in two areas, preaching and witnessing, that Weakland saw Cousins's fullness as Christian, as priest, and as bishop. "He was an exemplary preacher; he lived the message he taught. He proclaimed Christ, he lived Christ."

True indeed, powerful. But what struck me with even greater force was a paragraph about "a person who grew through suffering."

> The trust he showed others was not always reciprocated. He was an archbishop at a difficult time in the history of the Church. He was proud to have been a Father of the Second Vatican Council. He trusted in the Holy Spirit and willingly implemented the spirit of the Council. Not all eagerly followed his example and his enthusiasm. We can be forever grateful in the Milwaukee Archdiocese for his trusting attitude toward others in that post-conciliar period. Yet he never exaggerated his sufferings. He often told me that he thought it was more difficult being a bishop now than in those years right after the Second Vatican Council. . . . I will be forever grateful to him for the example he showed us all of how a Christian could be often misunderstood and maligned, but should never bear any anger or ill-will or bitterness toward others. He showed us all what it means to be Christlike at times of trial and suffering.

On April 24, 1994, in a vein similar to much of the above, the archbishop preached in his cathedral for the 150th anniversary of the archdiocese. The centerpiece was the Good Shepherd of John 10:11-18. Very touchingly he recalled how as a child he loved to be carried on the shoulders of his father or his uncles. "One had to hold tightly under the chin or one would topple backwards. More importantly, one had to trust the grown-ups that they had a secure grasp of your legs and would never let go." Then he told his listeners: "Picture yourselves as riding the shoulders of the Good Shepherd, Jesus Christ. He has you firmly in his grasp. He is carrying you along. He is holding us [the archdiocese] tightly as we face the future. Today we renew our confidence and trust in him and his providence."

The response to the Good Shepherd on this anniversary day? Commitment and courage. Commitment: in the past this meant "many sacrifices, especially to build the large and beautiful churches needed for worship and the schools needed for education." Today (1994) the sacrifices may be different: "fidelity to the faith community by regular Mass attendance, deeper reflection on the gospel and its meaning in our daily lives and work, more acts of charity and love toward the whole of society, less anger and no violence . . . being shepherds to others in need." This might take even more backbone and strength of character than in the past. But always remember that the Good Shepherd carries us in the face of these challenges.

Courage: like the Good Shepherd, we may have to risk all. "We face an uncertain future." Unending global conflicts? Endless local unrest and violence? Large-scale conflicts stemming from major religious differences? Our response is to "risk all by being examples of nonviolent, loving, and caring people." Rising above divisiveness, preaching a different gospel, respecting human life and every person, not threatened by differences, open to learning from others, saying no to violent solutions, to a drug, pornographic, sexist, racist, dishonest, selfish culture—to a culture of death. Neither isolationists hiding from the world nor imperialists with all the answers. True voices for justice to the poor and less fortunate.

If we ride on the shoulders of Christ, everything looks different, almost awesome. We do not see the future, but we know it is in God's hands. Today we renew our trust. The Good Shepherd will carry us securely.

Christian Hope and *Kairos*

The theme of Christian hope was reasserted dramatically on July 29, 1990, at an ecumenical church service celebrating the tenth anniversary of Germanfest in Milwaukee's Marcus Amphitheater, a celebration that thanked God "for the many graces and gifts that have come to the citizens of German origin" in Milwaukee and the surrounding area. Specifically, the archbishop explained that the primary purpose churches should have in mind when celebrating such occasions is that "from examining the good things of the past and from understanding the present moment, we commit ourselves to building a better future. Thus, in faith we look backwards in order to sharpen our vision to look forward."

The present moment, the tenth anniversary, Weakland declared, is "an extraordinary moment." It is what we call a *kairos*, "an unrepeatable opportunity in the history of God's kingdom," where "the events that are happening so fast around us not only change world history but present new opportunities for our faith."

One such event was a long dream becoming a reality: the unification of Germany. Unbelievably rapid and without bloodshed. A unification "that can only take place with sacrifice and mutual understanding and love." An "exciting moment that challenges all Germans, but all of us as well, to new understandings of what it means to be a single family of God."

A second event is "the new sense of freedom in all the countries of Eastern Europe and in Russia." Despite all their suffering, the faith of these people "remained indomitable and their search for freedom of religious expression remained unquenchable." Especially influential for such faith have been not only Cardinal Wyszynski but the great Lutheran Bishop Dibelius, whose "prophetic words were a resonating counterpoint to so much of the Marxist jargon that filled the political halls in the post-War years."

But the new moment, the *kairos*, created by the faith of these people "is a great challenge for the future." A receding Marxism and its atheistic ideology "could so easily be supplanted by a new pragmatic atheism in the form of materialism and consumerism." Disastrous, too, "if we permitted this new moment to dissipate its energy into factional wars; new forms of collaboration and new sacrifices will be demanded so that all peoples can respect the worth and dignity of each other and live in peace." St. Paul's "boast of our hope" (Rom 5:1-5) excludes easy solutions; it is realistic enough to accept "the afflictions that come with striving for peace and enduring the sufferings that must be ours" to bring about a kingdom of love and justice. And, of course, "the real source of Paul's hope is his recognition of the action of the Holy Spirit in our midst."

Seven years later a fresh *kairos* intrigued the archbishop: the proximity of a new millennium. On September 27, 1997, he preached on
"Hope in the Face of Crisis" at the LARC (Lutheran, Anglican, Roman
Catholic) Millennial Conference in Madison, Wisconsin. How to use
"this special gift of God to our generation in a positive and constructive way"? God's gift is not a knowledge of the day and hour when
Christ is coming in his glory. It is rather the opportunity to hear the
apocalyptic passages of the New and Old Testaments "with fresh ears,
with fresh insights, with fresh understanding." In that literature the
archbishop discovered five special aspects of Christian faith that "the
millennium should reinforce, all of them being a part of our hope and
trust as we face the future, all of them in one way or another being but
different strains of the same theme."

1. The millennium should strengthen our larger vision of who Jesus
Christ is: the Lord of history, "majestic in his divinity, more than a
human brother, Christ reaching his full stature and assimilating us to
him, to his Body." Here, now, in our midst. We, all the baptized, "are
growing into the fullness of Christ's Body. Christ and his Body, the
baptized, are now one." Our vision should embrace "that 'high' Christology that we may have been avoiding of late." The same Christ who
taught, cured, talked, and forgave "stands before the throne of the
Almighty as our Lord, the Lord of all. With Christ as the Lord of our
history, why should we fear?"

2. We must regain the immediacy of the apocalyptic literature, the
urgency of the New Testament. "Enkindle in your own hearts that
same desire for the full presence of Christ in our midst that was so
clear in the early Church." Seek every sign of the presence of Christ in
Church and world today. Let the immediacy of the coming of Christ
as described in the apocalyptic literature become a reminder of the immediacy of Christ's presence in the here and now.

3. The failure of the Enlightenment to produce a perfect society by
human reason is replaced in the new millennium by the realization
that "only Christ can bring such fulfillment and such perfection, both
to us as individuals and societies." The apocalyptic literature will
again remind us that "market economy, democratic processes, and all
the lip service we give to seeking solutions to racism, violence, exploitation of others, will not work until we are remade into Christ's
image and likeness." Let Christ be Christ, the Savior in our midst.

4. The apocalyptic literature will also help us form ourselves into a
people, a Church. In that literature no one stands alone. The Church

is a gathering of all the elect. "We are being formed into the living Body of Jesus Christ." The younger generation, spiritual, prayerful, with an instinct for the holy, has an aversion to the institutional Church. Perhaps, as they hear the apocalyptic passages read in the assembly, they will see that one of the important aspects of our belief in Jesus Christ, and in the Church that he founded, is that it must contain that Spirit of unity and oneness and be a catalyst for bringing people together, not dividing them.

5. The apocalyptic literature, much of it written during persecution, stresses patient endurance as we live and wait in the end times. It will not let us be naïve about evil. "Evil or good is not the total possession of one or the other person or institution. Good and evil create a ragged line down through all people and all human constructs. Evil must be fought against, within our Churches, in ourselves, in our society, in the world." We leave final judgments to Christ; we take from our hearts all that keeps us from recognizing Christ's presence in others. The millennium will be truly God's gift to our generation if our waiting for Christ becomes a search for his presence here and now.

Jewish-Christian Relations

The theme of "trial and suffering" leads naturally to a critical, delicate, troublesome area for the preacher. In "An Interfaith Remembrance: Commemoration of the Holocaust," a sermon delivered on April 17, 1983, at the War Memorial Center in Milwaukee, the archbishop noted the importance of remembrances: "They provide the stimulus and framework for our present commitments; they become the promise for our hope in the future." But remembrance has two facets. It is easy "if we remember the *saving* acts of God, the triumph of good over evil. It is so much more difficult to remember the past when that good is still unclear, when the power of evil dominates the memory, when we abhor even to recall the event because of the horror it generates." In the latter category rests the Holocaust. "As Christians we remember it with shame, with guilt, with a sense of implausibility. Most of all, we remember it with a fear that the roots of that evil could still be found among us. To the Jew, the very existence of a good, wise, merciful, and loving God is at stake in such a remembrance."

For Weakland, "even the remembrance of painful, negative horrors must lead to positive commitments": first, a renewal of our covenant with God, reliance on His mercy, God calling us back to Him, "away from all those ideologies that made mere human strength and ingenuity and superiority the center of an egotistic universe." Second, all of us

> must commit ourselves this day to eradicate all attitudes and biases that are the source of hatred toward others or of an intrinsic sense of superiority over others. . . . For us Christians there is yet an unfinished task as we seek to root out all those attitudes that directly or indirectly led up to or provoked the Holocaust or the silence of its onlookers.

Third, our part in that covenant also means building mutual trust and confidence now. "We want to bond ourselves together in love this day."

A later section of that courageous homily gave me pause, evoking an experience of my own. The archbishop said he might make bold "to add one last hope and prayer, namely, that for all of us who remember the Holocaust this day, suffering will become redemptive and cathartic, not paralyzing and repressive." This same hope I treasured in 1964, in a White Plains (New York) synagogue, where I tried to make a small beginning toward reconciliation by focusing, as Weakland did, on the famous Suffering Servant passage in Isaiah 52:13ff. I had read that for the last eight centuries most Jewish interpreters had seen in the Servant the Jewish people, had seen in his sufferings not only the agony of the Captivity but the sufferings of the whole Jewish people. I wanted to suggest the redemptive power of Jewish suffering—for them and for me.

It was, at best, a magnificent failure. From certain reactions, then and later, especially from the young, I was forced to conclude that a theology of redemptive suffering makes little or no sense if your history includes (among much else) the Holocaust. That experience was confirmed years later by an article on the Center for Jewish-Christian Learning at the University of St. Thomas in St. Paul, Minnesota:

> Christians have always believed, and Vatican II reaffirmed, that suffering yields sanctity. The Jewish people, in contrast, see no value, spiritual or otherwise, in suffering. Its value is that, as we use our free will to eliminate it, there will be less. "Suffering, as such, does not confer privilege," said Elie Wiesel in his appearance at the center. It is not because I suffer that I have certain rights.
>
> "But the main reason why we talk is not for the dead—it is too late for the dead. We are talking for the next generation, for the children. . . . Our past may become our future unless we are careful."[12]

---

12. Bill Wagner, "Still Working for Understanding: Christians and Jews," *St. Anthony Messenger* 100, no. 3 (August 1992) 36–41, at 40.

I am not disparaging the archbishop's effort to preach a suffering that is redemptive and cathartic; such preaching is profoundly Catholic. That message comes through beautifully and fittingly in a sermon preached in St. Joseph Church, Fond du Lac, Wisconsin, on January 5, 1990, celebrating the deaths of two Sisters of St. Agnes, Maureen Courtney and Teresa de Jesús Rosales. Both were martyred while serving the Mesquito Indians in Nicaragua—"a kind of senseless martyrdom, from a human point of view."[13] Their offering will not have been in vain if we see it as a sign of Christ's victory over death, over all hatred and sin. If we are encouraged by their example to move from here to make this world a place of peace and love through the mutual service we give to one another, then senselessness will be turned into fullness of life.

I do suggest that when preaching on the Holocaust, especially in the presence of our Jewish sisters and brothers, we do so aware that with their history they "see no value, spiritual or otherwise, in suffering."

Jubilee Homilies

Inasmuch as the Catholic celebration of the new millennium found such widespread inspiration in the Jubilee of Leviticus, I thought it pertinent to study three homilies preached by Archbishop Weakland in this context: anticipation of the Jubilee Year, its formal opening, and its closing.

In preparation for the Jubilee Year (2000), the archbishop preached a homily on November 7, 1999, during a joint worship service sponsored by the Milwaukee Catholic-Jewish Conference. For the Jewish people, he recalled, the Jubilee Year proclaimed a new beginning: "The Jubilee Year was to make possible a creative, refreshing renewal that would be characterized by previously unheard-of fervor. In other words, a Jubilee Year was to afford for the individual and for the community a fresh start." In our day, he declared, this means that "we have to change interiorly. At the end of the Jubilee Year we cannot be the same people who began it." For Christians, a conversion—the Greek *metanoia*: "changing our attitudes so as to change the course of our lives and of our society." Our Catholic tradition speaks of three stages in the conversion: acknowledge our wrongs, seek forgiveness,

---

13. Sister Maureen came from Milwaukee, Sister Teresa was a native Nicaraguan. The two sisters were murdered on New Year's Day, 1990. There are three versions of their deaths: (1) in an ambush, (2) when the vehicle Maureen was driving rode over a grenade, (3) at the hands of U.S.-organized terrorists.

and resolve to reform. That evening the archbishop sensed "a need to walk through these three stages."

First, the archbishop acknowledged before his fellow Jewish citizens of Milwaukee the wrongs "we Catholics" have done. As the appointed leader of the Roman Catholic community, he asked the Catholics present to answer "Amen" to three affirmations if they felt in conscience able to do so:

- I acknowledge that we Catholics have through centuries acted in a fashion contrary to God's law toward our Jewish brothers and sisters.
- I acknowledge that such actions harmed the Jewish community throughout the ages in both physical and psychological ways.
- I acknowledge that we Catholics, by preaching a doctrine that the Jewish people were unfaithful, hypocritical, and God-killers, reduced the human dignity of our Jewish brothers and sisters and created attitudes that made reprisals against them seem like acts of conformity to God's will. By doing so, I confess that we Catholics contributed to the attitudes that made the Holocaust possible.

But since "only the victims can impart absolution," the archbishop asked God publicly for forgiveness in the name of the Roman Catholic community and asked the Catholics present to say "Amen" (if able in conscience) to five requests for forgiveness. In brief, for (1) hurtful and harmful statements through the centuries; (2) statements implying abandonment by God, deicide, punishment by God as a people; (3) statements reducing their human dignity to "non-people"; (4) teaching and preaching that may have led up to and contributed to the horrors of the Holocaust; (5) any contributions on the part of Milwaukee Catholics to movements denigrating Jews and threatening their well-being.

But since such assertions, to have any force, must be supported by a firm purpose of amendment, the archbishop asked Catholics present to say "Amen" (if able in conscience) to three affirmations. In brief, (1) that the God both communities worship will not be divided by our human hatreds; (2) that the God we worship together does not reject the covenant made and that we will struggle to learn what the continuing love of God for both communities means for the way we will live together in the same society; (3) that our faith compels us to see each other as bearing the same image of God within us, and therefore we must see each other not as rivals before the same God, but as brothers and sisters in that one God's love.

The archbishop went on to ask Jews and Catholics alike to say "Amen" if they could in conscience agree on four points. In brief, (1) that all persons are sacred in God's eyes as images of God; (2) that all of us are responsible for one another as brothers and sisters; (3) that we are called to be prophets, the voices of the voiceless, speaking out against injustices toward some of our members; (4) that when someone is hurting, we must, as individuals and as a society, not just form a committee, not expect action from the state or others, but reach out ourselves with works of charity.

In a Vesper service in his cathedral on November 28, 1999, the first Sunday of Advent, Archbishop Weakland opened the Jubilee Year. He began with a theology behind the Jubilee in Leviticus: the land belongs to God; we are only tenants thereon; it has to revert back to God. Similarly with our Jubilee: in Luke 4, Jesus announces a year of favor from the Lord, a jubilee. To live in God's kingdom is to live in that constant jubilee. The signs of that kingdom? When the poor hear the glad tidings, captives have liberty proclaimed to them, the blind recover their sight, and the oppressed go free.

All of us are in some ways captive, in bondage. The archbishop offered his own list from Milwaukee. In physical bondage: the poor, those without health care, single parents, working folk stressed out trying to make ends meet, the homeless, those with homes but without heat. In spiritual bondage: the variously addicted, those who feel unwelcome or uncomfortable in our churches, those hurt by the Church, the divorced in second marriages, the depressed and the isolated, the angry and the fearful, those discouraged or with low self-esteem.

Such are the people the Jesus of Luke 4 would list as captives today, of whom he would say: "I came to pronounce a year of favor to all of them, that they be freed up from all these bondages that keep them from being the kind of people I want, people to love and honor me, people who are freed up to contribute and take their place in society."

Where to begin? "With ourselves, learning how God loves us, that we all belong to God, that God cares for each one of us; then we reach out to others and announce the Good News to them." Give others "the sense that somehow they are worth something and that Christ came to give us all the fullness of freedom, the kind of freedom that is spiritually full because we are at one with God, and with Christ, and with each other."

Such is our Jubilee dream: God came to free us; how can we help? The Jubilee is saying, "Let's begin!" *God* will build the kingdom . . . in and through *our efforts.*

Twelve months later, on November 26, 2000, Archbishop Weakland preached at a Vesper service in his cathedral to close the Jubilee Year. It was the feast of Christ the King. In harmony with 1 Corinthians 15:25-27, he declared that everyone living in the archdiocese these many years, and everything that was done therein, including the Jubilee Year, "is just a prelude to that final act when Jesus hands everything over to the Father, and we and this earth will be transformed." Specifically, in the name of all present, he wanted to thank God for all that the religious men and women had contributed to the archdiocese. His gratitude stemmed from two separate aspects of their contribution.

First, thanks to the religious for *being* who they are. Even if they were to *do* nothing, they would still be incredibly valuable to the Church because of the total commitment of their life to the Lord. It is to the Church more than to the world that the religious witness. Moving forward, the Church often compromises with the culture of the day. Every so often it is important for the religious to witness to the fact that there is more to the following of Christ than perhaps what we in the Church get involved in day after day. They keep the final picture before our eyes, the end of time, when Christ will hand the kingdom over to his Father.

The religious do this by their three vows. The vow of obedience is a witness to the Church that what is really important in life is not our will but God's will for us, that God's plan comes first, as it did in the life of Jesus. The vow of poverty tells an acquisitive society to go through life simply, as those sent out by Jesus were to travel light. The vow of chastity tells a culture permeated by sex that there are higher values in life, such as our relationship to Christ, which will find its total fulfillment at the end of time. Briefly, religious remind us that it is the kingdom of God that comes first, the importance of freeing ourselves to be one with Christ now and for ever.

Second, thanks to the religious for all they have *done*. The archbishop singled out two activities of high importance. First, education: universities, colleges, high schools, grade schools, with special tribute to the influence of the sisters. Second, continued sensitivity to justice issues. There follows a sentence probably clear to Catholics in Milwaukee, somewhat obscure to the outsider. "I know at times it's irritating to me, but keep it up. It's an important witness, a witness to the Church." I have vague recollections of actions for justice that may have overleaped generally accepted bounds of propriety.

The archbishop's conclusion I found especially insightful. "No single Christian can perfectly imitate the totality of who Jesus Christ was and is." Benedict did it in his way; so too Francis of Assisi and Clare, Francis de Sales and Jane Frances de Chantal, Teresa of Avila, John of the Cross, and Thérèse the Little Flower. Each "was an example of really only a small aspect of Jesus Christ. We need all these witnesses." Still, somehow all the religious, through their lives and especially their spirituality, "are able to show forth for us those virtues that bring Christ to us, that make us see Christ more clearly, and the wonders of who and what Jesus Christ was and is."

Re: September 11, 2001

Ever since terrorists destroyed the World Trade Center in New York and part of the Pentagon in Washington, raising unprecedented fears across our nation, I have been intrigued by the attention (or lack of attention) given to the event in Catholic preaching. Archbishop Weakland dealt with September 11 at some length in his homily on September 23, 2001. The gospel for that Sunday, the parable of the Dishonest Steward (Luke 16:1-13), was difficult to relate to the unparalleled bombings; he would have preferred a gospel with a clearer connection to that disaster. Still, he said, this is the gospel God has given us on this Sunday. So then, a connection should be sought.

Archbishop Weakland felt that he had found a connection in verse 8: "The master commended that dishonest steward for acting prudently. For the children of this world are more prudent in dealing with their own generation than are the children of light" (NAB). About to be dismissed for "squandering [his master's] property" (v. 1), he proceeds to make friends of the debtors by reducing what they owe. In the archbishop's interpretation, the manager had been giving himself a commission—a commission that he renounced in order to curry favor with the various people in debt to the master. Here I suggest that the archbishop's explanation is very much in line with that favored by biblical expert Joseph A. Fitzmyer, S.J.:

> [The manager] lent his master's goods or land to fellow Jews at an interest apparently customary to the practice of his day, even though unauthorized to do so by his master. This was his profit. Such a practice, however, was in violation of the Torah and especially of the Pharisaic, rabbinical interpretation of it (see Dt 15:7-8; 23:20-21; Ex 22:24; Lv 25:36-37). However, as far as the courts were concerned, there were ways of getting around the law. . . . The manager, in the interests of ingratiating himself with others than his master, now that his job is vir-

tually lost, has summoned the debtors and ordered them to write new receipts or bonds which represent the real amounts owed to the master. . . . The manager has, therefore, merely foregone his own profits on the transaction. In this case his subsequent conduct is hardly dishonest, since he is renouncing what in fact was usury.[14]

The archbishop's application? Taking a bad situation and turning it around. How can we, without justifying an evil situation such as 9/11, make good come from it? "We are so caught up in immediacy" that we fail to plan for the broader future. He asked his listeners to look within: How do I react to misfortune, to evil, to my own sinfulness, my own liabilities? He told the story of an Oxford student lamenting the fact that he had been raised an orphan. Weakland suggested that he turn that liability into an asset—visit orphanages, help orphans. Think how to turn a deficit into something positive, somewhat as the manager made friends with various debtors. Today we should experience a new bonding, communities as well as individuals. In the Dominican Republic at the time of the New York and Washington bombings, Weakland found that *he,* the American, was the victim; *he* was hugged in sympathy, *he* was the object of grieving, of affection. Also, from the parable, a new hope, rising above material things. Are we ready for that? The images of 9/11 are still too much with us. After the grieving, the sense of loss, yes the humiliation, a going out to others, to the poor of the world. How was it that the image of G.I Joe giving candy to children changed into the ugly American? The gospel suggests that we move from our woundedness to the long-term issues: building a kingdom of peace, justice, and love.

The archbishop had dealt briefly with moral issues raised by the bombings in a sermonette delivered on September 26, 2001, at a noon prayer service in Red Arrow Park near City Hall, a service where he joined Mayor John O. Norquist and clergy from United Methodist, Islamic, and Sikh faiths. The archbishop called his address "A Prayer in Time of Need." Addressed to "God of Peace, Love, Justice, and Mercy," the prayer was presented in the form of sense lines. Among the needs expressed: how to create a world in which people of all nations, races, and religious beliefs can live in peace and harmony; how to find Christ in the Eucharist and in those in need; the Spirit of courage and a strong desire for peace; a sense of justice tempered with God's gift for peace; rooting out vengeance and hatred from our hearts and from all

14. Joseph A. Fitzmyer, S.J., "The Story of the Dishonest Manager (Lk 10:1-13)," *Theological Studies* 25 (1964) 23–42, at 35–36.

called to serve our nation; rooting out the causes of dissension, hatred, and hopelessness; rightful indignation over conditions in our society that force others to live in poverty, surrounded by violence; healing for our grief and calm for our fears; courage to ask deeper questions about how we live the gospel in our daily lives; how we relate to others, how to share more justly the gifts given us; a deeper understanding of those who differ from us, their hopes and desires, their fears and anxieties.

Conclusions for Effective Preaching

What have I found particularly impressive about Archbishop Weakland's preaching? First, the "one thing necessary": an intimate link between Scripture and concrete human issues—the gospel applied to living people. The homily is not simply exegesis of Scripture, nor is it a lecture on the sins in our culture. Basic to the archbishop's homilies are the liturgical readings, but never in abstraction from the needs of people in pain, from "the signs of the times." We saw it in a number of instances above: for example, in the courageous Jubilee homily stemming from Leviticus 25 that called for Milwaukee's Catholics to acknowledge wrongs done to Jews, seek forgiveness, and resolve to reform.

In so doing, the archbishop was following, consciously or not, the most helpful Church document on the liturgical homily, *Fulfilled in Your Hearing: The Homily in the Sunday Assembly*, produced in 1982 by the Committee on Priestly Life and Ministry of the National Conference of Catholic Bishops of the United States. The homily is there defined as "a scriptural interpretation of human existence which enables a community to recognize God's active presence." The homilist is described as a "mediator of meaning." In other words, explains homily expert Robert P. Waznak, S.S.,

> the homilist is primarily an interpreter, not a teacher. The document insists that the homily does not "primarily concern itself with a systematic theological understanding of the faith." The liturgical gathering is not primarily an educational assembly.... To return to a pre-Vatican II understanding of the liturgy as a platform for doctrinal and moral instruction would be an unfortunate leap backward. It would rob Catholics of a rich homiletic tradition and do irreparable harm to our renewed liturgical tradition as well.[15]

15. Robert P. Waznak, S.S., "The Catechism and the Sunday Homily," *America* (Oct. 22, 1994) 18–21, at 19.

A second impressive aspect of Weakland's preaching is his knowledge and use of theology. Theology not as an abstract science but as the Church's ceaseless struggle to grasp what God has said and what God might be saying now. Theology in that sense is indispensable for effective preaching and is a constant in the archbishop's homilies. It is clear to me that he did not close his last theological tome when the oil of holy orders caressed his fingers or when he was ordained a bishop.

Third, Weakland listens: not only to God in his heart and in the proclaimed Word, but to people—his own flock, to women and men of other faiths, and to the voices of a world wider still. Paradoxically, he believes this may well be the only area in which he has incurred Rome's serious displeasure. "I'm in trouble," he remarked to friend theologian Martin Marty, "because I listen to women." Marty continues:

> He has groups in which women speak of their experiences. Rome wasn't interested in hearing what women thought about childbearing and birth control. . . . He said: "But that's not all I do. I also want to know how profound articulators of the culture do it. So, this summer is my Muriel Sparks summer. A couple of years ago was my Flannery O'Connor summer. . . . Every summer I read the entire corpus of a woman author, because artists see some things that we don't normally see."[16]

Fourth, Weakland the preacher comes through as a man of prayer. Vatican II made it clear that the homily is "part of the liturgical action," is "part of the liturgy."[17] And the homily is, or should be, worship. For, in theologian Gerard Sloyan's pithy definition, "To worship is to be in the presence of God in a posture of awe."[18] And a bit later: "To sum up: preaching is an integral part of the worship act. One speaks in the assembly to facilitate the people's prayer."[19] Here Vatican II was pointed and pellucid: "The two parts which in a sense go to make up the Mass, viz., the liturgy of the word and the eucharistic liturgy, are so closely connected with each other that they form but one single act of worship."[20] Very simply, the homily is liturgy, the

---

16. Martin Marty, "Preaching Rhetorically: Thanks, Aristotle and Apostles," delivered at the 2001 Gladstone Festival of Preaching, March 5–6, 2001, McMaster Divinity College, McMaster University. Text available online at *McMaster Journal of Theology and Ministry* 4 (2001): http://www.mcmaster.ca/mjtm/4-2.htm (accessed September 13, 2002).

17. SC 35 and 52.

18. Gerard S. Sloyan, *Worshipful Preaching* (Philadelphia: Fortress Press, 1984) 7.

19. Ibid., 15.

20. SC 56.

homily is worship, therefore the homily is prayer. Archbishop Weakland's homilies are vocal prayers. That comes through explicitly in a prayer that accompanied his 2001 Stewardship Appeal:

> Loving and gracious God,
> You did not hesitate to give us your Son, Jesus Christ.
> He in turn gave of himself for us,
>   not only on the cross,
>   but in every moment of his life among us.
>
> When he saw the hungry, he fed them;
> When he saw the lame, he cured them;
> When he saw the sick, he healed them;
> When he saw those without a teacher, he taught them;
> He gave of himself so that others might have a fuller life;
> In this way, he taught us to give.
>
> Loving and gracious God,
> You ask us to be like your Son Jesus:
>   to open our hearts to the needy,
>   to teach those spiritually hungry,
>   to reach out to the unwanted.
> Do you dream of a world without hunger,
>   without hopelessness?
>
> If so, strengthen us to open our hearts
>   as you did, as your Son Jesus did,
>   to the endless possibilities of being
>   neighbor to all in need.

But a person of prayer, a prayerful preacher, is not limited to vocal prayer. In harmony with the Benedictine tradition, the man of action that is the Archbishop of Milwaukee is a contemplative in action. A contemplative in the definition of Carmelite William McNamara: a man who "looks long and lovingly at the real." The "real" here is not some abstract "pie in the sky." The real is all that is: the sun setting over the Swiss Alps and a sparkling glass of Burgundy, a striding woman with windblown hair and a child licking a chocolate ice cream cone. The real is the rain in your face and the idea in your head. The real is Christ Jesus. Yes, the real is sin and sickness, war and the Holocaust—where the real draws forth compassion, which is another name for love.

The real for Archbishop Weakland includes each Jesus who is hungry or thirsty, a stranger or naked, ill or in prison. Real are the six million Jews of the Holocaust; real are the ghettoes structured by

Christians, the forced baptisms, the shoulders shrugged and the backs turned. Real is every man, woman, and child in physical or spiritual bondage, aching only to be loved, to be treated with dignity as an image of the Lord. Terribly real is each Jesus on his or her Calvary.

The Voice That Utters the Word

Several brief comments on the voice that expresses the word. Three tapes have been illuminating. One homily, dating from November 7, 1993, dealt with the Gospel parable of the Ten Virgins (Matt 25:1-13). The archbishop stressed the final verse: "Stay awake, for you know neither the day nor the hour." It is one of those texts, he noted, that tell us "what it's all about." He suggested that we do not take such texts seriously enough. We take Christ's second coming for granted, but not as something to be concerned about right now. And yet we should be as ready for Christ's final appearance as we are for each Eucharist. And if we are genuinely ready for each Eucharist, each coming of Christ sacramentally, beneath the appearances of bread and wine, we are ready for his final coming "on clouds of glory." Ready now.

Together with the content, what I admired time and again was the tone: not classical oratory, not the commanding artistry of a Fulton Sheen, though these qualities emerge every so often, as when he speaks of the Holocaust or Catholic-Jewish history. Conversational on the whole, direct address, persuasive rather than fault-finding, with a gentle firmness that draws acceptance. Now and then a surprising analogy, as when we are encouraged to prepare for a crucial event, somewhat vague, perhaps far off (second coming), by relating it to an important event of today, happening this day, perhaps every day (our experience of Eucharist). Rarely dry or abstract; consistently imaginative, but imagination in search of truth alive, in pursuit of Christlike action.

Another attractive quality: much in a short space, with humor and love. At Midnight Mass on Christmas 1996, the archbishop preached on peace—peace when there was so little peace. He insisted that genuine Christmas peace has three aspects. (1) Peace within ourselves. This means accepting ourselves for who we are, sensing the presence of God in our lives, hence a basic self-esteem. What keeps us from having it? Some are perpetually angry, blaming others, blaming God, blaming parents. Some are full of fear, afraid to take risks. If you want to be at peace inside, you have to be at peace with your God. (2) Peace with others. The obstacles? Prejudice; dividing people into good guys and bad guys. When we stereotype people, we don't have to deal with them. Get rid of selfishness, narcissism, using other people, exploiting them. See other people as God's gift. Delicate gifts, like the ornaments hanging so fragilely on a Christmas branch. (3) Peace in society. There will be no peace (e.g., in Rwanda, where there are Catholics on both sides) till we have justice—not charity alone. We have to work constantly for a just society—Christ in our personal lives, Christ in others, Christ in society. Imagine all our churches across the world tonight committing themselves to being persons of peace. "Blessed are the peacemakers" (Matt 5:9). No wasted words; no clichés; conversational, person to person.

Finally, an Easter sermon, April 16, 1995, that exemplifies so much of the above. Many Christians, Weakland noted, have a preference for Christmas, with its child, its exchange of gifts. Easter is somewhat more abstract; offers an empty tomb. Good Friday is more easily grasped. And yet Easter is the most important of our feasts. Each Sunday celebrates Easter. It is not God touching down and leaving us; it is God staying with us. Nothing human can be excluded. He became one of us in every stage, from birth to death. Easter is God's commitment to us: God lives on among us, hands over his Spirit to us. The Spirit is poured out on everyone. In baptism God becomes one with each of us. The Greek Church has always stressed divinization—a strong word: God shares God's life with us. The Lord walks with us. In baptism we put on Christ—each of us. It doesn't depend on how we feel. On the paschal feast the archbishop recalled his childhood, when the whole house smelled of bread. Such is the grace that permeates everything we are. That's why the theme of Easter is hope; God stays with us. In our current crisis God is working in and through us. Yes, things will change, but there will always be a Church, an archbishop. The risen Lord will be among us. God seems silent at times; even martyrs have asked God, "Why don't you speak?" Easter is a renewal of our belief, our hope, that God is with us, despite the silence. Put your hopes on the altar. Easter permits us to say: God stays with us; Christmas did not say that.

What engaged me, held my attention? The archbishop was talking to me. To me. And at the same time to a much larger world.

A preacher for all seasons, a preacher for a Church universal, a preacher for a human family wherein terror threatens to replace the peace of Christ.

Chapter Four
The Bishop's Teaching Office

Francis A. Sullivan, S.J.

In the course of the John Courtney Murray lecture that I gave at Fordham University in May 2001, I mentioned the statement of the Second Vatican Council that bishops receive teaching authority through their episcopal ordination. During the question period that followed the lecture, one of the participants said that he didn't see how teaching authority could be the result of being ordained a bishop. He insisted that a person acquires teaching authority through the conferral of a doctorate, followed by a career of successful teaching and scholarly publication. In matters of faith, therefore, he would recognize theologians, rather than bishops, as possessing teaching authority.

In my reply I tried to explain, rather summarily, the difference between the teaching authority of bishops and that of theologians. That this difference is not always clearly understood is illustrated by an incident that the late Father Raymond Brown recounted in his book *Priest and Bishop: Biblical Reflections.*[1] Here is his account of it.

> Sometimes the role of the bishop as official theologian has been misunderstood, as if the episcopal office somehow substituted for theological investigation and gave the occupant a divine insight. I can remember an incident which happened just before Vatican II that illustrates the difficulty. A bishop, now deceased, was welcoming several Scripture scholars who had been invited into the diocese to address the clergy. He remarked that he envied the modern seminarians because they had good professors in Scripture, whereas his own course had been hopeless and consequently he never felt confident about even the exegesis needed for

1. (Mahwah, N.J.: Paulist Press, 1971) 76–77.

preaching. At the end of these kind words, he cautioned the scholars that they should advise the audience that their conclusions about Scripture were only opinions, for the bishops were the only official theologians of the Church and only they could speak authoritatively about Scripture. Here was a man innocently claiming that he could speak authoritatively about a subject in which, as he had just admitted, he had not even elementary competence!

Among the several misunderstandings that this episode illustrates, I think the first is Father Brown's own expression "the role of the bishop as official theologian." I would say that while episcopal ordination makes a man an official teacher, it does not make him a theologian. The bishop in the story seems to have thought that his episcopal ordination made him the only official exegete in his church. Again, I would say that episcopal ordination does not make a man an exegete. In other words, there is a very real difference between the teaching authority given to bishops by their ordination and the teaching authority that theologians and exegetes acquire through years of scholarly achievement in their fields.

Of course, it is possible that a man who is already a professional theologian can be ordained to the episcopate. (This has happened quite frequently in Germany, where theologians like Joseph Ratzinger, Karl Lehmann, and Walter Kasper have been chosen as bishops.) However, the great majority of those ordained to the episcopate are not professional theologians, nor do they have the time or opportunity to acquire such competence after ordination. The following questions need to be answered, therefore. (1) What is the nature of the teaching authority that the Catholic Church attributes to its bishops? (2) How can one explain and justify the belief that a man receives teaching authority by ordination to the episcopate? In the rest of this article I shall offer my answers to these questions.

The Nature of the Bishop's Teaching Authority

While the Catholic Church attributes teaching authority to all the members of the episcopal college (which they can exercise, for instance, in an ecumenical council), in this essay I shall focus on the teaching authority of the diocesan bishop. I shall begin by recalling the teaching of the Second Vatican Council about the effect of episcopal consecration. Settling a question to which different answers had previously been given, the council declared: "Episcopal consecration confers, together with the office of sanctifying, the offices also of teaching and ruling, which, however, of their very nature can be exercised only in hierarchical communion with the head and members of the college" (LG 21). The "Preliminary Explanatory Note," in the light of which Pope Paul VI insisted that Chapter Three of *Lumen Gentium* be interpreted, explains that in that sentence, the word *munera* ("offices" or "functions") was used, rather than *potestates* ("powers"), because a further canonical determination is required in order for these offices to be "ordered to action."[2] This applies particularly to the teaching office of the diocesan bishop, which becomes "ordered to action" as teaching authority for the faithful of a particular diocese by his canonical mission as its bishop. A further qualification of a bishop's teaching authority is that it can be exercised only in hierarchical communion with the head and members of the episcopal college. "Hierarchical communion" has a sacramental basis in the common sharing of valid episcopal orders and has also a juridical component in the mutual recognition of respective rights and duties among the members of the college and between them and the bishop of Rome. This means that a schismatic bishop could not exercise the teaching function that he had received at his consecration.

The paragraph of *Lumen Gentium* to which we have referred further describes the effect of episcopal ordination by saying that through it "the grace of the Holy Spirit is given, and a sacred character is impressed in such a way that bishops, eminently and visibly, take the place of Christ himself, teacher, shepherd and priest, and act in his person." I think we are more accustomed to say that bishops act *in persona Christi* when they celebrate the Eucharist, but here they are said to "take the place of Christ" and "act in his person" also when they exercise their office as teachers and pastors. The sense in which this is true is suggested in LG 20 by the application to bishops, as successors to the apostles, of the saying of the Lord: "Whoever listens to you listens to me. Whoever rejects you rejects me" (Luke 10:16, NAB). It is further explained in LG 25 when it describes bishops as "teachers endowed with the authority of Christ," and also in DV 10, when it says that their authority to interpret the word of God "is exercised in the name of Jesus Christ."

It is the understanding of the Catholic Church, therefore, that a bishop's teaching authority is based not on scholarly competence in

---

2. Austin Flannery, O.P., ed., *Vatican Council II: A Completely Revised Translation in Inclusive Language* (Northport, N.Y.: Costello Publishing Company, 1996) 93, "Preliminary Explanatory Note," par. 2.

theology or exegesis, but on the combination of episcopal ordination and hierarchical communion, which qualifies him to teach in the name of and with the authority of Jesus Christ. However, in order for teaching authority to be effective, a teacher must be recognized as authoritative by those to whom his teaching is directed. Students recognize the authority of a teacher in view of the reputation he has gained through his achievements as a scholar. The recognition of the teaching authority of bishops is based rather on the belief of the Catholic faithful that bishops, as successors of the apostles, teach in the name of Christ, so that the words of Christ, "Whoever listens to you listens to me," apply to them. What is distinctive about the nature of the bishops' teaching authority, then, is that its possession is based on a sacrament, and its recognition is based on faith.

According to the principle expressed by the Latin axiom *"agere sequitur esse,"* we can expect that the exercise of episcopal teaching authority will correspond to its distinctive nature. This expectation is confirmed by the description that is given in *Lumen Gentium* of the ways in which bishops exercise their teaching function. "Among the more important duties of bishops, that of preaching the Gospel has pride of place"; "[they] are heralds of the faith, who draw new disciples to Christ"; "they cause that faith to radiate, drawing from the storehouse of revelation new things and old"; "they make it bear fruit and vigilantly ward off whatever errors threaten their flock"; "[they] are to be respected by all as witnesses of divine and catholic truth; the faithful, for their part, should concur with their bishop's judgment, made in the name of Christ, in matters of faith and morals, and adhere to it with a religious docility of spirit" (LG 25).

It is obvious that bishops exercise their teaching function in a way that is very different from that of university professors of theology and with a kind of authority that theologians cannot claim. An important part of a bishop's teaching is done from the pulpit; few professors of theology would be happy to have their lectures described as "preaching." In the exercise of their teaching function, bishops are described as "heralds" and "witnesses" of the faith; these terms hardly apply to the function of the university professor. When a theologian expresses his judgment about a controverted question, he makes it on the basis of his expertise in the matter and expects his students to accept if they are convinced by the reasons he gives for it; a bishop expresses his judgment in a matter of faith and morals in the name of Christ, and his subjects have an obligation to adhere to it with "a religious docility of spirit." The responsibility that bishops have to "ward off whatever errors threaten their flock" is the clearest indication that their teaching function is rightly described as "pastoral." This is the term that St. Thomas Aquinas used of the bishop's *magisterium,* when he distinguished it from that of the professor of theology in a university.

In the vocabulary of the medieval schoolmen, the word *magisterium* meant the "mastery" of anyone who teaches, without its modern restriction to official teaching by members of the hierarchy. The symbol of teaching authority was the chair, and they knew two kinds of such chairs: that of the bishop in his cathedral and that of the professor in the university. So St. Thomas spoke of two kinds of *magisterium: magisterium cathedrae pastoralis* and *magisterium cathedrae magistralis.*[3] For St. Thomas, both these instances of *magisterium* involved authority. The bishop's authority was based on his role as a prelate *(ex officio praelationis),* while the theologian's authority was based on his knowledge of theology.[4]

Pastoral teaching authority is based on the nature of the Church as *congregatio fidelium:* a community united in the profession of the same faith. In order to remain united in the same faith, the Church has to have a common creed and a common understanding of the basic truths of its faith. Hence the pastors who are responsible for the well-being of the community have a special responsibility regarding its common profession of faith. When conflicts arise as to the terms of its creed or to its interpretation, those with pastoral responsibility must have the authority to judge which of the conflicting opinions is in accord with the faith of the Church. They likewise have the responsibility of protecting the faithful from errors that would draw them away from the true faith.

According to the Catholic understanding of the matter, it is part of God's design that in every age of the Church there should be successors of the apostles, not, to be sure, as immediate recipients of revelation, but as authorized witnesses, with authority from Christ to preach and teach his word and, when necessary, to settle questions that arise concerning the normative faith of the community. It is in this sense that Vatican II speaks of bishops as "judges of faith" (LG 25). This, of course, does not mean that they are superior to the word of God. A passage of *Dei Verbum* expressly denies this. Since it throws

3. *Quodl.* III, 9, ad 3.
4. *In IV Sent.,* d.19, q. 2, a. 2, q[a.] 2, ad 4.

a good deal of light on the notion of a pastoral teaching authority, I shall quote it and offer some comments on it.

> This magisterium is not superior to the word of God, but is rather its servant. It teaches only what has been handed on to it. At the divine command and with the help of the holy Spirit, it listens to this devoutly, guards it reverently and expounds it faithfully. All that it proposes for belief as being divinely revealed it draws from this sole deposit of faith (DV 10).

Since "the magisterium" in this passage is the subject that "teaches," "listens," and "proposes," it obviously refers to the persons who exercise the magisterium; hence these terms apply to bishops in the exercise of their teaching authority. Since each term brings out an aspect of their pastoral teaching role, each deserves comment, substituting "the bishop" for "the magisterium."

The bishop is not superior to the word of God, but is rather its servant. The bishop does not have authority over the word of God, but over human interpretations of it, especially those that are in conflict with the faith of the Church. His is an authority within the community of faith; he has a ministry to the word, and to the people who have accepted this word. It is a service to the unity of the Church in the profession of the true faith.

The bishop teaches only what has been handed on to him. The term "what has been handed on" is used here with the same inclusive meaning which it has in DV 8, where the council says: "What was handed on by the apostles comprises everything that serves to make the people of God live their lives in holiness and increase their faith." In other words, it means the whole "sacred deposit of the word of God, which is entrusted to the church" (DV 10). It is significant that Vatican II says that it is to the *Church* (and not just to the magisterium) that the deposit of the word of God has been entrusted. Likewise, it is "the Church, in its doctrine, life and worship" that "perpetuates and transmits to every generation all that it itself is, all that it believes" (DV 8). This is a salutary corrective of some earlier treatises on the subject that focused almost exclusively on the transmission of the deposit of faith by the magisterium.

The bishop listens to the word of God devoutly. This phrase tells us that before a bishop can teach what the Church has handed on to him, he must first listen to it; before he can belong to the "teaching Church" *(Ecclesia docens)* he must belong to the "learning Church"

(Ecclesia discens). And since "the sacred deposit of the word of God has been committed to the Church," it follows that the bishop has to listen devoutly to this word as it is handed on from generation to generation "in the doctrine, life and worship of the Church." He cannot isolate himself from the Church and listen only to himself. An important part of his listening to the word of God as handed on in the Church will be to "consult the faithful," as Cardinal Newman put it.[5] Another part will be to consult the theologians and exegetes who spend their lives studying the word of God.

The bishop guards the word of God reverently. This phrase suggests the special responsibility of the pastoral magisterium and the reason why it is properly "conservative"; the bishop's teaching role is not to penetrate into the depths of the mysteries of faith (the task of the theologian), but rather to safeguard the priceless treasure of the word of God and to defend the purity of the faith of the Christian community.

The bishop expounds the word of God faithfully. Here the adverb "faithfully" is another indication that the primary concern of the pastoral teacher is fidelity to the original deposit of faith. The bishop must explain the word of God in his teaching, but he does not take upon himself the specific function of the theologian, whose role it is to seek a deeper understanding of the faith, making use of knowledge gained from philosophy and other sciences in the process.

"With the help of the holy Spirit." While the Holy Spirit dwells in all the faithful and arouses and sustains their "sense of the faith" (LG 12), Catholics believe that the sacrament of episcopal ordination, which confers on bishops the function of pastoral magisterium, is a divine pledge of a special assistance of the Holy Spirit in the fulfillment of their teaching office. However, this divine assistance is not such as to render them immune from error in their teaching as individuals. It is only when all the bishops, together with the pope, are in agreement that a particular doctrine must be held definitively that a bishop shares in the charism of infallibility.

The fact that the teaching of an individual bishop is not infallible can be raised as an objection against the doctrine of Vatican II quoted above, namely, that "the faithful . . . should concur with their bishop's judgment . . . and adhere to it with religious docility of spirit." A person might well ask how one can be obliged to adhere to a judgment that is not infallible and therefore could be erroneous. The

---

5. John Henry Newman, *On Consulting the Faithful in Matters of Doctrine*, ed. John Coulson (Kansas City: Sheed & Ward, 1961).

answer to this question depends on a correct understanding of what is meant by "religious docility of spirit."[6] The key point is that the direct object of "religious docility of spirit" is not the bishop's judgment as such, but the authority with which he teaches in matters of faith and morals. "Docility" is the attitude of will that is a proper response to what one recognizes as legitimate teaching authority. It is a willingness to be taught, a willingness to listen and learn, a willingness to give one's assent to what is proposed. In most cases, such an attitude of docility on the part of Catholics who respect the teaching authority of their bishop should normally result in their adhering to his judgment by giving it their intellectual assent.

However, docility, which is an attitude of the will, does not automatically result in assent, which is a judgment of the mind. It is possible that persons who respect the authority of the bishop and are willing to be taught by him can have such strong doubts about the truth or soundness of a particular judgment their bishop has made that they cannot give it their sincere assent. Such persons have to be mindful of their own fallibility and not be over-confident in the correctness of their own judgment when it differs from that of their bishop. Their attitude of docility should move them to consult well-informed persons who might be able to solve their doubts.

However, it is possible that after having done their best to overcome their doubts about their bishop's judgment, they could still be unable to give it their sincere assent. In that case, they would have fulfilled their obligation to respond to their bishop's authority with "religious docility of will." This is the proper response to teaching that is authoritative but not infallible. It is the nature of such teaching that, as authoritative, it always calls for a response of willingness to assent to it, but as not infallible, it may in a particular instance be erroneous and objectively not warrant assent.

Having at least briefly discussed the nature of the teaching authority that the Catholic Church attributes to its bishops, we come to our second question.

How Justify the Belief That Teaching Authority Is Conferred by Episcopal Ordination?

The Catholic Church believes that it is an element of the divinely willed structure of the Church that by valid episcopal ordination a

---

6. The Latin phrase is *religioso animi obsequio.*

man is incorporated into the college of bishops, which succeeds to the apostles in their threefold office of teaching, ruling, and sanctifying. Most Protestants question this belief on the grounds that there is no clear evidence in the New Testament that either Jesus himself or his apostles ordained a bishop for each local church or established a permanent church order in which each local church would be led by a bishop in apostolic succession. In fact, most Catholic scholars now agree that one cannot prove that bishops are the successors of the apostles in their teaching authority on the basis of the New Testament evidence alone. They generally agree that the Catholic conviction about this must also be based on our belief concerning the guidance of the Holy Spirit in the development of the Church's structure during the first few centuries of the Church's life.

The Catholic argument can be developed in the following steps: (1) In the subapostolic period of the New Testament, those who carried on the apostles' ministry combined a role of pastoral leadership with responsibility for handing on the apostolic faith and protecting the community from being led astray in its belief. (2) During the course of the second century, Christian churches came to be led by bishops who were recognized as successors of the apostles and authoritative teachers of the genuine apostolic tradition. (3) As the churches received certain writings as the written norm of their faith, so they received the teaching of their bishops as the living norm of their faith. The Holy Spirit, who maintains the Church in the true faith, must have guided the Church in its reception of these norms of its faith, since error about the norms would have led to untold errors in faith. Therefore the Holy Spirit must have guided the Church in recognizing its bishops as successors to the apostles in their pastoral teaching authority. Such evident guidance of the Spirit justifies the belief that it is an element of the divinely willed structure of the Church that pastoral teaching authority is conferred by episcopal ordination. In what follows, I shall develop briefly each of these points.

1. *Teaching ministry in the subapostolic period of the New Testament.* The authentic letters of St. Paul provide abundant evidence that he shared his ministry both with his missionary co-workers and with those whom he left in charge of the local churches that he had founded. The later books of the New Testament indicate that after Paul's death his ministry was carried on by members of both of these groups. The address that the author of Acts has Paul give at Miletus to the presbyters/overseers of Ephesus makes it clear that Paul expected them to continue his work in that local church. The Pastoral Letters can hardly

be understood except in the light of the assumption that co-workers like Timothy and Titus inherited Paul's ministry when he was no longer on the scene. A closer look at these texts shows that those who carried on the apostles' ministry in the subapostolic period of the New Testament combined their pastoral care of the Christian community with responsibility for handing on the apostles' teaching and refuting errors that would have led the faithful astray.

Paul's address to the local leaders of the church of Ephesus. Luke tells us that Paul made a first brief visit to Ephesus at the end of his second missionary journey, leaving Priscilla and Aquila there and promising to return (Acts 18:18-21). He did return, at the beginning of his third missionary journey, and stayed for three years (Acts 19). After a brief visit to the churches in Greece and Macedonia, Paul was on his way to Jerusalem when he stopped at Miletus, a port city about forty miles from Ephesus. Luke tells us: "From Miletus he had the presbyters of the church at Ephesus summoned" (Acts 20:17, NAB), and then reports the farewell speech that Paul addressed to them. Needless to say, this speech is a Lukan composition, which in this respect followed the practice of ancient historians. In it Paul warns his hearers about what will happen in the future, when he is no longer with them. Written some twenty-five years after Paul's death, this is more likely to reflect the situation at the time of writing than when the speech was actually delivered. For this reason, we can be more confident that it tells us about local ministry in Pauline churches during the subapostolic period than when Paul himself was alive.

What it tells us is that in the church at Ephesus there was a group of presbyters who were responsible for giving it pastoral care. Paul's exhortation contains the following description of their role: "Keep watch over yourselves and over the whole flock of which the holy Spirit has appointed you overseers, in which you tend the church of God that he acquired with his own blood " (Acts 20:28, NAB). The word translated by "tend" is the Greek *poimainein,* which means literally "to shepherd"; correspondingly, the Christian community is described as a "flock" (Greek *poimnion*). It should be noted that "pastors" (literally "shepherds") and teachers are also named among the gifts of the risen Christ to the Church in the Letter to the Ephesians (4:11). In that text, the fact that "pastors" and "teachers" are linked by the same definitive article suggests that the same persons had both of these roles.

In introducing his account of Paul's speech, Luke described the men whom Paul summoned to Miletus as "the presbyters of the church at

Ephesus" (Acts 20:17, NAB). On the other hand, in the speech he has Paul say to them: "Keep watch over yourselves and over the whole flock of which the holy Spirit has appointed you overseers, in which you tend the church of God" (Acts 20:28, NAB). The word "overseers" translates the Greek *episkopous*, the word that will eventually come to mean "bishops." Paul began his Letter to the Philippians by greeting "all the holy ones in Christ Jesus who are in Philippi, with the overseers and ministers" (Phil 1:1, NAB). From this undisputed letter we know that Paul did use the term *episkopoi* of local leaders in his churches. The fact that Luke puts this term on Paul's lips, although he himself had described these same men as presbyters, suggests that he may have known that Paul spoke of local leaders as *episkopoi* rather than as *presbuteroi*. It also suggests that in Luke's day, local church leaders could be called either "elders" or "overseers," without a clear distinction between the terms.

It is evident from Paul's farewell address that he had prepared these men for their ministry and that he expected them to carry it on after his departure. He had prepared them by his teaching, his admonitions, and his example. "I did not at all shrink from telling you what was for your benefit, or from teaching you in public or in your homes" (Acts 20:20, NAB). "I did not shrink from proclaiming to you the entire plan of God" (Acts 20:27, NAB). "For three years night and day I unceasingly admonished each of you with tears" (Acts 20:31, NAB). "In every way I have shown you that by hard work of that sort we must help the weak" (Acts 20:35, NAB).

Paul expected them to carry on his pastoral care of the church: "I know that after my departure savage wolves will come among you, and they will not spare the flock. And from your own group, men will come forward perverting the truth to draw the disciples away after them. So be vigilant. . . . And now I commend you to God and to that gracious word of his that can build you up and give you the inheritance among all who are consecrated" (Acts 20:29-32, NAB).

As teaching the truth of the gospel and defending it against all perversions had been paramount in Paul's ministry, so it was also to be a primary care of those who would carry it on after his departure. They had received from Paul, along with the pastoral care of the Christian community of Ephesus, responsibility for the purity of its faith, with authority to oppose any who would "come forward perverting the truth to draw the disciples after them."

The Pastoral Letters. The two Letters to Timothy and the Letter to Titus have, from ancient times, been called "pastoral" because of their contents, which deal primarily with the pastoral care of the churches of Ephesus and Crete, entrusted to Timothy and Titus. They present themselves as written by Paul, but most modern scholars judge them to have been written some years after Paul's death by one (or two) of his disciples. Hence they are thought to reflect church structure as it had developed during the subapostolic period.

The authentic letters of Paul tell us how Paul shared his missionary and pastoral task with Timothy and Titus, frequently sending them on delicate missions to the churches that they had evangelized together. In the Pastorals they are presented as still working under Paul's direction, sent by him to churches that he had founded with their help: Timothy to Ephesus, and Titus to Crete. As they are working under Paul's direction, so also they have received from him the pastoral authority that they exercise in those communities. In our liturgical calendar they are called "bishops," but Paul did not leave them as permanent residential leaders of those churches; they were still missionaries and were to rejoin Paul when they had completed their present task (Titus 3:12; 2 Tim 4:9, 11, 21). This task was not evangelization, but the pastoral care of established Christian communities. This care involved the teaching of sound doctrine and the choice and appointment of local leaders who would likewise combine pastoral care with responsibility for the faith of the community.

A major concern of these letters is the danger of false doctrine, which Timothy and Titus were to counteract by their sound teaching. Thus Paul says to Timothy: "I repeat the request I made of you when I was on my way to Macedonia, that you stay in Ephesus to instruct certain people not to teach false doctrines" (1 Tim 1:3, NAB). "Until I arrive, attend to the reading, exhortation and teaching" (1 Tim 4:13, NAB). "Teach and urge these things. Whoever teaches something different and does not agree with the sound words of our Lord Jesus Christ and the religious teaching, is conceited, understanding nothing" (1 Tim 6:2-4, NAB). A key idea of these letters is that the true doctrine of Christ is a sacred "deposit" or "trust," which must be kept safe and handed on incorrupt. Thus 1 Timothy concludes: "O Timothy, guard what has been entrusted to you. Avoid profane babbling and the absurdities of so-called knowledge. By professing it, some have deviated from the faith" (1 Tim 6:20-21, NAB). The same instruction is given in 2 Timothy: "Take as your norm the sound words that you heard from me, in the faith and love that are in Christ Jesus. Guard this rich trust with the help of the holy Spirit that dwells within us" (2 Tim 1:13-14, NAB).

The men whom Timothy and Titus were to appoint as presbyters and overseers in the churches under their care were also to combine the roles of leadership and teaching. Among the qualifications of one to be chosen as an *episkopos* was that he be *didaktikos:* "able to teach" (1 Tim 3:2, NAB). While all the presbyters had a role of leadership, some also had a ministry of teaching: "Presbyters who preside well deserve double honor, especially those who toil in preaching and teaching" (1 Tim 5:17, NAB). Timothy is instructed: "What you heard from me through many witnesses entrust to faithful people who will have the ability to teach others as well" (2 Tim 2:2, NAB). Likewise Titus is told that among the qualifications of an *episkopos* is that he must be a person "holding fast to the true message as taught so that he will be able both to exhort with sound doctrine and to refute opponents" (Titus 1:9, NAB). Joseph Fitzmyer has summed up this evidence by saying:

> In the Deutero-Pauline letters, then, we have a clear picture of a number of emergent details regarding the function of teaching in different local churches. The author himself clearly writes as a *didaskalos* guaranteeing the "sound doctrine," and he relates the teaching of it to the office of *episkopos,* who is to be concerned for it and for the judgment and confutation of what is opposed to it.[7]

2. *During the second century the churches came to be led by bishops who were recognized as successors of the apostles and authoritative teachers of the apostolic tradition.* The postapostolic development of ministry was consistent with what took place during the period of the New Testament. Just as during the subapostolic period the need was recognized for a structure that would provide stable and continuing leadership in the churches, and that need was met by the development of the presbyterate, so also in the second century the grave threat that Gnosticism posed to the unity of the church and its genuine apostolic faith led to the development and general acceptance of the episcopate as a form of leadership that could more effectively meet those threats.

However, the few Christian writings that we have from the late first and early second century do not allow us to reconstruct the process by which the Christian churches moved from the leadership of a group of presbyters to the leadership of a single bishop. The few documents of

7. Joseph A. Fitzmyer, "The Office of Teaching in the Christian Church According to the New Testament," in *Teaching Authority and Infallibility in the Church,* ed. Paul C. Empie and others (Minneapolis: Augsburg Publishing House, 1980) 207.

the period that we possess suggest that the development of the episcopate took place at varying rates of speed in various regions of the church. The first documented example of a bishop whose role corresponded to that of a modern diocesan bishop is Ignatius of Antioch, who is known to us from the seven letters that he wrote while on his way to Rome, where he suffered martyrdom about the year 117. I shall cite one of the numerous passages of those letters in which he exercised his teaching authority to defend the genuine doctrine about Christ from the error of docetism.

> Be deaf, therefore, whenever anyone speaks to you apart from Jesus Christ, who was of the family of David, who was the son of Mary, who really was born, who both ate and drank, who really was persecuted under Pontius Pilate, who really was crucified and died while those in heaven and on earth and under the earth looked on; who, moreover, really was raised from the dead when his Father raised him up, who—his Father, that is—in the same way will likewise also raise us up in Christ Jesus who believe in him, apart from whom we have no true life. But if, as some atheists (that is, unbelievers) say, he suffered in appearance only (while they exist in appearance only!) why am I in chains? And why do I want to fight with wild beasts? If that is the case, I die for no reason; what is more, I am telling lies about the Lord. Flee, therefore, from these wicked offshoots that bear deadly fruit; if anyone even tastes it, he dies on the spot. These people are not the Father's planting.[8]

One of the seven letters written by Ignatius was addressed to Polycarp, the bishop of Smyrna, who also suffered martyrdom, but many years later, when he was eighty-six years old. An authentic eyewitness account of his martyrdom is preserved in the form of a letter written by the presbyters of Smyrna to the church of Philomelium. Two passages of this letter witness to the fact that Polycarp was recognized as an outstanding teacher of the faith, not only by his fellow Christians but even by those who cried out for his execution. The account of his martyrdom includes the detail that when the herald proclaimed that Polycarp had confessed that he was a Christian, "the entire crowd, Gentiles as well as Jews living in Smyrna, cried out with uncontrollable anger and with a loud shout: 'This is the teacher of Asia, the father of the Christians, the destroyer of our gods, who teaches many not to sacrifice or worship.'"[9] The expression "teacher of Asia" (refer-

8. Letter to the Trallians, 9-11, in *The Apostolic Fathers*, ed. J. B. Lightfoot and others (Grand Rapids, Mich.: Baker Book House, 1992) 165.
9. The Martyrdom of Polycarp 12:2, in *The Apostolic Fathers*, 237.

ring to the Roman province of Asia) shows that Polycarp was recognized, even by pagans and Jews, as the foremost Christian teacher of that region. That he was similarly esteemed by his own presbyters is shown by their description of him as "the most remarkable Polycarp, who proved to be an apostolic and prophetic teacher in our own time, bishop of the holy church in Smyrna."[10]

While there are considerable gaps in our knowledge about the development of the episcopate, we are on solid historical ground when we affirm that by the end of the second century, every Christian church about which we have information was being led by a single bishop, that these churches recognized their bishops as the rightful successors to the apostles, and that they received their teaching as normative for their faith. We have clear evidence about this in the writings of Hegesippus, Irenaeus, and Tertullian. We shall consider briefly what these writers tell us about the teaching role exercised by bishops during the second century.

Hegesippus was a Christian writer concerned about the heresies that had sprung up in the second century. Seeking certainty about the true doctrine, he traveled from the East as far as Rome, visiting bishops along the way. The church historian Eusebius has preserved a passage of his writing in which he spoke of what he learned during his journey. Here is what Eusebius wrote about Hegesippus.[11]

> Hegesippus, in the five treatises that have come down to us, has left us a very complete record of his own opinion. In these he shows that he traveled as far as Rome and mingled with a great many bishops, and that he received the same doctrine from all. It is well to listen to what he said after some remarks about the epistle of Clement to the Corinthians: "And the church of the Corinthians remained in the true word until Primus was Bishop of Corinth. I associated with them on my voyage to Rome and I spent some days with them in Corinth, during which we were mutually stimulated by the true Word. And while I was in Rome I made a list of succession up to Anicetus, whose deacon was Eleutherus, and Soter succeeded Anicetus, and after him Eleutherus. In each succession and each city all is as the Law, the Prophets, and the Lord preach."

From this account it is not certain which of those named by Hegesippus was bishop of Rome at the time of his arrival there, but he

---

10. The Martyrdom 16:2, in *The Apostolic Fathers*, 239f.
11. *Historia Ecclesiastica* 4:22, trans. Roy J. Deferrari, Eusebius Pamphili, *Ecclesiastical History*, Books 1–5 (New York: Fathers of the Church, 1953) 253–254.

must have arrived no earlier than 155, when Anicetus became bishop, and before 189, when Eleutherus died. We can conclude from his testimony that before the end of the second century, the church in each city was being led by a bishop, that these bishops were recognized as the authoritative teachers of the faith, and that they all taught the same faith.

Our next witness is Irenaeus, Bishop of Lyons and a contemporary of Hegesippus. From the fact that Irenaeus tells us that in his youth he had seen Polycarp, the Bishop of Smyrna, one can conclude that he himself was a native of the Roman province of Asia. Like Hegesippus, he traveled from the East to Rome, and he was probably in Rome at the time when Polycarp paid his visit to Anicetus, around 155, as his account of that visit suggests the presence of an eyewitness.[12] It may have been at Rome that he became familiar with the teachings of the Gnostics Valentinus and Marcion, as he mentions the fact that both of these heretics were active in Rome during the episcopate of Anicetus (155–166).[13]

Irenaeus went on to Gaul and became a presbyter of the church of Lugdunum (Lyons). While a presbyter, he was commissioned by that church to carry a letter to Eleutherus, Bishop of Rome, telling him of the persecution that took place at Lyons in the year 177. On his return to Lyons he was chosen as its bishop. His lasting memorial is the work that he wrote to refute the Gnostic heretics, entitled *Exposure and Refutation of the Knowledge falsely so called*. Only fragments remain of the original Greek text; however, a complete and faithful Latin translation has been preserved, to which reference is usually given with the Latin title *Adversus Haereses*. Against the claim of the Gnostics to possess a secret, more perfect tradition, known only to the elite of their group, Irenaeus appealed to the tradition that was handed down by the apostles and continued to be transmitted in the Christian churches by the bishops who succeeded one another as teachers down to his own day. Here is one of the passages in which he speaks of the teaching office of the bishops and the key role that they had played in handing on the apostolic tradition.

> The tradition of the Apostles is there, manifest throughout the world in each church, to be seen by all who wish to see the truth. Further we can

---

12. The account was given in a letter he wrote to Victor, Bishop of Rome (189–199), quoted by Eusebius, *Historia Ecclesiastica* 5:24.

13. *Adversus Haereses* III.4.2-3.

list those who were appointed by the Apostles to be bishops in the churches and their successors to our own day. What they taught and what they knew had nothing to do with these [Gnostic] absurdities. Still, even if the Apostles had known hidden mysteries which they taught the "perfect" apart from the rest, surely they would have passed on such knowledge above all to those to whom they entrusted the churches. For they wished the men whom they designated as successors and to whom they left their teaching office to be perfect and beyond reproach in all things. So, if these men were to accomplish their task faultlessly, it would be a great gain, but, if not, the greatest disaster.[14]

The key idea for Irenaeus is that the apostles entrusted the safeguarding and transmission of their message to those to whom they entrusted the care of the churches. Pastoral care of the faithful included responsibility for the soundness of their faith. The apostles handed on their own teaching office to those whom they left as their successors. Writing as a bishop himself, Irenaeus no doubt was aware of the many pastoral duties incumbent on bishops, but he focuses on their role as teachers and reliable transmitters of the apostolic faith.

Our next witness is Tertullian, a North African layman, whose writings date from 196 to 220. In works that he wrote against the Gnostic heretics, he argued that only what had been handed down in the apostolic churches was the genuine apostolic tradition and that apostolic churches could be identified by their series of bishops going back to the apostles or apostolic men who had founded these churches. Here is a passage in which he developed this argument.

If any heresies claim to plant themselves in the age of the apostles in order to make it seem that their ideas were handed down by the apostles because they existed under the apostles, we can say: Let them show the origins of their churches, let them unroll the list of their bishops, (showing) through a succession coming from the very beginning, that their first bishop had as his authority and predecessor someone from among the number of the apostles or apostolic men and, further, that he did not stray from the apostles. In this way the apostolic churches present their earliest records. The church of Smyrna, for example, records that Polycarp was named by John; the church of the Romans, that Clement was ordained by Peter. In just the same way, the other churches show who were made bishops by the apostles and who transmitted the apostolic seed to them. Let the heretics try to invent something like that. But

---

14. *Adversus Haereses* III.3.1, trans. Robert B. Eno, in *Teaching Authority in the Early Church* (Wilmington, Del.: Michael Glazier, 1984) 45–50.

after their blasphemy, nothing is beyond them. Even if they can come up with something, it will do them no good. Their very teaching, when compared with that of the apostles, from its diversity and internal contradictions, will show itself for what it is—that it has no apostle or apostolic man at its origins because just as the apostles did not contradict each other in their teachings, so the next generation taught nothing contrary to what the apostles had preached, unless, of course, you believe that they preached something different from what they had learned from the apostles. This is how they will be challenged by those churches which cannot historically claim as founder either an apostle or an apostolic man because they came much later. New churches are still being founded every day. Since they are in agreement on the faith, they are to be considered no less apostolic because of their kinship in doctrine. Thus let all heresies challenged by our churches to furnish this two-fold proof show for what reasons they consider themselves apostolic. But in fact they are not apostolic. They are not received into peace and communion by churches that are in any way really apostolic, because the diversity of their teaching proves that they are in no way apostolic.[15]

Tertullian's argument took for granted that the apostles and "apostolic men" who founded churches had left bishops in charge of them and that the bishops of his day were the successors of those original bishops. It seems evident that for him this was not a matter of controversy. What he wished to prove, rather, was that the Christian churches of his day could rightly claim to be apostolic, on the grounds that they could do what the heretical sects could not do, namely, "unroll the list of their bishops, showing through a succession coming from the very beginning, that their first bishop had as his authority and predecessor someone from among the number of the apostles or apostolic men." His argument focused on the apostolicity of the Catholic churches, proven by the fact that they could provide a list of their bishops going back from the present incumbent to one appointed by an apostle or by an "apostolic man."

Tertullian, of course, was aware of the fact that there were churches that could not trace their list of bishops back to apostolic times, simply because they had been founded more recently. However, these also had a valid claim to apostolicity because they shared the same faith with the churches founded by apostles and were in full communion with them. Tertullian emphasized the apostolicity of the churches as a guarantee of the genuine apostolicity of the faith that had been

15. *De Praescriptione Haereticorum* 32, trans. Eno, in *Teaching Authority*, 60–61.

handed down in them, but he did not stress the teaching role of the bishops, as Irenaeus had done. However, this is implied by his argument that the genuine apostolic tradition was to be found in the churches which could either "unroll the list of their bishops" back to an apostle or "apostolic man" or which were in full communion with such churches.

We come now to the third and final point of our justification of the belief that episcopal ordination confers an authoritative teaching office. Building on the previous points, it proceeds as follows.

In the second century the episcopate provided the instrument that the church needed to be able to maintain its unity and orthodoxy in the face of the danger that threatened it from the spread of Gnosticism. This danger was particularly evident in the church of Rome, where various exponents of this heresy established themselves and formed communities of their followers, claiming to possess a secret apostolic tradition that surpassed what was being taught in the ordinary Christian communities. Most modern scholars are agreed that the development of the episcopate was the Church's answer to this threat to its unity, but they differ in their assessment of its significance. Protestants judge it to have been a merely natural response to the need for stronger leadership, while Catholics believe they have good reasons to recognize it as guided by the Holy Spirit. One good reason is based on the theological significance of the reception by the Church of the norms for its faith.

The consensus to which the Christian churches arrived during the second and third centuries concerning the reception of four Gospels, the letters of St. Paul, the Acts of the Apostles, and the Catholic Epistles substantially fixed the canon of the New Testament. By virtue of this consensus, the Church recognized that collection of writings as normative for Christian faith. It is obvious that an erroneous decision about the norm of its faith would have led the Church into incalculable errors on particular matters of faith. If one believes that the Holy Spirit maintains the Church in the true faith, one must also believe that the Holy Spirit guided the Church in its discernment of the books that would constitute the written norm for its faith.

The fact that in the course of the second century the Gnostics also appealed to these writings made it evident that the Church needed another norm by which to be able to judge which interpretation of the New Testament corresponded to the authentic apostolic faith. The Gnostics claimed that their interpretation was based on a secret tradition originating from one of the apostles and handed down by a succession of their teachers. The response of Christian writers, such as Hegesippus, Irenaeus, and Tertullian, was to appeal to the tradition handed down from the apostles by the succession of bishops in the churches. The fact that in all those churches one found the same "rule of faith," in contrast to the great diversity of Gnostic teachings, proved that the churches that were led by bishops had maintained the genuine apostolic doctrine. These writers, from different regions of the Church, witness to the recognition of the bishops as the rightful successors of the apostles and as authoritative bearers of the apostolic tradition, whose teaching was normative for Christian faith.

It would have been just as disastrous for the Church to have made the wrong decision about the living norm of faith as it would have been to make a wrong decision about its written norm. We have just as good reason to believe that the Church was guided by the Spirit in the recognition of its bishops as successors of the apostles and authoritative teachers of the faith as we have to believe that it was guided by the Spirit in its discernment of the books that make up the New Testament.

From this it follows that there is also good reason to believe that the development of the episcopate itself was guided by the Spirit, since it was to play such a primary role in maintaining the Church in the true faith. Without the leadership of its bishops, the early Church could hardly have achieved a consensus on the canon of Scripture, nor could it have overcome the very real threat that Gnosticism posed to its unity and orthodoxy. While most Catholic scholars agree that the episcopate is the fruit of a post-New Testament development, they maintain that this development was so evidently guided by the Holy Spirit that it must be recognized as corresponding to God's plan concerning the structure of his Church. And this is how they would explain and justify the teaching of Vatican II that "the bishops have by divine institution taken the place of the apostles as pastors of the church in such wise that whoever hears them hears Christ and whoever rejects them rejects Christ and him who sent Christ" (LG 20). It is on these grounds as well that they would justify the teaching of Vatican II that the sacramental consecration by which a man becomes a member of the episcopal college also gives him a share of the teaching authority which the apostles received from Christ and which has been handed on in uninterrupted succession by those who have carried on the apostles' ministry as teachers, priests, and pastors of the People of God.

Chapter Five

Reflections on
What an Abbot of a Monastic Community Brings to the Role of Bishop in the Church

Most Reverend Daniel W. Kucera, O.S.B.

The responsibilities of a bishop in the Church in the modern world can be as diverse and complicated as the ecclesiastical and secular environment in which he is called to leadership. There is no uniform way of preparing for these responsibilities. Each candidate brings to the episcopacy his own gifts, experiences, and background. I have been invited to reflect on what an abbot of a monastery brings to the role of a bishop, since Archbishop Rembert Weakland and I share this common background. It is an honor to do so for this festschrift, noting his completion of a quarter of a century of episcopal service to the local, national, and universal Church. This service was forged and tempered by his years as abbot of a monastery and as abbot primate of the Benedictine Order.

While responsibilities vary with time and place, there is a basic theological focus at the heart of the episcopal office: Feed my lambs; feed my sheep. From apostolic times, the bishop is seen to hold the place of Christ in the Church. This theological truth is reiterated in our times in the basic document of the Second Vatican Council on the nature of the Church (LG 7). It is also incorporated into the allocution to the faithful in the rite of ordination of a bishop: "In the person of the bishop with his priests around him, Jesus Christ, the Lord, who became High Priest for ever, is present among you." By its proximity to this early tradition, the Rule of St. Benedict and its monastic structure build on this concept of a spiritual father. The abbot is the presence of Christ in the community. It is this primary focus that an abbot brings to the episcopal office.

The role of an abbot, like monasticism itself, has a long and rich history reaching back to the early centuries of the Church. St. Benedict, the founder of Western monasticism, lived in the sixth century. He was the beneficiary of several centuries of eremitical and cenobitical tradition going back to the Desert Fathers. He lived in a time of civil and social turmoil. It was his genius to adapt this earlier tradition and blend it into the concept of a cohesive and stable monastic community in which monks vowed to remain for life under the guidance of an abbot. The monastery was a mirror of the local church, and the abbot was analogous to the bishop. The role of the abbot was defined not by his position at the head of a community, but rather by his relationship to the persons he served. He was the spiritual father around whom the community gathered.

In such an arrangement, the abbot was a pivotal figure, since he provided the sense of unity and direction for the community. St. Benedict treats of the abbot in two specific chapters of his Rule, although the abbot's interaction with the community is, naturally, visible throughout. The Rule has come to be a veritable vade mecum for spiritual leadership and forms the basis of the abbatial experience one brings to the episcopal office.

In Chapter 2 of his Rule, St. Benedict outlines the qualities of an abbot. He says: "To be worthy of the task of governing a monastery, the abbot must always remember what his title signifies and act as a superior should. He is believed to hold the place of Christ in the monastery, since he is addressed by a title of Christ, as the Apostle indicates: 'You have received the spirit of adoption of sons by which we exclaim, abba, father'" (Rom 8:15).[1]

From this basic theological premise, St. Benedict proceeds to indicate how the abbot goes about fulfilling his responsibilities. He is to teach by word and example. He is to be even-handed and avoid favoritism. He is to accommodate and adapt himself to each one's character and intelligence. Above all, he is not to show too great a concern for the fleeting and temporal things of this world, neglecting or treating lightly the welfare of those entrusted to him. Rather, he is to keep in mind that he has undertaken the care of souls for whom he must give an account. St. Benedict concludes: "That he may not plead lack of resources as an excuse, he is to remember what is written: Seek first

---

1. *RB 1980: The Rule of St. Benedict in Latin and English with Notes,* ed. Timothy Fry, O.S.B., and others (Collegeville, Minn.: The Liturgical Press, 1981) 171, 173.

the kingdom of God and his justice, and all these things will be given as well" (Matt 6:33).[2]

Chapter 3 of the Rule ("Summoning the Brothers for Counsel") reminds the abbot of the need to share responsibility and to consult the community before decisions are made. The abbot is to call the whole community for counsel on important matters, since St. Benedict says: "The Lord often reveals what is better to the younger."[3] The abbot is cautioned to settle everything with foresight and fairness. In transacting ordinary business of the monastery, he is to "take counsel with the seniors only, as it is written: 'Do everything with counsel and you will not be sorry afterward'" (Sir 32:24).[4]

At the end of his Rule (Chapter 64), St. Benedict deals with the election of an abbot and offers his final advice: "He ought, therefore, to be learned in divine law, so that he has a treasury of knowledge from which he can bring out what is new and what is old (Matt 13:52). He must be chaste, temperate and merciful. . . . He must hate faults but love the brothers. . . . he should use prudence and avoid extremes."[5] Finally, St. Benedict gives a bit of psychological advice: "Excitable, anxious, extreme, obstinate, jealous or oversuspicious he must not be. Such a man is never at rest. Instead, he must show forethought and consideration in his orders."[6]

No abbot, then or now, can totally fulfill St. Benedict's expectations. Still, the day-to-day interaction with the monks gives the abbot ample opportunity to grow in his own spiritual life and to hone his leadership skills. From the moment he enters the novitiate, a monk learns what it means to live in the "school for the Lord's service," as St. Benedict calls the monastery.[7] He joins a stable monastic family striving for the same spiritual and material ends. He shares communal prayer and common activities. He works at the apostolates of community, perhaps heading one or the other in time. He shares the wisdom and experience of older monks and participates with them in decision-making. By the time he is elected abbot, he has had many opportunities to develop his abilities.

The abbatial position will test those leadership abilities further. The abbot will come to realize what it means to be Christ in the midst

2. Ibid., 177.
3. Ibid., 179, 181.
4. Ibid., 181.
5. Ibid., 283.
6. Ibid.
7. Ibid., 165.

of his brothers, what it means to gather the opinions of his brothers into cohesive decisions and balanced programs. If called to the episcopal office, he brings with him a venerable tradition of leadership and consultation that translates well into service to the larger Church. Above all, he has his vade mecum, the Rule of St. Benedict, with its wisdom and prudence as his handy reference.

Part Two

THE BISHOP
AS SUBJECT AND AGENT
OF DIALOGUE

Chapter Six

Episkopé and Episcopacy in Modern Orthodox-Catholic Dialogue: An Orthodox Perspective

John H. Erickson

The subject of *episkopé* and episcopacy has figured prominently in modern ecumenical discussion. This is hardly surprising. In the search for visible unity, questions relating to reconciliation of ministries, and especially to the nature and role of the ministry of *episkopé* or oversight, have been particularly difficult to resolve. The Faith and Order Commission of the World Council of Churches has undertaken extensive work in this area. Its major contributions include the study *'Episkopé' and Episcopate in Ecumenical Perspective,*[1] the ministry section of the Lima document *Baptism, Eucharist, Ministry,* or *BEM,*[2] and two consultations devoted to *'Episkopé' and Episcopacy and the Quest for Visible Unity.*[3] In addition, a number of bilateral dialogues, typically involving Churches that have episcopal ministry and those that do not also have addressed this subject.

Modern Orthodox-Catholic dialogue has addressed this subject as well, but from a different perspective. For the most part, Orthodox and Catholics have a common understanding and practice of ministry, including episcopal ministry. The chief point of difference between them has to do with the ministry of a particular bishop, the bishop of Rome, and not with episcopal ministry *per se.* When the Joint International

1. Faith and Order Paper No. 102 (Geneva: WCC Publications, 1980).
2. Faith and Order Paper No. 111 (Geneva: WCC Publications, 1982) and many other editions.
3. Papers and reports published in Faith and Order Paper No. 183, ed. Peter C. Bouteneff and Alan D. Falconer (Geneva: WCC Publications, 1999). The present essay is a revised and expanded version of my contribution to the volume in question, "*Episkopé* and Episcopacy: Orthodox Perspectives," 80–92. Used with permission.

Commission for Theological Dialogue Between the Catholic and Orthodox Churches was being organized, it was agreed that discussion should
begin with what Orthodox and Catholics have in common rather than
with what divides them. The historic episcopate was one of those common elements. Closer examination of the way in which *episkopé* and
episcopacy have been treated in modern Orthodox-Catholic dialogue reveals how far these two Churches have come in their own quest for
unity. In addition, the wealth of theological reflection offered in the principal documents of this dialogue may provide new perspectives for others who are engaged in discussion of this central ecumenical issue.

In a survey of the contribution of modern Orthodox-Catholic dialogue to the subject of *episkopé* and episcopacy, the most obvious
sources requiring comment include:

- The 1988 "Valamo Statement" of the Joint International Commission for Theological Dialogue Between the Catholic and Orthodox Churches ("The Sacrament of Order in the Sacramental
  Structure of the Church with Particular Reference to the Importance of Apostolic Succession for the Sanctification and Unity of
  the People of God"), along with portions of the Joint International Commission's 1982 "Munich Statement" ("The Mystery
  of the Church and of the Eucharist in the Light of the Mystery of
  the Holy Trinity").[4]
- Responses of the U.S. Orthodox-Catholic Theological Consultation to the "Valamo Statement" and the "Munich Statement," issued in 1989 and 1983 respectively.[5]
- Other statements of the U.S. Orthodox-Catholic Consultation, including "The Pastoral Office" (1976); "An Agreed Statement on the
  Lima Document: *Baptism, Eucharist and Ministry*" (1984); "Apostolicity as God's Gift in the Life of the Church" (1986); and "An
  Agreed Statement on Conciliarity and Primacy in the Church"
  (1989).[6]

Most of these texts date from the 1980s, the most recent international contribution being the 1988 Valamo Statement. Unfortunately,

---

4. Most conveniently available in English, with further bibliographical orientation,
in John Borelli and John H. Erickson, eds., *The Quest for Unity: Orthodox and Catholics in Dialogue* (Crestwood, N.Y.: St. Vladimir's Seminary Press; Washington: United
States Catholic Conference, 1996) 131–149 and 53–64, respectively.

5. *Quest for Unity*, 152–155 and 65–88, respectively.

6. *Quest for Unity*, 120–124, 125–130 and 152–155, respectively.

Orthodox-Catholic dialogue has done very little to advance our understanding of the subject of *episkopé* since then. After its meeting in Valamo, the Joint International Commission was expected to meet next in Munich in 1990 to prepare a statement on "Ecclesiological and Canonical Consequences of the Sacramental Structures of the Church: Conciliarity and Authority in the Church." No doubt this would have included further consideration of *episkopé* and episcopacy. By then, however, in the wake of the collapse of communism in Eastern Europe, this dialogue faced new challenges. Discussion turned from relatively abstract issues of ecclesiology to practical issues relating to "uniatism" and proselytism.

But even the 1988 Valamo Statement is less recent than its date suggests. Some sections consist simply of quotations from the 1982 Munich Statement (pars. 46-48 quote Munich II.4 and III.4). Even greater portions of the text, as well as its basic structure, are taken from the "Orthodox-Roman Catholic Reflections on Ministries" published in 1977 on the basis of still earlier discussions.[7] To appreciate fully the strengths and limitations of work of the Joint International Commission on the subject of *episkopé* and episcopacy, therefore, it is important to keep in mind who the principal theologians were that contributed to the preliminary stages of its work, and also what their particular theological insights and points of emphasis were. On the Catholic side, one certainly would have to keep in mind the contributions of such giants as Louis Bouyer, Emmanuel Lanne, and Jean-Marie Tillard. On the Orthodox side, one name stands out—that of Metropolitan John Zizioulas, the main Orthodox contributor both to the "Reflections on Ministries" and to the work of the Joint International Commission, whose published articles from this period also touch on many aspects of *episkopé* and episcopacy.[8]

---

7. "Reflexions de théologiens Orthodoxes et Catholiques sur les ministères," *La Documentation Catholique*, no. 1738 (March 9, 1978), 262–265 [English translation in *Origins*, 702–704.] Catholic participants in these discussions included Charles Moeller, Pierre Duprey, Louis Bouyer, Gustave Martelet, and Jean-Marie Tillard; Orthodox included Metropolitan Damaskinos of Tranoupolis (now of Switzerland), Ion Bria, John Zizioulas and, in the earlier meetings, Bishop Vassilios of Aristis and Olivier Clément. These discussions appear to have been undertaken in order to "jumpstart" official international Orthodox-Catholic dialogue.

8. These include "La continuité avec les origines apostoliques dans la conscience théologique des Eglises Orthodoxes," *Istina* 19 (1974) 65–94 [English translation "Apostolic Continuity and Orthodox Theology: Towards a Synthesis of Two Perspectives," *St. Vladimir's Theological Quarterly* 19 (1975) 75–108; reprint in *Being as Communion*

It would be difficult to overestimate the importance of Zizioulas's contribution to the discussion of *episkopé* and episcopacy. He is not an isolated figure, however. His work in ecclesiology in many respects builds upon insights developed earlier by Nicholas Afanasiev and other exponents of "eucharistic ecclesiology." In addition, many of his central concerns and presuppositions are shared by the principal Catholic theologians involved in this discussion. Among other things, Zizioulas, like so many other modern theologians both Orthodox and Catholic, appeals repeatedly to the witness of the Fathers, above all to the ante-Nicene Fathers. Inevitably, therefore, discussion of modern Orthodox-Catholic statements on *episkopé* and episcopacy leads us back to the ecclesiology of the first centuries of the Church.

There are two reasons why modern Orthodox statements relating to *episkopé* and episcopacy have concentrated on the period between the New Testament and the Council of Nicaea. First, it is argued that this period provides an important, indeed normative, point of reference for ecclesiology and theological reflection. As Zizioulas puts it, "It is not any idea of the bishop but that of the ancient church that I regard as normative for the Orthodox doctrine."[9] Second, it is argued that the pattern of episcopacy in this period—subsequent to the unique and irreproducible apostolic age but prior to the establishment of Christianity as a state religion under Constantine—may be of particular relevance in our own postapostolic but also post-Constantinian age. Among other things, it may be more acceptable to non-episcopal communities than the Constantinian-era pattern that determined the course of the sixteenth-century debates between Protestants and Catholics.[10]

Within this early period, three main aspects of episcopal ministry have been discerned. Each can conveniently be associated with a particular Church Father: Ignatius of Antioch, Irenaeus of Lyons, and Cyprian of Carthage.

(Crestwood, N.Y.: St. Vladimir's Seminary Press, 1985) 171–208]; *"Episkopé* and Episkopos in the Early Church: A Brief Survey of the Evidence," in Episkopé *and Episcopate in Ecumenical Perspective* (Geneva: WCC Publications, 1979); *"'Episkopé* et Episkopos dans l'Eglise primitive," *Irénikon* 56 (1983) 484–501; "The Bishop in the Theological Doctrine of the Orthodox Church," *Kanon* 7 (Vienna, 1985) 23–38.

9. Zizioulas, "The Bishop in the Theological Doctrine of the Orthodox Church," 26.

10. See Kallistos Ware, "Patterns of Episcopacy in the Early Church and Today: An Orthodox View," in Peter Moore, ed., *Bishops, But What Kind? Reflections on Episcopacy* (London: SPCK, 1982) 1–2.

- For Ignatius, the bishop is above all the president of the local eucharistic assembly. It is he who gathers the diverse gifts of the local community into unity, as they become one body of Christ through participation in the one eucharistic loaf. He is an *alter Christus*, a living icon who constitutes "the focus and visible centre of unity within the church,"[11] who expresses "the fullness, unity and multiplicity of the eschatological community in each place."[12]

- For Irenaeus, the bishop is above all an authoritative teacher and witness to the apostolic faith, an *alter apostolus*. His outward continuity in succession back to the apostles through his predecessors in the same see "serves as the sign and guarantee of inward continuity in apostolic faith."[13] Thus he is a living link between his local church and the apostles. He expresses "the historical continuity of the church in time"[14]—a continuity not merely of structures but of apostolic faith.

- For Cyprian, the bishop is part of a worldwide episcopal college, co-responsible with his brother bishops for maintaining the unity and good estate of all the churches. An *alter Petrus*, he expresses "the communion and unity of the church in space."[15] He is therefore a conciliar being. He possesses the fullness of episcopal grace not in isolation but in union with all the other bishops, and he serves as the bond of unity between his own local church and all the other local churches.

How can these three images of *episkopé* be held together in a coherent synthesis so that the Irenaean ministry of the word is organically joined to the Ignatian ministry of sacrament and not simply parallel to it, so that the Cyprianic ministry of wider oversight is organically joined to both and not simply an external administrative office? This question has been important for the internal life of the Churches—whether Orthodox, Catholic, or Protestant—at several points in their history, especially at times of division and conflict. Today this question is significant as the Churches strive for reconciliation and mutual recognition of ministries. Whether tacitly or explicitly, the Churches and the major Christian traditions they represent have acknowledged the importance of all three perspectives, but they

11. Ibid., 2.
12. Zizioulas, "The Bishop in the Theological Doctrine of the Orthodox Church," 35.
13. Ware, "Patterns of Episcopacy," 12.
14. Zizioulas, "The Bishop in the Theological Doctrine of the Orthodox Church," 35.
15. Ibid.

have brought them together in different ways, sometimes employing differing organizing principles, sometimes emphasizing elements that other traditions have neglected or subordinated. At the risk of over-simplification, I offer here some very broad characterizations of how the Ignatian, Irenaean, and Cyprianic images of *episkopé* have been employed by Orthodox, Protestants, and Catholics.

If one were to correlate these early Fathers with modern confessional emphases, one might argue that magisterial Protestantism has tended to look to Irenaeus for its inspiration and orientation. Though not preoccupied with certain aspects of historical continuity, such as the maintenance of institutional forms, it has strongly emphasized the role of the ordained ministry in witness to and proclamation of the apostolic faith, on the basis of apostolic scripture. While perhaps willing to acknowledge continuity in the apostolic succession of bishops as an important *sign* of continuity in apostolic faith, Protestants have generally been unwilling to see it as a *guarantee* of faith. Indeed, at the time of the Reformation they were willing to abandon the "historic episcopate" to the extent that this was experienced as an obstacle to apostolic preaching and faith. Certainly they would reject the tendency in some older presentations of Catholic sacramental theology to look on apostolic succession above all as a mechanism for ensuring the preservation of "valid" sacraments, to the point of detaching it from broader aspects of the life and faith of the Church community.

Here we may note a certain affinity with the Orthodox. Often to the bewilderment and annoyance of their ecumenical partners, the Orthodox have insisted that mutual recognition of sacraments and ministry is inseparable from mutual recognition of faith. Recognition depends not just on agreement about the subject immediately under consideration (e.g., eucharistic doctrine) but on agreement about the faith in its totality. Thus it is not so surprising that the Bari Statement (1987) of the Catholic-Orthodox Joint International Commission stopped well short of the mutual recognition of baptism that some had been expecting or that its Valamo Statement (1988) stopped short of mutual recognition of ministry, even though there would appear to be no substantial differences between the Churches on either subject.

Roman Catholic presentations of ecclesiology have historically taken their cue from Cyprian's dictum *episcopatus unus est.* Their point of departure has been the unity of the episcopate as a collective body, a single college having as its single head the veritable successor of Peter. While Catholic theologians like Tillard, Lanne, Legrand, and

Komonchak have adopted many elements of the Ignatian perspective, relating the ministry of the bishop to the life and faith of the local church, they have done so in the face of an ecclesiological tradition that has tended to value universality over diversity and particularity.

The continuing strength of the Cyprianic perspective is evident, for example, in the *Communionis notio* of the Congregation for the Doctrine of the Faith, which argues for the priority of the universal over the local, as well as the *Codex Iuris Canonici* (1983) and the *Codex Canonum Ecclesiarum Orientalium* (1990), which are far more concerned with issues of episcopal collegiality (especially the relationship between primacy and episcopacy) than with the place of the bishop within the communion of his local church.[16] Archbishop Rembert G. Weakland, veteran Catholic co-chairman of the U.S. Catholic-Orthodox Theological Consultation, has observed:

> We Roman Catholics use the phrase "Universal Church" more often than we realize. It is a phrase that most characterizes our ecclesiological position. . . . Especially since Vatican II, we have evolved an elaborate thinking on how the universal church is present in the local church and realized there. We Roman Catholics almost always begin with such universalism and then proceed to local manifestations. . . . The Orthodox begin with the local church and the celebration of the eucharist on the local level. The local eucharistic community—rather than the concept of a universal church—is their starting point.[17]

While this characterization of Roman Catholicism certainly is on target, the characterization of Orthodoxy requires some qualification. Certainly there have been periods in Orthodox Church history when a universal, "Cyprianic" perspective has been present in significant ways. While episcopal conciliarity usually has been emphasized more than primacy, some rather papal-sounding statements can be found that call attention to the role of the ecumenical patriarch as head of a universal episcopate, responsible for shepherding the Church understood as a universal organism. Toward the end of the Byzantine period, for example, Patriarch Philotheus Coccinus spoke of himself as "leader of all Christians found anywhere in the *oikoumené*," "protector and

16. On this subject see my article "The Code of Canons of the Oriental Churches (1990): A Development Favoring Relations between the Churches?" *The Jurist* 57 (1997) 286–306, and elsewhere in translation.

17. "Roman Catholic and Orthodox Dialogue: The Larger Picture," *Ecumenism* 107 (1992) 31.

guardian of their souls," "the father and teacher of them all," who, because he cannot physically be present everywhere,

> chooses the best among men, the most eminent in virtue, establishes
> and ordains them as pastors, teachers and high priests, and sends them
> to the end of the universe . . . so that each, in the country and place ap-
> pointed him, enjoys territorial rights, and episcopal see, and all the
> rights of Our Humility.[18]

Over the centuries, Irenaean and Cyprianic elements have never
been entirely absent from Orthodox practice and reflection. But they
certainly have been overshadowed in modern Orthodox presentations
of ecclesiology by the Ignatian image of the local eucharistic community. Afanasiev, for example, goes so far as to oppose the "eucharistic
ecclesiology" of Ignatius to other approaches, most notably to the
"universal ecclesiology" of Cyprian. Others have been more nuanced.
Zizioulas, for example, sees in Hippolytus's *Apostolic Tradition* a synthesis between the iconic approach of Ignatius and the historical approach of 1 Clement and Irenaeus.[19] So also, in contrast to Afanasiev,
he tries to hold together the approaches of Ignatius and Cyprian, insisting that "the nature of the eucharist points not in the direction of
the priority of the local church but in that of the *simultaneity* of both
local and universal."[20] Still, as this statement suggests, his point of departure remains the Eucharist as revealed in the letters of Ignatius, the
Didaché, and other early Christian texts.

While modern eucharistic ecclesiology has made some significant
contributions to ecumenical discussion, reading the impact of eucharistic ecclesiology on the internal life of the Orthodox Churches is
more difficult. From Orthodox responses to *BEM*, for example, one
could easily conclude that official Church agencies are still much
more influenced by textbook scholasticism than by the works of
Afanasiev or Zizioulas. Blame for this should not be laid solely on
ponderous officialdom. Modern Orthodox (or for that matter Catholic
or Protestant) appropriations of Ignatius have certain inherent limitations that make their application to modern Church life problematic.

18. Letter to the Russian princes, in Miklosich and Mueller, *Acta et diplomata* (Vienna, 1860) 521. On "Eastern papism," see A. Pavlov, "Teoria vostochnogo papisma v
novieshei russkoi literature kanonicheskogo prava," *Pravoslavnoe Obozreniie,* 1879.

19. In *"Episkopé* and *Episkopos* in the Early Church," note 8, above.

20. "The Local Church in a Perspective of Communion," in *Being as Communion,*
133; see his more fully articulated statement of the same point in "Apostolic Continuity and Orthodox Theology," note 8, above.

Exponents of eucharistic ecclesiology have tended to uphold an idealized second-century Church order as normative in every detail for all ages and situations, and they have been inclined to ignore or dismiss evidence not conforming to that model. They have not taken seriously enough either the ecclesiological diversity one finds in the New Testament texts or the many developments since the days of Ignatius. For example, Afanasiev altogether fails to address the fact that since the third or fourth century, the presbyter-centered parish has been the most common locus of Christian community. Zizioulas does acknowledge this, insisting against Afanasiev that "the local church as an entity with full ecclesiological status is the *episcopal diocese* and not the parish." In his view, the emergence of the presbyter-centered parish "destroyed the image of the church as a community in which all orders are necessary as *constitutive* elements," ultimately making both deacon and bishop and even laity redundant. But by opting for the diocese as the fundamental ecclesial organism, says Zizioulas, "the Orthodox Church has unconsciously brought about a rupture in its own eucharistic ecclesiology." At this point, he laments, one can only hope that "one day the bishop will find his proper place, which is the eucharist, and the rupture in eucharistic ecclesiology caused by the problem 'parish-diocese' will be healed."[21]

It is alarming to learn that the Church suffers from a disruption in its most vital structures so serious that for most of its historical existence it has only been able to *hope* for restoration of proper wholeness. It is even more surprising to discover how simple is the remedy Zizioulas proposes: "creation of small episcopal dioceses," which "would enable bishops really to know their flocks and be known by them" and thus "automatically improve the pastoral quality of the episcopacy," which "would reduce the load of administration which the bishops have at present, thus enabling them to function primarily as presidents of the eucharist, which is their ministry *par excellence.*"[22]

Can re-creation of the Ignatian local church really advance the Church's mission of redemptive integration today, when the context in which the Church is placed has changed so dramatically? In the context of the ancient *polis*, the eucharistic structures of the local church could and did powerfully proclaim and manifest Christ's victory over the divisions of this fallen world. But simply replicating those

---

21. *Being as Communion,* 251.
22. Ibid., 251, note 6.

structures in today's "global village" might well perpetuate and exacerbate these divisions by identifying the Church with the special interests of this or that natural, purely human community. Without a significant infusion of "Irenaean" and "Cyprianic" elements, replication of "Ignatian" structures would inevitably lead to an absence of common witness and action on broader levels (the world, the nation, the region, even the city—for surely a megalopolis like Mexico City or Athens would have to be broken up into "smaller dioceses"). At the very least, it would result in wasteful duplication of programs.

How has modern Orthodox-Catholic dialogue responded to the challenge of integrating the perspectives of Ignatius, Irenaeus, and Cyprian? It is hardly surprising that eucharistic ecclesiology, especially as articulated by Zizioulas, plays a prominent role, particularly in the work of the Joint International Commission. But before examining the relevant texts in greater detail, it is important to note the broader theological context into which these texts situate their discussion of ministry and episcopacy.

Both the 1982 Munich Statement and the 1988 Valamo Statement, echoing points made elsewhere by Zizioulas, draw attention to the importance of a pneumatologically conditioned Christology for a proper understanding of ecclesiology and therefore of episcopal ministry. In contrast to "Christomonistic" approaches that see the Church chiefly in terms of structures instituted by Christ long ago, the statements call attention to the Spirit's role in constituting the Church in each new moment and situation. As the anointed one of God, Christ is not an isolated individual who lived in a past that is increasingly distant from us. He "is present through the Spirit, in the church, his body, from which he cannot be separated" (Valamo, sec. 9, *Quest for Unity*, 132).

Because Christ's ministry is present to us only through the Spirit, ecclesial ministry is necessarily *charismatic*. For the same reason, it is *relational*. The nexus of relationships established by the Spirit creates a new way of being, which transforms both the one ordained and those for whom he is ordained, making it futile to debate whether ordained ministry in the Church is functional or ontological in nature. As Zizioulas writes, "In the light of love and in the context of the notion of communion, ordination binds the ordained person so deeply and existentially with the community that in his new state after ordination he cannot be conceived in himself at all—he has become a relational entity."[23] Finally, ecclesial ministry has an *eschatological* dimension.

---

23. "Ordination and Communion," *Study Encounter* 6.4, 190.

By the power of the Spirit it builds up the Church so as to reveal it in the space and time of this world as "the anticipated manifestation of the final realities, the foretaste of God's kingdom" (Valamo, sec. 22, *Quest for Unity*, 135).

A proper understanding of the relationship of pneumatology to Christology can help to correct distortions possible in the Ignatian, Irenaean, and Cyprianic approaches to *episkopé*.

- Without a pneumatological perspective, the "episcopo-centrism" of Ignatius can too easily become "episcopo-monism," in which the diverse other gifts of the Spirit in the local church are suppressed, supplanted, or simply ignored, so that the bishop comes to be seen as the unique possessor and source of all spiritual gifts, rather than the one who discerns their presence and authorizes their use for the upbuilding of the community.
- Without a pneumatological perspective, the Irenaean apostolic succession can too easily be reduced to the historical transmission of authority through hands on heads, ignoring the importance of ecclesial context or even the apostolic faith itself. Similarly, the Irenaean insistence on apostolic faith can too easily be reduced to the maintenance and mechanical transmission of the faith, as though it were an inert deposit rather than a living confession.
- Without a pneumatological perspective, the Cyprianic emphasis on the unity of the episcopate can too easily detach the episcopate from the whole body of the faithful, placing it over and above the Church rather than in its midst, and can degenerate into an insistence on institutional uniformity, to the detriment of true conciliarity.

The great merit of Orthodox-Catholic dialogue has been this recognition of the importance of pneumatology for ecclesiology. Among other things, it has made possible a balanced and coherent understanding of the relationship of the one and the many (Ignatius), the local and the universal (Cyprian), the historical and the eschatological (Irenaeus). One of the fruits of this approach is the 1982 Munich Statement, especially Sections II and III (*Quest for Unity*, 57–64), a text that merits repeated reading.

The Church, the Munich Statement argues, cannot be understood simply in sociological categories. It is above all a sacramental reality that "finds its model, its origin and its purpose in the mystery of God, one in three Persons" (II.1, *Quest for Unity*, 58). At the same time, the Church is not an abstraction; rather, it is a "local" reality, "placed" in the midst of the world to be the prototype of renewed human community. It is a *koinonia* that most fully realizes itself in the eucharistic assembly of the local church, gathered around the bishop or the priest in communion with him as one body. This *koinonia* is eschatological, in that it antici- pates the newness of the last times through continuing repentance and confession, conversion and reconciliation. It is also kerygmatic, "not only because the celebration 'announces' the event of the mystery but also because it actually realizes it today in the Spirit" (II.2, *Quest for Unity*, 58). Of this *koinonia*, "the entire assembly, each one according to his rank, is *leitourgos*." While being the gift of the triune God, *koinonia* is also the response of men and women who, "in the faith which comes from the Spirit and the Word . . . put into practice the vocation and the mission received in baptism: to become living members, in one's proper rank, of the body of Christ" (II.2, *Quest for Unity*, 59).

Within this context of communion, the bishop exercises a ministry that is "not merely a tactical or pragmatic function (because a presi- dent is necessary) but an organic function" that is "closely bound to the eucharistic assembly over which he presides" (II.3, *Quest for Unity*, 59). Within the communion of the local church, the bishop "delivers the word of salvation and the eucharistic gifts," but he also "'receives' from his church, which is faithful to tradition, the word he transmits." The bishop also

> stands at the heart of the local church as minister of the Spirit to dis- cern the charisms and take care that they are exercised in harmony, for the good of all, in faithfulness to the apostolic tradition. He puts him- self at the service of the initiatives of the Spirit so that nothing may pre- vent them from contributing to building up koinonia.

After thus developing the Ignatian aspect of the bishop's ministry, the Munich Statement considers the Irenaean question of apostolic succession. The communion of the bishop and his community "lies within the communion of the apostolic community" (II.4, *Quest for Unity*, 60).

> In the ancient tradition . . . the bishop elected by the people—who guarantee his apostolic faith, in conformity with what the local church confesses—receives the ministerial grace of Christ by the Spirit in the prayer of the assembly and by the laying on of hands (cheirotonia) of the neighboring bishops, witnesses of the faith of their own churches. His

charism, coming directly from the Spirit of God, is given him in the apostolicity of his church (linked to the faith of the apostolic community) and in that of the other churches represented by their bishops.

Thus apostolic succession means more than a mere transmission of powers. "It is a succession in a church which witnesses to the apostolic faith, in communion with the other churches which witness to the same apostolic faith."

The Munich Statement then turns to the relationship between the eucharistic celebration of the local church and the communion of all the local churches as the one body of Christ (cf. Cyprian). The ontological identity of the local churches "comes from the fact that all by eating the same bread and sharing in the same cup become the same unique body of Christ into which they have been integrated by the same baptism" (III.1, *Quest for Unity*, 61). From this understanding that the Church is a communion of local churches flows the understanding of how the bishops of the churches are related in their common responsibility for *episkopé* in the Church. "Attachment to the apostolic communion binds all the bishops together, linking the *episkopé* of the local churches to the college of the apostles" (III.4, *Quest for Unity*, 63).

> Because the one and only church is made present in his local church, each bishop cannot separate the care for his own church from that of the universal church. When, by the sacrament of ordination, he receives the charism of the Spirit for the episkopé of one local church, his own, by that very fact he receives the charism of the Holy Spirit for the episkopé of the entire church.

Thus, "the *episkopé* for the universal Church is seen to be entrusted, by the Spirit, to the totality of local bishops in communion with one another."

This selection of quotations from the Munich Statement suggests its theological richness. It challenges not only Orthodox and Catholics but also others engaged in the ecumenical enterprise to go beyond familiar institutional and juridical conceptions, beyond a "Christomonistic" approach to ecclesiology. At the same time, the careful reader may well ask how closely the situation described in the text actually corresponds to the life of either the Orthodox or the Catholic Church. For example, while "in the ancient tradition" the bishop may have been "elected by the people—who guarantee his apostolic faith, in conformity with what the local church confesses"—is this in fact the case today?

Similarly, one may ask whether the pneumatological perspective professed by the Joint International Commission has fully penetrated all aspects of its own work. An extended example from its Valamo Statement may illustrate this point. After discussing "Christ and the Holy Spirit" (Section I) and "The Priesthood in the Divine Economy of Salvation" (Section II), the statement goes on to "The Ministry of the Bishop, Presbyter and Deacon" (Section III). The statement emphasizes that these are not to be viewed in isolation, since "the various ministries converge in the eucharistic synaxis" (par. 24, *Quest for Unity*, 135). But notwithstanding the subtitle of this section of the statement, presbyters and deacons are treated only very briefly (in pars. 41-43, *Quest for Unity*, 138–139). Reference is made to other charisms in the Church only once, when the importance of the "particular charisms" of women "for the building up of the body of Christ" is mentioned (par. 32, *Quest for Unity*, 137)—and the point of that paragraph is to indicate that "our churches remain faithful to the historical and theological tradition according to which they ordain only men to the priestly ministry."

The Valamo Statement is certainly "episcopo-centric," though it would be ungracious to call it "episcopo-monistic." The problem is that it fails to situate episcopacy within a broader and more comprehensive understanding of ministry. Symptomatic of this failure is its inconsistent use of the term "minister/ministry." As the U.S. Orthodox-Catholic Consultation points out in its critique of the Valamo Statement, at some points "all the baptized faithful are seen as exercising diverse ministries. At other points a distinction is implied between this general ministry of all the faithful and that of the ordained. . . . In other cases, ministry/minister can mean only the ordained; and in at least one instance . . . it can mean only the one who assembles the community and presides in the celebration of the sacraments" (par. 9, *Quest for Unity*, 145).[24] By relying so heavily on eucharistic ecclesiology, with its essentially cultic view of ministry, the Valamo Statement missed an opportunity to develop more fully the pneumatological perspective that it sketches in its opening paragraphs.

24. See also the U.S. Consultation's comments about the earlier Munich Statement: "The text should have discussed the diversity of ministries within the one body (cf. II.1, par. 4); likewise some reference to the priesthood proper to all the faithful would have been in order. The relation between the bishop's ministerial priesthood and that of all the faithful is not adequately explored. The relation of the bishop and the presbyter is not sufficiently addressed" (par. 10, *Quest for Unity*, 67–68).

Let us now turn from the Joint International Commission's appropriation of Ignatius to its appropriation of Irenaeus, to its understanding of apostolic succession and episcopal ordination. In the Valamo Statement, as in the earlier Munich Statement, the Commission affirms that "the apostolic tradition concerns the community and not only an isolated individual, ordained bishop" (par. 45, *Quest for Unity*, 139). But sometimes the Valamo Statement appears to revert to a less-nuanced conception, or at least to a now-dated vocabulary. For example, we are told that "through his ordination each bishop becomes successor of the apostles" (par. 49, *Quest for Unity*, 140; cf. par. 40, *Quest for Unity*, 138). Equally infelicitous is a sentence not yet quoted from the Munich Statement: "The bishop receives the gift of episcopal grace (1 Tim 4:14) in the sacrament of consecration effected by bishops who themselves have received this gift, thanks to the existence of an uninterrupted series of episcopal ordinations, beginning from the holy apostles" (par. 3, *Quest for Unity*, 59). This appears to revert to a hands-on-heads understanding of apostolic succession. Also striking is the concluding sentence of the Valamo Statement's discussion of episcopal ordination: "What is fundamental for the incorporation of the newly elected person in the episcopal communion is that it is accomplished by the glorified Lord in the power of the Holy Spirit at the moment of the imposition of hands" (par. 27, *Quest for Unity*, 136). Up to this point, the text had been following practically verbatim the 1977 "Orthodox-Roman Catholic Reflections on Ministry." Why was this sentence interpolated at this point? Should it be regarded as inconsequential, or does it represent the "bottom line" of the Joint International Commission's thinking on "valid orders"?

This question has considerable ecumenical importance, since its implications go beyond the Orthodox-Catholic dialogue to their dialogue with Christian traditions lacking "apostolic succession" as it has been experienced in those two churches. On the one hand, the U.S. Orthodox-Catholic consultation stated in its own 1986 study of "Apostolicity as God's Gift in the Life of the Church" that "apostolicity seems to consist more in fidelity to the apostles' proclamation and mission than in any one form of handing on community office" (par. 10, *Quest for Unity*, 128; cf. the U.S. critique of the Valamo Statement; par. 25, *Quest for Unity*, 149). This statement would appear to leave room for further discussion of how the community office can be handed on without compromising apostolicity. The Joint International Commission, on the other hand, seems more inclined to pit the

Orthodox-Catholic understanding and experience of apostolic succession against that of other traditions. Consider these two passages from the Joint Commission's 1993 Balamand Statement on "uniatism":

> On each side it is recognized that what Christ has entrusted to his church—profession of apostolic faith, participation in the sacraments, above all the one priesthood celebrating the one sacrifice of Christ, the apostolic succession of bishops—cannot be considered the exclusive possession of one of our churches (par. 13, *Quest for Unity*, 177).
>
> Everyone should be informed of the apostolic succession of the other church and the authenticity of its sacramental life (par. 30, *Quest for Unity*, 181).

While these passages were written as part of an effort to resolve an exceptional crisis in Orthodox-Catholic relations and while the statement in which they occur was not part of the Commission's original agenda, they do suggest that Catholics and Orthodox may have difficulty maintaining their professed pneumatological perspective on ecclesiology when they leave the rarefied realm of pure theological discussion for the real world of inter-Church relations.

While the work of the U.S. Orthodox-Catholic Theological Consultation has been less voluminous than that of the Joint International Commission and has not directly addressed the subject of episcopacy, it may have implications for the broader issues raised in this paper.

At many points the statements of the U.S. Consultation reveal the same Ignatian perspective that we have seen in those of the Joint International Commission. Sometimes, however, they sound a more Irenaean note, especially in the 1986 agreed statement on "Apostolicity as God's Gift in the Life of the Church." It affirms that

> we call the church apostolic first of all because the church continues to share this mission (namely, that of the apostles, who were "endowed with the authority and freedom to act authentically on behalf of the one who sent them") in history, continues to be authorized by the risen Lord, through its continuing structures, as his legitimate representative (par. 5, *Quest for Unity*, 126).

But in addition to this historical aspect, apostolicity has an eschatological dimension, so that "here and now the life of the church—whether expressed in authoritative teaching, in judgment and discipline or in the eucharist itself—is being molded, corrected and governed by what has been received from the past *and* by what is awaited at the last day" (par. 7, *Quest for Unity*, 126–127). So also, when we speak of our faith as apostolic, we do not mean simply that its content has been received from the apostles. The *depositum fidei* is not "an inert object, relayed in purely mechanical fashion from generation to generation by duly authorized ministers" (par. 8, *Quest for Unity*, 127). Rather, it remains a living confession, both content and act. In the life of the Church and of each Christian, apostolicity is continually experienced in the baptismal act of receiving and giving back the Church's apostolic faith. "Apostolicity therefore is by no means unique to or limited to the realm of hierarchical ministry. For just as we share by baptism in the royal and prophetic priesthood, so also by this baptismal confession we too become bearers of the church's apostolicity" (par. 9, *Quest for Unity*, 127).

Within this broader context, what can be said of "those structures which attest to and assure the unity of the churches in their apostolic confession" (par. 11, *Quest for Unity*, 128)? The U.S. Consultation returned to this question in its 1989 agreed statement on "Conciliarity and Primacy in the Church." The Church, both locally and universally, is the locus of ordered charisms. Within the local eucharistic community "permanent offices of leadership have been established . . . as a service of love and a safeguard of unity in faith and life" (par. 5, *Quest for Unity*, 153); but the same Spirit who sets in order the local church also "manifests his presence in the institutions which keep local communities in an ordered and loving communion with one another." The text goes on to add that "the two institutions, mutually dependent and mutually limiting, which have exercised the strongest influence on maintaining the ordered communion of the churches since apostolic times, have been the gathering of bishops and other appointed local leaders in synods, and the primacy or recognized pre-eminence of one bishop among his episcopal colleagues" (par. 6, *Quest for Unity*, 153–154). Holding together these two important aspects of the Cyprianic conception of episcopal ministry remains the greatest problem still to be resolved by the Orthodox-Catholic dialogue.

As this perusal of documents resulting from international and U.S. Orthodox-Catholic dialogue suggests, the two Churches for the most part share a common understanding and practice of ministry, including episcopal ministry. The chief point in dispute is "the particular form of primacy among the churches exercised by the bishops of Rome" ("Conciliarity and Primacy," par. 7, *Quest for Unity*, 154). Their agreement is evident in the common affirmations set forth in those documents, as well as in the critical observations by the U.S. Consultation on the ministry section of *BEM:*

In general, the document BEM presents as possible, even laudable opinions, certain aspects of ordained ministry that we consider normative for the church's life and structure. These normative aspects include the threefold ministry; the historical succession of office holders in the episcopal ministry; the exclusive conferral of ordination by those entrusted with the episkopé of the community; and the presidency of the eucharist exclusively by an ordained minister. . . . In addition to the document's emphasis on episkopé as necessary ministry in the church, we affirm that episcopal office is a constitutive element of the structure of the church (*Quest for Unity*, 74).

The fact that Catholics and Orthodox can make such statements together suggests that wider reconciliation, encompassing those groups that do not regard such aspects of ministry as normative, may indeed be difficult to achieve. Nevertheless, the wealth of theological reflection on ministry offered in the principal documents of Orthodox-Catholic dialogue may provide some new perspectives for all who are engaged in the quest for Christian unity and may enrich future discussion of this central ecumenical issue.

Chapter Seven

The Roman Catholic Bishop in Ecumenical Perspective

Michael Root

The Second Vatican Council was a defining event not only for the modern Catholic Church but also for the ecumenical movement. Prior to the council, the relation between the ecumenical movement and the Catholic Church had been tentative and cautious, despite the ground-breaking work of such figures as Yves Congar. The council's affirmation in its Decree on Ecumenism *(Unitatis Redintegratio)* that the growth of the ecumenical movement was "fostered by the grace of the Holy Spirit" (UR 1) and its exhortation that "all the catholic faithful . . . take an active and intelligent part in the work of ecumenism" (UR 4) marked a sea change in that relation. Since the council, the Catholic Church has taken a leading role in every form of ecumenical discussion.

The ecumenically significant actions of the council were not limited to those explicitly concerned with ecumenism. Of at least equal significance were the many actions that signified a new direction in Catholic thought and practice, e.g., the affirmation of religious freedom, the discussion of Mary within the context of ecclesiology, or the understanding of the Church as People of God. In each case, developments internal to Catholic theology meshed with ecumenical developments, fostering a fruitful convergence. The internal evolution of Catholicism opened up new ecumenical possibilities.

A possible exception to this pattern lay in the council's new understanding of the bishop. The council itself, of course, was a decisive affirmation of the role of the bishops in the leadership of the Church. In the decades following the council, national bishops' conferences and individual bishops have played a significant role in bringing the ecumenical promise of the council to at least partial fruition. But the affirmations of the council about the episcopal office, while furthering internal Catholic developments that many non-Catholics would applaud, are also ecumenically ambiguous. On the one hand, they were an important affirmation of collegiality in the Church, a principle non-Catholics have stressed as important in any possible reunion.[1] On the other hand, when these affirmations are read in an exclusive manner, they create new ecumenical difficulties. In this essay in honor of the ecumenical work of Archbishop Weakland, I will describe how this conciliar teaching both opens and closes certain ecumenical doors, explore the historical background of its most significant feature, and finally note some possible paths forward.

The Ecumenical Significance of Vatican II on Episcopacy

From its inception in the mind of John XXIII, the Second Vatican Council was to have a primarily pastoral rather than doctrinal focus. In the course of developing its extensive range of documents, however, the council inevitably touched upon and elaborated doctrine. This doctrinal development was of particular importance in relation to episcopacy.

Pius XII, in his encyclical *Sacramentum Ordinis* of 1947, had already affirmed the sacramental character of the ordination or consecration of a bishop (DS 3860). The council went further and affirmed that in this sacrament a bishop receives "the fullness of the sacrament of Orders" (LG 21, 25). This fullness can be contrasted with the ordination of a presbyter or priest. Priests "share with bishops the one identical priesthood and ministry of Christ" (PO 7), but they are "dependent" on the bishops "in the exercise of their power" (CD 15). As the ordination formula for the priesthood approved by Pius XII put it, the priest or presbyter receives an "office of second rank" (*secundi meriti munus*, DS 3860).

This affirmation of the fullness of priesthood received by the bishop in his consecration had significant implications for the understanding of the relationship between the individual bishop and the pope. In his episcopal ordination the bishop receives not only the office of sancti-

---

1. Paul C. Empie and T. Austin Murphy, eds., *Papal Primacy and the Universal Church*, Lutherans and Catholics in Dialogue, no. 5 (Minneapolis: Augsburg Publishing House, 1974) 20, par. 24.

fying but also the offices of teaching and governing (LG 21). The concrete exercise of these teaching and governing offices are always to be carried out in communion with the episcopal college and thus with the bishop of Rome, but Vatican II made clear that "bishops, as successors of the apostles, enjoy as of right in the dioceses assigned to them all ordinary, special and immediate power which is necessary for the exercise of their pastoral office" (CD 8).

This affirmation is of obvious ecumenical significance. In the wake of Vatican I, non-Catholics worried about a papal centralism that seemed to reduce the diocesan bishop to a "vicar of the pope." Vatican II's teaching explicitly addresses that worry. "The bishops, as vicars and legates of Christ, govern by their counsels, persuasions, and example the particular churches assigned to them as vicars and legates of Christ . . . . The pastoral charge . . . is entrusted to them fully, nor are they to be regarded as vicars of the Roman Pontiff; for they exercise a power which they possess in their own right" (LG 27).

The council's understanding of episcopacy was a central aspect of its more comprehensive ecclesiology of communion. The bishops constitute a crucial bond of communion within the Church. On the one hand, the bishops "are the visible source and foundation of unity in their own particular churches" (LG 23). The particular church or diocese is thus defined in relation to its bishop; it is "a section of God's people entrusted to a bishop to be guided by him with the assistance of his clergy" (CD 11). On the other hand, the bishops form a college, in succession to the college of the apostles. "Together with its head, the Supreme Pontiff, and never apart from him, [this college] is the subject of supreme and full authority over the universal church" (LG 22). Each bishop is thus "bound to be solicitous for the entire church" (LG 23). The unity of the Church as communion is bound up with the unity of the episcopal college. "It is in and from these [particular churches] that the one and unique catholic church exists. And for that reason each bishop represents his own church, whereas all of them together with the pope represent the whole church in a bond of peace, love and unity" (LG 23). In addition, these universal and local roles of the bishop cannot be separated, since, as noted, the teaching and governing offices of each bishop within the diocese can only be exercised in communion with the wider college. In many ways the office of bishop is thus the hinge upon which the communion ecclesiology of Vatican II turns.

Ecclesiologies of communion have proven highly influential in ecumenical discussions over the last twenty-five years. The specifically episcopal focus of Vatican II has been particularly attractive to Catholic-Orthodox discussions, as can be seen in the 1988 statement of the international Orthodox-Roman Catholic Joint Commission for Theological Dialogue, "The Sacrament of Order in the Sacramental Structure of the Church." Vatican II's language of "the fullness of the priesthood" is adopted in relation to episcopal ordination, and the central role of the bishop in the unity of the local church is affirmed.[2] The essential unity of the local church with the universal communion of churches is said to be "expressed and realized in and through the episcopal college" (par. 26).

The attractiveness of this theological approach for Orthodox-Catholic relations is understandable. It builds on their shared, mutually recognized (or at least recognizable) episcopate[3] and meets the Orthodox concern for a balance between primacy and collegiality among the bishops. In this dialogue statement, however, one can already sense the problem that will emerge in relations with other Churches. One Orthodox commentator referred to the 1988 statement as "episcopo-centric."[4] When such weight is placed on the episcopal office, what consequences follow for relations either with Churches with a claim to a valid episcopate not recognized by the Roman Catholic Church (e.g., with Anglicans or some Lutherans) or with Churches that lack or have rejected the episcopal structure altogether (e.g., most Reformed)? If the sole competent minister of the sacrament of orders is a validly consecrated bishop,[5] then the implica-

---

2. Joint Commission for Theological Dialogue between the Roman Catholic Church and the Orthodox Church, "The Mystery of the Church and of the Eucharist in the Light of the Mystery of the Holy Trinity," in *Growth in Agreement II: Reports and Agreed Statements of Ecumenical Conversations on a World Level, 1982–1998,* ed. Jeffrey Gros, Harding Meyer, and William G. Rusch (Geneva: WCC Publications, 2000), pars. 25, 28, p. 675.

3. The nature of the Orthodox recognition of any ministry or sacrament outside the Orthodox communion is a complex matter. Nevertheless, it can be safely said that the Catholic episcopate is recognizable by the Orthodox, even if not recognized outside communion.

4. John H. Erickson, *"Episkopé* and Episcopacy: Orthodox Perspectives," in *Episcopé and Episcopacy and the Quest for Visible Unity: Two Consultations,* ed. Peter C. Bouteneff and Alan D. Falconer, Faith and Order Paper 183 (Geneva: WCC Publications, 1999) 88.

5. *Code of Canon Law: Latin-English Edition,* trans. Canon Law Society of America (Washington: Canon Law Society of America, 1983), can. 1012. In an ecumenical context, see "Roman Catholic Church Response to 'Baptism, Eucharist and Ministry,'" in *Churches Respond to BEM: Official Responses to the "Baptism, Eucharist and Ministry" Text,* vol. 6, ed. Max Thurian (Geneva: WCC Publications, 1988) 35. Neither explicitly

tion seems to follow naturally that ordained ministries in such Churches necessarily suffer from a *defectus* [UR 22]. While, as will be noted below, *defectus* might be translated either as "defect" or as "lack" or "absence," official translations of conciliar and later texts have consistently opted for the more severe "lack" or "absence,"[6] apparently implying that the ordained ministry is simply not present in Churches that lack what the Catholic Church recognizes as a valid episcopate. Since only a validly ordained priest is the minister of the Eucharist,[7] questions are obviously raised about the Eucharist in such Churches. Interestingly, *Unitatis Redintegratio* (no. 22) makes only the somewhat mild statement that the sacrament in such Churches "has not retained the authentic and full reality *[genuinam atque integram substantiam]* of the eucharistic mystery."[8] Whereas the sacrament of order apparently is simply absent, the Eucharist only lacks its full and authentic substance. Nevertheless, this paragraph does seem to imply that because of the *defectus* of order and the resulting defect in the Eucharist, these bodies can be referred to only as "ecclesial communities" rather than as Churches.

These negative conclusions turn on both the reiteration of the word "only" and the focus on the all-or-nothing character of the category of validity. If the affirmations about episcopacy and its role in the Church are understood in an exclusive and all-or-nothing manner, then the negative conclusions follow with a certain inevitability. Such an understanding can be found in recent Vatican texts,[9] most notably the Declaration *Dominus Jesus* from the Congregation for the Doctrine of the Faith, with its assertion that "the ecclesial communities which have not preserved the valid episcopate and the genuine and

---

states that the "sole" competent minister is a bishop, but the context and use of the statement in the BEM response seem to imply such.

6. The English of UR 22 on the Vatican web site translates *defectus* as "absence," as does Flannery [Austin Flannery, gen. ed., *Vatican Council II: The Conciliar and Post-Conciliar Documents* (Northport, N.Y.: Costello Publishing Co., 1984) 469]. Abbott [Walter M. Abbott, gen. ed., *The Documents of Vatican II* (New York: America Press, 1966) 364] and Tanner [Norman P. Tanner, ed., *Decrees of the Ecumenical Councils* (London: Sheed & Ward, 1990) 919] both use "lack." "Lack" is used in this context also in the official translation of *Ut Unum Sint* [John Paul II, *Ut Unum Sint: On Commitment to Ecumenism* (Vatican City: Libreria Editrice Vaticana, 1995), par. 67, p. 79] and "absence" in the official translation of the *Catechism* [*Catechism of the Catholic Church*, 2nd ed. (Rome: Libreria Editrice Vaticana, 2000), par. 1400, p. 353].

7. *Code of Canon Law: Latin-English Edition*, can. 900.

8. My translation.

9. For example, *Ut Unum Sint*, no. 67.

integral substance of the eucharistic ministry, are not churches in the proper sense."[10] The decisive ecumenical question is then whether such an exclusive, all-or-nothing understanding is convincing.

Historical Background: Bishop and Priest—One Order or Two?

A look at the history of the theology of the episcopate and the development of the present divide may be helpful. We cannot return to an earlier time, but a knowledge of how paths diverged may help us to see how they might come together again.

The Medieval Background

The sacramentality of episcopal consecration and reception only by the bishop of the fullness of the priesthood were not part of the consensus of medieval theology. As is well known, medieval theologians and canonists argued whether the episcopate was a distinct order or only, as Peter Lombard taught, an "office and dignity" within the order of the priesthood.[11] The majority of medieval theologians held that the episcopate was not a distinct order, although many canonists held that is was.[12] The theologians' opinion was not arbitrary, nor, as with similar, later Protestant opinions, was it based upon New Testament data. Rather it reflected the broader realities of the priestly ministry of the time.

The argument of Aquinas is revealing. In the Supplement to the *Summa Theologiae,* he explicitly addresses the question "Whether the episcopate is an order?" (Q. 40. art. 5). His clear but not unqualified answer is no. He cites a general rule he had earlier stated, that every order is ordered to the sacrament of the Eucharist *[ordinatur omnis ordo ad eucharistiae sacramentum].* He is here reflecting the common medieval understanding of priesthood almost exclusively in relation to the Eucharist (with a secondary reference to absolution within confession).[13] "Order, considered as a sacrament imprinting a character, is

10. Congregation for the Doctrine of the Faith, "Dominus Jesus: On the Unicity and Salvific Universality of Jesus Christ and the Church," *Origins* 30 (2000) 216, par. 17.

11. Petrus Lombardus, *Sententiae in IV Libris Distinctae,* 3rd ed. (Grottaferrata: Editiones Collegii S. Bonaverturae Ad Claras Aquas, 1981), IV, dist. 24.13.

12. Bernard Cooke, *Ministry to Word and Sacraments: History and Theology* (Philadelphia: Fortress Press, 1976) 580; Hermann J. Pottmeyer, "The Episcopacy," in *The Gift of the Church: A Textbook on Ecclesiology in Honor of Patrick Granfield, O.S.B.,* ed. Peter C. Phan (Collegeville, Minn.: The Liturgical Press, 2000) 344f.

13. Kenan B. Osborne, *Priesthood: A History of the Ordained Ministry in the Roman Catholic Church* (New York: Paulist Press, 1988) 206; Cooke, *Ministry to Word and Sacraments,* 581.

specially ordered to the sacrament of the Eucharist, in which Christ himself is contained, because by a character we are configured to Christ himself" *(ad 2)*. In relation to the Eucharist, "since the bishop has not a higher power than the priest, in this respect the episcopate is not an order" *(Resp.)*. Christ is no more or less present in a Mass celebrated by a priest than in a Mass celebrated by a bishop. If the priestly ministry is defined in relation to the power to preside at the Eucharist, without reference to the specific activities of the bishop, then priests and bishops are of the same order. Aquinas notes that "at his promotion a bishop receives spiritual power in respect to some sacraments" *(ad. 2)*, and so "in another way order may be considered as an office in relation to certain sacred actions" *(Resp.)*. Nevertheless, these other actions do not relate to the Eucharist, and so "this power does not have the nature of a character. For this reason, the episcopate is not an order in the sense in which order is a sacrament" *(ad. 2)*.

The medieval tendency to see the priesthood exercised by presbyters as the fullness of priesthood was rooted in the ecclesial realities of the time. The shift from the more "episcopal" patristic understanding of priesthood to the more "presbyteral" medieval understanding reflected parallel changes in Church structure. The early patristic norm was the bishop as head of a relatively small episcopal area, of a "local church" in the vernacular sense.[14] In the course of the late patristic and early medieval periods in the West, however, a decisive change took place. For a variety of historically complex reasons, "the local parish became the real focus of Church life, not the diocese, nor the urban baptismal Church, with its station churches or satellite rural churches."[15] As dioceses came to include more people and often greater geographical areas, the place where the typical Christian experienced Christian community and received the sacraments was the parish. The parish became the true assembly, the altar community.

This new reality was particularly prevalent in large parts of the Holy Roman Empire with its far-flung dioceses. The lived reality of ordained ministry necessarily changed also. The presbyter/priest, not the bishop, became the effective ordinary minister of the sacraments received by a typical layperson and the effective head of the primary

14. "The first 'bishops' in the monarchical sense were bishops of local churches; they were not diocesan superintendents in the later sense." John Knox, "The Ministry in the Primitive Church," in *The Ministry in Historical Perspectives*, ed. H. Richard Niebuhr and Daniel D. Williams (San Francisco: Harper & Row, 1983) 25.

15. Osborne, *Priesthood*, 172.

Christian community for most Christians. This ecclesial change is a significant aspect of the background of the medieval view of priesthood. John Zizioulas sees the medieval understanding of ministry as a function of this larger structural change: "It is clear that what stands behind this radical change [in ministry] is the emergence and establishment of the parish as a eucharistic gathering presided over by presbyters without the presence of the bishop."[16]

The medieval theology of episcopacy cannot be seen as an odd, rootless aberration, a period of unclarity between the theologically preferable patristic and modern discussions. The medieval understanding reflected ecclesiastical shifts, shifts that to a significant degree still shape Church life. These shifts undercut patristic understandings of the bishop as the head of a true eucharistic assembly and minister of the sacraments. To a significant degree, the debates over ministry and episcopacy that have played a role in Church division since the 1530s derive from the difficulties of theologically understanding the implications of this shift.

The Protestant Extension of Medieval Premises

The theological understanding of episcopacy was never a central concern for Martin Luther. Nevertheless, it is indicative that while doubts exist whether Luther actually nailed the 95 Theses on indulgences to the door of the Castle Church in Wittenberg on October 31, 1517, there is no doubt that he sent them on that day to his own bishop and to other bishops.[17] It was Archbishop Albrecht of Mainz who then informed Rome about Luther.[18] As the Reformation became a matter of the reform of churches and not just theological debate, the decisive question was whether a bishop would permit such a reform. A community effectively left the communion of the Catholic Church when it rejected the jurisdiction of the local Catholic bishop. Much of the discussion about a possible rapprochement between Lutherans and Catholics at the Diet of Augsburg in 1530 thus centered around the conditions under which the Lutheran estates would again come

16. John Zizioulas, "*Episkopé* and *Episkopos* in the Early Church: A Brief Survey of the Evidence," in Episkopé *and Episcopate in Ecumenical Perspective,* Faith and Order Paper 102 (Geneva: World Council of Churches, 1980) 38.

17. Erwin Iserloh, *The Theses Were Not Posted: Luther Between Reform and Reformation,* trans. Jared Wicks (Boston: Beacon Press, 1968) 46–56 and 76–97.

18. Martin Brecht, *Martin Luther: His Road to Reformation 1483–1521,* trans. James L. Schaaf (Philadelphia: Fortress Press, 1985) 206.

under the jurisdiction of the Catholic bishops.[19] It is no accident that the longest article in the Lutheran statement drawn up for the Diet, the *Augsburg Confession,* is Article 28: "Concerning the Power of Bishops," and differences over episcopal jurisdiction were among the issues that led to the failure of the negotiations at the Diet.[20]

The two major branches of the Reformation in Continental Europe, Lutheran and Reformed, differed in many ways, especially in relation to ordained ministry. Nevertheless, they agreed on one crucial point: no essential difference exists between a pastor/presbyter and a bishop. In this respect, they were in continuity with much medieval theology. The two traditions went on, however, each to draw conclusions from this principle that differed both from each other and from the consensus of medieval opinion.

The Lutheran Reformers stated a desire to preserve the medieval episcopal order, and in Scandinavia they succeeded in doing so, preserving a succession of consecrations in Sweden/Finland, while losing such a succession in Denmark/Norway/Iceland.[21] In the Holy Roman Empire, where no bishop successfully broke with the Catholic Church and the political order made the creation of new Lutheran bishoprics practically impossible, episcopal order could not be preserved, despite significant attempts on the part of Lutheran leaders to do so.[22] In this situation, the Lutherans drew a conclusion not drawn by their medieval predecessors. If bishop and presbyter belong to the same order, then, in a situation of emergency, a church can use the services of a presbyter to preside at an ordination.

The most detailed and official Lutheran argument on this matter comes in the section on "The Power and Jurisdiction of Bishops" in Philip Melanchthon's *Treatise on the Power and Primacy of the Pope.*

19. Wilhelm Maurer, *Historical Commentary on the Augsburg Confession,* trans. H. George Anderson (Philadelphia: Fortress Press, 1986) 59–236.

20. Jared Wicks, "The Lutheran *Forma Ecclesiae* in the Colloquy at Augsburg, August 1530," in *Luther's Reform: Studies on Conversion and the Church* (Mainz: Verlag Philipp von Zabern, 1992) 295 and 302.

21. On the history of episcopacy in the Scandinavian Lutheran churches, see the helpful historical essays in *Together in Mission and Ministry. The Porvoo Common Statement with Essays on Church and Ministry in Northern Europe* (London: Church House Publishing, 1993).

22. These efforts are described in detail in Dorothea Wendebourg, "The Reformation in Germany and the Episcopal Office," in *Visible Unity and the Ministry of Oversight: The Second Theological Conference Held Under the Meissen Agreement Between the Church of England and the Evangelical Church in Germany* (London: Church House Publishing, 1997) 49–78.

This text was written for the meeting of Lutheran princes in Schmalkalden in 1537 and came to be included among the Lutheran Confessions. Like many other Reformers, Melanchthon appeals to New Testament data and to the authority of Jerome to show that the distinction between bishop and presbyter did not exist in the New Testament and was a later invention of the Church. Melanchthon's argument is, however, theological and not simply an appeal to authority:

> The gospel bestows upon those who preside over the churches the commission to proclaim the gospel, forgive sins, and administer the sacraments. In addition, it bestows legal authority, that is, the charge to excommunicate those whose crimes are public knowledge and to absolve those who repent. It is universally acknowledged, even by our opponents, that this power is shared by divine right by all who preside in the churches, whether they are called pastors, presbyters, or bishops.[23]

Melanchthon here gives a Lutheran variant of the medieval argument. The essential activities of ordained ministry have been expanded to include the proclamation of the gospel, and reference to the sacrifice of the Mass has been replaced by language of the administration of the sacraments. But the form of the argument is the same: the ministries of the presbyter and the bishop do not differ in relation to what is definitive and essential to ordained ministry. Thus they are not truly two orders.

Melanchthon extends the argument, however, by arguing that the distinction between presbyter and bishop thus cannot be *jure divino.* "The reality itself implies this *[idque res ipsa loquitur]*, for, as I stated above, the power *[potestas]* is the same."[24] If the distinction is not *jure divino*, he insists, it can only be *jure humano.* If bishop and priest have the same power and if the distinction between them is *jure humano*, then in a situation of necessity, a church can and may authorize a priest to do whatever a bishop does. "Consequently, when bishops either become heretical or are unwilling to ordain, the churches are compelled by divine right to ordain pastors and ministers for themselves, using their own pastors *[adhibitis suis pastoribus]*."[25]

---

23. Pars. 60-61; Robert Kolb and Timothy J. Wengert, eds., *The Book of Concord: The Confessions of the Evangelical Lutheran Church* (Minneapolis: Fortress Press, 2000) 340.

24. Par. 63; Kolb and Wengert, *Book of Concord*, 340; translation altered.

25. Par. 72; Kolb and Wengert, *Book of Concord*, 341; translation altered. Both the recent Kolb/Wengert and the older Tappert translations omit the final phrase, which is included in the critical edition of the Book of Concord (*Die Bekenntnisschriften der*

Beginning in 1535, Electoral Saxony, the home of both Luther and Melanchthon, began regularly to ordain pastors. These ordinations were presided over by pastors who, while carrying out what amounted to episcopal duties of oversight, had not themselves been consecrated as bishops.[26]

The Lutheran tradition defended presbyteral ordinations as a matter of necessity, and even where the traditional episcopal order was not preserved, bishop-like offices were established with a variety of names: superintendent, dean, etc. The Reformed tradition, beginning from the same premise of the unity of bishop and presbyter in one order, drew more radical conclusions. While Calvin himself was willing to tolerate an episcopal polity, he insisted that "the Holy Spirit willed men to beware of dreaming of a principality or lordship as far as the government of the church is concerned."[27] The Reformed tradition came at least to prefer, and sometimes to insist upon as biblically normative, a presbyterian polity in which the "parity of ministers" was realized in oversight though the presbytery, the college of presbyters, without an individual who functioned in a way similar to a bishop.[28]

On the one hand, the Reformed break with episcopacy looks far less traditional than the Lutheran attempt to preserve some or most features of the received polity. On the other hand, an argument can be made that the classical Reformed presbyterian system represented a break with medieval distortions for the sake of a return to early patristic practice. The letters of Ignatius testify to a church with a variety of ministries: the bishop, collegially united with other bishops, surrounded by a council of elders and assisted in the care of the needy by a cadre of deacons, all serving within what amounted to what later would appear to be a large parish. The medieval church in the West

---

evangelisch-lutherischen Kirchen, 9th ed. [Göttingen: Vandenhoeck & Ruprecht, 1982] 492.23]. On the history and significance of this phrase, see Arthur Carl Piepkorn, "The Sacred Ministry and Holy Ordination in the Symbolical Books of the Lutheran Church," in *Eucharist & Ministry,* ed. Paul C. Empie and T. Austin Murphy, Lutherans and Catholics in Dialogue, no. 4 (Minneapolis: Augsburg Publishing House, 1970) 110–111.

26. Hellmut Lieberg, *Amt und Ordination bei Luther und Melanchthon,* Forschungen aus Kirchen- und Dogmengeschichte 11 (Göttingen: Vandenhoeck & Ruprecht, 1962) 181–191 and 216–223.

27. John Calvin, *Institutes of the Christian Religion,* Library of Christian Classics (Philadelphia: Westminster Press, 1960) 1072.

28. For a summary of polity in the Reformed tradition, see John H. Leith, *An Introduction to the Reformed Tradition: A Way of Being the Christian Community,* 2nd ed. (Atlanta: John Knox Press, 1981) 145–173.

significantly narrowed this diversity: the permanent diaconate disappeared, and the sense of an essential difference between priest and bishop was lost. The relation between bishop and presbyter was fundamentally altered. The classical Reformed polity, with a pastor, united with other pastors in a presbytery, advised by a group of ordained elders and assisted by deacons, in many ways was closer to early patristic practice than any other polity that came out of the sixteenth century.

Ecumenically, the decisive conclusion drawn by the Lutheran and Reformed leaders was that a pastor or group of pastors could preside at an ordination. In acting on this conclusion, the majority of Lutheran and almost all Reformed churches came to have an ordained ministry that the Roman Catholic Church has not been able to recognize as a valid ministry, with the results outlined above.

Two aspects of the logic behind the Protestant actions need to be noted. First, while the conclusion that a presbyter could ordain was not the consensus opinion of medieval theology, it was not unprecedented.[29] Huguccio of Pisa (died 1210), one of the most influential canonists of his time, held that anyone, if duly authorized, could confer whatever they had themselves received. Thus a priest could not consecrate a bishop but could, if rightly authorized, ordain a priest.[30] In two cases, popes of the early fifteenth century authorized abbots to ordain their own monks to the subdiaconate, diaconate, and priesthood (although it is not clear that the abbots ever actually did such). The abbots of Citeaux were authorized to ordain to the subdiaconate and diaconate from 1489.[31] The Reformers conclusion that presbyteral ordination was possible was thus not utterly new.

Second, in the medieval period and the early Reformation, arguments about episcopacy did not, as later, hang on a theological concept of an apostolic succession mediated by episcopal succession. In arguing that only a bishop can ordain a priest, Aquinas makes no mention

29. Secondary literature is not unanimous on just how far the precedent runs. Kenan Osborne states that who had the power to ordain was "quite an open question" in the early Middle Ages (Osborne, *Priesthood*, 193). Bernard Cooke, however, states that "there seems to be no questioning of the necessary function of the bishop in the action of episcopal or presbyteral ordination" during the same period (Cooke, *Ministry to Word and Sacraments*, 579).

30. Lawrence N. Crumb, "Presbyteral Ordination and the See of Rome," *Church Quarterly Review* 164 (1963) 27.

31. The documents authorizing these ordinations are presented in DS 1145, 1290, and 1435. They are discussed in detail in Crumb, "Presbyteral Ordination," 20–25.

of succession; rather, his argument turns on the bishop's relation to the total good of the Church.[32] Only with the republication of the relevant patristic texts, especially the new edition of Irenaeus produced by Erasmus in 1526, and with the turn to patristic sources to rebut opponents across the Reformation divide did a concept of episcopal succession come again to play an important role. Georg Kretschmar has shown that this concept enters discussion only at the very end of the 1530s, in the course of debates leading up to the failed negotiations at the Diet of Regensburg in 1541.[33] The discussions of episcopacy in the Lutheran confessions, all but the Formula of Concord written prior to this conceptual turn, thus do not address questions of succession at all. When the argument came to be made that episcopal succession is a necessary or even sufficient condition of a true ministry, the Reformers insisted that such succession is neither necessary nor sufficient.[34] Nevertheless, it should be noted that the Protestant decision to break with episcopacy was made without reference positively or negatively to concepts of succession.

The Response of the Council of Trent

As discussed above, Catholic doctrine on the relation between bishop and priest was by no means defined prior to the Reformation. Somewhat surprisingly, matters were only slightly more defined following the Council of Trent. Order and episcopacy were not discussed until the council's final period, beginning in 1562. The rejection or refutation of Protestant errors was determinative neither of the debate nor of the conclusions.[35] The decisive concerns were intra-Catholic, in particular the relation between episcopacy and papacy and the delicate question of the mandatory character of episcopal residence within the

32. "The episcopal power stands in the same relation to the power of the lower Orders, as political science, which seeks the common good, to the lower acts and virtues which seek some special good" (*ST*, Supplement, Q. 38, Art. 1, Resp.).

33. Georg Kretschmar, "Die Wiederentdeckung des Konzeptes der 'Apostolischen Sukzession' im Umkreis der Reformation," in *Das bischöfliche Amt: Kirchengeschichtliche und ökumenische Studien zur Frage des kirchlichen Amtes*, ed. Dorothea Wendebourg (Göttingen: Vandenhoeck & Ruprecht, 1999) 314–333. The paragraph above is highly dependent on Kretschmar's groundbreaking article.

34. For a vigorous expression of this argument, see Philip Melanchthon, "The Church and the Authority of the Word," in *Melanchthon: Selected Writings*, trans. Charles Leander Hill (Minneapolis: Augsburg, 1962) 130–186.

35. "The lengthy debate about the sacrament of orders (from September to December 1562) seems scarcely aware of the Reformation challenge." Cooke, *Ministry to Word and Sacraments*, 606.

diocese. A suggestion by Cardinal Guise in December 1562 of the proposition that "the bishops are appointed by Christ in the Church" was widely interpreted as implying mandatory residence and set off what a recent history of the Catholic Reformation refers to as "Trent's deepest crisis."[36] A definition that episcopacy existed *de jure divino* was seen as implying a diminution of the papacy.[37]

Trent's decree and canons on the sacrament of order thus say less than one might expect. Chapter 2 of the decree discusses seven major and minor orders without mentioning episcopacy and asserts only of priests and deacons that they are mentioned in Scripture (DS 1765). Chapter 4 does assert that the bishops succeed to the apostles and that, apart from *[praeter]* other ecclesiastical ranks, the bishops belong to the Church's hierarchical order. Bishops are able to confer the sacrament of confirmation and to ordain priests; "those of lower order" *[reliqui inferioris ordinis]* are not (DS 1768). No distinction is made between the capacity of a bishop to delegate confirmation to a priest and the capacity to delegate ordination to a priest. In fact, "nothing is said to indicate whether priests might also be 'extraordinary ministers' of ordination."[38]

Two of the canons address episcopacy. Canon 6 condemns those who deny that a hierarchy exists in the Church, instituted by divine ordination *[divina ordinatione institutam]*, which consists of bishops, priests, and ministers (DS 1776). It thus anathematizes those who would claim that hierarchy is a mere human invention but stops short of saying that hierarchy exists *jure divino*. Canon 7 condemns those who deny that bishops are superior to priests or who contend that the power to confirm or ordain is held in common by bishops and priests. It also condemns those who contend that "those who have not been rightly ordained and sent by ecclesiastical and canonical power, but come from some other source, are legitimate *[legitimos]* ministers of word and sacraments" (DS 1777). Interestingly, no mention is made of ordination by bishops, only of ordination by "ecclesiastical and canonical power." Even more important, ordinations not carried out by such power are not said to be invalid but only illegitimate.

Trent clearly wished to defend Catholic order and to reject what it saw as Protestant errors, especially the description of the episcopal ordering of the Church as, at best, a human invention to be retained and

---

36. Michael A. Mullett, *The Catholic Reformation* (London: Routledge, 1999) 61f.
37. Osborne, *Priesthood*, 273.
38. Ibid., 272.

abandoned at will or, at worst, a deformation of a biblically mandated ordering of the Church. Nevertheless, the council stopped significantly short of providing either the conceptual foundations for a communion ecclesiology in which episcopacy plays a major structuring role or the basis for the conclusion that Churches without a recognized, episcopally ordained ministry are without any valid ministry, without a valid Eucharist, and thus simply not Churches.

Conclusions

What can be concluded from this rapid historical overview? Immediately obvious is that the Reformers who broke with the episcopal ordering of the Church, although their action was undoubtedly a break with tradition, nevertheless were acting on principles that were also to be found in most medieval theology, most notably, the unity of episcopacy and priesthood in a single order. In this sense, the Reformers were in certain respects closer to the majority opinion of medieval theology than is contemporary Catholic theology. If the premise that lay behind their actions is granted, that the bishops with the canonical authority to ordain were persecuting the gospel and refusing to ordain evangelically minded clergy (a premise Catholic theologians then and now may not be willing to grant, but which is perhaps understandable in historical hindsight), then the Reformation break with episcopal order can be understood not as an uncatholic innovation, but as an emergency action guided by concepts shared with the theology of the immediately preceding centuries.

In addition, both medieval and Reformation theology can be said to have recognized the fundamental shift that took place in ecclesial life when the parish replaced the diocese as, experientially, the primary Christian community for most Christians. That change brought with it the new role of the priest or presbyter as, experientially, the primary ordained minister. This change is reflected in the Lutheran and Reformed insistence that a parish pastor exercises (or in principle can exercise, under certain conditions) the fullness of ordained ministry. Any modern ecclesiology of communion needs to take this still existing ecclesiastical reality into account.

What becomes the primary argument for a more episcopacy-centered understanding of ordained ministry, the succession of episcopal consecrations as the means by which the apostolic office is preserved and handed down in the Church, is mostly absent from medieval and early

Reformation debates. The Reformers' break with episcopal ordering predated the introduction (or re-introduction) of this argument (although the reality of episcopal succession of course existed).

On close examination, the rejection of the Reformers' teaching on ordained ministry by the Council of Trent turns out to be more restrained than that implied by more recent Catholic teaching. To say that non-episcopal orders are illegitimate is rather different from saying that they are invalid, and to speak of ordinations not carried out with ecclesiastical and canonical power is rather different from simply talking of non-episcopal orders. The oddity of the ecumenical consideration of episcopacy and orders is that Trent seems to have left more ecumenical doors open in this area than did the more intentionally ecumenical Vatican II.

Ecumenical Paths Forward?

The preceding discussion shows that the historical basis for an exclusive reading of recent affirmations about episcopacy and episcopal succession is shakier than might be thought. This history is not simply of antiquarian interest. The ecclesiastical reality that formed the background for the medieval and Reformation perception of bishop and presbyter as forming one order, namely, the parish presided over by the priest as the primary Christian community for the vast majority of Christians, is still with us. Has this reality been adequately understood theologically? In its statement on "The Ministry in the Church," the international Roman Catholic-Lutheran Joint Commission concluded:

> The existence of local congregational ministries and superordinated regional ministries on both sides is for both churches more than the result of purely historical and human developments or a matter of sociological necessity. Rather, they recognize here the action of the Spirit as this has been experienced and attested from the very beginnings of the church. The development of the one ministry of the church into different ministries can be understood as having an intimate connection with the nature of the church.[39]

In the immediate context of the dialogue, this statement may have been intended as a concession by the Lutherans that a distinct episco-

39. Par. 45; in Harding Meyer and Lukas Vischer, eds., *Growth in Agreement: Reports and Agreed Statements of Ecumenical Conversations on a World Level* (New York: Paulist Press, 1984) 263.

pate appeared in the Church under the guidance of the Spirit, but does this statement also have important implications for Catholic theology? Is the existence of presbyters in distinction from bishops part of the divinely willed order of the Church? If so, is this reality adequately accounted for in present Catholic ecclesiology?[40] Does Catholic ecclesiology make clear why there are parishes in addition to dioceses? Do the documents of Vatican II make clear why a Church that had bishops but no priest/presbyters would be disordered? If Vatican I's affirmations on the papacy needed to be supplemented by Vatican II's understanding of episcopacy, perhaps the present stress on episcopacy needs to be supplemented by a deeper reflection on the ministry of the truly local ministry of the parish priest.

Ecumenically, such reflection might have at least two consequences. First, it might provide a better context for understanding the actions of the Reformers in relation to ministry. Second, by providing a more complex picture of the Church as structured through its ministry, it might help open up a richer, more complex picture of the bonds of communion through which the Church lives out its unity.

If the communion that is the life of the Church is the community's participation in the common life of the Trinity, then everything that mediates the Church's participation in the life of the Trinity is a bond of communion: common baptism; common Eucharist; the common proclamation and reception of the gospel in faith; common prayer in the Spirit; common service, suffering, and martyrdom in the name of Christ. All the items in this list are not equivalent. Baptism, the Eucharist, and the faithful proclamation and hearing of the Word have an irreplaceable centrality in the Church's communion. The importance of ordained ministry and episcopacy (or, for that matter, papacy) to the Church's communion are related to their role in the Church's unity in faith and sacraments. The communion of the Church is thus held together by a structured variety of bonds. This truth has significance both for diachronic unity across time and for synchronic unity in one time.

The unity of the Church across time is often thought of in terms of its apostolicity, i.e., its continuity in the apostolic teaching, mission, and ministry. Orthodox theologians in particular have stressed that apostolicity is a function of the total life of the community, focused in but not reduced to the bishop. "In episcopal succession, therefore,

40. On this problem in Catholic theology, see Susan K. Wood, *Sacramental Orders* (Collegeville, Minn.: The Liturgical Press, 2000) 65f.

we have essentially succession of communities."[41] Susan Wood has argued for

> a theology of apostolic succession as both a succession of ministers who have received the laying on of hands and a succession of apostolic communities which have retained the apostolic faith. . . . These are not two separate and unrelated successions, but one succession in which the minister is in communion with the community, articulating, personifying and representing the apostolic faith of the community, and the community recognizing itself in its minister.[42]

John Zizioulas might add "in its ministers," for "apostolic continuity is realized through the bishop, not as an individual, but in his being surrounded by the college of the presbyterium."[43]

Precisely because apostolic continuity is thus a complex phenomenon, we can understand how episcopal succession has been diversely understood in the Church's history. Irenaeus understands succession as a succession of persons in the office of bishop in a certain city, a *successio localis* in which one person succeeds the previous one as bishop. It is not a succession of consecrations, in the sense of every bishop being consecrated as such by some other bishop, a *successio personalis*. Such a personal succession may have existed at the time, but it is not the succession of which Irenaeus speaks.[44]

If continuity is thus complex, should apostolic continuity in a community's ministry be understood to hang entirely on a succession of episcopal consecrations, so that if such a succession is broken, apostolic ordained ministry is simply not present? A strict adherence to such a position will need to face up to the historical difficulties of asserting any such a continuity in the first and second centuries. As Francis Sullivan concludes in a recent study: "Neither the New Testament nor early Christian history offers support for a notion of apostolic succession as 'an unbroken line of episcopal ordination from Christ through the apostles down through the centuries to the bishops of today.'"[45] Historical continuity or communion across time in

---

41. John Zizioulas, *Being as Communion: Studies in Personhood and the Church* (Crestwood, N.Y.: St. Vladimir's Seminary Press, 1985) 198.

42. Wood, *Sacramental Orders*, 43.

43. Zizioulas, *Being as Communion*, 196.

44. *Against Heresies*, Book III, ch. 3.

45. Francis A. Sullivan, *From Apostles to Bishops: The Development of Episcopacy in the Early Church* (New York: Paulist Press, Newman Press, 2001) 15f. The passage Sullivan quotes comes from the Vatican response to the *Final Report* of the Anglican-Roman Catholic International Commission.

the Church's ministry, even if focused in the ministry of the bishop, cannot be reduced to episcopal succession.

The synchronic communion of the Church also must be thought of as a complex reality. The collegiality of the bishops focuses a reality that cannot be reduced to them. If the Eucharist is the sacrament of the Church's unity, it is the priest, not the bishop, who visibly and physically represents Christ, the Church's head in whom all are one, to and within the vast majority of celebrations. More comprehensively, communion is realized in a wide variety of common actions by Christians of every sort. As Hermann Pottmeyer notes: "Not only the pope and the bishops are bearers of *communio,* but the rest of the members of the Church are as well."[46]

These bonds of communion are not of an all-or-nothing character. As Vatican II famously asserted, in their baptism non-Catholics share a real if imperfect communion with the Catholic Church (UR 3). In *Ut Unum Sint* (no. 11), John Paul II implied that in baptism a communion exists not just between non-Catholic Christians and the Catholic Church but also between the Catholic Church and non-Catholic Churches and ecclesial communities. The Lutheran-Catholic *Joint Declaration on the Doctrine of Justification* elaborates an extensive consensus on both the content and significance of the doctrine of justification, which "directs us in a special way toward the heart of the New Testament witness to God's saving action in Christ."[47] Such agreement in the central teachings of the faith, an agreement that had been thought through most of our history to be lacking, cannot be without relevance to a present common life in Christ, however imperfect.

Even in relation to the Eucharist, "validity" and "invalidity" are not the first and last words. As Cardinal Ratzinger wrote in 1993 to Bavarian Lutheran bishop Johannes Hanselmann:

> I count among the most important results of the ecumenical dialogues the insight that the issue of the Eucharist cannot be narrowed to the problem of "validity." Even a theology oriented to the concept of succession, such as that which holds in the Catholic and in the Orthodox Church, need not in any way deny the salvation-granting presence of the Lord in an evangelical Lord's Supper.[48]

46. Pottmeyer, "Episcopacy," 351.

47. The Lutheran World Federation and The Roman Catholic Church, *Joint Declaration on the Doctrine of Justification* (Grand Rapids, Mich.: Wm. B. Eerdmans, 2000), par. 17.

48. "Briefwechsel von Landesbischof Johannes Hanselmann und Joseph Kardinal Ratzinger über das Communio-Schreiben der Römischen Glaubenskongregation," *Una Sancta* 48 (1993) 348; my translation.

If a Lutheran or Reformed Eucharist communicates the salvation-granting presence of Christ, then it must also, in some way, communicate that communion with Christ and all who are in him, which is the fundamental reality of the unity of the Church.

If the actions of such communities "most certainly can truly engender a life of grace" and "must be held capable of giving access to that communion in which is salvation" (UR 3), then their essentially *ecclesial* quality needs to be emphasized. Vatican II's phrase "ecclesial communities" has a positive side, as was emphasized by the council's doctrinal commission: such communities

> are not merely a sum or collection of individual Christians, but they are constituted by social ecclesiastical elements which they have preserved from our common patrimony, and which confer on them a truly ecclesial character. In these communities the one sole Church of Christ is present, albeit imperfectly, in a way that is somewhat like its presence in particular churches, and by means of their ecclesiastical elements the Church of Christ is in some way operative in them.[49]

If so much must be said about the sacraments and the life of such ecclesial communities, what must then be said about the ministries that preach such a gospel, administer such rites, and guide such a community life? As Francis Sullivan has suggested, the logic that binds together ministry and ecclesiality need not flow in only one direction, implying that a body without a valid ordained ministry cannot be a Church in the proper sense. If a community is truly ecclesial, if it proclaims the saving gospel, hands on the Holy Scriptures, baptizes into Christ and the one Church, celebrates a Lord's Supper which, even if not valid in the eyes of the Catholic Church, mediates the saving presence of Christ, then is "invalidity" the only or even the first thing that should be said about its ministries? As Sullivan concludes: "One can hardly recognize the authentic Christian life of another community without forming a positive judgment about the ordained ministry that nurtured and fostered that life."[50]

The question whether the *defectus ordinis* of Western non-Catholic Churches is an utter lack or a defect in a reality that is nonetheless present must be assessed in this light. Walter Kasper (writing while still a professor and not yet a cardinal and president of the Pontifical

---

49. Cited in Sullivan, *Apostles to Bishops*, 233.
50. Sullivan, *Apostles to Bishops*, 236.

Council for Promoting Christian Unity) argued that if "many elements of sanctification and truth" exist outside the Catholic Church (LG 8), and if the Spirit of Christ uses these communities as means of salvation (UR 3), then "on material grounds *[aus der Sachlogik]*, and not merely on the basis of the word usage of the council, it becomes clear that *defectus ordinis* does not signify a complete absence, but rather a deficiency *[Mangel]* in the full form of the office."[51] If *defectus* is deficiency and not absence, then a real but imperfect communion exists between the Catholic Church and the Western non-Catholic Churches also in ordained ministry.

Such a shift need not negate the role episcopacy and episcopal collegiality play in the communion ecclesiology of Vatican II. It would, however, place the role of the bishop in the context of a more complex web of connections and relations that make up the communion of the Church. Such a contextualization would not only soften certain ecumenical judgments, it might make an actual reconciliation of ministries more possible. The international Roman Catholic-Lutheran Joint Commission suggested a "mutual recognition that the ministry in the other church exercises essential functions of the ministry that Jesus Christ instituted in his church and, which one believes, is fully realized in one's own church." Such a recognition would be "as yet incomplete," but it "would be an important step in helping us through further reciprocal reception to arrive eventually at full mutual recognition of ministries by the acceptance of full church and eucharistic fellowship."[52] Its subsequent text, "Facing Unity," provided a concrete outline for how such partial recognition could form the basis for a growth into full communion.[53]

Lutheran-Anglican relations in Northern Europe, Canada, and the United States over the past fifteen years have shown just such a progression.[54] On the basis of a more complex understanding of communion and apostolicity in which episcopal collegiality and succession

51. Walter Kasper, "Die apostolische Sukzession als ökumenisches Problem," in *Lehrverurteilungen-kirchentrennend? III: Materialien zur Lehre von den Sakramenten und vom kirchlichen Amt,* ed. Wolfhart Pannenberg (Freiberg i.B.: Herder, 1990) 345.

52. "The Ministry in the Church," par. 85; in Meyer and Vischer, eds., *Growth in Agreement,* 274.

53. In Gros, Meyer and Rusch, eds., *Growth in Agreement II,* 443–484.

54. For Northern Europe, see *Together in Mission and Ministry: The Porvoo Common Statement with Essays on Church and Ministry in Northern Europe* (London: Church House Publishing, 1993); for Canada, see Richard G. Leggett, ed., *A Companion to The Waterloo Declaration: Commentary and Essays on Lutheran-Anglican Relations in Canada* (Toronto: Anglican Book Centre, 1999); for the U.S., see Evangelical

play an important but not exclusive role,[55] Anglicans and Lutherans were able mutually to recognize each other's ordained ministries. This recognition was a moment in a process of growing together into a reconciled ministry that will include episcopal succession. In each of these agreements, Lutheran Churches that in the past have not claimed episcopal succession have entered succession as one aspect of life together. Important in all of these has been the recognition that while episcopal succession is an important sign of continuity in apostolic mission and ministry, ministries outside such succession are nevertheless recognizable as the ministry Christ and the Spirit gave to the Church. In this context, the Lutheran Churches were able to receive the succession broken at the time of the Reformation without repudiating the ministries they have exercised over the past four centuries. A more flexible approach to episcopacy as a bond of communion was thus able to be more effective in binding together a larger body of churches.[56]

Vatican II's ecclesiology of communion, within which episcopacy plays an important but specific role, is one of the many developments internal to Catholicism over the last century that is of great ecumenical promise. To realize that promise, however, an all-or-nothing and exclusive understanding of episcopacy and, especially, episcopal succession will need to be overcome. I believe a more flexible understanding is both in accord with Catholic theology and in accord with the intentions of much of the Reformation. The exact institutional form and theological understanding of episcopacy and ordained ministry that will accord with our theological convictions and fulfill our ecumenical hopes cannot now be described in detail, but we have enough sense of the goal to guide us forward.

Lutheran Church in America, *Called to Common Mission: A Lutheran Proposal for a Revision of the Concordat of Agreement* (Chicago: Evangelical Lutheran Church in America, 1999).

55. The decisive argument on apostolicity and episcopacy was made in Anglican-Lutheran International Continuation Committee, *The Niagara Report: Report of the Anglican-Lutheran Consultation on Episcope, Niagara Falls, September 1987* (Cincinnati: Forward Movement Publications, 1988).

56. In this area, the difference between the Lutheran Churches, which have consistently declared themselves open to episcopacy at least in principle, and the more anti-episcopal Reformed Churches becomes significant.

Chapter Eight

The Role of the Local Bishop in Catholic-Jewish Relations

Michael A. Signer

The Dialogue with a Human Face: The Local Bishop

The remarkable progress in Jewish-Catholic relations since the publication of *Nostra Aetate* nearly forty years ago has been one of the most exciting new directions in the post–Vatican II Church. It has been my unique privilege as a rabbi ordained just after the council to have observed these changes through my participation in dialogues with both clerical and lay members of the Church. As the years have passed it becomes clearer to me that I have been a participant in an almost unprecedented development in the history of our two communities. I have observed that the shape of the reconciliation between Jews and Catholics in America has been the product of the leadership by the American episcopate. This article is, in some fashion, both an expression of gratitude for the leadership by a generation of bishops and an effort to explain the background of the development of Catholic-Jewish relations since the council.

As I begin to write this article my gaze turns to a photograph taken more than twenty years ago. In that photograph I am standing with Timothy Cardinal Manning, Archbishop of Los Angeles, and Dr. Uri Herscher who was then Dean of Hebrew Union College in Los Angeles. Cardinal Manning is smiling and dressed in his roman collar with his pectoral cross invisible, tucked into his pocket. He had arrived driving his own car only moments before the photo. The occasion that brought us together was not a public ceremony honoring the cardinal, but a luncheon celebrating the priests and women religious who were concluding a week of study with members of the Hebrew Union College faculty. The priests and women religious who were in attendance surrounded him in good spirits and genuine welcome. I remember being surprised as they narrated how their bishop had cared for them and members of their family. The stories of very human moments were so distant from the image of the bishop I held since my own graduate studies about the role of the medieval bishop who exercised temporal power as well as spiritual. Within the next hour my "book learning" about the role of a bishop was displaced by the experience of listening to the cardinal's address to his priests and the members of the Hebrew Union College faculty.

When the cardinal spoke at lunch he reminisced about his early years in Los Angeles. He had come as a young priest from Ireland. On Sunday mornings he would walk two or three miles from his parish to hear the sermons given by Rabbi Edgar F. Magnin at Wilshire Boulevard Temple. Cardinal Manning explained that these excursions were "not permitted" Catholics in the 1940s, but he found the liturgy and sermons such a rich experience that he "transgressed" for a greater good. These Sunday adventures led to a deep friendship with Rabbi Magnin. The discovery of that friendship and the rich treasures within Judaism led him, as archbishop, to encourage Jewish-Christian dialogue.

Hearing the cardinal's message brought me to reflection on the ways that friendship and experience can have unprecedented consequences. During my early years of teaching in Los Angeles (1974–1985) I became the beneficiary of the Manning-Magnin friendship. I observed first-hand the possibilities for the ways that a local bishop could open the doors to dialogue. Through the agency of his ecumenical officer, Rev. Msgr. Royale Vadakin, Cardinal Manning initiated a rabbi-priest dialogue that published a number of significant pastoral statements; developed a Catholic-Jewish lay dialogue that focused on issues of pastoral concern; and developed a Catholic-Jewish women's dialogue that promoted amity and interreligious understanding. In addition, Cardinal Manning and Msgr. Vadakin encouraged an academic exchange between St. John's Major Seminary in Camarillo and Hebrew Union College to deepen an ecumenical interseminary exchange program sponsored by the National Conference of Christians and Jews. Dialogue was encouraged at all levels of education due to the initiative of the Archbishop of Los Angeles and the activity of those who served him.

This biographical reflection demonstrates that the renewed relationship between Christians and Jews has a human face. By that phrase

I mean that the dialogue is born in the human experience of the bishop and supported by a growing body of theological reflection and magisterial teaching. The reconciliation between the People of Israel and the People of God in Pilgrimage has been a process where experience and theological reflection have complemented one another. On some occasions the experience of friendship has directly advanced theological reflection.

In the article that follows I would like to develop this idea of reciprocity between experience and theology by describing how the relationship between the Roman Curia and local bishops' conferences reflects this symmetry with respect to Jewish-Christian relations. Then, I will turn to the writings about Christian-Jewish relations of two American bishops, Joseph Cardinal Bernardin of Chicago and Archbishop Rembert Weakland of Milwaukee. The article will conclude with some suggestions for future directions.

The Universal and the Local Church: Jewish-Christian Relations

In the autumn of 1999 a letter from the late John Cardinal O'Connor appeared in the *New York Times*. The contents of the letter were surprising to members of both Catholic and Jewish communities. The cardinal sent greetings to his Jewish friends along with "sincere love and true admiration for [their] fidelity to the Covenant." He also asked "this Yom Kippur that you understand my own abject sorrow for any member of the Catholic Church, high or low, including myself who may have harmed you or your forebears in any way."[1] In November 1999, Archbishop Weakland addressed the Jewish community of Milwaukee and presented a litany that sought reconciliation and forgiveness.[2] One month later the Archbishop of Denver, Charles J. Chaput, O.F.M. Cap., repeated the request of the Jewish community for "forgiveness for the wrongs committed by Catholics against the Jewish

---

1. The *New York Times*, September 9, 1999. The letter was submitted by Victor J. Barnett, Elie Wiesel, and James D. Wolfensohn with this caption: "This inspiring and courageous letter was sent by John Cardinal O'Connor to his many Jewish friends. We are publishing it because we believe it ought to be shared. We pray for his speedy and complete recovery so that he may continue his important work of bringing people of all faiths together for many years to come."

2. "Asking the Jewish Community's Forgiveness," *Origins* 29, no. 24 (November 25, 1999). We shall examine this text later in the article.

people in the past, and the ignorance and prejudice that still exist."[3] These three letters may be among the best publicized, but when I asked an on-line group of rabbis about their recent experience with their bishops, I received a flood of replies from across the United States that described public ceremonies where the local bishop had provided a penitential message about the past, and a promise for a more positive relationship in the future.[4]

This groundswell of support by local bishops for Jewish-Catholic relations reflected a rapprochement between these two communities that began with *Nostra Aetate* in 1965 at the end of the Second Vatican Council and continued through the efforts of Pope John Paul II to set a penitential program as part of the preparation for the Jubilee year 2000.[5] The public pronouncements by American bishops were two remarkable events that took place during the Jubilee year itself. The first event took place on the first Sunday of Lent. Pope John Paul II presided at a penitential liturgy at St. Peter's. During that ceremony, Cardinal Edward Cassidy read a prayer asking divine forgiveness for those sons and daughters of the Church who had mistreated the Jewish people during the first two millennia of Christianity. This ceremony was followed by the papal visit to Jerusalem where the Pope stood at the Western Wall, a place sacred to the Jewish people as the last remnant of the Jerusalem Temple, and the pontiff engaged in an act of Jewish devotion where he inserted a prayer into the wall. That prayer stated:

> God of our fathers
> You chose Abraham and his descendants to bring Your Name to the Nations:
> We are deeply saddened by the behavior of those
> Who in the course of history
> Have caused these children of Yours to suffer
> And asking Your forgiveness we wish to commit ourselves to genuine brotherhood with the people of the Covenant.

3. The letter was issued December 10, 1999. In that same week, the *National Catholic Reporter* ran a story entitled "Three Bishops say, 'I'm sorry'" (December 17, 1999) 7.

4. It was particularly gratifying to learn about the response by bishops in places as small as Las Cruces, New Mexico, or as large as Cleveland, Ohio. I was very moved by the letter that Rabbi David Jacobson of San Antonio, Texas, sent me while he was dying. His widow wanted me to know how much the friendship with his local bishop had meant to him over the years.

5. John Paul II's letter *Tertio Millennio Adveniente* and its implications for Jewish-Christian relations have been explored in *SIDIC* (Journal of the Service internationale de documentation judeo-chrétienne, January 1999).

With this simple prayer and the gesture at the wall the Pope brought the relationship of the Church and the Jewish people into a new phase. Clearly, Pope John Paul II's act drew worldwide attention to the Jewish-Christian relationship. Reconciliation between the two communities was not simply grounded in political considerations but in a deep theological reversal of the Church's approach to Judaism that had been expressed for so many generations in the "teachings of contempt."

The Pope's plans for the Jubilee, the message of bishops throughout America during that year, and even the papal trip to Jerusalem were not isolated phenomena. They were part of a chain of events that had been set in motion by the Second Vatican Council. *Nostra Aetate* was part of a new opening of the Church to the world, and a new spirit of dialogue within the body of the Church itself. Indeed, we might argue that it is precisely in the area of Jewish-Christian relations where the symmetry between the local churches and the universal Church has been demonstrated most clearly.

The signs of reconciliation have come both from Rome and from the local churches. In the wake of the council, Pope Paul VI established the Commission on Interreligious Relations with the Jews as part of the Pontifical Council for Christian Unity. This office of the Curia has issued documents for instructing the entire Church. Two documents focused on how the Church should proceed in establishing a relationship of amity with the Jews: "Guidelines and Suggestions for Implementing the Conciliar Declaration Nostra Aetate (n. 4)" (1975); and "Notes on the Correct Way to Present the Jews and Judaism in Preaching and Catechesis" (1985). These texts have been augmented at the level of local bishops' conferences in Australia, Canada, and the USA.[6] These bishops' conferences have focused on issues that implement the ideas suggested by the commission in Rome and make more concrete suggestions to those who minister in the churches.

On one issue, the Shoah, it is clear that a new different level of communication was reached in 1997 with the document "We Remember: A Reflection on the Shoah."[7] The issue of the role of the

6. These documents are available online at www.jcrelations.net and in printed format in the two volumes compiled by H. Croner, ed., *Stepping Stones to Further Jewish-Christian Relations* (New York: Stimulus Books, 1977), and *More Stepping Stones in Jewish-Christian Relations* (New York: Paulist Press, 1985).

7. Secretariat for Ecumenical and Interreligious Affairs/National Council of Catholic Bishops, *Catholics Remember the Holocaust* (Washington: United States Catholic Conference, 1998), contains the document by the Pontifical Commission (pp. 45–56),

Church during the period 1933-1945 when European Jewry was destroyed had been a major barrier in the post-conciliar movement toward improving relationships with the Jewish community. Many members of the Jewish community understood the Shoah to be the climax of centuries-long ecclesiastical denigration of Judaism and the failure by many in the Church to stop violence against the Jews. Leaders of the American Jewish community noted the failure of *Nostra Aetate* to address the issue of anti-Semitism and the Holocaust. However, when we examine the actions by the Bishop of Rome, John Paul II, and the specific contributions of Cardinal Bernardin and Archbishop Weakland, we shall observe that the Pontifical Council has expressed issues of deepest concern to the Jewish community more clearly at the local level than in Rome.

The road to a statement by the universal Church on the Shoah leads through the See of St. Peter and the Bishop of Rome. Pope John Paul II had made reference to the Shoah ever since his first visit to Auschwitz in 1979. Shortly after that trip he crossed the river Tiber and entered the synagogue of Rome to express his solidarity with the Jewish community there. During his worldwide travel the Pope has made it a point to meet with survivors of the Shoah.[8] Beyond these pastoral visits, the Pope has expressed his gratitude for Jewish philosophers like Martin Buber and Emmanuel Levinas for shaping his own theological views of the human person.[9] The papal solicitude for the Jewish community derives from his own childhood experience of friendship with Jews in Katowice.[10] Without reducing theology to biography, we would claim that the Pope's life experience and theological orientation provides support for the idea that reconciliation between Jews and Christians is rooted in reciprocal relationship between human experience and theological reflection.

---

as well as the documents issued by European bishops' conferences and statements by members of the American episcopate.

8. The Pope's statements have been collected in *Spiritual Pilgrimage: Texts on Jews and Judaism 1979–1995,* ed. Eugene Fisher and Leon Klenicki (New York: Crossroad, 1995).

9. *Crossing the Threshold of Hope,* ed. Vittorio Messori; trans. Jenny McPhee and Martha McPhee (New York: A. A. Knopf, 1994) 238–239, and Michael A. Signer, "Crossing the Threshold of Reconciliation: John Paul II and the Jews," *Reform Judaism* (Spring 1995) 36–40.

10. Darcy O'Brien, *The Hidden Pope* (New York: Daybreak Books/St. Martin's Press, 1998), provides details of John Paul II's childhood in Poland and narrates the rediscovery of his Jewish friend Jerzy Kluger in Rome.

At the urging of Pope John Paul II and leaders of the Jewish community, the Commission on Interreligious Relations with the Jews began its work on a document about the Shoah. Edward Cardinal Cassidy, the President of the Commission, promised at a 1989 meeting with Jewish leaders in Prague that a statement would be forthcoming. However, in 1995, the occasion of the fiftieth anniversary of the liberation of Auschwitz and the end of World War II, nearly every bishops' conference in Europe offered its own declaration about the Shoah. The Hungarian and German conferences made direct statements about the connection between the church teachings and anti-Semitism. The Dutch bishops declared that they were "filled with shame" that the tradition of anti-Judaism in the Church had created a climate of indifference. The Swiss bishops expressed regret that their country had not welcomed more refugees. Deeply moving expressions of shame, guilt and complicity appear in the pronouncements of the Germans, Poles, and the French. The French bishops offered a declaration of repentance and expressed a desire that the Church submit her own history to critical examination for the sins committed by members of the Church. In their letter to Rabbi Toaff, rabbi of the synagogue in Rome, the Italian bishops "want to do Teshuvah" [the Hebrew word for "repentance"] as they "recognize the truth, however painful, of the facts of our responsibility." Archbishop Oscar Lipscomb, speaking for the United States Bishops Conference, expressed regret for the failure of the U.S. to save more lives during those tragic times.[11] Cardinal Cassidy, President of the Pontifical Council for Christian Unity, praised these statements by local councils. In response to criticism of "We Remember," he considered it appropriate for bishops' conferences of the countries where the Shoah had occurred to make explicit references to anti-Semitism and the Christian anti-Judaism or "teachings of contempt." By contrast, "We Remember" was directed to the universal Church and required a more generalized approach to the problem.[12] While many Jewish critics of "We Remember" considered Cardinal Cassidy's explanation as an evasion by the Curia to take responsibility

11. All the statements by the European bishops' conferences can be found in *Catholics Remember the Holocaust* (note 7 above).

12. Cardinal Edward Idris Cassidy, "Reflections Regarding the Vatican's Statement on the *Shoah*" (May 1998) in *Catholics Remember the Holocaust*, 61–76. For a sharper response to criticisms of "We Remember," one should read Remi Hoeckman, O.P., "The Jewish-Christian Encounter: A Matter of Faith?" in Michael A. Signer, ed., *Humanity at the Limit: The Impact of the Holocaust Experience on Jews and Christians* (Bloomington, Ind.: Indiana University Press, 2000) 429–441.

for the Shoah, a more careful examination of his essay may indicate that his message was an emphasis on post-Vatican II ecclesiology: the local bishop or the national conference of bishops is the appropriate location for catechesis about the Shoah and about the future of Jewish-Catholic relations.

"Covenantal Responsibility": Joseph Cardinal Bernardin and Archbishop Rembert Weakland as Pastoral Teachers of Jewish-Christian Relations

Joseph Cardinal Bernardin and Rembert Weakland have been major figures in the post-Vatican II dialogue between Jews and Catholics. Their work in this area has been recognized by major organizations such as the American Jewish Committee or the National Conference of Christians and Jews. Bernardin and Weakland never held the high public visibility of John Cardinal O'Connor in New York nor undertook the burden of organizing episcopal responsibility for Jewish-Christian dialogue in the manner of William Cardinal Keeler. Yet they each held significant responsibility among their peers in the United States bishops' conference. However, they have written about many of the theological issues at the heart of the "new" relationship between the two communities. Their writings, often delivered in the form of public addresses to audiences of Jews and Christians, make significant contributions to the theoretical foundations of the dialogue. Many of Cardinal Bernardin's writings on Jews and Judaism were collected into the volume *A Blessing to Each Other: Cardinal Joseph Bernardin and Jewish-Catholic Dialogue.*[13] Archbishop Weakland's addresses remain in manuscript; however, their content should become more broadly known.[14]

As pastors and teachers of the Church, both Bernardin and Weakland address the theological foundations of the Jewish-Christian dialogue. In his keynote address to the Sixth National Workshop on Christian-Jewish Relations, Archbishop Weakland addressed the theme

13. Liturgy Training Publications, Chicago, 1996. See also *Selected Works of Joseph Cardinal Bernardin*, vol. 2: *Church and Society*, ed. Alphonse P. Spilly (Collegeville, Minn.: The Liturgical Press, 2000) 209–307.

14. The manuscripts were sent to me by the archdiocesan archives. I am most grateful to David Stosur for his help in gaining access to Archbishop Weakland's papers. (Editor's note: Mary Carian of the Salzmann Library at Saint Francis Seminary deserves the credit for making these papers available.)

"In the Image of God: The Challenge of Diversity."[15] He focused on the scriptural verse in Genesis 1:26 that Adam was created in the image of God. The fact that God states "let us make" is an indication that the Jewish-Christian relationship is founded on "a vision of reality that comes from faith, from the creative power of God active in the world's origin" and particularly with the world's family.[16] The free will of God to create Adam in the divine image endows humanity with a sense of dignity and worthiness.

At the core of the divine-human relationship is a free choice—the choice to enter into covenantal relationship. The covenant becomes the guarantee of human freedom. Weakland proposes that the creation narrative sets a temporal framework in which the *Urzeit* implies that all was unified and given to human beings, who would have power over it. At the *Endzeit* this order would be restored with a return to peace and harmony. In the time "in between," human beings face the challenge between order on the one hand and the demands of freedom and diversity on the other.[17] The covenant, the relationship between God and humanity freely chosen, is a way of getting back to the proper order. According to Weakland, "The challenge of diversity does not consist in reducing all to unity, but in maintaining the freedom that comes with the right order and that can be destroyed by disobedience, evil intention, and exterior coercion."[18]

The diversity of humanity in general and of the two faith communities that hold the creation story sacred provides the foundation for renewing the relationship between Jews and Christians. The mutual tasks are set in the "between time," where their mutual fidelity to the covenant impels them to establish the "proper order," an order that they must first re-establish between themselves. Weakland exhorts the two communities that "God's self-revelation to humanity was not complete in one event nor grasped in one response by Israel or by the Christian people." In this statement Weakland stands in a line of thinking that is also found in the German-Jewish philosopher Franz Rosenzweig (1886–1929), who makes a similar claim that "the truth

15. Rembert Weakland, "In the Image of God: The Challenge of Diversity," keynote address, National Workshop on Christian-Jewish Relations, Milwaukee, Wisconsin, October 26, 1981. All Weakland documents are from the Weakland Collection at Salzmann Library, Saint Francis Seminary, Milwaukee, Wisconsin.

16. Ibid., 1.

17. Ibid., 4.

18. Ibid., 5.

lies neither with us or with them [Christians]," but with God.[19] Learning to live in the "time between" comes from a careful scrutiny of the ways of God, who is a "good pedagogue" and "slowly brings about a realization of what his relationship involves."[20]

Weakland pushes the narratives of the Hebrew Bible to the forefront in another address, "The Interfaith Dimension of Social Ministry."[21] In this address he argues that Christians must read the Old Testament or Hebrew Bible to "put Christians on the right track." The emphasis in his exploration of the foundation of social justice is to begin with the idea that human beings are created in the image of God, because this implies the absolute dignity of each person on the globe. However, the dignity of each person can be worked out only in solidarity or relationship with other human beings. That solidarity is founded on the notion of covenant, or *Berit*. Weakland emphasizes that this covenant is made not only with individuals but with a whole people. When Christians read the Exodus narratives, they discover that: (a) God has a preference for the needy, the poor, and the voiceless; and (b) Christians rediscover their sense of community by reading the Hebrew Bible. These ideas also become clear in Jesus. It is to be noted that Weakland emphasizes "clear" in Jesus and not "clearer." He goes on to emphasize the point with his Christian audience that their covenant with Jesus is a "new covenant of a new people . . . so it is not that the old covenant exhausts all that is old, but simply brings it to a new dimension because it is still covenant and He is still calling us to be a people."[22]

Weakland attempts to demonstrate that the New Testament "goes beyond" the Old Testament in two areas: in the universality of God's love and justice and in the eschatological dimension. He emphasizes that these points are made in the Old Testament already but are made clearer in the New Testament. The sensitivity demonstrated by Weakland to the different dimensions of the relationship between the two testaments has been a continuing topic in the Jewish-Catholic dialogue. His position of the clear existence of significant ideas in the Old Testament or Hebrew Bible as supremely valuable to Christians is in the trajectory articulated by the recent document published by the

19. Franz Rosenzweig, *The Star of Redemption* (New York: Holt Rinehart and Winston, 1971) 415–417.

20. Weakland, "In the Image of God," 5.

21. Second Annual Social Ministry Conference, Archbishop Cousins Catholic Center, Milwaukee, Wisconsin, October 27, 1984.

22. "The Interfaith Dimension of Social Ministry," 3–5.

Pontifical Biblical Commission, *The Scripture of the Jewish People in the Christian Bible.*[23]

The understanding of the Scriptures has also been fundamental in the writings of Cardinal Bernardin. In his analysis of Bernardin's writings about Jews and Judaism, Fr. John Pawlikowski utilizes the term "covenantal partnership" to describe this approach to the relationship between the two communities. Bernardin begins with the problem of the substratum of Christian anti-Judaism that had colored theological assessments of Judaism. His statements demonstrate a willingness to challenge this harmful approach.[24] In 1984 Bernardin addressed the National Executive Council of American Jewish Committee and focused on the Crucifixion as the appropriate place to begin serious work in Jewish-Catholic relations. He indicated that the death of Jesus had been a source of conflict between Jews and Christians. The narration of Jesus' death and suffering has been the source of continuing stereotypes. After invoking the Second Vatican Council and recent New Testament scholarship as a major turning point in turning Christian negative images of Jews around, he indicated that "we need to stress that the religious ideals which Jesus preached and tried to implement in the social structure of his day, were shared by the most creative and forward-looking forces in Judaism of that period. Actually, Jesus and his followers stood in concert with a significant part of the Jewish community in opposing the unjust structure that existed at that time. His death bore witness to many of the same ideals proclaimed by other rabbis."[25]

The correlative change to this reversal of negative images of Judaism in the New Testament is to deepen appreciation of the Hebrew Bible. Christian scriptural reading by correcting stereotypes in the New Testament and emphasizing a positive appreciation for theological ideas in Hebrew Scripture can become a bridge between Judaism and Christianity rather than a barrier. Ultimately, a theology of the Cross could then become a source of confluence and not a basis of conflict.

23. Commission Biblique Pontificale, *Le peuple juif et ses saintes écritures dans la bible chrétienne* (Paris: Cerf, 2001) 17–26. The relationship between the two testaments is also discussed in the preface by Cardinal Joseph Ratzinger, *Many Religions—One Covenant: Israel, the Church and the World* (San Francisco: Ignatius Press, 1999) 1–13.

24. John T. Pawlikowski, "Covenantal Partnership—Cardinal Bernardin's Theological Approach to Catholic Jewish Relations," in *A Blessing to Each Other*, 17–22, provides an excellent systematic introduction to the thought of the cardinal in this area.

25. National Executive Council Meeting, American Jewish Committee, November 3, 1984, in *A Blessing to Each Other*, 48–49.

If Scripture is the foundation for a renewed dialogue between Jews and Christians, the content discussed in those conversations must surely be part of the agenda of the local bishop. It is clear from reading the speeches and articles of Bernardin and Weakland that they listened carefully to their American Jewish interlocutors. The concept of genuinely listening to the living Jewish community and its leadership was emphasized in the 1975 "Notes and Guidelines" published by the Vatican's Commission for Religious Relations with the Jewish People.[26] In numerous discussions the leadership of American Jewish communities put their agendas forward after the Second Vatican Council. They hoped for the Catholic Church to continue work on removing the sources of anti-Judaism from Christian teachings, whether in textbooks or in preaching and catechesis during Holy Week, or in Christian attendance at the Oberammagau Passion Play in Germany. In addition, American Jews wanted to promote a more profound understanding of their deep ties to the state of Israel and secure a commitment from the Catholic bishops that the Holocaust would receive appropriate treatment in their schools. These issues would play a significant role in the archdioceses of Milwaukee and Chicago, which had large and well-established Jewish communities and also a significant population of Holocaust survivors.

In his 1994 acceptance speech of an award from the National Conference of Christians and Jews, Archbishop Weakland stated,

> As we Catholics look to our past we see many reasons for questioning and self-examination. We were engaged in crusades; we were involved in pogroms; we taught prejudices that could well have led to the extermination of the Jews, seen as predestined by God for such punishment. In other words, as we look at the past, even the immediate past, we should not too easily say that it could never happen again. It could. Daily we see signs that it might.[27]

These words indicate the empathy necessary for dialogue with a Jewish community that was—and is—still on the path of learning to trust the Christian world. Cardinal Bernardin also emphasized the need for Catholics to "listen when you raise questions about alleged gospel representations that fail to portray the profound and positive influence of

---

26. "Guidelines and Suggestions for Implementing the Conciliar Declaration *Nostra Aetate 4*," in *A Blessing to Each Other*, 191–198.

27. Awards Night, Wisconsin Region of the National Conference of Christians and Jews, Pfister Hotel, Milwaukee, Wisconsin, June 2, 1994, p. 1.

Jewish tradition on the formation of Jesus' teaching and on the spirit of the early Church."[28] Bernardin articulated that the American bishops have had a special responsibility in four areas of implementing the ideas of *Nostra Aetate*: (1) the Hebrew Scriptures and the Catholic Church; (2) Jesus and the Jewish Tradition; (3) the Church and Judaism; (4) the themes emphasized by John Paul II, such as the spiritual bond that links Judaism to Christianity, the living heritage of Judaism, the permanent validity of the Jewish covenant, and the Holocaust.[29]

Weakland and Bernardin, in their respective ministries, never turned away from the difficult areas of the dialogue. They pressed forward with the issue of the Holocaust. Cardinal Bernardin became the co-chairman of the local efforts on behalf of the U.S. Holocaust Memorial Museum. In addition, he spoke with wisdom and understanding during the difficult period of misunderstandings between Jews and Poles about the Carmelite convent at the Auschwitz concentration camp.[30] Given the large number of Catholics with ties to Poland and Jewish survivors of the Shoah and their children who reside in Chicago, this required extraordinary pastoral skills. Cardinal Bernardin also gave emphasis to his solidarity with the American Jewish community as it struggled to free thousands of Soviet Jews from religious persecution.

While maintaining solidarity with the agenda brought by the American Jewish community, Weakland and Bernardin also asked members of the Jewish community to broaden the horizons of their agenda. Archbishop Weakland indicated that the dialogue is in the process of changing direction; it need no longer only be about the "negative" but can "push on in a positive way." He stated:

> It is important in any dialogue to remember that no group is static and no group is monolithic. Each group is changing according to the demands of the times. Catholicism today does not look like it did before Vatican Council II. Within both the Jewish community and the Catholic community there are differences of opinions and views. One is never dialoguing with an immovable object that looks the same from all angles. The

28. "American Jewish Committee," in *A Blessing to Each Other,* 46.

29. Center for Jewish and Christian Learning, College of St. Thomas, St. Paul Minnesota, September 28, 1988, in *A Blessing to Each Other,* 76–87.

30. His column in the archdiocesan newspaper, "A September Prayer" (September 28, 1989), and the address to the Chicago Board of Rabbis, "Together We Can Move Mountains: Reflections on Catholic Jewish Relations Today" (April 18, 1990), indicate the cardinal's abilities to address the pain suffered by both Catholics and Jews over the founding of a Carmelite convent on the grounds of the Auschwitz concentration camp. *A Blessing to Each Other,* 94–97and 98–108.

pluralism within each body must also be respected, because one is dia-
loguing with a richness that should not be reduced to easy accessibility.[31]

Cardinal Bernardin asked the Jewish community leaders to consider
making items from the Catholic community part of their agenda. He
suggested particularly the themes of reverence for life, ecology, and
economic justice.[32] In looking toward the future of the Jewish-Catholic dialogue, both Weakland and Bernardin articulated similar agendas: (1) a continuing discussion of the meaning of the Holocaust in
order to understand how each community remembers this historical
period and transmits that memory to future generations. The Shoah
should become part of Catholic educational practice. In addition, Cardinal Bernardin argued that the Catholic community must be prepared to submit its World War II record to a thorough scrutiny by
respected scholars. (2) A continuing discussion of theologies of Scripture and covenant. The council may have done away with the deicide
charge, but how this important shift of ideas will be put into practice
will require renewed pastoral efforts. This discussion will lead to a
continuing focus on liturgy and preaching. (3) A continuing discussion
of the Jewish people and the state of Israel. Archbishop Weakland argued that "Catholics have not taken seriously the Jewish position of
relationship to the land. For Catholics we lack a category of thought
in our religious systems where there is any parallel."[33]

The remarkable symmetry in outlining the future agenda for
Catholic-Jewish relations reflects the parallels that have already been
described in earlier parts of this essay. Two local bishops in American
communities made a commitment to carry out the ideas of *Nostra Aetate* 4. Each in his own diocese built a public intellectual agenda for
implementing the suggestions that came from the Vatican Commission for Religious Relations with the Jews. Without doubt, both of
these bishops joined with their confreres in validating the "Guidelines
for Catholic-Jewish Relations" of 1985 and "God's Mercy Endures For-

31. "Jewish Catholic Dialogue: Planning for the Future," Keynote Address, Killeen
Chair, St. Norbert College, De Pere, Wisconsin, March 19, 1992, pp. 5–6.
32. "Address to the Chicago Board of Rabbis and the Jewish Federation of Metropolitan Chicago" and "Address to Interfaith Clergy Institute of Metropolitan Chicago,"
in *A Blessing to Each Other,* 29–35 and 131–133.
33. The future agenda is discussed by Weakland in his address at St. Norbert College (see note 31). Bernardin addressed the issue of the future agenda during the course
of his visit to Jerusalem in 1995, particularly in his address, "Anti-Semitism: The Historical Legacy and Continuing Challenge for Christians," and "Homily at St. Savior
Parish," in *A Blessing to Each Other,* 164–166 and 167–169.

ever: Guidelines on the Presentation of Jews and Judaism in Catholic Preaching" of 1988.[34]

Conclusion: History, Theology, and Liturgy in Balance

I am moved in these concluding thoughts to turn to St. Thomas Aquinas on the role of the bishop: "There are different kinds of instruction in the Church. One brings conversion to the faith . . . and belongs to any preacher or any one of the faithful; the second concerns the basics of faith and belongs to ministers, mainly to priests; the third level of instruction is on Christian life and belongs to the godparents; the fourth is on the profound mysteries of faith and the completion of Christian life and belongs to bishops" (*Summa Theologiae*, III, q. 71, a. 4, ad 3). The local bishop, at some point, must bring the mystery of Christian faith and the completion of Christian life to the topic of the renewed relationship between Judaism and Christianity. In the Jewish community, each statement by the Vatican and the hierarchy is carefully discussed and scrutinized. This activity does not seem to have a parallel in the Catholic community except among theologians.

However, there seems to be hope that the new direction of the Catholic-Jewish relationship may reach the faithful through a new emphasis on penitence. The profound turn of Christian discourse during the last decade has been toward a theology of penitence and its relationship to the future of Catholic-Jewish reconciliation. Prayer for vision and reconciliation and fostering a true spirit of repentance were the final items of Cardinal Bernardin's address at Hebrew University in 1995. Repentance was the core of Cardinal Cassidy's speech to the meeting of Jewish leaders in Prague that set a Vatican document on the Shoah in motion. Archbishop Weakland's litany of repentance offered on the occasion of the Jubilee Year may be one of the most forward-looking compositions in the renewed history of the relationship. It was offered in a public setting. Members of the Jewish community were present. The archbishop asked the Catholics who were present to join in his confession and resolve. He then asked those members of the Jewish community who were present to affirm the "common resolve." Theoretical statements are important, but the concept of an assembly gathering to review, resolve, and confess on an annual basis seems to provide the communal bonding that will allow communities to traverse moments of fierce disagreement and even moments of despair.

34. These documents are printed as part of *A Blessing to Each Other,* 189–224.

Ultimately, the role of the local bishop in Catholic-Jewish relations may serve as a symbol of hope for the future. This hope may find its basis in the concluding essay written by Cardinal Bernardin, who insisted on writing the closing chapter of his collected speeches to the Jewish community. In that valediction he indicated that he had tried to listen to his Jewish friends. Their question was, "Where do we go from here?" Bernardin offered a simple but poignant reply, "Just keep going." He suggested that as a bishop he had sought every opportunity given to him as a local bishop to teach the message of *Nostra Aetate*. He averred that we teach, first, by words and ideas; second, by the programs and institutions we create. Bernardin suggested that the ideas need a mediating structure in order to become part of the world of human interaction. His true legacy in the area of Jewish-Christian relations was to be found in the joint programs that the archdiocesan office for ecumenical and interreligious affairs conducted with its partners. Therefore his advice was: "Continue to build the relationship between the two communities on friendship and then be sure to support it with structures of implementation and continuity. Then, keep going." The idea of building institutions to mediate ideas would seem to be at the heart of the episcopal office—shepherding the People of God on their pilgrimage by creating communities. However, Bernardin continued by gifting both communities with the heart-touching message out of his own experience. His words should be quoted because they touch upon the basic principle of human mortality that is our lot as Christians and Jews.

> Dialogue is sharing our faith experience. . . . As a Christian I believe that death is not the end, only a change from earthly life to life eternal. We can look at death as an enemy or a friend. If we see it as an enemy death causes anxiety. But if we see it as a friend our attitude is totally different. In faith I want to say to you that I see death as a friend.
>
> I want to tell you how much I love you and how much the Catholic-Jewish friendship has meant to me during the years I have been in Chicago. As we both go forth into the future that God has planned for us, I want you to know that the dialogue has been a blessing for me. After fourteen years I truly feel you have accepted me as Joseph, your brother.

In these words we can discern the great synthesis of the role of the local bishop in Jewish-Christian relations. Bernardin's message is one of experience, profound theological knowledge, deep personal faith, and institutional leadership. However, one should not lose sight of the fact that it was his acceptance as "brother" by the Jewish community that brought him the deepest satisfaction and became another reservoir of strength upon which he could draw as he looked forward to the "eternal life" beyond this life. While such a belief may leave us Jews in wonderment, it is the wonderment of appreciation. The balance between history, theology, and a life lived in hope of Teshuvah is one more proof that "love is strong as death."

Chapter Nine

Common Ground: A Ministry of Unity

Most Reverend Oscar H. Lipscomb

" For who is able to govern this vast people of yours?" (1 Kgs 3:9, NAB). All bishops, especially as they first assume the episcopal office, must in some way resonate with this question posed to God by Solomon at the outset of his kingly service, when he prayed for "an understanding heart." Nor is the challenge made any easier when a bishop hears, or perhaps later reads, a charge from the homily suggested in the rite of ordination to that office:

> As a father and a brother, love all those whom God places in your care. Love the priests and deacons who share with you the ministry of Christ. Love the poor and the infirm, strangers and the homeless. Encourage the faithful to work with you in your apostolic task; listen willingly to what they have to say. Never relax your concern for those who do not yet belong to the one fold of Christ; they too are commended to you in the Lord.[1]

Nor does the bishop's responsibility stop at the boundaries of his own diocese. A little later in the same homily he can hear or read these words: "Never forget that in the Catholic Church, made one by the bond of Christian love, you are incorporated into the college of bishops. You should therefore have a constant concern for all the churches and gladly come to the aid and support of churches in need."

But the bishop is not alone in this task. A consoling reading of the words of the fathers of the Second Vatican Council in the Dogmatic

---

1. International Commission on English in the Liturgy, *The Rites of the Catholic Church*, vol. 2 (Collegeville, Minn.: The Liturgical Press, 1991) 69.

Constitution on the Church *(Lumen Gentium)* provides the insight that God calls such an individual, empowers him through a reality that reaches back to the very beginnings of the Christian faith, is founded in the call and mission of the apostles, and remains with him, once he accepts the obligation, in his own work and effort on behalf of a local church. In such local churches, bishops have the challenging status as "vicars and legates of Christ," so that they speak with his voice and act with his authority in directing by their "counsels, persuasion, and example . . . their flock in truth and holiness" (LG 27). Bound to such a task by the office that he has accepted, the bishop can never forget his own humanity and frailty. Hence the council fathers, following the lead of Sacred Scripture (see Heb 5:1-2), are specific in urging compassion in his task of governance and offer this concrete advice: "He should not refuse to listen to his subjects, whose welfare he promotes as of his very own children and whom he urges to collaborate readily with him" (LG 27).

The end result of such a ministry is that unity for which Christ prayed in the priestly prayer that he offered to the Father the night before he died, as recorded in the Gospel of St. John (John 17:20-23). All the bishop's efforts, beginning with the witness of preaching and teaching, and extending to sanctification and good order, are designed to bring about a oneness in mind and heart on the part of the faithful that unites them to the mind and heart of Christ and leads to the Father. Such a ministry of unity in today's Church is by no means an easy or altogether successful task. It is one, however, to which a bishop must address himself "in season and out of season," and he should take encouragement from the words of the *Catechism of the Catholic Church*: "The very differences which the Lord has willed to put between the members of His body serve its unity and mission. For 'in the Church there is diversity of ministry but unity of mission.'"[2]

The Archbishop of Chicago, Cardinal Joseph Bernardin, had direct and extensive experience of both the unity and the division as a result of that remarkable local church and of his wider involvement with the Catholic Church in the United States and the Church universal through his service to it in a number of ways at the request of the Holy See. After some four years of study and consultation with bishops, priests, religious, and lay people, the cardinal, through the resources of

---

2. *Catechism of the Catholic Church* (Vatican City: Libreria Editrice Vaticana, 1994; distributed by The Liturgical Press, Collegeville, Minn.) no. 873.

the National Pastoral Life Center in New York, issued what has come to be thought of as the foundational document of the Catholic Common Ground Initiative entitled "Called to Be Catholic: Church in a Time of Peril," on August 12, 1996.[3] The opening statement captured nicely the situation as it was perceived: "Will the Catholic Church in the United States enter the new millennium as a Church of promise, augmented by the faith of rising generations and able to be a leavening force in our culture?" Recognizing a distinct moment of peril, the text went on to highlight many positive features of Catholic life in the United States: continued growth in numbers; openness and hospitality toward the poor and the stranger; strong examples of Christian faith and witness to the gospel within our culture; communities of worship and service; and all "deeply rooted endeavors that are kept alive by the hard labor and daily sacrifices of millions of Catholics."

There followed, however, a list of thirteen "urgent questions" that it was felt ought to be aired "openly and honestly" for the sake of the Church in the United States. The questions ranged, with no order of priority, through a host of concerns that touch the effort of every bishop in his diocese; for example: the changing roles of women; the organization and effectiveness of religious education; the eucharistic liturgy; human sexuality; the image and morale of priests and the declining numbers of priests and religious; lay positions and leadership in current Church structure; the capacity of the Church to embrace minorities; the survival and excellence of Catholic education; the manner of decision-making in consultation for Church governance; the responsibility of theology to authoritative Church teaching. And the list is by no means exhaustive.[4]

Part III of the document began by asking what it might take for the Church in the United States to emerge from a host of polarized positions and the partisanship they represented, which resulted in paralysis. The answer was reassuring: "Jesus Christ, present in scripture and sacrament, is central to all that we do; He must always be the measure and not what is measured." The text continued to note that there should be respectful dialogue among the parties and at the same time reaffirmed the full range and demands of authentic unity as well as acceptable diversity. The goal was not just to "dampen conflict" but a way

3. "Called to Be Catholic: Church in a Time of Peril," in *Catholic Common Ground Initiative: Foundational Documents* (New York: Crossroad, 1997) 34. Hereafter *Foundational Documents*.

4. Ibid., 37–38.

to make, as Cardinal Bernardin himself often noted, "our conflicts constructive." Accountability was then further explained as recognition and adherence to the Catholic tradition, but as well to a Spirit-filled, living Church in which non-essentials are susceptible to change in keeping with needs. There was a recognition that, historically, there has always been wide room for legitimate debate, discussion, and diversity in the Church, but it did rule out, for example, "pop scholarship, sound-bite theology, unhistorical associations and flippant dismissals." Notice was also taken of a certain fundamentalism that narrows the richness of the tradition to a text or decree, or an appeal to individual or contemporary experience that ignores the richer tradition, over the centuries, or "the living magisterium of the Church exercised by the bishops and the Chair of Peter."[5]

The cardinal gave a news conference and responded with a written press statement in August 1996, further explaining the goals and methods of the project (shortly to be known as the "Initiative"), while completing the formation of a committee that, at his invitation, would continue to foster and promote the idea. The committee met for the first time on October 24, 1996, with Cardinal Bernardin present, in Chicago. At that time his health had deteriorated drastically, and he had requested that I take the position as chair of the group, since he could no longer do so. I agreed, and at the close of the committee meeting, the cardinal gave one final address, appropriately entitled "Faithful and Hopeful." In it he fleshed out precisely the ground rules for the kind of dialogue in which the Initiative hoped to engage as a part of its response to some of the questions raised in "Called to be Faithful." They represented a classic exercise in civility and charity, always at the service of the truth and of the gospel. This remarkable churchman left us with a quotation from the conciliar document *Gaudium et Spes*, the Pastoral Constitution on the Church in the Modern World. It was a plea for the Church to become a sign of sincere dialogue as part of its mission to enlighten the world. Cardinal Bernardin said:

> I close with the following words of that passage: "Such a mission requires us first of all to create in the Church itself mutual esteem, reverence and harmony, and acknowledges all legitimate diversity; in this way all who constitute the one people of God will be able to engage in evermore fruitful dialogue, whether they are pastors or other members

5. Ibid., 40–41.

of the faithful. For the ties which unite the faithful together are stronger than those which separate them: let there be unity in what is necessary, freedom in what is doubtful, and charity in everything" (no. 92).[6]

For some five years now, as chairman of the Catholic Common Ground Initiative Committee, I have been closely associated with the work of this endeavor and have been grateful for the insights and growth that it has offered to me in my office as diocesan bishop. Twice yearly the full committee meets; on one occasion a national dialogue follows; on the other, a lecture from such individuals as Cardinal Basil Hume and Cardinal Avery Dulles, S.J. The National Pastoral Life Center in New York continues to staff the work of the committee and currently publishes a newsletter for some three thousand interested individuals or institutions. Committee members have spoken to a wide range of symposia in colleges and universities, dioceses, and Catholic lay organizations. While I have spoken on the Initiative in our local church, and we have had meetings in some parishes, no formal dialogues have emerged.

Still, there can be no denying that much of the process in which I have participated has found its way into my pastoral style of responding to needs in our archdiocese. By and large I have learned the virtue of "listening" in a way that involves far more than simply remaining silent in the course of a discussion or dialogue. The almost monthly meetings of our priests' council and the quarterly meetings of the Archdiocesan Pastoral Council have emerged with more of a dialogic process than in previous times, and a number of diocesan boards and commissions seem to reflect this same result. In this, however, I must confess that the result is due largely to informed and professional lay leadership that has taken a role in assuring such a development.

There is no doubt in my mind that the most influential moments in which Catholic Common Ground activities have touched my life as a diocesan bishop have been my participation in the annual dialogues. Notable among these, and for reasons that will be obvious, was the Second Cardinal Bernardin Conference, which took place in Oconomowoc, Wisconsin, in 1998, addressing the theme "Church Authority in American Culture." The group comprised some forty invited guests and four panelists. Avery Dulles, S.J., spoke on "*Humanae vitae* and *Ordinatio sacerdotalis.*" He phrased the question nicely in these words:

6. Cardinal Joseph Bernardin, "Faithful and Hopeful," in *Foundational Documents*, 76–77.

> The basic question is whether to accept the long-standing Catholic tradition, authoritatively confirmed by the ecclesiastical teaching office and by the pope as its supreme exponent, or to maintain a critical distance from the tradition and the magisterium and give weight to new perspectives that enjoy greater support in society at large.

He felt that Common Ground existed because, as he said,

> in spite of the ideological cleft, it is possible for reasonable adherents of each side to appreciate their adversaries' point of view. Few conservatives are so extreme that they deny all mutability in the tradition or question the possibility that the Church might have something to learn from the developments in secular society. The Church itself encourages its members to be men and women of their own time and to proclaim the faith within the framework of new cultural situations.[7]

Father Joseph Komonchak spoke on "Authority and Its Exercise," concentrating on the pastoral letters of the United States bishops to illustrate "exercises of authority at the level of the Episcopal Conference." One of the more telling points of Father Komonchak's presentation questioned whether a purely formal approach to authority is sufficient for the kind of discussion that the panelists were presenting. He noted that "in addition to a discussion of the formal or *de iure* grounds of authority, we need to discuss also the conditions of effective or *de facto* authority, which I believe reduce considerably the often-claimed uniqueness of teaching authority in the Church."[8] To support such a contention, Father Komonchak cited a classic letter from John Henry Newman to the Duke of Norfolk, who raised a serious objection to the conversion of his son to the Catholic Church. The heart of Newman's response concerning external coercive force in the Church, or "ecclesiastical prohibition to doubt," is captured by one sentence: "Thus it [ecclesiastical prohibition] avails in neither case; while he loves and trusts, it is not needed; when he does not love and trust, it is impotent." Hence, Father Komonchak concluded, "If, in fact, exercises of teaching authority in the Church, whether by pope, bishop, or episcopal conference, are today ineffective, Newman's remarks might usefully turn our attention beyond questions of formal authority to consider how to restore the admiration, trust, and love that it presup-

---

7. Avery Dulles, S.J., "*Humanae vitae* and *Ordinatio sacerdotalis*," in *Church Authority in American Culture*, Second Cardinal Bernardin Conference (New York: Crossroad, 1999), 21. Hereafter *Church Authority*.

8. Joseph A. Komonchak, "Authority and Its Exercise," in *Church Authority*, 36.

poses for its effective exercise." And he immediately added, "I'm struck by the presence in both quotations of the word *trust*."[9]

The third presentation was by Father James A. Coriden and centered on discipline rather than doctrine. Its primary emphasis was on the exercise of the power of governance, and within such a power more specifically, executive or administrative authority exercised by bishops and pastors in the ordinary course of their ministry. Father Coriden noted that the exercise of such administrative leadership depends upon the concrete circumstances and its setting within the Church. He further explained, "The Roman Catholic Church in the United States has its own ethos of authority." Recognizing that it differs from other Christian Churches, and even from other Catholic Churches elsewhere in the world and in some respects, he listed several diverse factors that form background and substance to this ethos: ". . . for example, a Catholic sense of what communion implies, high esteem for the episcopal office, [and] American individualism." A final and more important introductory note preceded consideration of cases: "Christians cannot even begin to discuss authority in the Church without reflecting on its essential counterpart, freedom."[10]

Against such a background, Father Coriden offered an analysis of three cases: general absolution, reconciliation of the divorced and remarried, and conflict resolution through mediation. He suggested that as we considered the three cases to be presented with respect to the exercise of authority, the following points or questions ought to be asked: "Who had the right to make the decision? How should that authority have been exercised in order to be authentic and effective? And should the decision have been made at all, as over and against allowing freedom of expression or action?"[11]

At the close of his analysis, the panelist located the prime focus on issues such as freedom and authority in the common tradition, especially the biblical. He listed aspects of such a biblical dimension of authority in the Church, its exercise ultimately from Christ, and for the reasons of salvation, so that the community, living in faith, shared in all its members in the powerful gifts of the Spirit. His conclusion from such a biblical context: "Authority as service is rooted in the identity and mission of Christ. It defines the very nature of authority in the

9. Ibid., 38–39.
10. James A. Coriden, "Cases and Observations," in *Church Authority*, 47–48.
11. Ibid., 48–49.

Church, not simply the style of its exercise."[12] Father Coriden closed his presentation with a consideration of the principle of subsidiarity, a firmly embedded dimension of Catholic social teaching, and ways in which it has been applied within the Church at different levels. He cited the preface of the 1983 Code of Canon Law, which urges the greater application of this principle. Finally, Father Coriden recognized the requirement of good order in the Church but noted that "those in authority and those subject to authority are both responsible for that order." He ended with a question concerning discipline in the Church: "[H]ow close an order is required, and how differently can Catholics in their communities act and still remain in communion?"[13]

The fourth panelist, Dr. Philip Selznick, was expressly invited from outside the Catholic tradition for insights on the exercise of authority in America as a societal phenomenon. The remarkable insights of this paper served to place those of the other panelists in context and rested upon a wealth of historical and sociological analysis. In a subtitle of an area styled "The Erosion of Authority," Professor Selznick concluded:

> A major outcome is the erosion of parental, religious, and political au-
> thority. In all these areas we see a substantial waning of loyalty and obe-
> dience. Americans have never been comfortable with subordination, but
> the spirit of modernity makes subordination especially difficult to accept.
> An egalitarian temper, suspicious of all elites, saps the self-confidence of
> leaders and institutions. Authority becomes inherently unstable, anxious,
> and placative.[14]

In working toward an understanding and possible corrective of the above situation, Professor Selznick proposed "a union of trust and criticism." He offered what he called a "threshold meaning" of the key concept of authority as "a rightful claim to deference or obedience. The criterion of rightfulness distinguishes authority from power, and that is the beginning of wisdom." Subsequently, Professor Selznick dealt with four areas of the experience of authority and a need for what he characterized as the combination of trust and affirmative criticism in an analysis of authority within the American common law tradi-tion, science, family, and employment. He felt that each of the exam-ples offered a distinctive shape to the union of trust and what he later styled as "critical affirmation." Drawing from examples of such critical

12. Ibid., 56.
13. Ibid., 58.
14. Philip Selznick, "Authority in America," in *Church Authority*, 63–64.

affirmation in an overview of American history, centered, in part, on the contrast between the Declaration of Independence and the Constitution, Professor Selznick asked the question, "Can this healthy-minded spirit of critical affirmation be sustained? Can authority be trusted as well as questioned?" He then listed three aspects of cultural occurrence in America that he felt were the "weaknesses of our strengths and the humbling defects of our virtues." The three elements listed were plurality and relativism, indeterminacy and absolutism, and the sovereignty of will. Professor Selznick closed on this note with respect to the last:

> It should help us to see that will is not sovereign but rather transcended by requirements of participation in a moral order we can and must interpret, but cannot make. To serve this need, the Constitution must be understood as incorporating principles of justice, as well as claims of reasons and those of a distinctive heritage.[15]

The panelists' discussion that actually opened the dialogue (the written papers had been digested by all the participants and knowledge of their content was presupposed) was rich, free-flowing, and involved everyone. I will not make an effort to present it here, as the interplay between those speaking was highly personal, required knowledge of events in a continuum for their understanding, and can be read in the source cited. It took place with the best example of civil and charitable discourse, while never skirting the truth, but with recognition of valid points wherever they occurred, and at times with a sense of camaraderie and humor that enriched the whole process. Both panelists and those of us who shared in their discussion were very conscious of Common Ground in the whole exercise.

On the following day two general discussions took place among all the participants. I would like to highlight an exchange in the Second General Discussion during which Dr. Monika Hellwig asked Professor Selznick to expand upon a comment that he had made that the organizational structure of the Catholic Church contains "a rich elaboration of hierarchic structures and perhaps explication of the reasons that would help solve the problems." And then, she continued in her own words, "And I match that with another comment that you made, that careful attention, careful commitment really, to the purposes of institutions was the way to find judgments about whether the claims

15. Ibid., 71–73.

being made for authority in specific instances were valid in relation to the aims of the community."[16] Professor Selznick was very happy with the recapitulation by Dr. Hellwig and went on to elaborate the point, emphasizing that dialogue is in so many ways constitutive (inherent) in the idea of a community, and he added, "Dialogue is a requisite for effective authority. But dialogue presumes a framework of commitment so that people really listen to one another."

Professor Selznick's comments continued with the development of the notion of civility into piety, the result of authentic listening and exchange on the part of those committed to dialogue engaging the virtues of humility and loyalty. What is not in the text, but what I have in my own notes, is that Professor Selznick also used the word "charity" as a dimension of the development that engaged the community to proceed from civility to piety. (Here "piety" is not what we ordinarily think of in a secondary sense as "holiness," but the more pristine definition of the word in the classical sense as an obligation arising from justice and resulting in acceptance and even enthusiasm for such complex structures as the filial relationship in families.) The text continued with Professor Selznick's comments that I consider to be crucial:

> But it is not a genuine civility if you haven't really listened. If you really listen, as the listening deepens, you begin to consider what ideas and feelings you share. In effect you create a community of discourse. The richer that community of discourse the closer civility comes to piety. Piety is tamed by civility, but the two work in tandem. I say this because it suggests a way of thinking about how the elements of community come together, and how each element must accept a framework of constraint. Civility constrains piety; piety enriches civility and guides it as well.[17]

Father Dulles pointed out that there is indeed a constraint of the Holy Spirit, of God, of Christ, in limiting the authority of the hierarchy.

> I'm a little unsatisfied because we need to interpret truth in ways that will embrace the whole community. That is to say, to embrace all those who are outside the hierarchy and are, at some level, subject to its authority, but who are also members of a community that is the source of authority. So religious principles, ultimate sources of authority, have to be interpreted and applied with attention to the nature of the community, perhaps especially the way people experience their connection to the community.[18]

16. Second General Discussion, *Church Authority,* 141.
17. Ibid., 142.
18. Ibid., 142–143.

That exchange during the dialogues opened up for me the remark-able vistas that are ours with respect to "the whole community" and "the nature of the community." Here we are considering the Mystical Body of Christ, and Christ the Head is by no means apart from the community; nor is any single member apart from the community, re-gardless of status or place in the Body of Christ. It is important for me, as a bishop, never to lose sight of this fact or of the Christ-life that flows through all the members of his Body, making us one with each other in ways which can only be known by faith, but which are strengthened the more that faith grows in all of us. Ontologically the source of union is what Christ adds to our acceptance of membership in the Body to strengthen and solidify it in making us all "one" in him. Hence we return to the obligation and charge of the bishop to be a source of unity in the community that is the Body of Christ, of which he, too, is a part.

Part Three

EPISCOPACY
AND
CONTEMPORARY CULTURE

Chapter Ten

Developing a New Way of Teaching with Authority

Bradford E. Hinze

Introduction

St. Benedict, in his guide for monastic life, admonished future abbots that they "must never teach or decree or command anything that would deviate from the Lord's instruction."[1] On the day of judgment, not only will the abbot's teaching be examined, but also "his disciples' obedience will come under scrutiny" (2.6). The abbot is judged for his teaching, and his community members for their obedience. Here we see the teaching Church and the learning Church in its monastic form, or so it appears.

But the picture is far more complex, and we risk distorting Benedict's Rule if we stop there. Without a doubt, the abbot must exercise authority, leadership, guidance. But Benedict was equally insistent that when things need to be addressed in the community, "the abbot shall call the whole community together and himself explain what the business is; and after hearing the advice of the brothers, let him ponder it and follow what he judges the wiser course." Why, one might ask, would the abbot, the designated teacher, listen to his community members? "All should be called for counsel," Benedict urged, because "the Lord often reveals what is better to the younger" (3.3).

Not surprisingly, the Rule goes on to say a great deal about obedience and disobedience in monastic life and about correcting the erring monk. But what is remarkable and unexpected is that Benedict ends

---

1. *RB 1980: The Rule of St. Benedict in Latin and English,* ed. Timothy Fry, O.S.B. (Collegeville, Minn.: The Liturgical Press, 1981) 2:4. Thanks to Ann R. Riggs, who upon hearing me speak on the topic "Obedience in a Dialogical Church: Trinitarian Reflections On Listening," pointed me in the direction of the Rule of St. Benedict.

165

his treatise on this note: "Obedience is a blessing to be shown by all, not only to the abbot but also to one another as brothers, since we know that it is by this way of obedience that we go to God" (71.1). The Rule of St. Benedict unambiguously acknowledges the authority of the abbot in matters of teaching but recognizes with equal clarity that the teacher's authority is based on a deeper receptivity to the wisdom of the entire community, and indeed, that the community's call to obey the Lord is realized through mutual obedience to one another in the community.

Archbishop Rembert Weakland, a member of the Order of St. Benedict, has had considerable experience as abbot, having served as archabbot of St. Vincent's Archabbey, Latrobe, Pennsylvania, for four years (1963–1967), before becoming abbot primate of the Benedictine Order, a position he held for ten years (1967–1977). With deep gratitude, this essay honors his ministry as archbishop by reflecting on Benedict's Rule on the importance of mutual obedience in the interest of teaching with authority.

There is considerable evidence that Weakland sought to follow Benedict's advice to abbots on consultation and teaching even after he became bishop. One could say that in order to fulfill his episcopal responsibility as teacher, he regularly sought the counsel of community members before he taught. During March and April 1990, for instance, Weakland held six listening sessions with over eight hundred women around the Archdiocese of Milwaukee to discuss the Church and abortion; this process positively influenced his own teachings on this topic. In his response one detects an echo of Benedict's teaching: "Listening is . . . an important part of any teaching process; the church's need to listen is no exception."[2]

Also in 1990, Weakland established "The Archbishop's Consultation on Theological Issues" with a group of about ten theologians, chosen for three-year terms, from the Catholic schools of higher education in Milwaukee—Saint Francis Seminary, Sacred Heart School of Theology, Alverno College, Mount Mary College, Cardinal Stritch University, and Marquette University. This group met with him and Bishop Richard Sklba about once a month during the academic year to

---

2. Archbishop Rembert Weakland, O.S.B., "Listening Sessions on Abortion: A Response," *Origins* 20 (May 31, 1990) 33–39, at 35, which was originally accompanied by a 22,000-word report summarizing the listening sessions; also see *idem*, "Proposed Respect Life Act: Supporting Women," *Origins* 21 (March 12, 1992) 640–641.

discuss a selected issue in the Church with an assigned reading.[3] An even more important application of Benedict's Rule outside the monastic setting was provided by Archbishop Weakland's leadership role in the formation of the pastoral letter on economics prepared by the National Conference of Catholic Bishops (NCCB). It is the development of this latter collective process of generating Church teaching that is our focus here.

In developing pastoral letters on several disputed issues during the 1980s and 1990s, the U.S. bishops pioneered a new, explicitly dialogical approach to teaching. Beginning with the pastoral letter on war and peace, *The Challenge of Peace* (1983), and continuing with the letter on economics, *Economic Justice for All* (1986), and finally on women's issues, originally titled *Partners in the Mystery of Redemption: A Pastoral Response to Women's Concerns for Church and Society* (which was never approved by the bishops), a new process emerged of broad consultation with people representing different sectors of the Church and society. This approach developed by the NCCB, it will be argued, offers a new dialogical process of teaching with authority. As one commentator put it, "The process of broad consultation and public debate the committee [on war and peace] launched eventually became at least as important as the pastoral letter itself."[4]

For the purposes of this essay, we will focus on this process rather than on the content of these letters. Although this method of generating Church teaching reflects, as we will see, ancient practices and deep theological convictions about the exercise of Church leadership, we need to show how the U.S. bishops experimented with a genuinely new teaching process, that is to say, how they explored ways of structuring and institutionalizing dialogue in the exercise of the Church's teaching office. Without denying theological and practical questions and difficulties raised by this new approach, it will be argued that

3. Through these meetings of the bishops and theologians, bonds of communion were formed through dialogue. The theologians came to know the bishops and their concerns about their local church and about the larger issues in the global Church. The bishops came to know the theologians and seemed to appreciate their concerns, the state of the question in various fields, and the disputed questions. Outside these contexts, there were times when one of the bishops would be teaching in a public forum and one might hear an echo of conversations experienced long before. Likewise, the theologians were influenced by these encounters in how they viewed the needs of the Church and in how they sought to address them.

4. Jim Castelli, *The Bishops and the Bomb: Waging Peace in a Nuclear Age* (Garden City, N.Y.: Image Books, 1983) 81.

there are weighty theological and practical reasons for continuing this practice and developing it further in the interest of strengthening the authority of Church teaching.

Moreover, it is my firm belief that this dialogical procedure has a much wider range of applicability in the exercise of the Church's teaching office and all ministries of teaching, not only on sensitive and hotly debated pastoral and public issues but also on all kinds of doctrinal and practical topics. A genuinely dialogical approach to teaching provides the proper and most effective vehicle for teaching with authority on matters of faith and morals.

This essay begins with a brief review of the origins and development of this collegial, collaborative, and consultative process of episcopal teaching within the U.S. Church. Next, official criticisms by Roman officials of this process will be identified, and the pastoral and theological precedents explored. Finally, it will be argued that the U.S. Church has developed a distinctive dialogical approach to episcopal teaching with authority that makes a unique contribution to the global Church and has relevance for every exercise of Church teaching.

The U.S. Bishops' Dialogical Teaching Process: Origins and Structure

We begin by recalling the nature of the National Conference of Catholic Bishops (NCCB), the organizational structure established in the 1960s by which the U.S. bishops would come together in their capacity as chief pastors and official teachers to deliberate about and address matters pertaining to the life of the Church. The constitution of this group as a canonical entity developed in response to the Second Vatican Council's endorsement of the formation of national episcopal conferences that would promote greater collegiality among bishops at the national level.[5] The NCCB is composed of a variety of different committees, including those on doctrine, liturgy, education, and missions, as well as social development and world peace. Each committee is composed of a group of U.S. bishops, which has a staff, and there are experts (who could be lay persons) as consultants readily available to them.

---

5. The longer history of the bishops in the United States would begin with the Synod of Baltimore in 1791 and include the provincial and plenary councils of bishops during the nineteenth century and the formation of the National Catholic War Council in 1917, and the National Catholic Welfare Conference in 1919. See Vatican II's Decree on the Pastoral Office of the Bishops in the Church *(Christus Dominus)*, nos. 36–38.

The United States Catholic Conference (USCC) was formed during this same period of time and registered as a non-profit social service organization devoted "principally with affairs involving the general public, including social concerns, education, and communications."[6] The USCC also has committees and staffs that differ from those of the NCCB. The U.S. bishops comprise the membership of both organizations, the NCCB and the USCC, and they have the same officers. (As of July 1, 2001, the USCC and the NCCB combined as the United States Conference of Catholic Bishops [USCCB].) The NCCB and the USCC generate various kinds of statements: national liturgical norms, pastoral letters on some teaching of the universal Church that apply it to the local situation, and formal statements on sundry political and social issues.

Since its inception in the late 1960s, there has been a standard process used to generate *joint pastoral teachings* by the committees of the NCCB. There are two versions of this standard process. (Here I am prescinding from formal policy statements drafted either by a committee of the NCCB or by the USCC.) Its most commonly used form is as follows: pastoral teaching statements are written by a given committee assisted by its staff, often with informal input from individuals or a small circle of theological, moral, biblical, or public policy experts as needed. Once a draft has been prepared, it is sent to other bishops and sometimes to specific theologians or policy experts for reactions, written or oral. These responses become the basis for amendments to the drafted policy statements, which, when completed, are then brought before the NCCB for discussion, revision when needed, and final approval by the full body of bishops.[7] In a second version of the standard procedure, an ad hoc committee is formed to generate the working document. The *Pastoral Letter on Marxist Communism* (1980) was developed by such an ad hoc committee and approved by a wide margin.

After the successful completion of the letter on Marxism, two new ad hoc committees were formed in 1980 and given the charge to develop pastoral teachings—one on war and peace in the age of nuclear warfare and another on capitalism. Previously, in 1972, the bishops had created an ad hoc committee on the role of women in society and

---

6. "NCCB/USCC Mission Statement," in *Pastoral Letters of the United States Catholic Bishops*, vol. 4: *1975–1983*, ed. Hugh J. Nolan (Washington: USCC, 1984) 486.

7. In the past, committees of the USCC or the NCCB were able to make public statements on their own without the approval of the full body of bishops. Now it is possible to make interim statements but not new policy.

the Church; this committee had used ongoing consultations on this topic until, in 1982, the bishops approved their proposal to write a pastoral on the role of women. In each of these committees there was a group of bishops (war and peace, five; economics, five; women, six); consultants (war and peace, three; economics, six; women, six), and staff members (war and peace, two; economics, five; women, two). All of this reflected the standard procedure for ad hoc committees commissioned to prepare a pastoral document.

During the preparation of the pastoral on war and peace, however, a number of significant innovations in the process of generating Church teaching were introduced. This pastoral was slated by the executive committee of the NCCB to be addressed before the economic pastoral. The standard procedure for developing pastoral letters as it had been previously employed by ad hoc committees was initially operative. But this soon changed when people from various sectors of the Catholic community, experts and advocates from various sides of the issue, some members of other Christian Churches and other faiths, and representatives from government, as well as from political and public policy groups, showed considerable interest in the document and sought to voice their considered opinions on the matter. In the case of the letter on war and peace, what originally was expected to require four to six meetings before the first draft could be prepared took fourteen meetings (between July 1981 and June 1982). At these meetings, there were received, as reported by the second draft of the pastoral, "the views of a wide range of witnesses. . . . The witnesses were selected to provide the committee with a spectrum of views and diverse forms of professional and pastoral experience."[8]

Thus *the first innovation* was that a much wider consultation took place from early on in the process (self-consciously a "spectrum of views and diverse forms of professional and pastoral experience"). This practice of wide consultation was repeated in the preparation of the pastoral letters on economics and women; moreover, the ad hoc committee on women from the beginning conducted far more extensive consultations.[9] In each case the initial consultations were fol-

8. *"The Challenge of Peace:* Second Draft," *Origins* 12 (October 28, 1982) 326.
9. *Partners in the Mystery of Redemption: A Pastoral Response to Women's Concerns for Church and Society, Origins* 17 (April 21, 1988) 759. The chair of the committee, Bishop Joseph Imesch, noted in his letter when the first draft was made public: "This letter is written in a different style than the other pastoral letters. It is written in response to the consultations held in 100 dioceses, 60 college campuses and 45 military bases. The text contains a number of quotations from women who participated in

lowed by the drafting of a written document (usually with preliminary drafts circulated among the ad hoc committee members first before it was released for a larger audience).

The second innovation emerged initially as a breach of standard operations: once the first formal draft was approved by the committee, it was marked "Confidential," for distribution only to the bishops and selected theological and policy experts, but in this case it was leaked to the secular and religious press. Subsequently, each of the approved first drafts was made public, that is, released for publication in *Origins: NC Documentary Service.* These documents were thus discussed and debated in the public realm, not only among Catholics but at a variety of levels of society.

In *a third innovation*, written and oral reactions to the first draft were welcomed and encouraged, and responses were taken into consideration during the preparation of the next draft. The response to each of the initial drafts from every level of the Church and from diverse sectors of society exceeded expectations.[10] This meant that greater reflection on the reaction was needed, and the revising took longer. The ad hoc committee for the war and peace letter had to postpone the next discussion at the NCCB by six months. Once reactions from the bishops and the other participants were heard and read by the committee, a second revised draft was written and approved by the committee and was made public.

Making public the second draft was *the fourth innovation*, which led to the repetition of the previous procedure. Written and oral responses led to the preparation of the third draft, which was then discussed by the bishops at one of their bi-annual meetings, revised as needed, and given the final approval by vote of the bishops (two-thirds majority).

Each of the pastoral letters has its own history, but the basic pattern of public disclosure, open communication and dialogue among the bishops, between bishops and theologians, and bishops and consultants, both within the Catholic community and members of the larger society, and revisions of documents in light of this public discussion, were the same for the three documents. In the cases of the pastorals on war and peace and economic justice, the preparation of

---

these consultations." This "style" was significantly revised in subsequent drafts. See also "On File," *Origins* 14 (December 27, 1984) 460.

10. See, for example, Archbishop Joseph Bernardin, "Bishops Delay Peace Pastoral," *Origins* 12 (April 26, 1982) 170–171.

the first draft, including time for consultations, took two or more years. The time for written and oral reactions between the first and second drafts was approximately one year. The time for reactions between the second and third drafts was approximately six months. Each step of the document on women took longer: the preparation of the first draft, four years; the time between the first and second drafts, two years; the time between the second and third drafts, two years; and the time between the third and an additional fourth draft, six months.[11] The significance of the fact that the pastoral on women's issues was never approved merits further reflection, which I will provide below.

Unprecedented. Inspired idea. Brilliant plan. These are the words that come to mind when thinking about the development of this open consultative process. However, there were precedents, and the events that led to the development of this procedure suggest that it was the work of pragmatic reasoning in response to a dynamic set of circumstances, rather than an idea generated with considerable forethought. At the time it did not seem groundbreaking, but rather a spontaneous and practical adjustment of the established process of deliberation.[12] As such, the development of this consultative process was a self-conscious attempt to give everyone who so desired the opportunity to have his or her voice heard. More time was consequently needed to digest the many written responses sent, to offer time for concerned parties to address the committee, and to debate and discern prayerfully.[13]

11. The dissemination and approval of the final documents were as follows:
—*peace pastoral*, committee began July 1981; first confidential draft released June 11, 1982; second draft published October 28, 1982; third draft published April 14, 1983, and approved on May 3, 1983 (238 in favor, 9 against);
—*economic pastoral*, the committee began meeting in 1981; first draft released November 11, 1984; second draft released October 5, 1985; third draft released June 2, 1986 and approved November 13, 1986 (225 in favor, 9 against);
—*women's pastoral*, the committee began March 1984; first draft released April 21, 1988; second draft released April 5, 1990; third draft published April 23, 1992; fourth draft published September 10, 1992 and rejected on November 18–19, 1992 (137 in favor, 110 against, 190 needed for two-thirds majority approval). It should be recalled that the U.S. Catholic bishops created an ad hoc committee on the role of women in society and the Church in 1972; in November 1978 the bishops decided that women's concerns needed further attention; in November 1982 the committee proposed that the bishops address women's concern through pastoral actions. In 1983 the bishops unanimously approved a proposal to write a pastoral addressing these concerns.
12. Castelli, *The Bishops and the Bomb*, 81, reports that Cardinal John O'Connor spoke of the "spontaneous" character of these changes in procedure.
13. "Prayer, reflection and discernment are as much needed as computer printouts. Listening, praying, reflecting, take time and a certain distance." Archbishop Rembert Weakland, "The Issues: Between Drafts of the Pastoral," *Origins* 15 (May 1985) 9.

Several antecedents for this kind of broad-based consultation and public debate within the U.S. Catholic Church can be identified. One immediate precursor was the hearings on social problems, spoken of as a national consultation, initiated by the Committee for the Bicentennial, which had been formed by the NCCB in preparation for the celebration of 1976, the two hundredth anniversary of the American Revolution and the founding of the United States.

The second antecedent is related to the first. As part of this Bicentennial program prepared by the committee, in October 1976 thirteen hundred delegates from dioceses and associations gathered at the first Call to Action conference, held in Detroit. There discussion of internal Church issues and various social issues resulted in the approval of many progressive resolutions, and in the judgment of David O'Brien, "its results were more or less shelved" by the U.S. hierarchy.[14]

The third antecedent is more pervasive and diffuse, yet certainly more significant. Within the national ethos of United States citizens, we find a great awareness of the benefits (and frustrations) of public processes of deliberation based on representative governance. Without denying the hypocrisy revealed in how U.S. citizens of European ancestry treated Native Americans, Africans, and eventually Latin Americans and Asians, those who arrived in America after the new nation was formed came to be a part of the American experiment in democracy, sharing neither ethnic blood line nor language, but only a belief and hope in the God-given dignity and freedom of human beings, which is the bedrock of democratic societies. These aspects of the U.S. character were formed over generations by the influence of democratic practices during the history of this nation; they offer that singular combination of traditions, republican, liberal, and biblical, that helped to mold the character of U.S. citizens.[15] Herein lies a national charism, the fruit of a shared history in the exercise of freedom and the practice of democratic institutions. We must dig this deep and go back more than two hundred-plus years to find the impulses for the

---

14. David J. O'Brien, *Public Catholicism*, 2nd ed. (Maryknoll, N.Y.: Orbis Books, 1996) 244.

15. Paul Joseph Fitzgerald, *L'Église comme lieu de formation d'une conscience de la concitoyenneté: étude sur la rédaction en public de la lettre pastorale "Economic Justice For All" (1986)* (Villeneuve d'Ascq Cédex: France: Presses Universitaires du Septentrion, 1992), esp. 170–216, 217–287, and 373–402; O'Brien, *Public Catholicism*, 243–245 and 249–252.

process of collective participation, of shared responsibility, that the pastorals came to embody.[16]

In 1986, with *The Challenge of Peace* approved, the second draft of the economic pastoral distributed, and the committee on the women's pastoral established and meeting, the president of the NCCB that year, Bishop James Malone, articulated the achievement of the U.S. bishops this way:

> Together as a national hierarchy, we have found a new and collegial method of teaching. For centuries, hierarchies have been publishing pastoral letters, but for the first time the people of God have been involved in the formation in a more intense manner. For the first time, the church has taught not simply through a finished product, but through the process that led to the finished document. Teaching is not a unilateral activity. One is only teaching if someone is being taught. Teaching and learning are mutually conditional.[17]

St. Benedict would certainly agree.

The Resistance of the Roman Curia to a Dialogical Method of Teaching

Vatican officials in the Roman Curia voiced repeated concerns and grave reservations about the open and consultative processes used by the NCCB in drafting the pastoral letters we have been considering.[18]

---

16. The first meeting of the Ad Hoc Committee on War and Peace was held July 26, 1981. What was to be an initial set of four to six meetings, with some consultation, but also with the committee members wrestling with the details before the first draft was to be written, grew into a much longer process of consultation because of the high level of interest in addressing the committee. The first draft was finished during the committee's fourteenth meeting in May 1982. When the committee reconvened to discuss reaction to the draft on July 28–30, they were overwhelmed with the written responses, and because of the bulk of material to work through, they had to prolong the process. By the time the second draft was ready to be released in October 1982, there was much anticipation and an eager audience. The greatest hurdle to the process came in early 1983 when representatives of the Curia invited representatives of the drafting committee to come to Rome for a discussion about the document with members of the Curia and Europeans. Archbishop John Roach and Cardinal Joseph Bernardin made a public statement on April 10, 1983: "In the final analysis . . . the third draft is far more the product of reflection and dialogue within the Catholic community than of dialogue between the drafting committee and the administration." Quoted in Castelli, *The Bishops and the Bomb,* 151.

17. *Origins* 15 (November 20, 1986) 395; also see his comments at the meeting a year before, "Collegiality, the Council and the Synod," *Origins* 15 (November 21, 1985) 388–391.

18. Thomas J. Reese, *Inside the Vatican: The Politics and Organization of the Catholic Church* (Cambridge: Harvard University Press, 1996) 34.

These were articulated both in formal meetings with delegates of the U.S. bishops and in a variety of statements made during the years the consultation process was being utilized. Important questions were raised concerning what precise level of teaching authority should be attributed to these documents, the mixed public audience intended by the documents, and particular aspects of their content. These curial efforts to clarify the precise nature of the teaching developed in these pastoral letters provided the context in which questions germane to this essay about the dialogical process of teaching were raised.

The pastoral letter on war and peace and the one on women precipitated official discussions with Roman officials and representative ordinaries from other nations (Western European in the case of war and peace, and global on the women's pastoral). On January 18–19, 1983, a meeting between the U.S. committee on war and peace, representatives of the Roman Curia, and representatives of episcopal conferences throughout Western Europe was held in Rome. According to a Vatican communique, "this common dialogue" was recognized as

> an expression of episcopal collegiality and by reason of the interdependence of nations and churches in these grave matters, it is normal that a great communion of thought should be established between the episcopal conferences and with the Holy See in order to provide guidance along the path to peace for the people of God and all people of good will.[19]

Jan Schotte, who was at that time a monsignor (now cardinal) and the secretary of the Pontifical Commission of Justice and Peace (now the secretary of the Council of the General Secretariat of the Synod of Bishops), wrote the official Roman synthesis (interpretation) of the meeting, which was dated March 21, 1983. A major question that kept resurfacing in the exchange between curial officials and representatives of the U.S. episcopal conference concerned the bishops' teaching authority and how it functions. One way the issue was framed bears directly on the dialogical process of teaching. "Should a pastoral letter be limited to proposing only the teaching that is binding? Or should it also contribute elements to encourage a debate?" Certain "ecclesiological problems" were detected pertaining to the teaching mission of bishops and the nature or form their pronouncements should take.[20] One particular formulation states the issue sharply:

19. *Origins* 12 (February 3, 1993) 545.
20. *Origins* 12 (April 7, 1983) 690–696, at 692–693.

When bishops propose the doctrine of the church, the faithful are bound
in conscience to assent. . . . The concluding pages of the draft seem ambiguous when they refer to pluralism of opinions on the matters touched
upon in the pastoral and at the same time urge substantial consensus.
Substantial consensus must be based on doctrine and does not flow from
debate. It is wrong to propose the teaching of the bishops merely as a basis
for debate; the teaching ministry of the bishops means that they lead the
people of God and therefore their teaching should not be obscured or reduced to one element among several in a free debate (693).

One of the central concerns voiced by Schotte's synthesis was that the
faithful will probably be confused by entering into a dialogue or debate
about episcopal teachings where different levels of authority are inter-
twined. As a result, each bishop's teaching authority might be wrongly
applied and its credibility obscured. The episcopal conference *per se* as
a collectivity has no *mandatum docendi* (692).

On March 8 to 11, 1989, a special meeting was held between the
Pope and thirty-five U.S. metropolitans (i.e., cardinals and archbishops),
along with twenty-five members of the Curia, on the theme of evangelization. That the U.S. bishops' new way of teaching was a part of the
conversation is reflected in several statements.[21] Before the meeting,
Cardinal Joseph Bernardin of Chicago delivered a statement describing
what was distinctive about the United States, and some of the elements
that he mentioned contributed noticeably to the U.S. bishops' experiment with a new way of teaching: cherished freedoms and democratic
traditions, communication-oriented society, and government in the
open with maximum participation of governors and governed.

Cardinal Joseph Ratzinger, prefect of the Vatican Congregation for
the Doctrine of the Faith (CDF), spoke of "The Bishop as Teacher of
Faith" and gave the following comments about the importance of the
role of bishops as shepherds in light of *LG* 20, which states: "The sacred synod . . . teaches that the bishops have by divine institution
taken the place of the apostles as shepherds of the church in such wise
that whoever hears them hears Christ . . . ." Ratzinger comments:

"The pastoral ministry," the shepherd's office, is explained through the
notion of hearing. One is a shepherd according to the mind of Jesus
Christ, then, inasmuch as he brings people to the hearing of Christ. In
the background here the words of the prologue of John's Gospel calling

21. For the various statements from the meeting, see *Origins* 18 (March 23, 1989)
677–686.

Christ the Logos can be heard; resonant too is the ancient Christian idea that it is precisely the Logos who is the shepherd of men, guiding us sheep who have gone astray to the pastures of truth and giving us there the water of life. To be shepherds, then, means to give voice to the Logos, voice to the redeeming Word (681).

Ratzinger goes on to point out that a particular danger in the post-conciliar exercise of episcopacy reflects a diminishment of the ancient role of the Christian bishops to "the *mebaqqer* of the Qumran community . . . [who] were only 'supervisors.'" Instead of preaching the redeeming Word, the contemporary bishop is being pressured "to avoid polarizations, to appear as a moderator acting within the plurality of existing opinions, but he himself is not to become 'partisan' in any substantive way" (681). "Why to so large an extent have we bishops acquiesced in this reduction of our office to the inspector, the moderator, the *mebaqqer*? Why have we gone back to Qumran when it comes to this essential point of the New Testament?" (682).[22]

The post-conference statement of Archbishop John May, then president of the NCCB, indicates that the process of generating episcopal teaching was at issue:

Clearly, there were some differences of perspective in the room . . . but these differences have to do with approach and not with doctrine. The church's teaching is universal; the bishops of the United States work to support, defend and promote the teaching as do the curia officials in Rome. Many of the factors that make America distinctive are the ones that make her great—the freedom of thought and expression, the pluralism of cultures and religions, the democratic spirit which values the opinion of each individual. America is a "marketplace society," where ideas have to sell themselves on their own intrinsic merit. That this would conflict at times with the hierarchical nature of the church is not surprising. What we came to Rome to say (and it was received calmly and well) was that this spirit of America must influence our own approach in the States. Though the teaching of the church is one and universal, our approach to presenting this teaching must be custom-fitted to the United States.[23]

Just a year after that meeting in Rome between the Pope, certain U.S. prelates, and curial officials on evangelization, the Sacred Congregation

22. See the comments by Cardinal John O'Connor about "the emergence of consensus theology," but also his defense of the approach of the U.S. bishops. *Origins* 18 (March 23, 1989) 682–686, esp. 685–686.

23. *Origins* 18 (March 30, 1989) 726.

for the Doctrine of the Faith issued a series of concerns in a written response to the U.S. bishops after the second draft of the proposed pastoral letter on women appeared in April 1990. And on May 28–29, 1991, the third time in three years that the "ecclesiological problems" concerning the U.S. bishops' teaching procedure needed attention, the Roman Curia convened an international consultation to discuss the second draft of the women's document with representatives of the U.S. hierarchy and two U.S. women involved in the development of the pastoral. Also participating were representatives of various dicasteries of the Roman Curia (Cardinals Joseph Ratzinger, Alberto Bovone, Angelo Sodano) and eighteen bishops from around the world.[24] Here the first issue raised was "the precise nature of the document and the related question of methodology."[25] Cardinal Ratzinger presented an address during the opening session. He echoed concerns voiced previously to the U.S. bishops by the Congregation for the Doctrine of the Faith when the second draft first appeared.[26]

As with the war and peace pastoral, questions were posed about confusing the faithful by not distinguishing levels of authority in the text; but a distinctive concern about this text was that it allowed diverse voices from the community to be represented in the text without clearly indicating the bishops' own voice. Moreover, the complaint was registered at this meeting that the voices of women (who testified at the many hearings held by the ad hoc committee) were more conspicuous in the document than the voice of the bishops.

The issues raised by Roman officials were legitimate and real ones. On one level, the U.S. bishops in response readily agreed that in these deliberative processes one cannot have a disagreement about dogmas and dogmatic principles. They maintained, however, that there must be room for disagreement and collective discernment about how to apply these dogmatic principles in practical living and that this communal dialogical process would not undermine the deepest convictions of faith, but in fact affirm and bolster them.

At another level, however, this meeting on the women's pastoral illuminated a genuine conflict between two approaches to episcopal teaching. The Roman approach, based on a long history of practice, emphasizes the teaching authority of the bishop and bishops' confer-

24. Mozambique, Ireland, Canada, Brazil, Mexico, Italy, France, Germany, the Philippines, Poland, England, and Australia.
25. *Origins* 21 (June 13, 1991) 73.
26. Ibid., marginal note on p. 76.

ences as derived from previously established official Roman Catholic teaching. The aura of sacred authority is viewed as incompatible with public discussion and wide consultation. The approach being experimented with by the U.S. bishops was not intended to call into question official positions, but rather to create a context for the Church (bishops, theologians, and representatives of the entire People of God) to gather to speak and think together about a certain teaching so as to learn from one another and thus strengthen the Church's teaching. In both cases it is preserving and strengthening the authority of the Church's teaching that is at issue. The conflict centers upon the way in which episcopal authority is bestowed or generated and how this authority is best exercised.

The very same issues being raised by Roman officials concerning this experiment with a new approach to teaching were being discussed at other formal assemblies and in a variety of official documents released during this same period. The fundamental concern was to demarcate the distinctive roles of bishops, theologians, and the entire People of God and their interrelationships. We see this in the extraordinary synods on the collegiality of bishops with the pope and the role of episcopal conferences (1969), and on the twentieth anniversary of the conclusion of the Second Vatican Council (1985); the ordinary synod on the laity (1987); the meeting between the U.S. bishops with the Pope during his visit to the United States in September 1987; and the circulation of the *instrumentum laboris* "Theological and Juridical Status of Episcopal Conferences," prepared by the Congregation for Bishops in cooperation with other Congregations (January 1988).

I hasten to point out that while synods were convened to discuss the roles of bishops, priests, religious, and laity in the Church, none of the synods during the postconciliar period have addressed the role of theology and the authority of theologians in the Church. This has been left to the Congregation for the Doctrine of the Faith, which has articulated more and more precisely (one might say, narrowly) the role of the theologian in such a manner that her or his subservient role in relation to the work of the magisterium of pope and bishops has been increasingly accentuated. This trend is evident in the reinstatement of a Profession of Faith and Oath of Fidelity (1989); in the *Instruction on the Ecclesial Vocation of the Theologian* (1990); and in the revised 1983 Code of Canon Law (canon 812). It is also reflected in the Vatican's insistence that the U.S. application of *Ex Corde Ecclesiae* include the provisions for demanding that each Catholic theologian teaching in a Catholic institution of higher learning request and obtain a *mandatum* from the local ordinary.[27]

The work of the CDF in addressing the creative contributions of local churches merits special attention. Whereas Vatican II mitigated an overly centralized approach to Church authority and the Eurocentric character of official Catholic theology, the CDF's 1992 statement on *communio* ecclesiology consolidated Roman authority by positing the principle of the ontological and temporal priority of the universal Church over the local church. This explicit statement was accompanied, as if by way of applying the principle, by official CDF critiques of particular theological developments and theologians associated with different local churches and geographical regions: Latin American liberation theology, Asian interreligious dialogue and cultural relativism, African syncretism, European secularization, and, in North America and especially the United States, the problem of dissent. The CDF's interrogation and disciplining of individual theologians further illustrate the application of the same principle. Now the point is not whether there are bona fide concerns about regional theological developments or the work of particular theologians in those regions. The issue is, rather, whether authority is being exercised and judgments made about regional developments and theologians without a process of wide consultation and deliberation with representatives of diverse theological schools and the particular parties involved, in which mutual learning and teaching can take place.

The apprehensive reaction of Roman offices to the dialogical process of teaching being devised by the U.S. bishops is a part of the larger drama surrounding the Second Vatican Council. The council was a defining moment not only because of what it taught about the nature of the Church but also because of the experience of those who participated in the council, especially bishops and theologians, which mirrored this changing vision of the Church. Theory and practice coincided. The result was that the prevailing understanding of the Church in terms of a pyramidal, hierarchical, juridical view of the exercise of authority associated with the rise of papal power and Roman centralization was called into question and checked by a new emphasis on collegial relations among bishops and collaboration between

---

27. Amidst all this, the widespread consultation on the initial schema and revised drafts of a pontifical document on Catholic universities (which became *Ex Corde Ecclesiae*) during the 1980s reflects a production process that approximated the methods used by the U.S. bishops for a papal document.

bishops and theologians. At least as important was the affirmation of the wisdom and active participation of the entire People of God in the life of the Church, which provided the basis for postconciliar reflection on the need for bishops and theologians to consult representatives of the entire People of God (laity, religious, priests).

Performatively, a triadic vision of the Church as a community of dialogue and communication was coming into focus during the council: bishops, theologians, the entire People of God in dynamic interrelationships of learning and teaching.[28] The council's stated commission was more ambiguous: it mandated the promotion of collegiality among bishops; the event of the council modeled rather than taught in its documents the need for greater collaboration between bishops and theologians; and it laid the foundation for bishops and theologians to consult with the entire People of God in its larger doctrine of the Church as People of God and communion, without exploring in its documents the importance of such consultation.[29] Collegiality, collaboration, consultation are the terms used here to name these *three modes of acting in relationships—collegiality* among bishops; *collaboration* between bishops and theologians; *consultation* among bishops, theologians, and the entire People of God; together they are intended

28. My own views on the triadic relationships between the entire People of God, the magisterium (bishops and pope), and theologians, which I will return to below, have been developed in conversation with the work of Bernd Jochen Hilberath, who distinguishes and relates three levels of communication in the Church and three groups that participate in this communication: (1) everyday communication of faith—the process of tradition—by all the People of God; (2) doctrinal discourse stated by the magisterium; and (3) theological discourse of theologians. *Communio* and consensus are realized only when the magisterium and theology are in active dialogue with the entire People of God. See Bernd Jochen Hilberath, "Vom Heiligen Geist des Dialogs: Das dialogische Prinzip in Gotteslehre und Heilsgeschehen," in *Dialog als Selbsvollzug der Kirche?* Questiones Disputatae series, ed. Gebhard Fürst (Freiburg: Herder, 1997) 93–116, at 110–111; idem, "Welche Theologie brauchen wir in der Fortbildung?" in *Im Ursprung ist Beziehung: Theologisches Lernen als themenzenrierte Interaktion,* ed. Karl Joseph Ludwig (Mainz: Matthias Grünewald, 1997) 67–70; idem, "Der Wahrheit des Glaubens: Anmerkungen zum Prozeß der Glaubenskommunikation," in *Dimensionen der Wahrheit: Hans Küngs Anfrage im Disput,* ed. Bernd Jochen Hilberath (Tübingen: A. Francke Verlag, 1999) 51–80; idem, "Vorgaben für die Ausarbeitung der Communio-Ekklesiologie," in *Communio—Ideal oder Zerrbild von Kommunikation?* Quaestiones Disputatae series, ed. Bernd Jochen Hilberath (Freiburg: Herder, 1999) 277–297, at 291–297.

29. That the importance of consultation with the entire People of God (qua "laity") has not been sufficiently treated is evident in the fact that "dialogue is not a theme" in John Paul II's encyclical on the laity, *Christifideles Laici* (1988). Peter Neuner, "Das Dialogmotiv in der Lehre der Kirche," in *Dialog als Selbstvollzug der Kirche?* ed. Gebhard Fürst (Freiburg: Herder, 1996) 69.

to denote the inclusive, open, participatory form of learning and teaching Vatican II symbolized and began to articulate.[30]

The experience of collegiality and collaboration at the council can be described as a breakthrough event, but, as such, it was by no means a habituated practice. The postconciliar period is defined by the cultivation of closer collegial relations *(collegialis affectus)* among bishops and the development of the practices, that is, the learned skills, of collegial decision-making at many levels *(collegialis effectus)*.[31] The council left much unfinished business. The doctrine of the papacy and the practices of the Roman Curia, which emerged during the previous century, had now been resituated within a larger vision of the Church, but the doctrinal and practical ramifications were not yet worked through. Not surprisingly, the postconciliar period has witnessed a struggle between centralizing forces associated with the older, pre-Vatican II vision of the Church and the decentralizing focus on the power and contributions of local churches promoted by Vatican II. Against this backdrop, it is no wonder that the experimentation of the U.S. bishops met with resistance.[32]

30. I have used three different words in order to distinguish three types of collective action: collegial action among bishops, collaboration of bishops and theologians, and consultation with representatives of the entire People of God by bishops and theologians. One could, of course, use the designations collaboration and consultation interchangeably, even though further specification of which particular groups were involved and the nature of their involvement would have to be given. Dolores Leckey speaks of collaboration and consultation between the laity and the bishops, "Becoming a Collaborative Church," *Origins* 27 (August 27, 1987) 171–174; canonical issues are explored by James Provost, "Canon Law and the Role of Consultation," *Origins* 18 (May 4, 1989) 793–799.

31. The Vatican Congregation for Bishops, in its document "Theological and Juridical Status of Episcopal Conferences," contrasted sharply *actio collegialis (effectus collegialis)* and *affectus collegialis* (sometimes translated as "collegial spirit"), which is found in *Lumen Gentium* at the end of nos. 22 and 23 respectively (II. 2, *Origins* 117 [April 7, 1988] 733). This distinction is used in the document on episcopal conferences as the basis for arguing that a collegial spirit *and* action are strictly speaking possible in the full sense only by the entire college of bishops, whereas episcopal conferences foster a collegial spirit among bishops, but as a group are not capable of a collegial action (and do not have a *munus magisterii*) (ibid., sections IV–V, 734–735). This distinction, in my judgment, is being too sharply drawn here and is hard to justify historically and conceptually as a basis for denying to episcopal conferences the ability to achieve a collegial action in teaching. On this issue, see Joseph Komonchak, "The Roman Working Paper on Episcopal Conferences," in *Episcopal Conferences: Historical, Canonical and Theological Studies,* ed. Thomas J. Reese (Washington, D.C.: Georgetown University Press, 1989) 188–195; Brian Daley, "Structures of Charity: Bishops' Gatherings and the See of Rome in the Early Church," ibid., 56–57.

32. Hermann J. Pottmeyer has rightly insisted that we need to articulate precisely the achievement of Vatican II in the context of the longer history of the Church. "Kontinuität und Innovation in der Ekklesiologie des II. Vatikanus," in *Kirche im Wandel,*

Classical Precedents and Theological Warrants

The U.S. bishops' experimentation with a dialogical process of teaching was new in significant ways, but it was not without precedent in Church practice and theological warrant. It will be useful for our argument to identify examples of such practices and explore certain of these theological rationales.

Practices. One finds a variety of instances of dialogical practices in the early Church. Obviously, any historical examples of types of dialogical relationship deserve greater scrutiny. We will focus briefly on examples that in principle include collegiality among bishops, collaboration between theologians and bishops, and consultation between bishops, theologians, and representatives of the entire People of God. Two areas wherein dialogical relations of discernment were especially operative in the early Christian era were the selection of bishops and deposition of unworthy bishops because of erroneous teachings or lifestyles, and the readmission of lapsed Christians who had apostatized during persecution. Cyprian of Carthage (ca. 200–258) offers through his letters testimony to the importance of dialogue in these areas of ecclesial decision-making. He speaks in particular of the need to strive for consensus, both among a group of bishops and through the unanimous accord of the entire Church. As Paul Fitzgerald puts it,

> In the process of discerning questions which affected the entire community, the bishop stood in a reciprocal relationship to the other members of the local church. . . . The bishop [is understood as] the primary teacher of sound doctrine. But a good teacher is always a good learner [*doctus* and *docibilis*]. It is only by listening to the Spirit . . . who speaks through different members of the community . . . that the bishop can obey God and preserve both unity and orthodoxy.[33]

The most important precedent for the practices of collegiality, collaboration, and consultation is synods. This practice developed in the patristic period and has been renewed in the wake of Vatican II.[34] "The

---

eds. Giuseppe Alberigo, Yves Congar, and Hermann J. Pottmeyer (Düsseldorf: Patmos, 1982) 89–110; and idem, *Toward a Papacy in Communion: Perspectives on Vatican Councils I and II* (New York: Crossroad, 1998). Archbishop John R. Quinn has explored various challenges facing the magisterium during this period in *The Reform of the Papacy: The Costly Call To Christian Unity* (New York: Crossroad, 1999).

33. Paul J. Fitzgerald, "A Model for Dialogue: Cyprian of Carthage on Ecclesial Discernment," *Theological Studies* 59 (1998) 236–254, at 250–251.

34. See Michael Fahey, "Eastern Synodal Traditions: Pertinence for Western Collegial Institutions," in *Episcopal Conferences: Historical, Canonical and Theological Studies,*

term 'synod' was once applied to any gathering (local, regional, national, or ecumenical [here meaning universal]) called to discuss and sometimes to resolve church issues. In this sense it was synonymous with 'council.'"[35] But according to the revised Code of Canon Law (1983), "synod" is the term used to designate a number of different teaching and governing structures that are distinct from ecumenical councils, consistories of the College of Cardinals, regional councils, and episcopal conferences. Ordinary synods of bishops are the most common general sessions, convened every four years to address various issues related to particular groups within the Church (priesthood, family life, laity, religious life); and pastoral problems like faith, justice, evangelization, catechesis, penance, and reconciliation. Extraordinary synods of bishops are general sessions that take place to address in a timely manner urgent issues; they are rare (1969 on the collegiality of bishops with the pope and episcopal conferences; 1985 on the twentieth anniversary of the end of Vatican II). A special synod of bishops can be convened to address issues of a particular region or nation (recently in preparation for the millennium: Europe, 1991; Africa, 1994; Lebanon, 1995; Americas, 1997; Asia, 1998; Oceania, 1998). It is also proper, following canon law, to speak of diocesan synods, which are convened by a bishop in a local church with participants from that community. The synod process is dialogical by nature and indeed is designed in such a way as to obtain input from the whole Church.

To clarify this claim, it is helpful to consider the process involved in a synod of bishops, which by definition is called "to foster closer unity between the Roman Pontiff and bishops, to assist the Roman Pontiff with their counsel in the preservation and growth of faith and morals and in the observance and strengthening of ecclesial discipline, and to consider questions pertaining to the activity of the church in the world."[36] Subsequently we will comment on dialogue within diocesan synods.

The process of an ordinary synod of bishops offers the best example. The synod is a thirty-day meeting of the bishops, but in fact it is a much longer process. It begins with the preparatory process un-

---

253–266; "Episcopal Conferences in Light of Particular Councils During the First Millenium," in *The Nature and Future of Episcopal Conferences,* eds. Hervé Legrand, Julio Manzanares, and Antonio García García (Washington, D.C.: Catholic University of America Press, 1988) 30–56.

35. Reese, *Inside the Vatican,* 287, note 3.

36. Canon 342, *New Commentary on the Code of Canon Law,* ed. John P. Beal, James A. Coriden, and Thomas J. Green (New York: Paulist Press, 2000).

dertaken by the general secretariat of the synod of bishops, which consists of a general secretary and a council of fifteen members—twelve elected by the members of the synod and three chosen by the pope. The pope chooses the topic. The general secretariat, in consultation with experts (often from Roman universities), prepares the *"lineamenta,"* which is the *first document* outlining the topic and posing questions intended to foster discussion and educe responses from bishops' conferences. Collaboration between bishops and theologians and consultation with representatives of the People of God are encouraged at this stage. The bishop can consult with whomever he chooses: experts and the wider community, for example, "priests' councils, pastoral councils, religious educators, seminary professors, theologians, canon lawyers, or other experts."[37] Discussion may take place in the Catholic press and theological journals, and pre-synod symposiums are sometimes convened by the Curia. Episcopal conferences prepare written responses to the *lineamenta,* which are supposed to be confidential but do not always remain so.

The *second document* is the *"instrumentum laboris,"* the working paper drafted by a group of experts in the office of the general secretariat and then reviewed and revised after discussion of the council, with the final draft sent to the pope for approval. This document is intended to promote and sharpen further discussion throughout the Church. Thus it is sent to delegates and made public.

The *third document* is a report on the topic written by the reporter *(relator),* a person selected by the pope. The report is sent out at least thirty days before the synod. At the thirty-day synod the delegates are present as well as a number of people representing sectors of the People of God; these latter are able to contribute by addressing the assembly and participating in the small group sessions but have no vote. During the formal meeting of the full synod assembly, each delegate is allowed eight minutes to offer his opinion on the topic, but no dialogue on the topic is allowed.

In the final week of the synod each small group prepares the *fourth document* of the process, resulting in a set of documents that offer propositions or recommendations on the topic. These are submitted to a drafting committee comprised of the president, the synod reporter *(relator),* secretary, group reporters *(relatores),* and any assistants appointed

37. Reese, *Inside the Vatican,* 51. My description of the procedure used for the synod of bishops is drawn from Reese's longer analysis.

by the president, who prepare a *fifth document*, which is offered to the entire assembly for debate. The delegates prepare a *sixth document*, either a final report *(relatio finalis)*, which is drafted and approved, or since 1974, a brief "message to the People of God" and a list of recommendations to the pope, who will later write a *seventh document*, an apostolic exhortation on the synod. Theological collaborators reflecting various schools of thought and geographical regions are not active participants throughout the synodal process, as they were at Vatican II.

Diocesan synods differ from the extraordinary, ordinary, or special synods of bishops in that various representatives of the diocese are convened by the local bishop "to offer assistance to the diocesan bishop for the good of the whole diocesan community" (canon 460). The bishop convokes the synod; the participants include representatives of the People of God in the diocese: priests, religious, and laity; some are required by their position in the diocese to attend, others are invited. Free discussion of the questions raised is required, but the diocesan bishop is the sole legislator; "other members . . . possess only a consultative vote" (canons 465-466).

Synods provide the clearest practical precedent of collegial, collaborative, and consultative dialogue in the genesis of Church teaching; however, there is plenty of room for questioning whether dialogue has been undermined and cut short in these processes; and whether certain voices have not been invited or are not really heard and incorporated into the teaching that is developed or the course of action planned.[38] Leaving these questions open and aside for the time being does not diminish the significance of these synods and the dialogical modes of discernment in the Church they make possible, nor their role in providing a precedent for the new process devised by the U.S. bishops.

Theological Rationale. What is the theological rationale for a dialogical approach to Church teaching? Here we will introduce a num-

---

38. Questions have frequently been raised about whether practices of collegiality in deliberation at the synods are being undermined by structural patterns (the eight-minute speeches, no time for open discussion). Moreover, the role of the Curia in fashioning the final statement and taking the control away from the synod bishops has been criticized; for example, in the special synods of bishops in preparation for the new millennium, genuine discussion was cut short, and the final apostolic exhortations written as a report of the synod have been criticized for using a curial filter on the deliberations at the synod; wide-ranging discussions fostered by deliberations beforehand and in the small-group discussions during the synod were whittled and molded into a pre-established christological framework that united all the regional documents. Additional questions concern the extent of collaboration with theologians, as well as receptivity to the contributions of representatives of the entire People of God.

ber of classical theological tenets and important recent developments that contribute to a cumulative case for advancing such a dialogical approach to Church teaching. Let me first suggest this: It is no accident that increasing attention to the dialogical character and mission of the Church has taken place during the same period of time when the previous concentration on a christocentric ecclesiology has been reoriented in light of increasing attention to the significance of the Holy Spirit and the Trinity for understanding the Church. Why?

The pyramidal, centralized, hierarchical, and clerical approach to the exercise of Church teaching authority that reached its apogee at the turn of the twentieth century was based on a christological foundation for the sacramental office of bishop and priest, and a depiction of the nature of the Church as the Body of Christ, with the pope, bishops, and priests serving as representatives of the Head. The threefold powers of episcopal office—governing, teaching, and sacramental— were correlated with the kingly, prophetic, and priestly character of Jesus Christ. The Holy Spirit received at baptism, according to this theology, helped the laity in their spiritual lives to be obedient members in the Body of Christ, but there was virtually no attention given to the importance of baptism and the gifts of the Spirit for the mission of the Church as a whole in *liturgia, martyria,* and *diakonia.*

In Vatican II's *Lumen Gentium,* baptism in the name of the Father, the Son, and the Holy Spirit is presented as the doorway for all persons to realize over time their ecclesial identity and mission as members of the People of God, the Body of Christ, and as a part of the living temple of the Holy Spirit. Through the Spirit, Christians participate in the divine life of the Triune God and are called, in turn, to participate actively in the life of the Church in each of its dimensions. *Lumen Gentium* gave fresh attention to the Apostle Paul's teaching that the Spirit has bestowed on every individual special charisms for the good of the whole Church and world. Equally important, Jesus' anointing with the Spirit in his kingly, priestly, and prophetic identity is extended to every baptized Christian, not just to priests, bishops, and the pope.[39] Accordingly, it is the baptismal birthright and mandate of every member of the People of God to become an active agent in the

---

39. Richard R. Gaillardetz offers a learned analysis and theological reflection on the subject, the object, the exercise, and the reception of Church teaching in *Teaching with Authority: A Theology of the Magisterium in the Church* (Collegeville, Minn.: The Liturgical Press, 1997).

Church. Moreover, through the Eucharist the entire Christian community celebrates and realizes their communion with the Triune God and all People of God as they gather around the eucharistic table with the local bishop. In every action of the Church, the power of the Spirit is invoked *(epiclesis)* to effect the transformation of the community into the Body of Christ, striving toward ever greater communion for the greater glory of God the Father.

The renewed appreciation of the significance of the Triune God's self-communication as a communion of persons for the understanding of the Church has simultaneously fostered and been fostered by a new recognition of the dialogical and communicative nature of the Church as the living tradition of the revelation of God. Beginning with baptism and Eucharist, all the members of the Church are enabled to participate actively in the Trinitarian self-communication of God. The eschatological journey into the full truth of the Triune God involves ongoing learning and teaching, which can only be advanced by attaining a vital communion among the entire People of God, the magisterium (bishops and the pope), and theologians. And genuine communion among these three groups can only be attained through honest, mutual communication and dialogue with the entire Church. The ongoing challenge is to find structural ways, institutional practices, to promote this dialogue in keeping with our deepest convictions about God's identity.

One can discover an equally important and related theological basis for dialogical forms of learning and teaching in the Church by tracing the impact of the empowering and healing Spirit on the individual and ecclesial act of faith. In the act and habit of faith, which is at once both deeply personal and interpersonal, one is endowed with a gifted perception, a *sensus,* of reality. This *sensus fidei* signifies a transformation whereby one's vision is opened to recognize and receive, in a manner of affective knowing and loving, both active and receptive, the truth of the gospel, the apostolic faith of the Church.[40] Through the divine gift and cooperative human response of faith, one is initiated into a community of faith that shares this *sensus,* which enables one to speak of the *sensus fidelium,* the "sense of the faithful," understood as the basis for and promise of a *consensus fidelium,* the "consensus of the faith-

---

40. Ormond Rush, *"Sensus Fidei:* Faith 'Making Sense' of Revelation," *Theological Studies* 62 (2001) 231–261; John J. Burkhard, *"Sensus Fidei:* Theological Reflection Since Vatican II: Part I, 1965–1984; Part II, 1985–1989," *Heythrop Journal* 34 (1993) 41–59, 123–136; Daniel J. Finucane, *Sensus Fidelium: The Use of a Concept in the Post-Vatican II Era* (San Francisco: International Scholars Publications, 1996).

ful." *Lumen Gentium* speaks of the "supernatural sense of the faith which characterizes the people (of God) as a whole," providing the basis for "a universal consensus in matters of faith and morals" that cannot be mistaken (no. 12). Thus the sense of the faithful allows one to speak of the integrity and even the infallibility of the People of God.[41] In the words of John Henry Newman, "the *fidelium sensus* and *[fidelium] consensus* is a branch of evidence which it is natural or necessary for the Church to regard and consult, before she proceeds to any definition, from its intrinsic cogency; and by consequence, that it ever has been so regarded and consulted."[42]

The Trinitarian character of the Church as a communion of persons and the doctrine of *sensus fidei* and *sensus fidelium* provide the strongest theological justification for the dialogical character of Church learning and teaching in the genesis, recognition, and reception of doctrines. This is why in the *generation* of doctrines, the entire People of God, the faithful, have an authority in matters of faith and need to be consulted by bishops and theologians; this is why bishops need to exercise candid collegiality among themselves in their common work; and this is why there must be genuine collaboration between bishops and theologians. The *sensus fidelium* enables a *recognition* of the apostolic faith when it is taught, a confirmation of the deposit of faith within believers, an inner testimony of the Holy Spirit, and a prudential sense of how practices cohere with and apply these most basic beliefs.[43] This sense provides the foundation for the *reception* of authentic teaching by individuals and communities, not

41. Orthodox theologians stress that, contrary to the Roman Catholic emphasis on the hierarchy as the guardian of truth, the whole People of God are the guardian of the faith—bishops, clergy, and laity together. As [Kallistos] Timothy Ware puts it, "The proclamation of the truth is not the same as the possession of the truth: all the people possess the truth, but it is the bishop's particular office to proclaim." *The Orthodox Church* (Bungay, Suffox, Great Britain: Penguin Books, 1963) 255. Ware quotes Alexis Khomiakov: "The unvarying constancy and the unerring truth of Christian dogma does not depend upon any hierarchical order; it is guardian by the totality, by the whole people of the Church, which is the Body of Christ." Ware takes this quotation from W. J. Birkbeck, *Russia and the English Church* (London: SPCK, 1917) 94.

42. John Henry Newman, *On Consulting the Faithful in Matters of Doctrine*, ed. John Coulson (Kansas City: Sheed & Ward, 1961 [originally published in 1859 in the *Rambler*]), 55. Newman's background in rhetoric gave him a profound awareness of the *sensus communis* in the generation of authoritative, truthful teaching. On truth and the *sensus communis* in rhetoric, see Hans Georg Gadamer, *Truth and Method*, 2nd ed., tr. Joel Weinsheimer and Donald G. Marshall (New York: Crossroad, 1991) 17–30.

43. Gerard Kelly, *Recognition: Advancing Ecumenical Thinking* (New York: Peter Lang, 1996).

in passive compliance to the magisterium, but as an active dimension in authoritative teaching, an inner resonance in the faithful that confirms the truth of the gospel and the unfolding wisdom of the Spirit.[44] These beliefs validate the need for participatory forms of teaching and learning in which (1) broad-based participation in the production or revision of teaching occurs; (2) drafts of documents are made public and discussion is promoted; and (3) the reactions of members from a variety of sectors of the People of God are sought.

Practical and theological criticisms of dialogical teaching procedures, such as those raised by Cardinal Ratzinger and other representatives of the Curia, should neither be dismissed nor diminished. Could a dialogical approach to Church teaching be practically unhelpful and theologically tenuous? Can the sense of the faithful really serve not only as a source but also as a guardian in matters of faith and morals?[45] What role do theologians really have in the production of doctrine? Can bishops, theologians, and all the faithful be trusted to work together in the interests of the truth of the gospel and the good of the universal Church? Will outside influences put pressure on deliberations, undermine procedures, generate confusion, divert attention by concentrating on trivial matters? To formulate the argument in its harshest terms,

44. My own approach to reception and the dialogical character of tradition is consistent with and enriched by the work of Ormond Rush, *The Reception of Doctrine: An Appropriation of Hans Robert Jauss' Reception Aesthetics and Literary Hermeneutics* (Rome: Editrice Pontificia Università Gregoriana, 1996).

45. Cardinal Ratzinger puts it this way: "[T]he opinions of the faithful cannot be purely and simply identified with the *sensus fidei*. The sense of faith is a property of theological faith; and as God's gift which enables one to adhere personally to the truth, it cannot err. This personal faith is also the faith of the church, since God has given guardianship of the word to the church. Consequently what the believer believes is what the church believes. The *sensus fidei* implies then by its nature a profound agreement of spirit and heart with the church, *sentire cum ecclesia*." "[S]tandards of conduct, appropriate to civil society or the workings of democracy, cannot be purely and simply applied to the church. . . . Polling public opinion to determine the proper thing to think or do, opposing the magisterium by exerting the pressure of public opinion, making the excuse of a 'consensus' among theologians, maintaining that the theologian is the prophetic spokesman of a 'base' or autonomous community which would be the source of all truth, all this indicates a grave loss of the sense of truth and of the sense of the church." *Instruction on the Ecclesial Vocation of the Theologian* (May 24, 1990), no. 39. Elizabeth Groppe reports: "Joseph Ratzinger believes that some have taken *Lumen gentium's* theology of the People of God too far and he is critical of programs of reforms that 'in place of all hierarchical tutelage will at long last introduce democratic self-determination into the Church.'" *Yves Congar's Theology of the Holy Spirit* (Ph.D. diss., University of Notre Dame, 1999) 282, quoting Ratzinger, *Called to Communion: Understanding the Church Today* (San Francisco: Ignatius Press, 1996) 139.

will not wide participation and open debate simply bring about an erosion of Church authority, fuel cognitive and moral relativism, unleash a cacophony of voices and polarizing factions, foster a "herd mentality" following any fad? Will it not foster the desire to resolve important disputed matters by voting? In the end, have not the U.S. bishops simply opened the doors to a dubious ecclesial version of democracy?

To these real concerns at least two responses need to be made. On the one hand, the participatory process of teaching introduced by the U.S. bishops and supported by the precedents and theological rationales explored can properly be called democratizing. However, democratizing need not and, indeed in the case of the Church, cannot imply or entail one particular form of political philosophy, one political structure, especially one that settles every dispute through majority rule or voting.[46] Instead, there must be a way to enable the authority of the People of God, the authority of theologians, and the authority of the magisterium to work in communion, sharing responsibility in teaching. On the other hand, to consult widely and invite the reactions of various sectors of the Church to proposed teachings should not mean that the Church ends up, as it could be stated sarcastically, boldly and prophetically proclaiming the lowest common denominator of beliefs. That would be a disgrace. Instead, in order to be true to this process of "testing everything and holding fast to what is good," there is a need for genuine, prayerful discernment of spirits in which the voice of the Triune God is sought, heard, and heeded in the midst of this dialogical process.

In the case of the U.S. pastorals, one can argue that the U.S. bishops did in fact exercise their grace of office by going through a discernment process within this dialogical procedure. Their positions were enriched and their arguments strengthened by their dialogical approach, but at the end of the day they accepted their mandate (even though a *mandatum docendi* is not canonically ascribed to episcopal

---

46. My thinking about the legitimacy of speaking about the democratization of Catholic ecclesiology has been influenced by the work of Siegfried Wiedenhofer; for his comments and extensive bibliography, see "*Sensus fidelium*—Demokratisierung der Kirche?" in *Surrexit Dominus vere: Die Gegenwart des Auferstandenen in seiner Kirche (Festschrift J. J. Degenhardt)*, ed. J. Erns and S. Leimgruber (Paderborn: Bonifatius, 1996) 457–471; idem, "Synodalität und Demokratisierung der Kirche aus dogmatische Perspektive," in *Demokratische Prozesse in dem kirchen? Konzilien, Synoden, Räte, Theologie im kulturellen Dialog* (Graz, Wien, Cologne: Styria Verlag, 1998) 73–99; idem, "Kritische Übernahme: Kann die Kirche demokratisiert werden?" *Herder-Korrespondenz*, Monatshefte für Gesellschaft und Religion 52 (1998) 347–351.

conferences) to make the hard judgments and decisions, knowing full well that they would be held accountable for what they teach and, recalling Benedict's admonition, for the obedience of those who adhere to their teachings. The ecclesial community must be open to accept the hard truths spoken by prophetic voices in its midst; sometimes these voices are among the bishops, but sometimes voices of theologians or of other members prove prophetic. The discernment process must be sufficiently wide to receive this prophetic word wherever it breaks forth.

Conclusion

The U.S. bishops have developed, through experimentation, a new approach to teaching with authority, with greater collegiality, collaboration with theologians, and consultation with representatives of the People of God. This dialogical approach to teaching has significantly enhanced the credibility and authority of the written documents that have been generated through this shared form of responsible participation. Moreover, the teachings produced through this process are themselves stronger, richer, more substantive as a result.

That this approach to teaching has developed among U.S. Catholics is significant because it reflects the history and character of this regional church. And as such it reveals a distinctive American gift for fostering participatory forms of teaching and governance; one could truly say it is a charism from God—created desires, abilities, and skills purified and transformed by the power of the Spirit for the good of the Church. This is but one instance of a larger conviction that has emerged during this period of the breakdown of the Eurocentric vision of the Church: local and regional churches in every culture around the world have received charisms, that is, unique combinations of inherited, bestowed, and achieved environmental, social, cultural, and historical factors that are given to them for the good of their own community. Here is one way that *the principle of subsidiarity* is applied in ecclesiology: local churches have distinctive assets and abilities to address local issues, and consequently it is not necessary to go to a higher regional or international level of organizational structure to address these issues. On the other hand, there are times when the move to a higher level is warranted and needed, when the principle of subsidiarity must be applied in the opposite way. But there is more. In some instances the gifts received that have shaped practices cultivated in a local church out of their own efforts to address their own local issues not only can but should be received as goods by other local and regional churches and at times by the Church universal. Here we discover *the principle of dispersion,* by which graces received in a local or regional church are disseminated to other regional, national, international, and universal ecclesial collectivities.

In this day and age we prayerfully ponder and seek to discern what gifted teachings and practices the universal Church and other regional churches need to receive and learn from the churches in Asia, Africa, and Latin America. Likewise, the U.S. Catholic Church has certain charisms to offer. The U.S. is known for many things, but one of its greatest gifts, assets, and achievements has been its ability to develop, maintain, and improve—all through experimentation—structures of dialogue, institutional structures for reaching judgments and decisions, and for making possible collective action. These dialogical structures promote maximum participation in the processes of deliberation and public discussion of matters of common concern that enable participants to sharpen, strengthen, and revise positions when needed, without violence and without simply resorting to the exercise of coercive power. By developing this new approach to Church teaching, the U.S. bishops have tried to acknowledge and receive a certain set of regional cultural charisms without denying their limitations and their ability to be corrupted and hinder rather than help the larger designs of God.

The synodal structure provides the clearest extant institutional practice for implementing this new approach, which itself requires experimenting with procedures that promote greater collegiality among bishops, cooperation between bishops and theologians, and broad-based consultation with representatives of the People of God. This will involve revising the current procedure to allow more open discussion and debate at synodal gatherings; public disclosure of draft documents; and using reactions to draft documents by theologians representing diverse theological paradigms (or "schools") and representatives from various sectors of the Church, including the laity, as an impetus for discerning revisions. In order to strengthen the credibility and authority of official Church teachings more generally, there is also a need to apply this new approach, in modified forms, to the ways many documents are produced by the pope and the Roman offices. Ultimately, in fact, the theological and pastoral principles that undergird this approach to learning and teaching are worthy of integration at every level of learning and teaching in the Church. Local, regional, national, and Roman offices can generate great documents, but they risk being ineffective if they are not produced in the kind of communion between bishops, theologians, and the People of God made possible through ongoing communication.

As promising as this ancient yet new approach to teaching may be, the hard truth is that a dialogical approach to learning and teaching in the Church, under the conditions of finitude and sin, can and does break down or is frustrated for any number of reasons. There needs to be an honest exploration of the many ways this dialogical approach can fail or be jeopardized, including by the impact of well-funded and well-organized conservative groups applying pressure regionally or in Rome; public expressions of opinions dissenting from the official position and advancing changes in doctrine or practice; the risk of polarization and endless discussion without sufficient movement toward consensus and resolution; insufficient promulgation and catechetical follow-up; and non-reception that is widespread or in sectors of the Church.

The failure of the pastoral letter on women's issues provides but one instructive example. Why did it fail? A number of reasons have been given, including a premature discussion of certain contested issues in theological anthropology. But one recurring reason given for its failure was that certain topics, and specifically women's ordination, were considered taboo for open discussion based on the CDF statement *Inter Insigniores* (1976). It was only after the women's pastoral failed that an official silence was imposed by the apostolic letter *Ordinatio Sacerdotalis* (1994) and the CDF's "Response to the *Dubium* concerning the ordination of women" (1995). On December 6, 1992, after the pastoral on women's issues failed and before the apostolic letter and CDF response just mentioned were issued, Archbishop Weakland published an editorial in *The New York Times*, in which he identified two options for the discussion of women's issues:

> The first is to close the doors to all discussion on the ordination issue and accept the consequences. That means, first all, preparing to live in a church of reduced size, for many women and men would say goodbye to a church they feel is out of touch with the world. The church also would have to stop telling society to increase signs of respect for women and how to use women's abilities to the fullest: it would be seen as hypocritical.
>
> The other option is to keep the doors open to further discussion and continue the important, even if painful, dialogue between the church's tradition and modern insights. This dialogue involves listening to all

> voices, especially the wisdom of the laity, and, with prayer and reflection, seeing what God wants of the church today. For some of us, too much is unclear, and too much is at stake to close the doors now.

The official statements of 1994 and 1995 reflect the first option. During the 1992 NCCB meeting at which the women's pastoral was rejected, Bishop Joseph Imesch, chair of the ad hoc committee that prepared the document, addressed the assembly of bishops: "As a bishop I challenge you—and challenge myself—to reexamine the role of women in our dioceses, *to hear more than we allowed ourselves to hear,* and to cross a bridge from word to action."[47]

At a profound level of principle, what the U.S. bishops advanced by the dialogical approach they used in their pastoral letters was thoroughly consistent with what Pope John Paul II has stated in *Novo Millennio Ineunte*. There he acknowledges the necessity of "structures of participation" for advancing ecclesial communion at every level of the Church's life. When he states that pastors must be encouraged "to listen more widely to the entire People of God," he invokes St. Benedict's admonition to abbots that began this essay. And he offers this powerful quotation from St. Paulinus of Nola: "Let us listen to what all the faithful say, because in every one of them the Spirit of God breathes."[48] John Paul is here urging practices of participation in local churches. One could argue that he fails to explore the import of Benedict's teaching for episcopal, synodal, curial, and papal practices. In the local churches priests and pastoral councils "are not governed by the rules of parliamentary democracy, because they are consultative rather than deliberative; yet this does not mean that they are less meaningful and relevant" (no. 45). The distinction being drawn between consultation and deliberation is intelligible and perhaps practical. But a strict contrast between consultation and deliberation in this formulation seems to imply a restriction of the role of theologians and of the entire People of God in relation to the magisterium, instead of offering a fuller articulation of the dynamic interrelationships between them in a way

---

47. Emphasis added. The passage from Bishop Joseph Imesch was cited by Dolores Leckey in "Crossing the Bridge: Women in the Church," *Church* 17 (2001) 11–17, at 11.

48. John Paul II, *Novo Millennio Ineunte* (January 6, 2001), no. 45. I wish to thank Bryan Hehir, Walter Grazer and Thomas Schellabarger from the staff of the Social Development and World Peace Committee of the United States Conference of Catholic Bishops, Dolores Leckey, and David Coffey for their assistance.

that expresses the shared responsibility of all those involved in the teaching and learning process.

Genuine discernment is required, but there must be a way of understanding and practicing ecclesial teaching and learning that respects the participation of all those involved in this deliberative process, without reducing it to a system of rule by vote. The authority of Church teaching depends upon mutual obedience to the voice of the Triune God at work in the honest dialogical exchange of those in the Christian community, which is the only basis for a real communion of persons. This is a pathway opened up by St. Benedict, by the U.S. bishops in the process of preparing these three pastoral letters, and by individual bishops like Rembert Weakland. May we grow in mutual obedience for the greater glory of the Triune God.

Chapter Eleven

Partners in the Mystery of Redemption

Dianne Bergant, C.S.A.

During my entire life, the Archdiocese of Milwaukee has played an important role in shaping my understanding of Church. I was born in one of the western suburbs of Milwaukee and educated in the archdiocesan Catholic school system. It was within this local church that I was prepared for and received the sacraments. I knew the names of and lived under the guidance of various archbishops and auxiliary bishops. I participated in the celebrations of their consecrations and ordinations and in the sense of loss at their deaths. I had already left the home of my childhood when the changes inaugurated by the Second Vatican Council began to be implemented. Still, I have always been most grateful that my parents experienced that renewal within a local church that took seriously both the changes themselves and the preparedness of the people in the pews.

I joined a religious congregation that was founded in 1858 in the northern part of the newly established Diocese of Milwaukee. Father Casper Rehrl, the missionary priest whose dream it was to found a group of women religious to minister to the German-speaking immigrants in Wisconsin, won the support in this venture of Milwaukee's first bishop, the Most Reverend John Martin Henni. Hence my identity as a woman religious has been significantly influenced by the ecclesiological perspectives and realities of the leaders of the Milwaukee Archdiocese from the period of our founding to this very day. Consequently, regardless of where I have been sent to minister, I have always thought of myself as being in some way a daughter of that local church. It is, therefore, a distinct honor to add my reflections to this tribute to Milwaukee's former diocesan bishop, Archbishop Rembert Weakland.

Contemporary Women in a Post-Vatican Church

In Western societies during the nineteenth century, debate over gender issues assumed a decidedly public stance. At that time these issues were referred to as "The Woman Question." Those committed to them questioned any policy that employed gender as a factor in either granting or limiting civic rights. The suffragettes are an example of this early commitment. During the twentieth century, concern for gender issues gave rise to "The Women's Movement." Among other concerns, it wrestled with questions about the nature and function of gender in determining social roles. Today many advocates hold firmly to the belief that gender identity is a product of socialization. They reject the idea that social roles are divinely ordained, eternally determined, or universally applicable. Matters pertinent to issues of gender continue to be central questions in social sciences such as anthropology, politics, economics, and psychology.

Despite the admittedly secular tone of most of Western society, those who recognize the religious dimension to all of human life argue that there are theological implications to aspects of the social sciences. They discern definite relationships between gender perceptions and theological issues, particularly in the realms of morality, soteriology, and ecclesiology. Therefore, as attention focuses more explicitly on the question of appropriate gender socialization, corresponding theological questions become even more pressing. Since gender touches the very heart of one's self-identity, it has been impossible to relegate such interrelated questions to positions of secondary importance. On the contrary, whether welcomed or not, these matters have assumed a prominent place in the mainstream of both critical and popular discourse.

For its part, the Church, too, both local and universal, has had to come to grips with matters related to gender. It has not been an easy issue to deal with. This is not simply because women are disgruntled, though some certainly are. Nor is it exclusively because the Church is unwilling to change, though for many and varied reasons some within the Church are certainly resistant to change in such matters. Rather, the question of gender is a difficult issue to deal with because it is so complex. It encompasses fundamental dimensions of personal identity and social status, as well as influencing profoundly the nature of one's relationship with God and the character of one's membership within the believing community. How an individual or the Church as a body understands any one of the aspects of this network of perceptions will largely determine the position taken on other gender issues.

Vatican II challenged the entire Church to a more comprehensive and a richer understanding of its participation in the threefold mission of Jesus, which was to teach, to govern, and to sanctify. While declaring that those who are ordained carry out this commission in a way that is inherently different from the way open to the laity,[1] the council did insist that it is baptism and not ordination that actually confers the threefold commission. In view of this more comprehensive understanding, the question raised then is not *"Do* lay people, by virtue of their baptism, teach, govern, and sanctify in the name of Jesus?" but rather *"How do* lay people, by virtue of their baptism, teach, govern, and sanctify in the name of Jesus?"

Women who have been shaped by the teaching of Vatican II fulfill these Christian responsibilities in ways that often differ significantly from the way women served in an earlier generation. Many of them today have moved into areas of service that do not conform to the traditional gender roles. This change has been troubling to some who interpret it as an example of selfish modern women demanding what they consider to be their rights. For their part, the women believe that in doing this, they are simply acting as committed believers intent on assuming their Christian responsibilities.

Because of their commitment to the Church and their desire to serve, these women are increasingly attentive to the way the diocesan bishop fulfills his responsibility to teach, to govern, and to sanctify. They know that they are beneficiaries of the grace that flows from such ministry. However, they are also concerned about how that same bishop allows and encourages them to fulfill their own responsibilities. They take seriously the views expressed in official Church documents, such as the most recent statements issued by the USCCB's Committee on Women in Society and in the Church, namely, *Strengthening the Bonds of Peace*[2] and *From Words to Deeds.*[3] These two documents underscore the importance of three goals set forth by the bishops: (1) to appreciate and incorporate the gifts of women in the Church; (2) to appoint women to Church leadership positions; (3) to promote collaboration between

1. The question of ordination, with its gendered character and privileged status, though certainly an issue related to episcopal ministry, is beyond the scope of these reflections.

2. National Conference of Catholic Bishops, Committee on Women in Society and in the Church, *Strengthening the Bonds of Peace: A Pastoral Reflection on Women in the Church and in Society* (Washington: USCC, 1995).

3. National Conference of Catholic Bishops, Committee on Women in Society and in the Church, *From Words to Deeds: Continuing Reflections on the Role of Women in the Church* (Washington: USCC, 1998).

women and men in the Church. These goals identify some of the areas of episcopal responsibility as well as ministerial possibility for women. They also set the broad outline for the reflections that follow.

Diversity of Gifts

> There are different kinds of spiritual gifts but the same Spirit; there are different forms of service but the same Lord; there are different workings but the same God who produces all of them in everyone. To each individual the manifestation of the Spirit is given for some benefit (1 Cor 12:4-7, NAB).

This passage from the writings of St. Paul precedes the bishops' discussion of the first goal that they set for themselves. However, it is actually the biblical grounding for all three goals, and the reality that it describes is the impetus for the ministerial aspirations of many women in the Church today.

Gifts *(charísmata)* refer to activities of the Spirit, notably speaking in tongues and prophesying, that were usually operative during worship. Ministries *(diakoníai)* were services within the community that were often considered menial, like serving at table or collecting money. Paul may have included this reference in order to show that within the community of believers, no task is ignoble. Works *(enérgēmata)* were feats of great energy or divine power. Since all these gifts or ministries or works were manifestations of the Spirit, no one was to be considered superior to another. Further, they were not given for the self-aggrandizement of the one who received them; all were given for the benefit of the entire community.

The way the diversity of gifts is understood today depends upon one's anthropological presuppositions. Although many individuals and groups assert that women and men are in fact equal, their underlying assumptions frequently belie the implications of that assertion. They may operate out of a popular form of dual-nature anthropology in which complementarity is seen as inherent in nature. This anthropological perspective tends to make distinctions between mind and body, spirit and matter, culture and nature, etc., and it stereotypically aligns men with the first and more desirable component of the pair, and women with its "complement." Women are considered "natural" followers rather than leaders, supporters rather than administrators, dependents rather than providers, and the social roles open to them are assigned accordingly. Men have the really important roles, and women help.

This biased point of view is often justified by arguing from a literal reading of the creation account recorded in Genesis 2, where the woman is taken from the rib of the man, and by ignoring the account in Genesis 1, where equality in creation is undeniable. This kind of biblical interpretation suggests that the woman is derivative of the man. She is often referred to as the "weaker sex," in need of protection or direction. She is the man's helper, his "right hand," merely an extension of him, enjoying little identity apart from him. No one will deny that nature has determined the distinctive roles played by women and men in procreation, but one cannot help asking: Do these biologically determined distinctions apply to the psychological, social, intellectual, and spiritual realms as well? How has societal conditioning influenced role differentiation and/or personality development? To what extent does biology really determine destiny?

Based on these anthropological presuppositions, both theology and devotion have advanced definitions of and models for women that have shaped their collective and individual self-concepts. Who has not heard that it was the fickleness of the woman that opened the door to sin in the world, and that as a result of that sin, women must work out their salvation through childbearing and dependence upon their husbands? Probably the best-known example of the perfect woman is Mary, the obedient virgin called to an unquestioning act of faith. While this is certainly a noble model worthy of emulation, it should be seen as only one aspect of that extraordinarily strong woman depicted in the *Magnificat*. All too frequently the rejection by many women of the traditional, restrictive self-concept is judged by others to be unfaithfulness to a long-standing and acceptable biblical tradition, and is experienced by these women themselves as such. New self-definitions are often ridiculed, dismissed, or rejected outright as theologically unsound. Misunderstanding, criticism, and painful accusation are some of the obstacles that women must overcome if they themselves are to appreciate and incorporate their gifts into the life of the Church.

It is not enough to disclaim the dual-nature anthropology and to opt for a single-nature view of humankind. Since no human being is exempt from sexual differentiation, the fact of sexual differences cannot be dismissed lightly. However, the claims of androgyny are also misleading. Accordingly, some insist that women and men have both feminine and masculine characteristics, and maturity is reached when these characteristics are integrated within the individual. They hold that imagistic thinking is feminine, linear thinking is masculine; emotionality is feminine, rationality is masculine. In an attempt to redress exclusion by gender, they argue that both women and men must participate in any project in order to rectify a situation that is exclusively "masculine." As admirable as this approach may appear to be, it still springs from the stereotyping of human traits according to gender, a fundamental premise of dual-nature anthropology. The time has come for a new anthropological understanding, one that does not confuse sex (physiological reality) with gender (social or cultural conditioning).

Traditionally, women have been assigned roles that are somehow connected with nurturing and with the home, while men have assumed responsibility for the marketplace. Teaching children, nursing the sick, and various "family matters" were considered "woman's work," and men who felt called to such work were often made to suffer discrimination. While it was conceivable, though not always considered acceptable, that men might move into the realms assigned to women, it was almost impossible for women to gain assess to "a man's world." This was true not only of society at large but of the Church as well. Women cleaned and cooked and kept house and taught children and cared for the sick. Men made decisions and governed and built buildings and empires and taught adults and performed miracles of healing. On occasion women were allowed to help.

Pointing out such role stereotyping should not be construed as criticism of the specific work itself. On the contrary, the success of the Catholic school system and of Catholic health care in the United States should be credited in large part to the commitment of the women who willingly and lovingly spent themselves in this selfless work. As they gained expertise, they carefully honed the attitudes of mind and heart that were essential to these fields, attitudes of patience and understanding, of gentleness and sensitivity, of warmth and loving-kindness. In this it was more the needs of others than any explicit womanly nature that led them to develop characteristics that are more generally human than specifically feminine. Nor should women be disparaged today who choose to continue in traditional modes of service, whether within the home and neighborhood, the community, the school, health care, or the Church. If that is their choice, it should be seen as an example of the diversity of gifts or service or workings offered for the benefit of the Church. What has been challenged is role designation that is determined by gender alone, for it not only limits ministerial possibilities but risks failing to recognize the unique gifts given to the individual by the Spirit of God.

Within the recent past, many of these lines of gender distinction and discrimination have faded, and the primary criteria for assuming certain roles within the society at large as well as within the Church are competence and adequate preparation. To quote the bishops:

> Today, throughout the world, women hold positions of exacting leadership, as heads of government, judges, research doctors, symphony conductors, and business executives. They serve as presidents at Catholic colleges and universities and as administrators and faculty members at Catholic colleges and seminaries. They are also chief executives of Catholic hospitals and executive directors of Catholic Charities. An increasing number of Catholic theologians are women. Some women serve the diocesan churches as school superintendents and chancellors, as archivists and members of marriage tribunals. More and more women have responsible national positions in the Catholic Church *(Strengthening the Bonds of Peace)*.

It is clear that the bishops have committed themselves to support women in such ventures and to provide further opportunities for sharing women's God-given gifts with the rest of the community. Women have come to expect this support and to look for these opportunities from the religious leaders of the local churches within which they minister. They do this, not simply because they passively accept the conclusions reached by the bishops, but primarily because they themselves have become aware of the pressing needs of the Church, have discerned the gifts that they possess which might address those needs, and have been seized by a burning desire to serve the People of God.

Leadership Positions

In another of his letters, St. Paul exhorts the Christians to exercise faithfully the diverse gifts given to them for the building up of the entire Church. He employs the image of the human body to characterize both the diversity of the various bodily parts and the interdependence that exists among them:

> For as in one body we have many parts, and all the parts do not have the same function, so we, though many, are one body in Christ and individually parts of one another. Since we have gifts that differ according to the grace given to us, let us exercise them: if prophecy, in proportion to the faith; if ministry, in ministering; if one is a teacher, in teaching; if one exhorts, in exhortation; if one contributes, in generosity; if one is over others, with diligence; if one does acts of mercy, with cheerfulness (Rom 12:4-8, NAB).

The diversity found within the community is compared to the complexity of the human body. Each part has its own unique function, but all parts work for the good of the whole. This metaphor characterizes several aspects of the community. First, it portrays unity in diversity, a unity that is far from uniformity. Second, it underscores the lack of competition among members, one activity elevating itself above the others. Lowly service is no less important than charismatic gifts. Third, it points up the interdependence that exists within the community. Finally, these gifts are given by God, not bestowed by the Church.

In a very real sense, each one of the gifts mentioned in this passage presumes some exercise of leadership within the Church. Arguing from the image of the body, Paul insists that no one person has been given all of the gifts, and therefore no person exercises exclusive leadership within the Church. This does not deny the administrative authority of the diocesan bishop. After all, as bishop *(epískopos)*, it is his responsibility to oversee *(episkopéō)* the entire local church. He may be the first to teach, to govern, and to sanctify, but he is not alone in this.

The bishops themselves state, "*The Code of Canon Law* reserves only a few offices or ecclesiastical roles to the ordained. It provides that laity can 'cooperate' in the exercise in the power of governance" *(From Words to Deeds)*. In accord with this, many Church leadership positions are now occupied by women. On the national level, they serve as theologians, and they hold key positions within the bishops' conference. In dioceses they serve as chancellors, directors of Catholic Charities, and tribunal judges. They are directors of liturgy and worship, pastoral planners, and directors or administrators of parishes. In many and very significant ways, women do indeed participate in the governance of the Church.

It would be naive to think that this is evidence that the gifts that women have to offer the Church have been universally recognized and wholeheartedly welcomed. What might be the case in one diocese is often lacking in another. Even when women do occupy these positions of leadership, they often meet with patronizing attitudes, suspicion regarding their competence, and resistance to their manner of operation. However, significant progress in these matters has been made in the short span of time since Vatican II, and the bishops have committed themselves to continued improvement.

The commission conferred on all at baptism is threefold. Therefore, one can say that leadership is exercised not only in governing but also in teaching and sanctifying. Unfortunately, the leadership potential in these other areas is not always recognized, much less engaged as it might be. There seems to be a bias in favor of governing. But why? Is it because of its more public nature, because its consequences are more immediate and obvious, while learning and growing in holiness occur incrementally and in private? Whatever answers are given to these questions, one must admit that such a bias is diametrically opposed to the depiction of Jesus that is found in every one of the Gospels. There we see that his public life was spent in teaching and sanctifying. In fact, he rejected any form of leadership that was not also an exercise of service to others. Just as it is time to come to a new understanding of gender, it might be time to develop an appreciation of the transformative role played by ministries of teaching and sanctifying.

We begin with the ministry of teaching. The bishop may be the primary teacher in the diocese, but seldom is he the one that the community of believers thinks of first in this role. They know the teachers with whom they have immediate contact, and there are many women in that group. Women not only continue in the traditional roles of teacher and catechist, but they are frequently some of the most popular, and sometimes controversial, speakers on the lecture circuit. Books which are written by women and which treat every theological topic or avenue of spirituality are often best sellers, and they hold that pride of place for long periods of time. Although women are themselves excluded from ordination, they are prominently involved in the theological, ministerial, and spiritual formation of those men who will be ordained. In this way their influence as teachers spreads throughout the Church. By shaping the minds and hearts of students of all ages, women often play a significant role in exercising leadership within the Church.

Unfortunately, the degree to which one's occupation is valued is often gauged by one's status within the community and the salary that such an occupation can draw. As essential as teaching is to the health, development, and future of society or of the Church, the profession is seldom accorded the esteem that it deserves, and teachers themselves are generally rather poorly compensated. Perhaps this is the case because teaching was traditionally considered "woman's work," and neither women nor their work were highly valued. Bishops are in a position to change this attitude as it exists within the Church. They do this by showing their respect to qualified teachers, by honoring them when appropriate, by consulting them when their expertise can contribute to the bishops' own insight, and by supporting them in legitimate theological inquiry. In such ways bishops act as servants as well as overseers of their respective local churches.

Focusing on the role of sanctifier, a comparable scenario can be sketched. Without in any way diminishing the preeminent importance of the sacraments as signs and causes of holiness and the role of the ordained in their celebration, attention should be given to other avenues of spirituality. The Church can boast of a long tradition of spiritual direction or companionship and of retreat work. However, in the past such ministries were customarily performed by ordained men, probably due, in large part, to the prominence of the sacraments of Eucharist and reconciliation in these spiritual practices. This situation has been dramatically changed within the recent past. Not only have women proven to be exceptional spiritual guides, but in many places they outnumber the men engaged in such work. Nor do women work only with other women; they administer, direct, and teach in renewal programs that have high enrollments of men. They also offer retreats to communities of men religious. While it is true that bishops oversee the sacramental life of the local churches, it would not be uncommon to find women also ministering to the spiritual needs of that church.

There is a kind of bias operative in this area of ministry as well. Participation in the sacramental life of the Church is considered integral to one's spiritual health. In fact, it is mandated by canon law. Such is not the case with other spiritual practices. In the past many of these practices were often considered the domain of the spiritual elite, namely, the ordained, those who belonged to religious communities, and a few exceptional lay people. Today, while many serious believers consider these practices essential to their spiritual development, others view them as secondary undertakings, even diversions, of religious dilettantes. They argue that some have become so dependent upon such practices that they will not take a step in life without consulting their spiritual guide. One cannot help wondering whether, in previous times, the spiritual ministry of the ordained was scrutinized and summarily dismissed, as are some of the spiritual ministries to which women commit themselves today. However these ministries are perceived by their critics, women and men alike, in numbers beyond calculating, attest to the healing, growth, and transformation that such ministries have effected in their lives. Although they may not always be in the forefront of Church consciousness, in many ways spiritual ministries may be some of the most influential workings of the diocese. Aware of this and conscious of their own episcopal responsibilities, bishops exercise careful oversight of them.

For us to applaud the transformative influence of the work of others is certainly not to challenge the authority of the diocesan bishops. Nor is the involvement of lay people a case of tokenism on the part of the bishops. Rather, it demonstrates the kind of collaboration that has emerged within the Church since Vatican II. The bishops themselves acknowledge this:

> We pledge our partnership in all these endeavors. In no way should these commitments be construed as "ecclesial political correctness"; they are theologically correct. They are rooted in our baptism and in our understanding of the Holy Spirit who works in the Church to build it up through the gifts of its members *(Strengthening the Bonds of Peace)*.

Collaboration

The theological basis of the collaboration of which the bishops speak is the concept of the Body of Christ. The following quote appeared in *Called and Gifted for the Third Millennium,* a document that reflected on the call of the laity to holiness and ministry.[4] Recontextualized in a later document that addresses the role of women in the Church, it takes on an explicit gender focus:

> The Church's pastoral ministry can be more effective if we become true collaborators, mindful of our own weaknesses, but grateful for our gifts. Collaboration challenges us to understand that we are, in reality, joined in Christ's body, that we are not separate but interdependent *(From Words to Deeds)*.

Most people will agree that "collaboration" simply means working together. However, the social and religious contexts within which the word is used, and the anthropological perspectives of the people using it, can significantly affect the way it is understood. For instance, various groups of people may be invited or actually expected to work together in implementing someone else's project. The one whose project it is may consider this collaboration, while those implementing it may not. These latter may feel that true collaboration requires that all participate at

---

4. National Conference of Catholic Bishops, Bishops' Committee on the Laity, *Called and Gifted for the Third Millennium: Reflections of the U.S. Catholic Bishops on the Thirtieth Anniversary of the Decree on the Apostolate of the Laity and the Fifteenth Anniversary of* Called and Gifted (Washington: USCC, 1995).

every level of the project, from deciding whether or not there should even be a project to designing it and ultimately implementing it. Even the bishops' 1990 definition of collaboration is open to interpretation: "Here we speak of collaboration as 'the working together of all the baptized, each contributing specific, personal gifts' for the good of the Church" *(Gifts Unfolding).*[5] Who decides which particular gifts are desirable, whose individual gifts will be employed, and when specific gifts will be needed? Different people will answer such questions in different ways.

The two major documents that form the basis of the present reflections, *Strengthening the Bonds of Peace* and *From Words to Deeds,* clearly indicate the bishops' desire that full collaboration be actively pursued in all areas that are not proscribed by canon law.[6] They insist that collaborative ministry is not an option; rather, it is a visible sign of the Church's *communio.* Acknowledging the diversity of gifts bestowed upon the Church by the Holy Spirit, they are concerned that these gifts not be determined according to restrictive gender categories, with women "expected to carry out the behind-the-scenes tasks rather than assume the more visible roles of group leadership and facilitation" *(From Words to Deeds).* They are particularly concerned that women have a voice in decision-making processes.

Episcopal support notwithstanding, women still face many serious obstacles to full collaborative participation in the Church. First, we cannot underestimate the discriminatory implications of anthropological views that perceive women as derivative from or complementary to men. Such views have been fundamental to our social, political, psychological, and theological perspectives, and it will take a long time to replace them with new ones. This can only be done by calling attention to long-established discriminatory practices and policies whenever and wherever they show themselves. Both patience and courage are indispensable on the part of those who bring them to attention, as is humility on the part of those whose sensitivity needs to be heightened. Such situations are usually awkward and frequently painful. However, the health and growth of the Body of Christ requires it. Referring to a statement by John Paul II in *Mulieris Dignitatem,* the bishops insist that "the violation of women's equality also diminishes the true dignity of men" *(From Words to Deeds).*

5. National Conference of Catholic Bishops, Bishops' Committee on the Laity, *Gifts Unfolding: The Lay Vocation Today with Questions for Tomorrow* (Washington: USCC, 1990).

6. Opposition to this proscription is beyond the scope of this article.

A second obstacle has to do with theological preparation. While the doors of some schools of theology are still closed to women students, other institutions prepare women and men, candidates for ordination and lay people alike, for ministry that will be collaborative. While acknowledging and preparing for their distinctive roles in ministry, together they work on theological and pastoral projects, organize and participate in liturgical and other prayer experiences, and share in both the successes and the challenges of ministry. However, the theological education of lay students, the large majority of whom are women, is not subsidized to the extent that it is for candidates for ordination. The bishops have recommended that one of the ways of preparing women for leadership roles in the Church is to "provide opportunities and resources, including scholarships, for women to acquire the education, spiritual formation, and skills needed for church leadership positions" *(From Words to Deeds)*. There is much question as to the extent to which dioceses have acted on this suggestion.

Finally, once women have demonstrated both preparation and competence in a particular field in ministry, they are still faced with questions of secure employment, adequate financial compensation, and the freedom to fulfill the responsibilities expected. While there may be situations on both the national and local levels where employment commensurate to expertise is still not open to women, generally speaking tremendous strides have been made in this area since Vatican II. The question of adequate financial compensation is broader than the issue of gender. Difficulties arise from the fact that formerly ministry was performed by priests and religious, all of whom worked for low stipends rather than full salaries. Dioceses have established various salary arrangements for their clergy, whose number has significantly decreased, but lay people, the large majority of whom are women, now look for full salary with benefits. Though they may be moving toward more equitable arrangements, Catholic institutions face an upward battle in this regard.

Perhaps the most difficult employment issue facing women is the lack of freedom so many of them experience in the exercise of their duties. Despite the fact that the bishops' Committee on Women in Society and in the Church has set forth statements about collaboration between women and men in the Church, the way that this collaboration unfolds depends upon the actual people involved. Without denying the legitimate authority of the bishops of the dioceses and the pastors of the parishes, women often chafe under persistent patronizing oversight. They feel that their gifts are minimized, their expertise is dismissed, and their ability to fulfill their responsibilities is questioned. Sometimes this is a question of outright gender discrimination; at other times it is a question of unwillingness or inability to relinquish control. To compound this unfortunate situation, women often feel that they have nowhere to go for recourse. They feel beholden to men who have been appointed to their positions by their diocesan bishops. One cannot help but ask: If bishops set the agenda for collaboration, might they also have some responsibility to see that it is effectively realized?

A Look to the Future

What might women expect from the bishops in the future? They expect neither more nor less than what has been promised by the bishops themselves. In the concluding words of *Strengthening the Bonds of Peace*, we read: "We have seen that the true face of the Church appears only when and if we recognize the equal dignity of men and women and consistently act on that recognition." And again: "A Church that is deepening its consciousness of itself, that is trying to project the image of Christ to the world, will understand the need for ongoing, prayerful reflection in this area." And finally:

> For many years a dialogue among women and between women and men took place in the Church in the United States, as we tried to write a pastoral letter that would capture the vast range of concerns expressed by women. The pastoral letter was not approved, but the concluding recommendations were sent to the Executive Committee of the National Conference of Catholic Bishops for action by various Conference committees. We bishops pledge ourselves anew, through our committee structure, to continue the dialogue in a spirit of partnership and mutual trust and to implement the recommendations where possible.

In *From Words to Deeds* they reiterate their stand:

> As the Committee on Women in Society and in the Church, we commit ourselves to continuing our advocacy on behalf of women . . . we will educate ourselves about the particular needs, concerns, and gifts of women and how women's gifts can be affirmed and incorporated into church life . . . we will explore what new forms of church leadership may be needed for our time and take steps to ensure that women are prepared for these as well as existing leadership roles.

Acknowledging the challenge of these aspirations, they end their reflections on a note of profound spiritual sensitivity:

> We can meet this challenge only by living personally in the Spirit. We need to pray for each other, to discern how the Spirit is leading us, and to have both the humility and the fortitude to follow. Above all, we must remember that the work we do is not ours but God's—in whose name it begins, under whose guidance it continues, and in whose glory it ends.

To this, the women in the Church will say: Amen!

Returning to my opening comments, I must add that I am not only in some way a daughter of the church in Milwaukee, but I have also served that church in various ways. Therefore, I am in a position to reflect on its willingness to respect the diversity of gifts bestowed on it by the Spirit of God; to appoint women to leadership positions in various departments; to support collaboration between women and men in ministry. First, on several occasions I have been called upon to provide biblical and theological insights at archdiocesan convocations, at gatherings of the faculties of the seminaries established in the archdiocese, and at adult education programs developed within its boundaries. On such occasions, my expertise has always been welcomed and respected. Second, I have served two terms apiece on the boards of trustees of both seminaries. In each case, my contributions as a theological educator were as valued as were those of any other board member. Third, as a theologian involved in seminary education, I have always appreciated the collaborative atmosphere that pervades the Archdiocese of Milwaukee, an atmosphere that I have experienced firsthand, an atmosphere that is both set and encouraged by the diocesan bishop. Ministering under the leadership of Archbishop Weakland, I have always considered myself a partner in the mystery of redemption.

Chapter Twelve

The Challenge of Peace and *Economic Justice for All:* Reflections Twenty Years Later [1]

Kenneth R. Himes, O.F.M.

Besides his leadership of the Catholic community in Milwaukee, Rembert G. Weakland, O.S.B., has made valuable contributions to the life of the wider Church. One of those significant contributions was his role as chair of the committee that drafted the pastoral letter *Economic Justice for All.* [2] Although the bishops of the United States have issued a number of admirable statements on social issues, it is the pastoral letter written by the Weakland committee and *The Challenge of Peace,* [3] the pastoral letter written under the leadership of then Archbishop Joseph Bernardin of Cincinnati, that are most often cited as illustrative of the U.S. bishops' functioning as moral teachers on social matters.

It was in November 1980 that the bishops called for the establishment of two committees—one to draft a letter on Church teaching regarding war and peace in the nuclear age and another to draft a letter that would examine capitalism from the perspective of Catholic

1. This is a slightly modified version of the presidential address given to the fifty-sixth annual convention of the Catholic Theological Society of America (CTSA) that was held in Milwaukee from June 7 to June 10, 2001. The original appears as "Presidential Address. *The Challenge of Peace* and *Economic Justice for All:* Reflections Twenty Years Later," in *CTSA Proceedings* 56 (2001) 77–96.

2. National Conference of Catholic Bishops, *Economic Justice for All: Pastoral Letter on Catholic Social Teaching and the U.S. Economy* (Washington: USCC, 1986). Hereafter EJA.

3. National Conference of Catholic Bishops, *The Challenge of Peace: God's Promise and Our Response* (Washington: USCC, 1983). Hereafter CP.

teaching.[4] With the passage of years since the establishment of the two episcopal committees, it may be useful to reflect upon those two letters to see what lessons we can learn from them about how the Church might advance its social teaching.

Archbishop Weakland himself anticipated this reflection in an essay published shortly in advance of the formal vote of the bishops approving the economics pastoral. Before addressing questions he raised in that essay, I would like to comment upon an important premise of the two pastoral letters, namely, the legitimate role of the local church in acting upon the social mission.[5]

Local Church

It is no surprise to Church historians that developments in the wider society in which the Church exists often provide, at least by way of analogy, models for the Church in its social organization. The Church after Constantine borrowed and adapted elements of the imperial court. During the medieval era the Church took on features of feudal society.

Today we live in the era of globalization. One of the features of this multi-dimensional process suggests that even though there are processes at work that spread a universal culture, there is another set of processes at work that give a particular cast to the universal.

We are very far indeed from seeing a one-culture world, much less a Westernized world-culture. The spread of global markets and communications are forces for interaction, but one ought not ignore the stubbornness of the particular. There is still the tendency for people to define themselves by what makes them different from others in a par-

4. In addition to Archbishop Bernardin, the members of the committee on war and peace were George Fulcher, Bishop of Columbus, Ohio; Thomas Gumbleton, Auxiliary Bishop of Detroit, Michigan; John O'Connor, Military Ordinariate; and Daniel Reilly, Bishop of Norwich, Connecticut. Besides Archbishop Weakland, the members of the committee for the economics letter were Thomas Donnellan, Archbishop of Atlanta, Georgia; Peter Rosazza, Auxiliary Bishop of Hartford, Connecticut; George Speltz, Bishop of St. Cloud, Minnesota; and William Weigand, Bishop of Salt Lake City, Utah. Originally, Bishop Joseph Daley of Harrisburg, Pennsylvania, served on the committee but resigned due to illness and was replaced by Archbishop Donnellan.

5. While I am aware that the terminology is in dispute, I use the expression "local church" to designate not only a particular diocese but also a gathering of churches of a geographical or cultural region. Thus I will speak of the church in the United States as a local church. For an overview of the problem of local church/universal Church, see Joseph Komonchak, "The Local Church and the Church Catholic: The Contemporary Theological Problematic," *The Jurist* 52 (1992) 416–447.

ticular context. A woman professor in the company of a dozen women who work at other jobs will think of herself as a professor; in a room with twelve male professors she will think of herself as a woman.

In short, in an increasingly globalized world, there will still be strong drives to identify with ethnic, religious, and other forms of particularist difference. So today we find in our world tensions between forces that compress the world and intensify our consciousness of one world and other drives to identify the particular and distinctive amidst the global whole.[6]

If this is a central dynamic at work in the wider world, it should not strike us as curious that similar competing models are at work in the life of the Church. Forces that promote centralization and stress the universal experience of Church will spur a reaction in arguments for the particular charisms and identity of the local church.

From its origins through its various title and organizational changes, the social mission of the Church has loomed large on the U.S. episcopal conference's agenda. The bishops believed that an important dimension of the work of the conference was and is to identify the social agenda arising from the local or national scene.[7]

What has been called the Magna Carta of the local church is found in Pope Paul VI's apostolic letter *Octogesima Adveniens*, issued on the eightieth anniversary of *Rerum Novarum*. Here we find these three startling sentences:

> In the face of such widely varying situations it is difficult for us to utter a unified message and to put forward a solution which has universal validity. Such is not our ambition, nor is it our mission. It is up to the Christian communities to analyze with objectivity the situation which

6. For one assessment of the geopolitical implications of this tension, see Samuel Huntington, *The Clash of Civilizations and the Remaking of World Order* (New York: Simon and Schuster, 1996).

7. Helpful accounts of the early years of the episcopal conference are Elizabeth McKeown, "The National Bishops' Conference: an Analysis of Its Origins," *Catholic Historical Review* 66 (1980) 565–583, and Joseph McShane, S.J., *"Sufficiently Radical": Catholicism, Progressivism and the Bishops' Program of 1919* (Washington: Catholic University Press, 1986), esp. ch. 2. Evident in these historical studies is the importance of the social mission for the agenda of the episcopal conference.

Originally called the National Catholic War Conference, the name was changed shortly after the close of World War I to the National Catholic Welfare Conference. Following Vatican II, the name became the National Conference of Catholic Bishops, coupled with its public policy arm the United States Catholic Conference. With the recent approval of reforms, the organization as of July 1, 2001, is to be called the United States Conference of Catholic Bishops.

is proper to their own country, to shed on it the light of the Gospel's unalterable words and to draw principles of reflection, norms of judgment and directives for action from the social teaching of the Church.[8]

I called these sentences startling because, first, the Pope acknowledges a problem with formulating a teaching that is apt for the universal Church. Then he announces that formulating such a teaching is not the mission of the papacy. And finally, he endorses the role of the local churches within a given nation to both read their particular situation and formulate a response.[9]

The pastoral letters *Economic Justice for All* and *The Challenge of Peace* were written at a time when the words of Paul VI about the local church still were on the minds of our bishops. The significance of this passage has been diminished somewhat by a number of actions in subsequent years.[10] Given the public nature of the "friendly argument" between Cardinals Ratzinger and Kaspar, it is clear that there are contesting visions of how to understand the relationship of the universal and local church.[11] In *Octogesima Adveniens* one finds evidence that Paul VI's approach to the question gives a greater role to the local church than does that of John Paul II. The balance between these two dimensions of the social mission of the Church may be struck differently from one papacy to another, but it is unlikely, or at least unwise, that we stifle the role of the local church in the social ministry.

Certainly this was presumed by the body of U.S. bishops as they supported the creation of the Bernardin and Weakland committees. The belief that the leaders of the local church should exercise a pastoral teaching role by speaking to developments within their country was an aspect of episcopal ministry taken for granted.[12]

8. Paul VI, *Octogesima Adveniens*, May 14, 1971 (Washington: USCC, 1971), no. 4.

9. I do not mean to imply that prior to Paul VI's statement there was no sense of a local church already operative in the U.S. situation. What I am suggesting is that there was an evolving sense of the place for a local hierarchy in the life of a nation, and the statement in *Octogesima Adveniens* certainly gave impetus to a more proactive role.

10. For accounts of the actions I have in mind, see Mary Elsbernd, "What Ever Happened to *Octogesima Adveniens?*" *Theological Studies* 56 (1995) 39–60, and Richard Gaillardetz, "Reflections on the Future of Papal Primacy," *New Theology Review* 13 (November 2000) 52–66.

11. Walter Kaspar, "On the Church," *America* 184 (April 23–30, 2001) 8–14. For a report on the controversy and some of the internal Church politics involved, see Robert Leicht, "Cardinal in Conflict," *The Tablet* 255 (April 28, 2001) 607–608.

12. Yet, recall that it was precisely the *mandatum docendi* of an episcopal conference that was questioned by Cardinal Ratzinger at a meeting in Rome on January 18–19, 1983, which was called to discuss the peace pastoral. See the public report of the meeting by Jan Schotte, "A Vatican Synthesis," *Origins* 12 (April 7, 1982) 691–695, esp. 692.

I mentioned earlier that the significance of Paul VI's statement has been somewhat diminished in recent years. For example, there is an unintentional downside to the frequency and visibility of papal trips. On these trips the Pope engages in a modern form of evangelization, he affirms the distinctive gifts of the local church, and he often brings to the world's attention the injustices found in a local region. Due to the modern media, papal actions are now reported and captured for cameras that send images out to the entire world. This is a new and dramatic opportunity for witnessing to the gospel, and one that reaches far more people than will ever constitute the readership of an encyclical.[13]

At the same time there is a risk involved, one that turns the Pope into a "supra-episcopal figure," obscuring the authority of the local bishop. Despite the Pope's good intentions to come as a pilgrim or a universal shepherd uniting with the flock, he carries too much historical "weight" to really build up the local church. Instead, what occurs is that the focus is so much on John Paul II that the local authority is weakened.[14] In the popular mind the papal symbolization today combines three images: the guardian and touchstone of unity in faith, the holder of supreme juridical authority, and, finally, a living icon. The first image is patristic in origin, the second medieval, but the third, the living icon, is quite modern. It is this last dimension that has shifted popular attention from the ministry of the Petrine office to the person of the Pope himself.[15]

Clearly this trend did not start with John Paul II but with the rise of ultramontanism in the nineteenth century. Recall the slogan of that time that Catholics venerate three white things: the soul of the Blessed Virgin Mary, the eucharistic host, and the cassock of the pope.[16] In regard to the perennial quest to balance the local and universal experience of the Church, the net effect of this present, highly visible papacy may well be to perpetuate an imbalance between the local church and the universal Church.

13. See Gaillardetz, "Reflections on Papal Primacy," 57.

14. Ibid., 58.

15. Dominic Monti, O.F.M., "The Role of the Papal Office in the Life of the Church: Historical Reflections," unpublished ms. (Academic Convocation, Washington Theological Union, 1987).

16. A striking reference regarding the "personality cult" of the papacy is from a sermon of Bishop, later Cardinal, Gaspard Mermillod of Lausanne, who referred to three incarnations of the Son of God: "in the womb of a virgin, in the Eucharist, and in the old man in the Vatican." The "old man" was, of course, Pius IX. See J. Derek Holmes, *The Triumph of the Holy See: A Short History of the Papacy in the Nineteenth Century* (London: Burns and Oates, 1978) 153.

Behind the entire exercise of the development of the pastoral letters *Economic Justice for All* and *The Challenge of Peace* was a basic premise that, especially in matters of social teaching, the nation's bishops had an important role in identifying and speaking to the issues of moment that the Church should address. Out of a somewhat spontaneous episcopal reading of the signs of the times in 1980, a proposal was formulated to review and articulate Catholic teaching on modern warfare. Thus the Bernardin committee.[17]

In a similar way, the economics pastoral came to be after floor discussion on a statement about Marxism raised the issue of a need to assess capitalism from a Catholic perspective.[18] It was Archbishop Weakland who argued within the committee that what was needed was an assessment of a specific economy. Thus the letter became, not a document about capitalism, but a pastoral letter on the U.S. economy.

By these actions something new was emerging in the life of the U.S. church. Archbishop John Roach of St. Paul, perhaps optimistically, believed that there was a maturing relationship between the American bishops and the Vatican, one that would realize a deeper sense of collegiality within the episcopacy. This would lead the American bishops not only to "interpret the teaching of the Pope to the American church but also interpret the experience and insights of the American church to the Pope."[19]

Public Church

At the time of completing the economic pastoral, Archbishop Weakland suggested that underlying the process of writing the pastoral letters were "many ecclesial questions that will demand a broader vision and should provoke a deeper response on our part as a church." In Weakland's mind, "a new functional model of the church is at stake." Two questions that loomed large in this new model were (a)

17. James Castelli, *The Bishops and the Bomb* (New York: Image Books, 1983) 13–25.

18. In 1977 the bishops had approved a statement, at the request of the Vatican, condemning religious persecution in central Europe. During the discussion of the statement, Cardinal Carberry of St. Louis asked if there ought not to be a statement about the larger problem, namely, Marxism. The result was the decision to formulate a statement on Marxism (largely written by the philosopher Louis Dupré) that was approved in 1980. In the course of the discussion about the Marxism statement, Bishop Peter Rosazza made the point that an appropriate next step would be to examine capitalism from the perspective of Church teaching.

19. Thomas Reese, "American Bishops and Their Agenda" *America* (December 17, 1983) 393–394, at 393.

"how the church as a whole will enter into the debate in American society on political, social and economic issues"; and (b) how the clergy, especially the bishops, "will relate as teachers" to a "highly intelligent and trained laity."[20]

The pastoral letters had as their topics pressing moral concerns: the morality of national security policy and the moral dimensions of the U.S. economy. Yet, more was involved in the two pastorals than an ethical analysis of pressing social ills. It is clear that there was an implicit ecclesiology operative in the processes of drafting the letters, in the texts themselves, and in their reception. This implicit ecclesiology can be fairly summarized by two principles that roughly correspond with Weakland's two issues. One principle, the establishment of a public church, pertains to the external mission of Church and society, and the second principle, becoming a community of moral discourse, pertains to the internal issue of relations between bishops and laity.

First, however, the external principle: the Catholic Church is to be part of the "public church." The words "public church" signify ". . . those churches which are especially sensitive to the *res publica,* the public order that surrounds and includes people of faith."[21] The Catholic Church's social ministry will entail three things: (1) acceptance of responsibility for the well-being of the wider society; (2) respect for the legitimate autonomy of public institutions; and (3) a pledge by the Church to work with other institutions in shaping the common good of the society.[22] All three aspects demand a nuanced understanding of the relationship between Catholicism and the wider society.

Augustine asked: Should the Church care only for the City of God and be indifferent to the fortune of the city of humankind? Or should the Church seek to closely involve itself in the second city in order to transform it into a closer approximation of the City of God? Most Catholic theologians have taken positions that try to acknowledge both the different goals of Church and temporal society and the shared interests both have in a just social order. Yet choices have to be made, and we have seen the Church make different choices over the centuries.

Catholicism pursued a strategy of selective engagement organizationally, with many Catholic institutions playing an important role in

20. Rembert G. Weakland, O.S.B., "The Church in Worldly Affairs: Tensions Between Laity and Clergy," *America* (October 18, 1986) 201–205, 215–216, at 201.

21. Martin E. Marty, *The Public Church* (New York: Crossroad, 1981) 3.

22. Michael J. Himes and Kenneth R. Himes, O.F.M., *Fullness of Faith: the Public Significance of Theology* (New York: Paulist Press, 1983) 2.

providing social services, health care, and education to a wider society while also maintaining a strong subculture of sensibility and identity. This U.S. approach was substantially different from the dominant approaches found in European Catholicism during the same period, views that reflected either integralism or Catholic Action.

Clearly, then as now, a great deal of leeway exists for determining how the Church will act in society. Key to understanding which strategy will be adopted are the three reasons that real estate agents use to explain the value of a property: location, location, and location. So much depends on the social location of the Church when strategizing about its mission to society.

The bishops at the Second Vatican Council sought to articulate in *Gaudium et Spes* a framework for understanding the Church's role in worldly affairs. The religious mission of the Church is to witness to the reign of God. This religious mission has indirect political consequences for the Church's ministry. Working with institutions like government, schools, organized labor, business groups, and voluntary associations, the Church can play its role of serving the reign of God by defending human dignity, protecting human rights, promoting human unity, and assisting people to find meaning in their everyday lives.[23] To exclude responsibility for society is to restrict the presence of God's reign only to limited areas of human life. This is the privatization of the gospel.

Such a broad theological framework as sketched here still leaves room for debate on specifics. Faithful Catholics remain at odds over whether certain strategies for engagement are too sectarian or too compromised. My reading of Vatican II and the history of American Catholicism suggests that the style most appropriate to our social location is that of a public church. Still we must discuss how to be a public church. By choosing a place along a spectrum ranging from the model of pure witness to that of being an agent for social change, we place limits on what the Church can and cannot do in public life.

In both pastoral letters the bishops chose a particular strategy for being a public church, one that answered yes to three questions: (1) Do we as a Church expect to change a diverse and secular society? (2) Ought we to commit ourselves to energizing devoted church members? (3) Should we also speak to those people of good will who stand outside our tradition?

23. GS 40-43.

Among the chief ways within American society that a public church will serve the commonweal responsibly is by the cultivation of a morally sensitive citizenry. Democracies require this in order to survive. Citizens must have an overarching sense of the nobility and characteristics of the American experiment, as well as a critical understanding of the moral ills embedded in that experiment. Morally reflective and politically engaged citizens play a transformative as well as supportive role in political life. A morally serious politics fosters a spirit of commitment to something larger than oneself and encourages a redefinition of the self in light of ideals that generate moral claims upon a citizen.

I believe the entire enterprise of creating both *The Challenge of Peace* and *Economic Justice for All* exemplified the U.S. Catholic community acting self-consciously as a public church. There was no serious expectation that the letters of the bishops would simply become the new policies of the U.S. government. Nor was there any effort by coercive threats or intemperate warnings to deny the rightful independence of elected officials and professionals in serving the nation. What was evident was a keen sense of the duty that the Church had to bring its moral wisdom to bear on the important topics of the nation's security and economy. The pastoral letters were written in an attempt to communicate our moral tradition, an attempt to resurrect concern for public discussion to guide government and promote greater citizen participation in formulating public policy.

By becoming a public church, we partly answer Archbishop Weakland's search for a new functional model of Church, namely, "how the church as a whole will enter into the debate in American society on political, social and economic issues." Still questions remain for a public church pursuing such a strategy. When is compromise permissible, when is it no longer tolerable? Are there issues on which no compromise is possible? What are they? Are there issues on which the Church stands ready to compromise? Can we name these? When the Church's position is a dissent from the societal consensus on an issue, what can be demanded of those in public office and influential positions who must lead the society?[24]

We have seen substantial division caused by different answers to these questions. When applied to abortion, capital punishment, civil rights for homosexuals, welfare reform, armed intervention, physician-assisted

24. Weakland, "The Church in Worldly Affairs," 215–216.

suicide, and an array of other issues, we have seen a wide and not particularly consistent set of responses from church members. Nor has civility in debate been particularly evident on many of these topics.

A Community of Moral Discourse

Reflecting on the pastorals, Archbishop Weakland suggested that
maintaining unity between clergy and laity is important and that writing the pastoral letters enhanced the unity between bishops and laity.
This leads to the second principle on the ecclesiology of the pastoral
letters: the internal principle that the Church will be a "community of
moral discourse."

The letters spoke the Church's mind to the general citizenry and in
a special way provided guidance for American Catholics. This approach
to moral education took seriously much of what we have discovered
about how adults learn best: dialogical and participative models of education are preferable to monological approaches, especially in moral
education, where the aim is not solely informational but the personal
appropriation of knowledge, making the truth meaningful.[25]

Employment of a dialogical model of adult learning is evident in several ways when one examines the pastoral letters. First, there was the
process of writing the letters. A large number of consultations went into
their formulation. Numerous scholarly figures in the fields of biblical
studies, theology, ethics, national security, economics, business, and social activism, as well as people who have played central roles in public
policy in various presidential administrations, were brought into the discussions.[26] In addition to the direct engagement with the committees
through meetings, a wide array of people had opportunities to influence
the letters due to the general circulation of drafts of the text. This procedure permitted editorial writers, journalists, academics, and interested
citizens to enter the debate. In brief, there was a wide-ranging dialogue
prior to the formulation of the documents. It was, in the words of the
economics pastoral, a process "of careful inquiry, wide consultation, and
prayerful discernment." The bishops went on to say that "the letter has
been greatly enriched by this process of listening and refinement."[27]

25. See the pastorally wise work of Timothy O'Connell, *Making Disciples: A Hand-
book of Christian Moral Formation* (New York: Crossroad Publishing, 1998).

26. It should be noted that among the theologians consulted were persons who were
banned from speaking in several dioceses by bishops.

27. EJA 3. However, Archbishop Weakland acknowledged that "some opposition
came to that procedure [i.e., the consultations] from certain church quarters; namely,

A second means whereby the dialogical model was at work in moral education was in the presentation of the teaching. The authors acknowledged that there were different levels of teaching in the documents, so people could read the letters without feeling as if disagreement or doubt was unreasonable or unfaithful. This explicit statement of degrees of certitude to be ascribed to moral teaching was familiar to earlier generations of priests reared on theological notes in seminary manuals. But it was a set of distinctions not always clear to most Catholics. As Ladislas Orsy once observed, "many of the faithful experienced . . . a 'crisis of faith' after Vatican II because they thought 'the teaching of the church has changed,'" when what had changed were not doctrinal truths but less certain teachings lumped together as "Church teaching" and therefore unchangeable in the minds of many.[28]

In our present time a frequent concern is voiced that the faithful have a right to know the teaching of the Church on a given topic. Without in any way challenging that claim, one ought to add that "[t]he faithful have a right to be informed correctly, as far as possible, concerning what point of doctrine belongs to the core of our Christian beliefs and what does not."[29] Such knowledge of the authority by which the Church teaches, if clear to all, would permit the furtherance of probing and constructive conversation among disciples in the formation of conscience.

Today, however, we find not greater but less clarity regarding the authority of Church teaching. Subsequent to the pastoral letters, we have received the Vatican document on the "Profession of Faith and Oath of Fidelity."[30] The next year came the instruction entitled *The Ecclesial Vocation of the Theologian*, which referred to a category of teaching that heretofore had not received a great deal of attention—definitive but not infallible doctrine.[31] Although this category is sometimes called

---

the fear was expressed that it could give the impression that the bishops were deficient in their knowledge of social justice and thus their teaching authority would be diminished." Rembert G. Weakland, O.S.B., "'Economic Justice for All' Ten Years Later," *America* 176 (March 22, 1997) 8–10, 13–19, 22, at 9.

28. Ladislas Orsy, "Reflections on a Canon," in Ronald P. Hamel and Kenneth R. Himes, O.F.M., eds., *Introduction to Christian Ethics* (New York: Paulist Press, 1989) 353–358, at 355.

29. Ibid.

30. Congregation for the Doctrine of the Faith, "Profession of Faith and Oath of Fidelity," *Origins* 18 (1989) 661, 663.

31. Congregation for the Doctrine of the Faith, "Instruction on the Ecclesial Vocation of the Theologian," *Origins* 20 (1990) 117–126.

the secondary object of infallibility, it has never been clear which teachings fit this category. Then in 1998 *Ad Tuendam Fidem* instituted a change in the Code of Canon Law to reflect this middle category of teaching standing between definitive, infallible dogma and authoritative teaching.[32] Cardinal Joseph Ratzinger offered a commentary on the text that furthered the confusion, precisely because he gave examples of teachings in this category that were not persuasive.[33] Using his criteria, one might have to include certain past teachings on usury or slavery. Whatever the outcome of theological development in this area, and without wishing to deny the existence of such a middle category of teaching, it can still be said that we are in a situation where the clarity of the authority of a teaching has become more muddled.

A third indication of the dialogical educational model at work in the pastorals was the open-minded tone of the letters. *The Challenge of Peace* stated, "This pastoral letter is more an invitation to continue the new appraisal of war and peace than a final synthesis of such an appraisal."[34] Taking their lead from no. 13 of *Gaudium et Spes*, the bishops admit that "on some complex social questions, the Church expects a certain diversity of views,"[35] even if there are shared moral convictions. No pretense existed that the final word had been spoken, only the conviction that the Church must speak a helpful word when it can in moral formation and public debate. This same approach can be found in the economics pastoral, where it is expressly stated that "there are . . . many specific points on which men and women of good will may disagree. We look for a fruitful exchange among differing viewpoints."[36] Perhaps the clearest example of living with tentative conclusions is the position of the peace pastoral in accepting both the pacifist and the just war traditions in the evaluation of war. Living not only with complexity but ambiguity is a sign the bishops realize that to press for more certainty than reality permits is no virtue.

In terms of educational philosophy, the letters followed a collaborative model of teaching in which the search for truth is participatory and mutual. All are learners in the community of disciples, and the office of pastor does not exempt one from ongoing learning even as one

---

32. John Paul II, *"Ad tuendam fidem," Origins* 28 (1998) 113–116.

33. Joseph Ratzinger and Tarcisio Bertone, "Commentary on Profession of Faith's Concluding Paragraphs," *Origins* 28 (1998) 116–119.

34. CP 24.

35. CP 12.

36. EJA 22.

is called to teach. The image of teacher suggested by the letters is not the lecturer at the podium refusing to entertain questions from students, but a fellow seeker of truth inviting critical reflection. Such an image of teacher assumes that adults have relevant experience and an understanding of their experience worth sharing with others.

This approach fits well in the U.S. with a high percentage of educated laity and a university system wherein free expression and inquiry are part of the academic ethos. Teaching adults in this context requires effective communication and persuasiveness. It is the intrinsic reasonableness of a moral teaching, not the extrinsic authority of those supporting it, which is the best guarantee that a teaching will be taken seriously. Traces of defensive hostility to questions or the promulgation of conclusions not open to further examination quickly undermines credibility. As Cardinal Avery Dulles puts it: "Generally speaking, the pastoral leaders should not speak in a binding way unless a relatively wide consensus has first been achieved. For authentic consensus to develop, there is need of free discussion."[37] The reception of the pastoral letters was advanced by the intellectual humility by which the teaching was put forth. By knowing their audience, the bishops gained the good will of the wider public and the interest of their fellow Catholics.

Perhaps the newer educational model is more time-consuming and somewhat messy, but in a Church and society in which appeal to authority is less persuasive than reasoned exposition and argument, the dialogical model of teaching is preferable. The important point to grasp is that the internal principle of the pastorals' ecclesiology reflects a claim that is as much psychological as theological. How do adults learn? Education processes that invite active involvement—questioning, launching thought experiments, discussion, experiential testing—are more effective than education that stresses docility and passive receptivity as the means to learning.

An ecclesiological strategy for moral formation that follows from such an approach to adult education would call upon the Church to become a community of moral discourse.[38] The ecclesial community

37. Avery Dulles, S.J., "Doctrinal Authority for a Pilgrim Church," in Hamel and Himes, *Introduction*, 336–351, at 348.

38. "The Church should be defined by a communal thinking effort in which all members of the community participate and share—albeit in different measure—the same responsibility." Klaus Demmer, M.S.C., *Shaping the Moral Life: an Approach to Moral Theology* (Washington: Georgetown University, 2000) 30.

ought to be a place where adult believers can gather to address the troubling issues of the day. In so many ways American society envelops people in a world of unreflective activity that prevents careful moral reflection. Stampeded into partisan debate and bombarded by information from all sides, the adult Catholic needs a time and place where thought, conversation, prayer, and moral discernment can occur. In their pastoral letters the bishops, in effect, suggested that the Church is an apt location for serious moral conversation. The letters constitute an invitation to envision a Church in which moral formation occurs through honest dialogue, mutual correction, and communal discernment.

The strategy of building a community of moral discourse ought to be the answer to the second of Archbishop Weakland's questions about the new functional model of Church: "how the clergy, especially the bishops, 'will relate as teachers' to a 'highly intelligent and trained laity.'"[39]

At the same time as it strengthens its pastoral strategy to generations of educated adult Catholics, the Church will also promote its presence in American public life. On the one hand, a vibrant community of moral discourse will feed and nourish the practices and institutions of a public church. On the other hand, a strong public presence in society must be coupled with the Church's internal life to avoid moral education becoming an introspective and private moral quest. Both the internal and external principles of the Catholic Church advance the life and mission of the Church, and failure in implementing either principle will harm the prospect of the other.

A Broader Vision

In his reflections on writing the economic pastoral, Archbishop Weakland observed that many questions emerged, questions that, in his words, "will demand a broader vision." Ten years later, in 1996, Weakland noted that the statistics cited in the pastoral letter for economic inequality "have become decidedly worse, not better." Yet, "there does not seem to be the will to take any corrective measures." On the topic of poverty, the need remains, but in Weakland's words, "missing now is the will . . . to take the big steps necessary to alleviate poverty, not just to reduce the number of people on welfare." In the

---

39. Weakland, "The Church in Worldly Affairs," 201.

area of unemployment "[t]he search for real jobs that bring sufficient wages and decent benefits is still often in vain."[40] Added to the lack of motivation or political will is another problem, seen more clearly ten years after the pastoral was written, and that is "the growing tendency to blame government for all our problems. It has become common-place today to hear speeches, one after the other, about the ineptitude of government. The solution then to all problems is to have as little government as possible."[41]

I cite the archbishop's remarks because they go to the heart of see-ing things with a broader vision. The real battleground in politics and the economy is not first to be found on Capitol Hill or Wall Street, or even in the corporate boardroom, on the factory floor, or on the mili-tary base. The most contested space is inside our heads, the realm of the imagination. By winning over people's loyalty at the level of imag-ination, that is, the images and metaphors we employ about our ex-perience, a public figure achieves a far broader goal than getting agreement on a particular topic of public life.

A number of years ago, while still teaching at Harvard, Robert Reich, the former Secretary of Labor, wrote a book entitled *Tales for a New America*.[42] He maintained that underlying all the campaign speeches and interviews given by politicians are a few basic stories that we tell and re-tell to ourselves. According to Reich, they are our "national parables." He sketched four of these narratives.

1. *The Rot at the Top.* This story has the lesson that Americans ought to oppose any group from becoming too powerful. It is a story of evil elites, be they corrupt business leaders, government officials, or cultural aristocrats. It is a tale of corruption in high places and plots against the public. Investigative reporters feed this belief. So, too, certain detective portrayals like Humphrey Bogart's Sam Spade and Jack Nicholson in *Chinatown* or real-life detectives like Frank Serpico find that the rot at the bottom of the society can be traced back up to the top.

2. *The Triumphant Individual.* In this parable the hard-working little person who is self-disciplined, faithful to the task, and willing to take a risk gets the reward of wealth, fame, and honor. The lesson is consis-tent: Anyone can make it in the U.S.A. if you work hard and persevere. Ben Franklin's *Autobiography*, Abe Lincoln's tale of a log-splitter who

---

40. Weakland, "'Economic Justice for All' Ten Years Later," 22.
41. Ibid., 18.
42. Robert Reich, *Tales for a New America* (New York: Random House, 1987).

becomes president, and the Horatio Alger stories are examples of this parable. We have films like *Rocky, Hoosiers,* and *Rudy.*

3. *The Benign Community.* The third parable paints a picture of friendly neighbors who roll up their sleeves and pitch in to help one another. It evokes a sense of patriotism, community pride, and self-sacrifice. This story has roots in the religious heritage of America. Perhaps the version most familiar to us today is Frank Capra's film *It's a Wonderful Life,* in which Jimmy Stewart learns that he can count on his neighbors' goodness as they once counted on him. The parable's moral: we must preserve and nurture community.

4. *The Mob at the Gates.* This last parable is about the darkness that lies just beneath the surface of democracy. It is a story that warns of how tenuous is the hold on civil order and how perilously close we are to chaos. It is a tale of mob rule, crime and indulgence, of society fragmenting due to excess. We find the *Federalist Papers* worrying about the instability of democracy. In the movies the parable is found in the lonely hero facing down social chaos: Gary Cooper in "High Noon" or Clint Eastwood as Dirty Harry. The meaning of the story is the need to impose social order lest the rabble take over.[43]

Reich maintains that these stories are familiar to us all. They undergird our ideologies, and shape our public consciousness. The stories can be put together in a variety of ways to emphasize one or the other lesson. For example, in the Progressive Era the Rot at the Top was linked with the Triumphant Individual to make the case that big business, in the form of emerging monopolies, had blocked the progress of the honest small businessperson. With Franklin Roosevelt the importance of the Triumphant Individual was replaced by the Benign Community parable. The Great Depression had taught a lesson in national solidarity as friends and relatives banded together to survive the effects of hard times and poverty. At the same time Roosevelt used the Rot at the Top to describe those he called "economic royalists" who took advantage of the lowly worker. Ronald Reagan used the Rot at the Top parable to attack government bureaucrats while celebrating the entrepreneur as the Triumphant Individual. Reagan warned about the Mob at the Gates in the person of welfare cheats, drug addicts, illegal immigrants and Central American revolutionaries. The Benign Community became a nostalgic appeal to the values of small town America where people voluntarily help one another without government mandates.[44]

43. Ibid., 8–13.
44. Ibid., 15–16.

We could extend this analysis to cover all types of political rhetoric, but the point is clear: every person, every community of persons, uses narrative to interpret the world. We all have a perspective on life by which we sort out its meaning, and this perspective is shaped by the images and metaphors that take up residence in our imagination. Narratives transmit these images and metaphors through our imaginative entry into the world portrayed.

It is to the realm of the imagination that Catholic social teaching must more often be directed. Only then will the Church be able to rally the political will to act. If Catholic social teaching can appeal to the imagination, it will be able to present its case persuasively to a wider public.

How we move from basic images, metaphors, parables, and stories to particular choices is not a simple trail of deduction. It is more a matter of discernment, arising out of our understanding of what is going on around us, and a judgment as to what behavior is most fitting, given how we see things. That is why so often we cannot "prove" to people that our moral judgments are right. What we can do is explain to others how we see the matter in light of our vision of reality, a vision formed within our imagination.

Explaining to others the way we see life and why we do what we do can be a more difficult task than at first considered. Forcing our moral vision into the procrustean bed of cost/benefit analysis or other dominant forms of public policy debate distorts the Catholic imagination. We cannot easily explain the social teaching of the Church to a culture whose imagination has been formed in ways that make the major elements of Catholic social teaching seem foreign.[45] One possible remedy is to find resonance between Catholic teaching and the neglected strands of American public discourse, the biblical and civic republican languages. As Robert Bellah and his colleagues argued when the economics pastoral was being written, these alternative forms of public discourse are necessary to supplement the dominant individualism of the culture.[46] Only then will themes like the common good, solidarity, and an option for the poor be understandable.

45. As Andrew Greeley makes clear: "Worldviews are not propositional paragraphs that can be explicated and critiqued in discursive fashion. Rather they are, in their origins and in their primal power, tenacious and durable narrative symbols that take possession of the imagination early in the socialization process and provide patterns which shape the rest of life." *The Catholic Imagination* (Berkeley, Calif.: University of California Press, 2000) 133.

46. Robert Bellah and others, *Habits of the Heart* (Berkeley, Calif.: University of California Press, 1985).

It is within the context of national parables, public languages, and American culture that we can appreciate the pastoral letters, especially *Economic Justice for All*. What that pastoral did was reassert certain biblical and civic republican ideas to demonstrate how they cast our economic life in a new light. The letter tried to enrich our public discourse by interjecting overlooked themes from the biblical and republican traditions into the national debate on the economy. By doing this, one might ascertain points of tension and points of agreement between Catholic teaching and the present reality of the economy.

Essentially, the economics pastoral was an effort by the bishops to move us toward a more communitarian self-understanding. That, in turn, might permit us to reframe the national parables used in our public speech. Thus the most significant aspect of the pastoral letter is chapter 2, where the bishops recall the meaning of justice in the Bible and then explain the meaning of justice today with biblical rather than liberal individualist premises.

It is by challenging the way in which we understand ourselves as a people that the power of the pastorals should be measured. Can we recapture a more communitarian vision of American life? Is it possible to recover the Benign Community parable in a manner that is less nostalgic, one with a more inclusive definition of community? Or must we continue to equate the American promise with successful individuals on the make?

If the categories in which we think of ourselves can be modified, then the possibilities for new policies become greater. The ideological framework must be altered if we are to change the operational structures of the economy. Therefore, it is correct, I believe, to see the letter as being in many ways an exercise in cultural critique more than economic analysis.[47] By that I mean that the letter should be read as a call to retrieve other interpretive strands of American experience besides the individualist one. Both critics and supporters of the Church's social mission should admit that such an agenda is closer to a religious community's strengths than the task of drawing up a blueprint for economic policy.

That is why the specifics of policy in chapter 3 of the letter came only after a lengthy discourse on the Catholic vision of economic life

---

47. At the end of their letter the bishops state: "In addition to being an economic actor, the Church is a significant cultural actor concerned about the deeper cultural roots of our economic problems." EJA 358.

in chapter 2. Apart from that context, the policies look less persuasive. The key, I believe, was the communitarian theme being espoused. If that were to take root, some of the specifics look more plausible. Without that change of key, few people will sing along with the bishops as they read the lyrics found in the policy sections of the document.

Both pastoral letters employed a similar strategy of seeking to speak to two audiences using two modes of discourse. Although the economics pastoral more successfully integrated the two modes of discourse, there were sections of both pastoral letters that relied upon biblical and explicitly theological language and sections that were cleansed of such language. The rationale presented for this was that policy language had to be accessible to more than Catholics and other Christians, whereas at other times the letters sought to inform the conscience of believers.

One difficulty with this approach, however, became obvious in the secular press's coverage of the economics letter. Going back and reading newspaper articles from the late fall of 1986, one is struck by how little attention was given to the first eighty-four paragraphs or so of *Economic Justice for All*. The entire treatment of biblical themes and most of the explanation of Catholic social teaching were largely ignored by secular journalists. For that reason the policy recommendations in chapter 3 received some harsh criticism and some praise, but also a measure of indifference, since in the minds of the secular press the bishops were offering little more than standard New Deal policies. The inability to convey the bishops' message was due to the neglect of the first part of the pastoral letter. I believe something similar happened in the case of the peace pastoral. In both cases the policy sections were treated by commentators as if they could stand alone and often were reported with little reference to the preceding materials.

The press coverage was a warning that we have not fully heeded in our social teaching. It is important for us to demonstrate that our social activism is an expression of our faith. We need to root our social teaching and activity in our theology. In this regard, I am reminded of a passage in *The Good Society*,[48] the sequel to *Habits of the Heart*. At one point the authors tell of a distinguished Protestant theologian who visited Washington "to advise a group of church board members, agency staffers, and activists." The theologian is quoted:

---

48. Robert Bellah and others, *The Good Society* (New York: Alfred Knopf, 1991).

After I'd spent a while laying out lines of theological justification on some of their major issues, one of the lobbyists raised his hand and asked, "What's the point of this? We agree on the issues. The point now is to organize and get something done about them." I turned to the director who had asked me down there, and said, "I'm sorry if I'm wasting your time. Just say so and I'll stop right now." That's part of their problem, of course, particularly the poli-sci types. They're so theologically inarticulate that they can't persuade anybody in the churches who doesn't already agree with them, and even then they come across as political partisans, not as reflective Christians.[49]

Bellah and his colleagues are recounting the experience of a scholar in a mainline Protestant church, which is seen as declining in its power to shape the ethos of a society. I cite the example to show the risk we run if we fail to be consciously and explicitly theological in explaining our social mission. The risk is that in trying to speak to a diverse nation, a public church can ignore its first audience—the people in the pews who remain unpersuaded or uninterested in the social mission.

For this reason, among others, it is imperative that we fashion a truly public theology— a recent term for the traditional concern to relate faith to the social ideas and movements shaping the world in which the Church exists. Both pastoral letters distinguished between the audience of Church and society. Without denying a legitimate distinction, I think it is an overdrawn divide when it is used to suggest that how one teaches should be dramatically different, speaking in theological language in one case, and in a style of public discourse cleansed of religious language and symbols to the second audience.

Public theology, understood as an "effort to discover and communicate the socially significant meanings of Christian symbols and tradition,"[50] can serve the two audiences identified by the pastoral letters. First, it can introduce into public conversation the wisdom that is resident within the Catholic tradition. The criticism of modernity's privileging of one type of discourse opens the door onto the public square for alternative forms of public discourse. The critique of modernity has made clear that "public reason" itself is a term of dispute, since all models of "reason" have communal and historical origins. It is not im-

49. Ibid., 192.

50. David Hollenbach, "Editor's Conclusion," in David Hollenbach, Robin Lovin, John Coleman, J. Bryan Hehir, "Theology and Philosophy in Public: A Symposium on John Courtney Murray's Unfinished Agenda," *Theological Studies* 40 (1979) 700–715, at 714.

mediately evident, therefore, why the reasoning of a particular religious community ought to be barred from the public square, for if it is intelligible and persuasive, it can make a contribution. And we ought not simply to presume that religious language and symbolism are unintelligible to those outside the religious tradition.

David Tracy's proposal that we evaluate not the origins of public discourse but its effects seems wise.[51] His position on the disclosive nature of a religious classic can be a way to go forward in making an argument for public theology. If the Catholic theological tradition can offer a wisdom that enriches public life, there seems to be no reason, in principle, why it should not be accepted as legitimate discourse in a pluralistic society. The argument that a public theology must be ruled inappropriate is not a case that should be settled in an *a priori* manner. Thus, in retrospect, the pastoral letters may have been a bit too timid in their presentation; the bishops were too quick to censor themselves in pursuit of a means whereby they could speak to an audience beyond the Catholic community. A public theology is an integral part of the functioning of a public church.

The second aim of public theology serves the task of creating a community of moral discourse. Recall that a major argument of *Habits of the Heart* was that unless we as a people use our alternative biblical and republican languages, we will cease being able to think in them. In effect, we will lose them if we do not use them. The pastorals sought to inform the consciences of Catholics in their understanding of the moral dimensions of national security policy and economic life, to help church members find alternatives to the dominant formulas of only national interest and narrow self-interest when discussing weapons and markets. The effort to explore what national security and economic life look like when viewed within the framework of Catholic teaching was an important exercise of teaching within a local church.

If educated American Catholics, so successfully assimilated into the cultural mainstream, cannot retain or discover the wisdom of our theological tradition for thinking about the meaning of the good life, the good society, and the global common good, then the social mission of the Church is in peril. For that tradition to be resurrected we need a vibrant public theology and new methods of transmission so that it may be appropriated by adults.

51. David Tracy, "Particular Classics, Public Religion, and the American Tradition," in Robin Lovin, ed., *Religion and Public Life* (New York: Paulist Press, 1986) 115–131.

Conclusion

The pastoral letters were important milestones in the development of American Catholicism. In the desire for a genuine inculturation of the Catholic faith within American culture, the Catholic community matured in two ways. First, it found its voice within the universal Church, and second, it discovered its place within a diverse society. Still, twenty years after the Bernardin and Weakland committees were first formed, we are left with challenges aplenty.

Catholics on the left of the bishops now ask whether the sense of local church that motivated the bishops twenty years ago has withered to the extent that enforced docility trumps creativity and self-initiative in naming and responding to the pastoral agenda before us. For others to the right, the issue is whether some U.S. Catholics will develop a sense of Church that, in practice if not in theory, ignores its ties with the universal Church.

A second set of questions pertains to the quest to become a public church. Will an assimilated Catholic population merely echo the dominant viewpoints and conventional wisdom of the wider culture? Will American Catholicism be simply co-opted by an affluent middle-class culture of comfort? Voices from Latin America faulted the economics pastoral for being too accepting of free-market economics, while others within our own nation maintained that the bishops sacrificed their prophetic voice in the peace pastoral by the determination not to condemn reliance upon a nuclear deterrent. In reply, others wonder whether the desire to speak a prophetic word and offer a clear alternative to business as usual would make Catholics so eccentric to public life that the social mission of the Church would become marginal to practical efforts of transforming society.

A third set of questions surrounds the effort to become a community of moral discourse. Can a Church that has a hierarchical teaching office develop strategies for teaching that effectively influence the moral formation of future adult Catholics? How can those charged with fulfilling the role of teacher in the community find processes that respect the diverse gifts and insights of a large, intelligent, and articulate Catholic population? Will the voices of the broad community of disciples be heard in the formulation of teaching? And will that teaching be received critically and appropriated personally by adult believers? Can the Church become a place where individuals want to participate so that they can wrestle with serious moral questions and clarify their viewpoints?

To a great extent, by focusing on activities like the pastoral letters the educational aspect of the social mission of the Church becomes paramount. Much of the activity subsequent to the publication of the letters was educational in nature. Yet Archbishop Weakland could observe that much of Catholic social teaching "has not been assimilated by our Catholic population."[52] It has not been formative of many Catholics in this nation. This may not be due to its rejection but to our inability to formulate a social teaching that resonates with the imagination of our people, tapping into the images and metaphors by which our people live. Have we as a Church focused on tutoring the imagination or passing on propositional formulas, be they liberal or conservative ones? Here is the issue of shaping a broader vision.

Subsequent to the completion of the writing of this essay, the church in the United States has been profoundly wounded by revelation of the sexual abuse scandal among its clergy and the woeful lack of leadership by the bishops in addressing it. The public voice of the Church will no doubt suffer due to this tragic episode. The bishops of the United States have taken their lumps at the hands of many critics, and rightly so. But Rembert Weakland and other pastoral leaders of this local church produced documents such as the pastoral letters *The Challenge of Peace* and *Economic Justice for All*. In the cooperation with theologians and other scholars evident in those letters, we can note the partially fulfilled promise of mutually rewarding collaboration between bishops and scholars. In the serious efforts to advance moral insight on public matters, we can see in our bishops the somewhat successful attempt to become a Church that enriches our society and invites the faithful to deeper discipleship.

I have suggested several ways in which the pastoral letters leave room for improvement or represent unrealized hopes. But it was pastoral leaders with wisdom, integrity, and skill who provided reasons for those hopes in the first place. At a time when the Catholic community needs to find common ground and heal rifts that hinder its witness to the gospel, we can do worse than recall the experience of what the local church of the U.S. can be when it tries to be a public church and attempts to create a community of moral discourse with a broad vision.

52. Weakland, "The Church in Worldly Affairs," 202.

Chapter Thirteen

The Bishop and the Proclamation of Biblical Justice

John R. Donahue, S.J.

Pity a poor bishop. He is expected to be a holy and dedicated priest, a wise and compassionate pastor, a caring guide to his clergy, one who mediates the teaching of the magisterium, an inspiring leader who energizes the lay talent in a diocese, a prophet who speaks out against evil and injustice in contemporary society, a careful steward and manager of the diocesan resources while remaining sensitive to the needs of the poor, all topped off by civic leadership, ceremonial occasions, and engagement in various commitments of the United States Conference of Catholic Bishops, while remaining abreast of the latest complex moral issues that did not even exist a decade or more ago. The surprising thing is that so many bishops have done these things so well.

The Bishop and Contemporary Catholic Social Teaching

The Second Vatican Council and the recent Synod of Bishops have been the major instances of magisterial reflection on the vocation of the bishop. The Decree on the Pastoral Office of Bishops in the Church *(Christus Dominus)*, after speaking of the relationship of the bishop to the Church universal, addresses the role of the bishop in his diocese.[1] Following the traditional division of teaching, sanctifying, and shepherding, the first role discussed is teacher, where "one of their principal duties" is to "proclaim to humanity the gospel of Christ."[2] This mission involves preaching and concern for the doctrine of the Church at

1. CD 11-35.
2. CD 12.

all levels, in accord with the vision of the Church articulated in the first sentence of The Church in the Modern World *(Gaudium et Spes):*

> The joys and hopes, the grief and anguish of the people of our time, especially of those who are poor or afflicted, are the joys and hopes, the grief and anguish of the followers of Christ as well. Nothing that is genuinely human fails to find an echo in their hearts.[3]

Two phrases of these citations—"proclaim to humanity" as those to be addressed by episcopal proclamation of the gospel, and "the people of our time, especially those who are poor or afflicted"—have given bishops a mandate to be concerned not only for Catholics in their dioceses but for all people, and especially for those who are suffering economic deprivation.

Contemporary Catholic social teaching builds on a corpus of papal and episcopal statements spanning more than a century, beginning with *Rerum Novarum,* issued by Pope Leo XIII on May 15, 1891, which dealt with problems associated with emerging modern capitalism (care for the poor, the rights of workers, the right to private property; the duties of workers and employers; the need for Christian morality; the role of public authority). This was followed by major encyclicals of Pope Pius XI, Pope John XXIII, with the intervening work of the Second Vatican Council, followed by a major encyclical and apostolic letter of Pope Paul VI, statements of the 1971 Synod of Bishops, and three major encyclicals by Pope John Paul II. The present Pope constantly addresses issues of poverty, human dignity, human rights, and protection of the innocent in his many pastoral visitations. The papal teaching has engendered many important statements by national groups of bishops, especially in the United States, beginning with "The Program of Social Reconstruction" (1919) and culminating in the pastoral letter *Economic Justice for All"* (1986), which was preceded and followed by teaching documents on the major social issues of our time.[4]

---

3. GS 1.

4. National Conference of Catholic Bishops, *Economic Justice for All: Pastoral Letter on Catholic Social Teaching and the U.S. Economy* (Washington: USCC, 1986), hereafter EJA. An excellent collection of documents is David J. O'Brien and Thomas A. Shannon, eds., *Catholic Social Thought: The Documentary Heritage* (Maryknoll, N.Y.: Orbis Books, 1992). This is the most up-to-date collection of documents and contains good introductions and brief commentaries. The older collections (Gremillion, Byers) remain helpful, since they often cover statements not found elsewhere, along with important introductions and comments. Surveys can be found in John A. Coleman, ed., *One Hundred Years of Catholic Social Thought: Celebration and Challenge* (Maryknoll,

The pontificate of Pope John Paul II has witnessed both an expansion and an intensification of the Church's concern for social justice. In addition to the three major social encyclicals, *Laborem Exercens* (1981), *Sollicitudo Rei Socialis* (1987), and *Centesimus Annus* (1991), he has spoken and written extensively on issues such as the need for human solidarity, the dangers of rampant capitalism, concern for threats to life in all its forms, and responsibility of rich nations to their poorer neighbors (often using the parable of the rich man and Lazarus in Luke 16:19-31 as an image of the neglect of the rich nations for the poor people at their doorstep), and has consistently articulated the "preferential option for the poor."[5] Despite attacks on this expression by Catholic conservatives, the Pope has continued to use this language with ever stronger applications.[6] In announcing the "Great Jubilee" (1993), he stated: "From this point of view, if we recall that Jesus came to 'preach the good news to the poor' (Matt 11:5; Luke 7:22), how can we fail to lay greater emphasis on the Church's preferential option for the poor and the outcast"?[7]

Most recently the *instrumentum laboris* ("working paper") for the 2001 Synod of Bishops devoted a whole section to the bishop as "promoter of justice and peace," stating forcefully:

> The Bishop, therefore, needs to take every occasion to stir in people's consciences the desire to live together in peace and to promote a shared determination to dedicate themselves to the cause of justice and peace.

N.Y.: Orbis Books, 1991). Especially helpful are: David J. O'Brien, "A Century of Catholic Social Teaching: Contexts and Comments"; John A. Coleman, "Neither Liberal or Socialist: The Originality of Catholic Social Teaching"; Archbishop Rembert G. Weakland, O.S.B., "The Economic Pastoral Letter Revisited." See also Michael Joseph Schuck, *That They Be One: The Social Teaching of the Papal Encyclicals, 1740–1989* (Washington: Georgetown University Press, 1991). An outline of major documents with discussion questions can be found in Michael J. Schultheis, Edward P. DeBerri, and Peter Henriot, *Our Best Kept Secret: The Rich Heritage of Catholic Social Teaching* (Washington: Center of Concern, 1987).

5. The literature on the moral teaching of Pope John Paul II is vast. See especially Gerard Biegel, *Faith and Social Justice in the Teaching of Pope John Paul II* (New York: Peter Lang, 1997); John Conley and Joseph Koterski, eds., *Prophecy and Diplomacy: The Moral Doctrine of John Paul II* (New York: Fordham University Press, 1999); and the essays in Charles E. Curran and Richard A. McCormick, eds., *John Paul and Moral Theology* (Mahwah, N.J.: Paulist Press, 1998) 237–375.

6. Archbishop Weakland has described this option in more inclusive terms as "the clear choice to come to the aid of the poor," in *Faith and the Human Enterprise: A Post-Vatican II Vision* (Maryknoll, N.Y.: Orbis Books, 1992) 100.

7. Apostolic letter *Tertio Millennio Adveniente* (Washington: USCC, 1994) 51.

It is an arduous task requiring dedication, enduring strength and constant education, above all directed towards the new generations so that they will commit themselves, with renewed joy and Christian hope, to the construction of a more peaceful and friendly world.[8]

The synod's final message to the People of God, "The Bishop: Weaver of Unity, Father and Brother of the Poor," cites statistics that 80 percent of the world's population survives on only 20 percent of the income, and 1.2 billion people "live" on less than one dollar a day, and affirms: "A drastic moral change is required. Today the social teaching of the church has a relevance which we cannot overemphasize. As bishops we commit ourselves to making this teaching better known in our churches."[9]

When combined with a century of social teaching and a constant stream of statements from the National Conference of Bishops on issues related to social justice, clearly the task of the bishop in this area is formidable. Since summaries of Church teaching are readily available, I will mention some of the more significant elements.

1. **The essential link between the social and religious dimension of life: the social, that is, the human, construction of the world is not "secular" in the sense of being outside of God's plan.**[10] Religion is not to be relegated to the Sunday morning world nor to the sphere of private devotion but should inform a person's public life in community.

2. **The dignity of the human person.** Made in the image and likeness of God, all people have a human dignity and fundamental rights that are independent of their gender, age, nationality, ethnic origin, religion, or economic status, embodied in the statement of the U.S. bishops that "the dignity of the human person, realized in community with others, is the criterion against which all aspects of economic life must be measured."[11] This dignity demands that

8. Synod of Bishops, Tenth Ordinary General Assembly, "The Bishop: Servant of the Gospel of Jesus Christ for the Hope of the World," *Instrumentum laboris* (Vatican City: General Secretariat of the Synod of Bishops and Libreria Editrice Vaticana, 2001), no. 142; available from http://www.vatican.va/roman_curia/synod/documents/rc_synod_doc_20010601_instrumentum-laboris_en.html; Internet; accessed 16 October 2002.

9. Published in *Origins* 31/22 (November 8, 2002), sec. 10.

10. The Second Vatican Council stated: "One of the gravest errors of our time is the dichotomy between the faith which many profess and their day-to-day conduct. . . . Let there, then, be no such pernicious opposition between professional and social activity on the one hand and religious life on the other" (GS 43).

11. EJA 28.

the fundamental questions to be posed to any economic system are: What does it do to people? What does it do for people? How do people participate in it?[12] In its concern for the dignity of the human person, Catholic social teaching has consistently affirmed the precedence of labor over capital, the importance of humane working conditions over efficiency of production, and the subordination of prosperity to the demands of love and justice.

3. **Promotion of the common good.** While affirming the dignity of the human person, Catholic social teaching has rejected radical individualism and consistently stressed that the fullness of human life is found in community with others. "The common good is the sum total of all those conditions of social living—economic, political, cultural—which make it possible for women and men to readily and fully achieve the perfection of their humanity."[13] The common good is not the "general" good, but the good of the community, which can demand that the needs of the poor take precedence over the privileges of the wealthy.

4. **A deep concern for the poor and all those who are marginalized or adversely affected in a given economic situation.** As articulated in the pastoral of the American bishops,

> [The option for the poor] imposes a prophetic mandate to speak for those who have no one to speak for them, to be a defender of the defenseless who in biblical terms are the poor. It also demands a compassionate vision that enables the Church to see things from the side of the poor and powerless and to assess lifestyle, policies, and social institutions in terms of their impact on the poor.[14]

5. **The common ownership of the goods of the earth and the summons to stewardship of the world's resources.** From the early Church writers to the present statements, the creation accounts of the Bible have been invoked to affirm that creation is God's gift to the whole human family and that "misuse of the world's resources or appropriation of them by a minority of the world's population betrays the gift of creation."[15]

6. **A growing sense of global solidarity.** This has emerged since the pontificate of John XXIII and Vatican II. We belong to one human

12. Ibid., 1; also Rembert G. Weakland, "How to Read the Economic Pastoral," in Weakland, *Faith and the Human Enterprise*, 95–107.

13. See Schulteis, De Berri, and Henriot, *Our Best Kept Secret*, 22.

14. EJA 52; see also nos. 87-89.

15. Ibid., 34.

family and as such have mutual obligations to promote the development of all people across the world.

One of the great strengths of this teaching has been its desire to address two distinct audiences: Roman Catholics and other Christians who share a similar vision, and people of good will, believers or not. The language and grounds for action draw on a developing tradition of natural law, enhanced by recent philosophical reflection on human rights. While Pope John Paul II frequently employs biblical texts and motifs in his social teaching, this represents a relatively recent trend.

The Biblical Renewal and Social Justice

Over the past fifty years, since the emergence of the biblical renewal with *Divino Afflante Spiritu* (1943), and stimulated by Vatican II, the Church in the United States has become much more of a Bible-reading, Bible-praying community. Vatican II mandated that Scripture be the soul of moral theology and stressed the need to ground ethics and theology in the biblical revelation.[16] These movements had impact on the two major letters of the U.S. bishops in the 1980s, *The Challenge of Peace* and *Economic Justice for All.* As chair of the committee that drafted the latter document, Archbishop Weakland argued that no matter how difficult the problems of interpretation and application of the biblical material, *if the document was to influence preaching and daily Church life,* there should be a scriptural section that would put people in touch with the major texts and social themes of the Bible.[17]

The biblical renewal has also expanded the notion of justice, and this expansion will be the major focus of this essay.[18] Biblical justice is similar to, but very different from, the necessary and precise understandings of justice that emerge from the philosophical tradition dating back to Aristotle and modified in Thomistic thought.[19] Even though justice is at once a transcendental and an analogous concept that is applied differently in specific situations, some major understandings and distinctions are almost universally accepted. Since ex-

16. OT 16.

17. Oral communication of Archbishop Weakland to the drafting committee.

18. This essay proposes primarily to survey aspects of "biblical justice" and to provide resources for further study. A much more lengthy treatment can be found in John R. Donahue, *What Does the Lord Require? A Bibliographical Essay on the Bible and Social Justice* (St. Louis: Institute for Jesuit Sources, 2000).

19. An excellent summary of these is provided in EJA 68-72.

cellent studies of traditional and contemporary usages of justice are readily available, I will direct my attention to some thoughts on "biblical justice."

"Traduttore"/"Traditore." A major problem confronting an initial reflection on justice in the Bible is that the Bible has a rich vocabulary of justice and injustice, which do not yield to a one-to-one correspondence in English.[20] The principal biblical terms are *ṣĕdāqāh* (used 523 times, along with *ṣedeq* 119 times) and *mišpāt* (422 times), which are very often used together. Space does not allow adequate exploration of the labyrinth of terms used for "justice" and their translations into Greek, Latin, and contemporary versions, so the emphasis will be put on the above terms and a major translation problem. In most contemporary English versions, *ṣĕdāqāh* is translated as "righteousness," and *mišpāt* is rendered as "justice" (or "judgment").

Biblical terms do not have the precision of concepts based in philosophical analysis, so distinctions between "justice" and "charity" or "justice" and "holiness" are much more murky in the Bible. A classic instance of the larger semantic fields embraced by these terms is the famous covenant renewal text of Hosea 2:21-22 (2:19-20 in RSV and NRSV).

> I will espouse you to me forever;
>> I will espouse you in right and in justice *(bĕ ṣeded wĕ bĕ mišpāt)*,
>> in love *(bĕ ḥesed)* and in mercy *(bĕ rahămîm)*;
> I will espouse you in fidelity *(b 'ĕmūnāh)*,
>> and you shall know the Lord (NAB).[21]

---

20. The major studies are: Eliezer Berkovits, "The Biblical Meaning of Justice," *Judaism* 18 (1969) 188–209; Pietro Bovati, *Re-establishing Justice: Legal Terms, Concepts and Procedures in the Hebrew Bible*, trans. M. J. Smith, *Journal for the Study of the Old Testament*, Supp. 105 (Sheffield, Eng.: JSOT Press, 1994); Léon Epsztein, *Social Justice in the Ancient Near East and the People of the Bible* (London: SCM Press, 1986); Barbara Johnson, "*mišpāt*," *Theological Dictionary of the Old Testament* 9:86–99, and *ṣādāq*, in *Theologisches Wörterbuch zum Alten Testament* 12:239–264; H. G. Reventlow, Y. Hoffman, eds., *Justice and Righteousness: Biblical Themes and Their Influence*, JSOT Supp. 137 (Sheffield, Eng.: JSOT Press, 1992); J. Pedersen, *Israel: Its Life and Culture*, vols. 1–2 (London: Oxford University Press, 1926) 337–340; K. H.-J. Fahlgren, *Sedàkà, nahestehende und entgegengesetze Begriffe im Alten Testament* (Uppsala: Almquist & Wiksell, 1932) 81. Fahlgren describes justice as *Gemeinschafttreue*, i.e., fidelity in communal life; Moshe Weinfeld, *Social Justice in Ancient Israel and in the Ancient Near East* (Minneapolis: Fortress Press; Jerusalem: Magnes, 1995).

21. See also Jer 22:15-16, where the doing of justice is equated with knowledge of the Lord.

The Revised Standard Version, the New Revised Standard Version, and virtually every other English edition translate *ṣĕdāqāh* as "righteousness" and *mišpāt* as "justice." Some other important examples would be:

> Right *(mišpāt)* will dwell in the desert
>   and justice *(ṣĕdāqāh)* abide in the orchard.
> Justice will bring about peace *(šalōm);*
>   right will produce calm and security (Isa 32:16-17 NAB).

A major problem arises in English from the connotations of the terms "righteous" and "righteousness" (generally used to translate the *ṣdq* word group). The Oxford English Dictionary defines righteousness as "justice, uprightness, rectitude, conformity of life to the requirements of the divine moral law, virtue, integrity."[22] The term was first introduced into English biblical translations under the influence of Cloverdale (1535). The problem is that in most people's mind "righteousness" evokes primarily personal rectitude or personal virtue, and the social dimension of the original Hebrew is lost. This has resulted in a virtual "biblical dialect" in which "righteousness" is relegated to the sphere of religion and personal piety. Imagine, for instance, people's reaction if we had a "department of righteousness" or we talked about "social righteousness."

The centrality as well as the richness of the biblical statements on justice is the very reason why it is difficult to give a "biblical definition" of justice, which, in the Bible, is a protean and multifaceted term. "Justice" is used in the legal codes to describe ordinances which regulate communal life (e.g., Exod 21–23) and which prescribe restitution for injury done to person and property as well as for cultic regulations. The Hebrew terms for "justice" are applied to a wide variety of things. Scales or weights are called just when they give a fair measure, and paths are called just when they do what a path or way should do—lead to a goal. Laws are just, not because they conform to an external norm or constitution, but because they create harmony within the community. Acting justly consists in avoiding violence and fraud and other actions that destroy communal life and in pursuing that which sustains the life of the community. Yahweh is just not only as lawgiver and Lord of the covenant; his saving deeds are called "just deeds" because they restore the community when it has been threat-

---

22. *The Compact Edition of the Oxford English Dictionary*, vol. 2 (Oxford: Oxford University Press, 1971) 2584.

ened. The justice of Yahweh is not in contrast to other covenant qualities such as steadfast love *(ḥesed)*, mercy *(raḥămîm)*, or faithfulness *('ĕmūnāh)*, which is virtually equated with them.

In general terms, the biblical idea of justice can be described as *fidelity to the demands of a relationship.*[23] God is just when he acts as a God should, defending or vindicating his people or punishing violations of the covenant. People are just when they are in right relationship to God and to other humans. In contrast to modern individualism, the Israelite is in a world where "to live" is to be united with others in a social context either by bonds of family or by covenant relationships. This web of relationships—king with people, judge with those pleading a cause, family with tribe and kinsfolk, the community with the resident alien and suffering in their midst, and all with the covenant God—constitutes the world in which life is played out. The demands of the differing relationships cannot be specified *a priori* but must be seen in the different settings of Israel's history.

An important perspective has been offered by J. P. M. Walsh, who underscores the social dimension of *ṣedeq* by describing it as "consensus" about what is right.[24] People in all societies have some innate sense of this, even though it differs in concrete situations. Biblical revelation of *ṣedeq* involves the consensus that is to shape God's people. Walsh relates *ṣedeq* to *mišpāt*, the implementation of justice *(ṣedeq)* by action (juridical or otherwise). Finally, he treats *nāqām* (lit. "vengeance") as the process by which "consensus" or sense of rightness is restored. The thrust of Walsh's whole work is that the biblical tradition gives a different vision of these seminal concepts than the modern liberal tradition. In the biblical traditions these terms define a consensus against the misuse of power and disclose a God who is on the side of the marginal.

Recent commentators have also stressed the social dimension of *ṣ*d*q*h* and *mspt*. For example, Walter Brueggemann, arguably the premier Old Testament theologian today, describes *ṣĕdāqāh* as "equitable, generative social relations."[25] In commenting on Amos 5:24, Barbara Johnson, author of two foundational studies of these terms,

23. See John R. Donahue, "Biblical Perspectives on Justice," in *The Faith That Does Justice: Examining the Christian Sources for Social Change*, ed. John C. Haughey (New York/Ramsey, N.J.: Paulist Press, 1977) 69. The definition is similar to the descriptions now proposed by Barbara Johnson; see note 20 above.

24. J. P. M. Walsh, *The Mighty From Their Thrones* (Philadelphia: Fortress Press, 1987).

25. Walter Brueggemann, *Isaiah 1–39*, Westminster Bible Companion (Louisville: Westminster/Knox, 1998) 48.

writes: "Here *ṣedeq* is understood as the normative principle and *mišpāt* as the standard of conduct which must conform to *ṣedeq* (cf. Ps 119:160)."[26] Especially significant is the conjunction of *ṣĕdāqāh* and *mišpāt* by hendiadys (the use of two terms to convey single meaning), which many recent scholars interpret as "social justice" (e.g., Isa 1:27; 5:16; 9:7; 32:16; 56:1; Ps 72:2; 89:14).[27]

Reflections on "Biblical Justice"

The massive contributions of biblical studies over the past half-century have been a mixed blessing for many seeking to proclaim biblical justice. For Catholics especially, the Bible has provided a rich source for reflection on issues of social justice. At the same time, a rigorous reading of the texts in their original context can so emphasize the difference between the world behind these texts (e.g., small agrarian or monarchic societies) and our modern complex structures that many feel it is anachronistic, for example, to apply Isaiah's criticisms of injustice to our world today. In addition, a proliferation of different methods and different schools of interpretation have left people doubting if anything consistent can be said about the Bible. While we are aware of these problems, certain working guidelines can be proposed.

1. Often more important than the preparation of the sermon or the class is the preparation of the preacher or the teacher. The great Protestant ethicist James Gustafson has commented that the Bible does not offer revealed morality but revealed reality and summons us to ask what God is requiring and enabling us to do; that is, the Bible tells us the kinds of people we are to become if we are to hear its message faithfully.[28] The first task is increased knowledge of pertinent biblical texts in their historical and literary context, but read with a concern for issues of social justice. Allied to this is a "hermeneutics of suspicion" about interpretations that support individualized piety. Philip Esler states that Luke's writings are read through a layer of *embourgeoisement* to foster middle-class values.[29] One way to avoid this is to be-

---

26. Johnson, "*mišpāt*," 93.

27. This has been developed in the important doctoral dissertation of Thomas LeClerc, "*Mišpāt* (Justice) in the Book of Isaiah" (Ph.D. diss. Harvard University, 1998).

28. J. F. Gustafson, *Can Ethics Be Christian?* (Chicago: University of Chicago Press, 1975), esp. 156–159.

29. Philip Esler, *Community and Gospel in Luke-Acts: The Social and Political Motivation of Lucan Theology*, Society for New Testament Studies Monograph Series 57 (Cambridge: Cambridge University Press, 1987) 53.

come aware of the social dimension and the social context of biblical material.

2. The Bible is both a historical document and a canonical and sacred text for a believing community. It is proclaimed in liturgy and is "the soul of theology." Though virtually no one feels that the Bible offers concrete directives or solutions to today's complex social problems, it is the foundation of a Judeo-Christian vision of life. It discloses the kind of God we love and worship. This God is interested in the world, in human history, and in the manner in which humans live in community. This is pervasive throughout both Testaments. In one sense, the "faith that does justice" is simply an application of the great command to love God with one's whole heart, mind, and soul and one's neighbor as oneself. What the Bible relentlessly affirms from the law of Moses to the Pauline summons to "bear one another's burdens, and in this way . . . fulfill the law of Christ" (Gal 6:2 NRSV) is that the love of neighbor is manifest especially in care for the weak and the powerless. When such a pervasive motif is found in multiple biblical literary genres (laws, prophets, wisdom teaching) that are handed on and reinterpreted over a millennium, it can be seen as central to biblical revelation.

3. Some principle of analogy is helpful for application of the biblical texts. Though the social and cultural situation of biblical texts is very different from our modern, post-industrial society, there are profound analogies, especially at the level of human behavior. Amos's criticism of the ostentatious rich (2:6-7; 4:1; 6:4-7), the plight of the poor man in Psalm 10, or the blindness of the wealthy to the needy at their gates (Luke 16:19-31) are hauntingly familiar in our own day. Paul's concern for the poorer churches of Palestine and even his collection strategy (2 Cor 8–9) have relevance to a church in the United States increasingly divided along socioeconomic lines. Paul Tillich once defined the task of theology as one of correlation of the symbols of the faith (where symbol is understood as sacred text and sacred tradition) with the existential question of a given age. In our age socioeconomic questions are the most pressing, and conversion, study, and imagination are necessary to achieve the task of correlation.[30]

4. Often the best way to speak about the inner meaning of justice as understood in the Bible is not to talk explicitly about justice, but

---

30. Paul Tillich, *Systematic Theology*, vol. 1 (Chicago: University of Chicago, 1951) 59–66.

about what justice means and about its related terms, for example, treating people with dignity; awareness of God's love for the "outsider"; fidelity to the demands of relationships on one's life; lovingkindness and compassion. One must get in touch with the parables and stories of Jesus in which the fundamental meanings of justice are affirmed, for example, the Good Samaritan, and the Rich Man and Lazarus.

Central Themes of "Biblical Justice"

At the risk of oversimplification, I would like to highlight some of the central themes and motifs of "biblical justice," drawing on resources from both Testaments.

A Theology of Creation. The biblical understanding of creation is not primarily about the origin of the world but about *its purpose.* Genesis 1:1–2:4 is punctuated by the refrain "God saw how good it was."[31] This is a blessing. As a preamble to the whole Bible, this account proclaims that the proper response to creation is praise and thanksgiving, even amid suffering and catastrophe. Two obvious implications of Genesis 1:1–2:4a are that (1) the response to creation is reverence and praise, not exploitation, and (2) humanity shares a solidarity with both the inanimate and animate world in owing its existence to the word of God. Other expressions of this: "The earth is the LORD's, and all that is in it" (Ps 24:1 NRSV); men and women crowned with honor and glory have dominion over the work of the Lord's hands (Ps 8:5). The New Testament builds on this foundation. The Christian prays, "Your kingdom come; your will be done *on earth* as it is in heaven" (Matt 6:10 NRSV). Jesus announces and symbolizes the presence of the kingdom by "mighty works" that touch the suffering of people in the here and now. When Jesus calls the poor "blessed . . . for theirs is the kingdom of heaven" and promises that those who suffer persecution for the sake of justice will be satisfied (Matt 5:3-10), he is proclaiming that *they are to be the beneficiaries here and now of his kingdom proclamation.* The kingdom is to transform those conditions under which they live.

The Christ-event as the foundation of Christian faith demands responsibility for the world. This is a corollary to the theology of creation theme. Christian faith in the death and resurrection is not simply faith in the promise of eternal life but faith in the *victory over death* achieved

---

31. See especially the fine treatment by Claus Westermann, *Creation* (Philadelphia: Fortress Press, 1974).

in Jesus. Through baptism Christians participate *already* in this victory: "We have been buried with him by baptism into death, so that, just as Christ was raised from the dead by the glory of the Father, so we too might walk *in the newness of life*" (Rom 6:4 NRSV). The Christian contrast is *not* between earth and heaven or between material and spiritual reality, but between the "old age" and "the new" (see esp. Rom 8; 2 Cor 5:16-21). Fundamental to new life in Christ is the experience of power: "With great power the apostles gave their testimony to the resurrection of the Lord Jesus" (Acts 4:33 NRSV; see 1 Cor 1:18-31; 2 Cor 12:9-13). The Christian is to be a *witness in mission* of the victory over death and the transforming power of the resurrection.

Covenant, Law, and Justice. In contrast to a philosophical foundation for justice, biblical justice is mediated by God's self-disclosure and human response. Paradigmatic for this is the covenant between God and the people. When Israel was freed from the slavery of Egypt, this freedom, as Michael Walzer has noted, was to be a bonded freedom—not simply freedom from external oppression but a freedom expressed in commitments to God and others.[32]

The distinctive understandings of justice are revealed in the law codes of Israel, and especially in their concern for the powerless in the community. Though examining the history and scope of the law codes is beyond the purpose of this essay, I will mention a few things that are important for a biblical foundation of social justice today.[33]

The codes themselves comprise: (1) the Covenant Code (Exod 20:22–23:33), parts of which date from northern Israel in the ninth century B.C.E. and which reflect pre-monarchic rural life, though, like the rest of the Pentateuch, it receives its final shape after the Exile; (2) the Decalogue, found in two versions (Exod 20:1-17 and Deut 5:6-21), which represent early covenant law; (3) the Deuteronomic code (Deut 12–26), which embodies traditions from the seventh century B.C.E. and perhaps from Josiah's reform, but which was incorporated into the full-blown "Deuteronomic history" only after the Exile; (4) the Holiness Code (Lev 17–26), put together after the Exile and often attributed to priestly circles. It is also similar to the thought of Ezekiel.

32. Michael Walzer, *Exodus and Revolution* (New York: Basic Books, 1985).

33. See the excellent treatments in Walter Harrelson, *The Ten Commandments and Human Rights* (Philadelphia: Fortress Press, 1980; rev. ed. Macon, Ga.: Mercer University Press, 1997); J. David Pleins, *The Social Visions of the Hebrew Bible: A Theological Introduction* (Louisville: Westminster John Knox, 2001) 41–91; and Norbert Lohfink, "Poverty in the Laws of the Ancient Near East and the Bible," *Theological Studies* 52 (1991) 34–50.

I will confine my comments on the legal texts to those sections that deal with the powerless (often made concrete as "the poor," "the widow," "the orphan," and "the stranger in the land").

Norbert Lohfink (whom I follow extensively here) has cautioned against viewing concern for the poor, etc., as "unique" to Israel's faith. A survey of a number of Mesopotamian texts (such as the Code of Hammurabi) and Egyptian wisdom texts shows a similar concern for *personae miserae*, with the exception of care for "the stranger in the land," which is distinctive to Israel.[34] While the content of concern is similar, the foundation and motivation are different. In Israel, care for such persons is part of the "contrast society" that is created through the Exodus. Also in Israel, this concern functions more as a critical principle against the misuse of power, while in some of the surrounding cultures it is a way in which those in power dampen down revolutionary tendencies of the people and thus maintain a divinely sanctioned hierarchy of power. Also, as Paul Hanson notes, in Israel responsibility for the well-being of such people devolves on the covenant community as a whole and not simply on the king.[35]

Concern for the powerless emerges first as part of the Covenant Code (see above). For our purposes, the first important section is Exodus 22:21-27. Here God says, "You shall not wrong or oppress a resident alien, for you were aliens in the land of Egypt" (v. 21, NRSV; note the motivation of a contrast society). The following verse proscribes abuse of the widow and the orphan, with the promise that God will heed their cry and "kill with the sword" their oppressors. The section concludes with the prohibition of lending to the poor at interest and enjoins restoring a neighbor's cloak taken in surety for a loan. Here also the motivation is God in his role as the protector of the poor: "And if your neighbor cries out to me, I will listen, for I am compassionate" (Exod 22:27 NRSV).

The next section contains a series of laws on the proper administration of justice. One of the first states: ". . . you shall not side with the majority so as to pervert justice; nor shall you be partial to the poor in a lawsuit" (Exod 23:2-3 NRSV). The prohibition of "partiality" to the poor in the specific context of a lawsuit does not contradict the concern for the marginal, since verse 6 immediately says that "you

---

34. Norbert Lohfink, *Option for the Poor: The Basic Principle of Liberation Theology in Light of the Bible* (Berkeley, Calif.: BIBAL Press, 1988).

35. Paul D. Hanson, *The People Called: The Growth of Community in the Bible* (San Francisco: Harper and Row, 1986).

shall not pervert the justice due to your poor in their lawsuits" (there is no corresponding statement on the rich or powerful), and verse 9 repeats the command to protect the alien. In verses 10-11, in a more cultic setting, the code mandates a sabbath year of leaving land fallow "so that the poor of your people may eat."

The second major block of legal material that deals with the poor comes from the Deuteronomic legislation of Deuteronomy 12–26. Lohfink points out that the ideal in the Covenant Code of a contrast society without oppression and poverty was in fact not realized, and locates Deuteronomy in this context. While retaining an ideal that "there will be no one in need among you, because the LORD is sure to bless you" (Deut 15:4 NRSV; cf. Acts 4:34), Deuteronomy realistically states: ". . . there will never cease to be some in need on the earth," and commands, "Open your hand to the poor and needy neighbor in the land" (Deut 15:11 NRSV). More strongly than the other codes, Deuteronomy commands justice and compassion for the powerless (Deut 15:1-18; 24:10-15; 26:11-12).

The historical significance of Deuteronomy is as evidence for a continuing concern in Israel's law for the *personae miserae*, which attempts to institutionalize the covenant ideal through law and practice. The significance of Deuteronomy in its present canonical location is that it is cast in the form of farewell speeches from Moses to the people on the brink of the Promised Land. The land is God's gift on condition of fidelity to the covenant (Deut 12:1 NRSV: "These are the statutes and ordinances that you must diligently observe in the land that the LORD, the God of your ancestors, has given you to occupy"). When read *after the Exile*, this can be seen as a warning against an infidelity that allows to develop the kind of society that is in opposition to the Exodus event and the Sinai covenant.[36]

The Holiness Code (Leviticus 17–26) contains provisions similar to those of Deuteronomy. In Leviticus 19:9-10 and 23:22, gleanings from the harvest are to be left for "the poor and the alien," though, as Lohfink points out, specific mention is not made of "the widow and the orphan," who now seem to be subsumed under "the poor." The Holiness Code also spells out in detail other provisions for the poor, very often those who have come suddenly upon hard times (Lev 25:35-42, 47-52).

36. On the social importance of covenant, see especially Walter Brueggemann, *A Social Reading of the Old Testament*, ed. Patrick D. Miller (Minneapolis: Fortress Press) 43–69.

Leviticus is also more concerned with the details of repayment of debts and cultic offerings made by the poor (Lev 12:8 = Luke 2:24).

The significance of Leviticus is twofold. First, though it is primarily a cultic code concerned with the holiness of the people and the means to assure that holiness, it manifests a practical concern for the poor in the land. As John Gammie has shown in his excellent study, there is no tension between Israel's concern to be a holy people consecrated to God and a people concerned about justice.[37] Secondly, and perhaps less positively, Leviticus seems to represent a relaxation of some of the earlier provisions for the poor. Lohfink argues that the stipulations of the jubilee (Lev 25:8-17, 23-25; 27:16-25), when debts are canceled every fiftieth year, would hardly benefit the majority of people who lived in poverty and would represent a step back from the sabbath year legislation of Deuteronomy. The Holiness Code may also reflect the radically changed postexilic political situation, when the monarchy was extinct and people had limited ability to enshrine the ideals of the covenant in law. This period also represents the beginning of apocalyptic thought, when many groups projected the hope of God's justice and a society free of oppression and poverty to a new heaven and new earth that would be ushered in by cosmic cataclysm.

The events of salvation history, especially the leading out from Egypt and the covenant at Sinai, are thus the foundations in Israel of a society that seeks justice and manifests concern for the marginal. This concern is incorporated in law and custom, which take different shapes in different historical circumstances, stretching over five centuries. As founding documents not only of the historical people of Israel but also of the Christian Church, they offer a vision of life in society before God that is to inform religious belief and social practice.

The laws of Israel have two great values. First, they show that religious belief must be translated into law and custom, which guide life in community and protect the vulnerable. Paul Hanson states this well in describing *torah* as "faith coming to expression in communal forms and structures."[38] In our contemporary pluralistic society, the Church and its episcopal leadership rightly strive to infuse the legislative process with a vision of social justice.

Secondly, although these traditions do not offer concrete directives for our complex socioeconomic world, they offer a vision of a "contrast

---

37. John G. Gammie, *Holiness in Israel* (Minneapolis: Fortress Press, 1989).
38. Hanson, *The People Called*, 47.

society," not ruled by power and greed, where the treatment of the marginal becomes the touchstone of "right relationship" to God. Christians today must ask soberly how our lives provide a contrast society, and whether, when we think of our "right relation" to God, the concerns of the marginal in our own time have been really made concrete in our attitudes and style of life.

Biblical Justice, the Poor, and the Prophetic Critique of Wealth. If there is one pervasive biblical motif in both Testaments, it is concern for the poor and marginal, which is the subject of an increasing number of studies. The question of the poor raises many problems, from their identity (e.g., economically poor or spiritually poor), to the social location of statements concerning them, to different evaluations of a response.[39] Since the biblical vocabulary for the poor is much richer than ours, at the risk of seeming overly technical I will indicate some of these. There are five principal terms for the poor.

1. '*ānî* (plural '*ăniyyîm*) probably derives from a root '*nh*, meaning "bent down" or "afflicted," and occurs eighty times in the Old Testament; in the Greek translation of the Old Testament (= LXX) translated by *ptōchos* ("beggar" or "destitute person") thirty-eight times, by *penēs* or *penichros* ("needy person") thirteen times, and by *tapeinos* ("lowly"; cf. Luke 1:52) nine times, or *praus* ("gentle") four times;

2. '*ānāw* (plural '*ānāwîm*) derives from the same root as '*ānî* and was often confused by copyists (e.g., at Qumran); used twenty-five times, translated most often by *tapeinos* and *praus* ("humble" and "lowly"), but also by *ptōchos* and *penēs*;

3. '*ebyôn* (the term "Ebionites" derives from this); root is very debated, from word meaning "lack" or "need," or "wretched," "miserable"; used sixty-one times in the Old Testament (especially in the Psalms, twenty-three times); appears often in stereotyped formula

---

39. The literature on the poor in the Bible is immense. See especially "'*ebyon*," in *The Theological Dictionary of the Old Testament*, G. J. Botterweck and H. Ringgren, eds. (Grand Rapids, Mich.: Eerdmans, 1974–) 1:27–41; "*dal*," ibid., 3:208–230; and "*ptochos*," in *The Theological Dictionary of the New Testament*, ed. G. Kittel, trans. G. W. Bromiley (Grand Rapids, Mich.: Eerdmans, 1964–) 6:885–915; and "The Poor," in *Harper's Bible Dictionary*, ed. P. J. Achtemeier (San Francisco: Harper & Row, 1985) 807–808; F. C. Fensham, "Widow, Orphan and the Poor in Ancient Near Eastern Legal and Wisdom Literature," *Journal of Near Eastern Studies* 21 (1962) 129–139; A. George, ed., *Gospel Poverty: Essays in Biblical Theology* (Chicago: Franciscan Herald Press, 1977), a very important collection of essays by leading French biblical scholars; the essays by George on the Old Testament and Dupont on the New Testament are highly recommended.

with *'ānî*, e.g., Deut 24:14; Jer 22:16; Ezek 16:49; 18:12; 22:29; translated by the Septuagint as *penēs* twenty-nine times, *ptōchos* ten times, and *adynatos* ("powerless") four times;

4. *dal*, from a term that means "be bent over" or "bend down," "miserable"; used forty-eight times; the Septuagint translates as *ptōchos* twenty-three times; *penēs/penichros* ten times; *asthenēs* ("weak" or "sick") five times; also used in synonymous parallelism with *'ānî* (Isa 10:2; 26:6; Zeph 3:12; Ps 72:13; 82:3; Job 34:28; Prov 22:22) and *'ebyôn* (1 Sam 2:8; Isa 14:30; Amos 2:7; 4:1; 5:11; Ps 72:13; 82:4; 113:7);

5. *raš*, "poor," in a derogatory sense, with overtones of a lazy person responsible for his or her own poverty. Not found in the Pentateuch or the prophets, but in the Wisdom literature (e.g., Prov 10:4; 13:23; 14:20; 19:7; 28:3).

The New Testament vocabulary is not as rich, using almost exclusively *ptōchos* about thirty-five times; for *penēs*, see 1 Corinthians 9:9; *penichros*, Luke 21:2; *tapeinos*, Luke 1:52; Matthew 11:29; Romans 12:16; James 1:9 and 4:6.

The importance of the terminology is twofold. First, it shows that "poverty" was not itself a value. Even etymologically the poor are bent down, wretched, and beggars. While the Bible has great concern for "the poor," poverty itself is an evil. Secondly, the terminology (as well as the actual use) is a caution against misuse of the phrase "spiritually poor." Though later literature (the Psalms and Qumran) often equate the poor with the humble or meek, and though the poor are those people open to God, in contrast to idolatrous or blind rich people, the "prime analogue" of the term is an economic condition. When the "poor in spirit" are praised, as in Matthew 5:3, it is because in addition to their material poverty, they are open to God's presence and love. Certain contemporary usages of "spiritual poverty," which allow it to be used of extremely wealthy people who are unhappy even amid prosperity, are not faithful to the biblical tradition. Nor is an idea of "spiritual poverty" as indifference to riches amid wealth faithful to the Bible. The "poor" in the Bible are almost without exception *powerless* people who experience economic and social deprivation. In both Isaiah and the Psalms the poor are often victims of the injustice of the rich and powerful. Isaiah tells us that the elders and princes "devour" the poor and grind their faces in the dust (Isa 3:14-15); out of injustice they turn aside the needy to rob the poor of their rights (Isa 10:2); wicked people "ruin" the poor with lying words (Isa 32:7). In the Psalms the poor, often called "the downtrodden," are contrasted not simply with the rich but with the wicked and the powerful (Pss 10:2-10; 72:4, 12-14). Today poverty is most often not simply an economic issue but arises when one group can exploit or oppress another.

The Prophets and the Call for Justice. When a people forgets its origins or loses sight of its ideals, figures arise who often speak a strident message to summon them to return to God. In Israel's history the prophetic movement represents such a phenomenon. The prophet, as the Greek etymology of the name suggests *(pro-phemi)*, speaks on behalf of another. This has a dual sense. The prophet speaks on behalf of God; he or she is a "forthteller," who also speaks on behalf of those who have no one to speak for them, specifically the powerless and poor in the land.[40]

Like all topics treated in this essay, prophecy is a minefield of historical and literary problems, so I will limit my reflections to a few introductory comments and then highlight some prophetic texts that bear on prophecy and justice.

For many decades the social teaching of Israel was virtually identified with the prophetic message. There is a danger in this when prophetic religion was often contrasted with a religion of law or was seen as a criticism of all cultic activity. The reduction of the religion of Israel to prophetic ethics often fostered an undercurrent of anti-Semitism, since postbiblical Judaism was and remains heavily centered on Torah. The attitude developed among some Christian scholars that the Judaism after the prophets was a decline into legalism. Also, the somewhat naive interpretation of the prophets as anti-cultic was often seen as justification for the reduction of religious life to social activism or a neglect of communal liturgical life.

---

40. Helpful overviews of the prophets, especially regarding their social message, are: Paul J. Achtemeier and James L. Mays, eds., *Interpreting the Prophets* (Philadelphia: Fortress Press, 1987), a series of articles originally published in *Interpretation*. They treat mainly literary and historical problems, with the essays on Jeremiah by Brueggemann and Holladay especially helpful, as is the "Resources for Studying the Prophets" by J. Limburg. Walter Brueggemann, *The Prophetic Imagination* (Philadelphia: Fortress Press, 1978) and Joseph Blenkinsopp, *A History of Prophecy in Israel*, rev. and enlarged ed. (Louisville: Westminster John Knox, 1996), are excellent standard introductions to all aspects of the prophets. See also Carol J. Dempsey, *The Prophets: A Liberation-Critical Reading* (Minneapolis: Fortress Press, 2000); Hemchand Gossai, *Justice, Righteousness, and the Social Critique of the Eighth-Century Prophets*, American University Studies, Series 7, Theology and Religion 141 (New York: P. Lang, 1993); James Limburg, *The Prophets and the Powerless* (Atlanta: John Knox Press, 1977); James L. Mays, "Justice: Perspectives from the Prophetic Tradition," in David L. Petersen, ed., *Prophecy in Israel: Search for An Identity* (Philadelphia: Fortress Press, 1987) 144–158; also in *Interpretation* 37 (1983) 5–17.

Recent research on the prophets has underscored a number of things that are of importance in assessing the prophetic texts that I will list below.

1. **The prophets are generally "conservative" in the best sense of the word.** They hark back to the originating experiences of Israel to counter corrupting influences of urbanization and centralized power that developed under the monarchy, especially after the split between the northern kingdom (Israel) and the southern kingdom (Judea) after the death of Solomon (922 B.C.E.). Their works are also a collection of traditions, some going back to the originally named prophets, others additions by disciples and later editors. Much recent research has attempted to describe these levels of tradition.

2. **The prophets are not opposed to cultic worship, but to its corruption.** Jeremiah was the son of a priest; Isaiah used cultic imagery, associated with the Jerusalem temple; Ezekiel was steeped in the cult. Recent research on Amos, often popularly portrayed as a "righteous peasant," has suggested some contact with the Jerusalem temple.

3. **In assessing the prophetic texts on justice and concern for the marginal, careful attention must be given to the literary context of a given text, but more importantly to its historical context.** Amos, for example, prophesied at the northern court shortly before the fall of Samaria to the Assyrians (721 B.C.E.). During this time, however, the northern kingdom experienced material prosperity. Under the reign of Solomon a more prosperous upper class had emerged. This created a class with a vested interest in the accumulation of land and goods as capital. The old emphasis on the land as the inheritance of every Israelite disappeared (see 1 Kings 21, the story of Naboth's vineyard). James L. Mays describes this: "the shift of the primary social good, land, from the function of support to that of capital; the reorientation of social goals from personal values to personal profit; the subordination of judicial process to the interests of the entrepreneur."[41] Amos's harsh words against the prosperous must be set in this context.

Isaiah of Jerusalem (Isa 1–39) flourishes roughly during the same period. His political message to Judea is that they have turned away from the poor and the downtrodden, that they should return to God and should avoid types of political entanglement that would ultimately spell the downfall of the northern kingdom. Though Isaiah is eloquent on the demand for justice, the motivation is different from

41. Mays, "Justice," 9.

that of Amos or Hosea. The controlling principle of much of Isaiah's teaching was his conviction of the holiness and kingly power of God. Oppression of the weaker members of the community offended Yahweh's holiness, so Isaiah vehemently criticizes injustice; furthermore, it distorted cultic worship.

4. **Though the prophets criticize the misuse of power by those in authority, their message is reformist rather than revolutionary.** They do not envision a community without a king or laws and statutes. During the bulk of the postexilic period (especially after the codification of the law under Ezra and Nehemiah), when the people lack their own kings and live under the successive rule of foreign powers (Persians, the successors of Alexander the Great, the Romans), prophecy as a movement within Judaism virtually ceases. Biblical prophecy required a shared heritage of values by the rulers and the ruled, even when those in power did not live up to those values. When people have no control over their destiny and are subject to brutal power, prophecy can take the form only of protest, not of a call to reform.

The Gospel of Luke and the Critique of Wealth. Often an objection is raised that while the Old Testament prophets are strong in their concern for the poor and speak out against social injustice, by the New Testament period prophecy has died out and few voices are raised about social issues. Jesus is often portrayed as preaching primarily the imminence of God's kingdom and the need for individual conversion. Such views are certainly not those of Luke, and most likely not of the historical Jesus (though this would be the subject of an even longer essay).[42]

The Lukan writings comprise about one quarter of the whole New Testament. With the exception of the Letter of James, the Lukan writings contain the most explicit statements on wealth, poverty, and the use of resources.[43] Luke's special concern is manifest from his editing

42. One of the interesting things is that two scholars on opposite ends of the spectrum among contemporary Jesus researchers, J. Dominic Crossan and N. T. Wright, both agree on the prophetic nature of Jesus' ministry; see John Dominic Crossan, *The Historical Jesus: The Life of a Mediterranean Jewish Peasant* (San Francisco: HarperSanFrancisco, 1992), and N. T. Wright, *Jesus and the Victory of God: Christian Origins and the Question of God* (Minneapolis: Fortress Press, 1997).

43. The writings on Luke and economic questions are extensive. See especially John R. Donahue, *The Gospel in Parable: Metaphor, Narrative and Theology in the Synoptic Gospels* (Philadelphia: Fortress Press, 1988) 162–180, on Luke's parables that deal with the poor; "Two Decades of Research on the Rich and the Poor in Luke-Acts," in D. A. Knight and P. J. Paris, eds., *Justice and the Holy: Essays in Honor of Walter Harrelson* (Atlanta, Ga.: Scholars Press, 1989) 129–144; Jacques Dupont, *Les béatitudes*, 3 vols. (Paris: Gabalda, 1969, 1973), especially vol. 2:19–142; vol. 3:41–64; 151–206; 389–471,

of the Markan tradition, and most importantly by the incorporation of "L" material (= material found only in Luke), which is itself a combination of tradition and Lukan composition. Luke-Acts has also been that New Testament work most often invoked on issues of social justice and concern for the marginal.

The Lukan infancy narratives show a special concern for the *'ānāwîm,* people without money and power. In her *Magnificat,* Mary praises a God who puts down the mighty from their thrones, fills the hungry with good things, and sends the rich away empty (Luke 1:52-53). The first proclamation of Jesus' birth is to people on the margin of society ("shepherds," 2:8-14); the sacrifice offered at his presentation in the temple is that determined by law for poor people (Luke 2:24); Simeon and Anna (a widow) represent faithful and just people (2:25-38). Luke begins the public ministry of Jesus, not with the proclamation of the imminence of the kingdom (cf. Mark 1:15; Matt 4:17), but with Jesus citing Isaiah 61:1-2, "the good news to the poor" (Luke 4:17-19; cf. 7:22).

Material found only in Luke shows concern for the poor and for the danger of wealth. In Luke it is simply "the poor" who are blessed, and Luke adds woes against the rich and powerful (6:20, 24-26). Luke presents Jesus in the form of an Old Testament prophet who takes the side of the widow (7:11-17; 18:1-8), the stranger in the land (10:25-37; 17:16), and those on the margin of society (14:12-13, 21). At the same time, Luke contains some of the harshest warning about wealth found in the New Testament: the parables of the Rich Fool (12:13-21), of the Unjust Steward (16:1-8), and of the Rich Man and Lazarus (16:19-31). Wolfgang Stegemann has suggested that Luke's Gospel is not so much a message of consolation for the poor as a warning to the wealthy.[44]

---

a classic study that had immense impact on interpreting the Beatitudes not simply as promises of future bliss; "Community of Goods in the Early Church" in *The Salvation of the Gentiles: Studies in the Acts of the Apostles* (New York: Paulist Press, 1979) 85–102; "The Poor and Poverty in the Gospels," in *Gospel Poverty,* A. George, ed. (Chicago: Franciscan Herald Press, 1971) 25–52; John Gillman, *Possessions and the Life of Faith: A Reading of Luke-Acts,* Zacchaeus Studies (Collegeville, Minn.: Liturgical Press, 1991); Luke Johnson, *Sharing Possessions: Mandate and Symbol of Faith* (Philadelphia: Fortress Press, 1981); Walter E. Pilgrim, *Good News to the Poor: Wealth and Poverty in Luke-Acts* (Minneapolis: Augsburg Press, 1981), an excellent overview; W. Stegemann, "The Following of Christ as Solidarity between Rich, Respected Christians and Poor, Despised Christians (Gospel of Luke)," in L. Schottroff and W. Stegemann, *Jesus and the Hope of the Poor* (Maryknoll, N.Y.: Orbis Books, 1986) 67–120; W. Stegemann, *The Gospel and the Poor* (Philadelphia: Fortress Press, 1984), good for use in pastoral settings.

44. See the works cited in note 43.

Yet the Acts of the Apostles offer a somewhat different perspective. The early community is one in which goods are held in common and in which there is no needy person (2:41-47; 4:32-37). Shared possession rather than dispossession is the goal, and almsgiving is stressed (Acts 10:2, 4, 31; 24:17). In biblical terms, almsgiving is not an exercise in optional charity, but an obligation in justice so much so that in latter biblical thought justice is translated as "almsgiving."[45] Lydia, "the seller of purple" who was a worshiper of God, shows hospitality to Paul—an example of good use of resources (16:11-15)—while upperclass women and men accept the gospel (17:12).

From this sketchy overview it is clear that the Lukan writings present a dilemma. In the Gospel riches are evil when they become such a preoccupation that they dominate a person's whole life or when a person attempts to secure the future through them, as in the case of the rich fool (Luke 12:16-21). They are also evil when, as in the parable of Dives and Lazarus, they blind people to the suffering neighbor at their doorstep (Luke 16:19-31). Discipleship demands renunciation of one's goods and adoption of the itinerant lifestyle of Jesus. Acts does not develop the more radical statements of the Gospel. Here proper use of possessions through mutual sharing and almsgiving rather than total dispossession is commended. If hospitality to the missionary was such an important aspect of Acts (and Paul), there must have been a great number of Christians who retained their homes and resources. If almsgiving is praised, the community could not have been composed of the wandering dispossessed.

Many solutions have been proposed for this dilemma, ranging from the older view of a two-level morality—one for the committed disciple and one for the ordinary Christian—to views that Luke accurately portrays the difference between the teaching of the earthly Jesus and its accommodation in the ongoing life of a first century church.[46] In the latter case, the teaching of Jesus is only of historical interest and possesses no lasting value as a model or ideal for subsequent Christians.

I would suggest, somewhat tentatively, that attention to the social setting of the final composition of Luke-Acts offers guidelines for interpretation. Luke-Acts was put together most likely in a Hellenistic city between 85 and 95 C.E. At that time more and more people of relative means and higher social status were entering the Church. As I

45. Compare Proverbs 10:2, "Righteousness *(ṣĕdāqāh)* delivers from death," with Tobit 12:9 (LXX), "Almsgiving *(dikaiosynē)* delivers from death."
46. Surveyed in Donahue, "Two Decades."

noted earlier, economic difference in antiquity was accompanied by social discrimination and often scorn for "the lower classes." By stressing the radical poverty of Jesus and his first followers and by emphasizing their origins among people of low status, Luke reminds his community of their "roots." Though Jesus can be acclaimed as "Lord and Savior," titles normally reserved to the Roman emperor, he himself was of low status and died a criminal's death. His followers lived as a community without status and class division. At the same time, Luke adopts the Jewish tradition of almsgiving (Tobit 4:10 NRSV: "For almsgiving delivers from death and keeps you from going into the Darkness"), understood not as a work of supererogation but of obligation, and exhorts his community to a proper use of wealth by putting it at the service of others. The old Deuteronomic ideal of a community in which there are no needy persons has been resurrected by Luke (Deut 15:4; Acts 4:34).

Proclaiming Biblical Justice Today

The biblical tradition provides rich resources and diverse challenges both for bishops as leaders and teachers and for all Catholics trying to live out the gospel in their lives. As St. Paul stressed, the Church is a body composed of different gifts and different ministries, and not all are gifted in the same manner (1 Cor 12; Rom 12:3-8). The Church is also united in a solidarity of suffering; when one member suffers all do. In our complex society, every bishop as a pastor and leader in a local church is called upon to foster the diverse gifts of the community. This has been done in a myriad of ways that have transformed Church life. As teacher, through homilies, through writings, and through the inauguration and encouragement of diverse programs, the bishop can help people appropriate the biblical perspectives on Justice. At the risk of being a false prophet, I would like to add two concerns about the proclamation of social justice today.

First, the traditional "works of mercy" (e.g., direct aid to the poor; sheltering the homeless, welcoming the stranger [immigrant]; see Matt 25:31-46) do not exhaust the Church's ministry of social justice, which involves a criticism of those structures that engender poverty and proclamation to those in power of their obligation to be concerned about the less fortunate, even though the works of mercy have undoubtedly been a part of the Church's life from its infancy. The distinguished early Church historian Peter Brown has written:

The Christian community suddenly came to appeal to men who felt deserted. At a time of inflation the Christians invested large sums of liquid capital in people; at a time of universal brutality the courage of Christian martyrs was impressive; during public emergencies such as plague or rioting, the Christian clergy were shown to be the only united group in the town, able to look after the burial of the dead and to organize food supplies.[47]

Today both nationally and internationally the Church is a "light to the nations" in its direct response to the tattered cloak of suffering worn by such a mass of humanity.

The more difficult task is to appropriate the prophetic critique of wealth and injustice. The United States Church is an established and respected institution within a modern (or even postmodern) complex economic structure. The Church also depends on the resources and generosity of people of power and wealth. One of the most demanding tasks facing Church leaders today is similar to that facing the author of Luke-Acts: to address people of means, helping them to recall their "roots" as a church and guiding them in proper use of resources. Church leaders can raise the consciousness of people about those very kinds of issues that have distinguished Church teaching over the last century, and are called on to speak out as forcefully on issues of injustice as strongly as they have on protection of human life. This is certainly done by papal teaching and by the agencies of the national conference of bishops, but often this teaching, because of its volume and complexity, is not appropriated or communicated to local churches. It is also inevitable that as the Church really adopts the "option for the poor" and the powerless, it will alienate certain powerful groups and carry the cross of rejection. Throughout the world we continually see Catholics murdered when they exposed injustice and became advocates for the poor. Perhaps the United States Church is really much too established and secure?

A second concern touches upon the integrity of proclamation and practice. At times the social doctrine of the Church seems like something for external consumption rather than internal appropriation.

---

47. Peter Brown, *The World of Late Antiquity from Marcus Aurelius to Muhammed* (London: Thames and Hudson, 1971) 67. Helpful surveys of early Church teaching are: William J. Walsh and John P. Langan, "Patristic Social Consciousness—The Church and the Poor," in Haughey, ed., *The Faith That Does Justice*, 113–151, and Peter Phan, *Social Thought*, Message of the Fathers of the Church 20 (Wilmington, Del.: Michael Glazier, 1984).

Though the process is cloaked in secrecy, the average Catholic would be hard pressed to say that concern for social justice is a major criterion in the selection of the hierarchy. There are instances where bishops noted for their commitment to the poor and to their confrontation with powerful forces have been succeeded by those opposed to those very commitments. Theologians are often stronger in articulating a prophetic vision than living it. The Church has consistently been one of the strongest world advocates for human rights and just treatment of all people, yet outsiders wonder if these same concerns guide Church authorities when dealing with internal issues. At the Second Vatican Council, for example, Cardinal Joseph Frings called the procedures of the Holy Office a scandal, and Father Bernard Häring, commenting on his own trial before the Congregation for the Doctrine of the Faith, mentioned that he stood before Hitler's military court four times on life and death issues and would have preferred that again rather than the way he was treated by the members of the Holy Office. Rather sadly, he notes, one major difference was that the Nazi accusations were true—he was not submissive to that regime—while the Curial accusations were false.[48]

Yet both the Old and New Testaments summon religious leaders and people of faith to an integrity of belief and practice. Isaiah reserves some of his most bitter criticisms for those who exalt religious practice while neglecting the poor, e.g., "Hear the word of the LORD . . . . What to me is the multitude of your sacrifices? . . . Your new moons and your appointed festivals my soul hates . . . . even though you make many prayers, I will not listen," but rather "cease to do evil, learn to do good. Seek justice, rescue the oppressed, defend the orphan, plead for the widow" (Isa 1:10, 11, 14, 15, 16, 17 NRSV; see also Isa 29:13-14, cited in Mark 7:6 and Matt 15:8). Ezekiel harshly criticizes the shepherds of Israel because "you have not strengthened the weak, you have not healed the sick, you have not bound up the injured" (Ezek 34:1-24 NRSV, esp. vv. 1-5). Jeremiah criticizes Jehoiakim, who embarked on a program of lavish construction, "building his house by unrighteousness, and his upper rooms by injustice," in contrast to his father Josiah, who "judged the cause of the poor and needy" (22:13, 16 NRSV).

---

48. Bernard Häring, *My Witness for the Church*, trans. L. Swidler (New York: Paulist Press, 1992) 90–189 (with excellent documentation); see especially pp. 132–133 on comparison between two kinds of trials.

While beginning with blessings on the poor in spirit, the peacemakers, and those hungering for justice, Matthew's Sermon on the Mount concludes with harsh warnings against false prophets who address Jesus as "Lord" and perform mighty deeds in his name, without "bearing fruit" and doing the will of God (7:15-23 NRSV). The harsh criticism of religious hypocrisy by the Pharisees in Matthew 23 for stressing various observances while neglecting the weightier things of the law, "justice and mercy and faith" (23:23 NAB 1970), according to John Meier, is also directed at an emerging Christian "pharisaism."[49]

Along with Matthew, the Jewish Christian Letter of James is one of the strongest witnesses to the need for integrity of proclamation and action. James exhorts his hearers: "Be doers of the word, and not merely hearers" (1:22 NRSV), and offers a sardonic criticism of those who welcome the homeless and hungry person with a warm greeting, without giving them "their bodily needs" (2:15-18). Though Matthew and James are parade examples of the criticism of the gap between proclamation and practice, this warning echoes throughout the whole New Testament.

Conclusion

The earliest description of the roles of the *episkopos* combines leadership and sound teaching with "care of God's church" (1 Tim 3:5 NRSV), which is expressed in hospitality and concern for ordinary things of life (1 Tim 3:1-7; Titus 1:5-10). As the Church evolved into a more complex society, bishop theologians such as Chrysostom and Ambrose spoke out against the danger of wealth and the need to be concerned for the poor and the marginal. Today the challenges are even greater, and not simply because of the complex and interconnected nature of modern societies, but because the ethical and theological response must not only draw on the rich resource of Catholic social doctrine but must be rooted in the Word of God handed on in the Bible. In guiding the bishop's statement *Economic Justice for All* and in reflecting on its meaning a decade later, as well as in a steady flow of writings and addresses and in personal witness, Archbishop Rembert Weakland, O.S.B., made major contributions to an understanding of the role of bishops in the promotion of social justice.

49. John P. Meier, *Matthew*, New Testament Message (Wilmington, Del.: Michael Glazier, 1980) 264–265. See also Pope John Paul II, *Tertio Millennio Adveniente*, especially nos. 35-36; EJA 347, in reference also to the synod, *Justice in the World*, no. 40.

Chapter Fourteen

Aesthetics and Episcopal Leadership: Teaching, Sanctifying, and Governing Analogically

Edward Foley, Capuchin

Introduction

It may strike some as at least a stretch, if not downright odd, to pen an entry on aesthetics for a book focused on episcopal leadership. It is certainly not a topic ordinarily broached by those who study the episcopacy. The topic could be justified by the fact that this volume honors a particular bishop with distinguished artistic training who, throughout his lifetime, has demonstrated in word and deed his love for the beautiful. While this essay is especially crafted to honor Archbishop Weakland, there is yet no intention to so personalize this contribution that it appears only as an *hommage* to the man and not, at the same time, a vision for the office. Rather, taking inspiration from one bishop who embraces the artistic, the intent here is to demonstrate not only that episcopal leadership is aesthetic leadership by default, but that it also need be by intention.

It is a truism to suggest that bishops are not ordinarily appointed because of their aesthetic expertise. Pastoral leadership, piety, orthodoxy, organizational skills, fidelity, and even fiscal acuity are usually more determinative factors than a potential appointee's musical tastes or eye for form. If the aesthetic is admitted as part of episcopal ministry at all, it is ordinarily subsumed under the teaching ministry, where *Christus Dominus* seems to place it.[1] The thesis of this essay, however, is that aesthetics is not a subject about which bishops should teach; rather it is a fundamental mode for carrying out their central ministries of teaching, sanctifying, and governing. While not the only

1. CD 12.

mode for rendering these services to the Church, the aesthetic is certainly an essential one for doing so. Fundamentally, the aesthetical is a necessary, if often unacknowledged, way of being bishop.

Aesthetics is generally understood as a branch of philosophy that addresses issues of judgment and perception of the beautiful, fine arts, or a wider range of objects or events considered moving or sublime.[2] It is not in this general sense, however, that the term will ultimately serve us here; rather, in making the turn to episcopal ministry, we will employ it more narrowly with a specific theological meaning. In his work on theological aesthetics, Alejandro García-Rivera opines that, rather than a science of sensory cognition, aesthetics can be recast as the science that asks "What moves the human heart?"[3] Employing this insight, theological aesthetics could be conceived as that approach which asks, "What moves the human heart *to God?*" Thus, while concerned with issues of perception, taste, judgment, and the like, the foray into theological aesthetics always places such issues in a decidedly religious context and with an explicit spiritual purpose. It is, as García-Rivera notes, making a connection with Beauty through the beautiful.[4]

Of Arts and Classics

David Tracy's magisterial *The Analogical Imagination* is a work of systematic theology that sets out to argue that all theology is public discourse.[5] Given this purpose, it might surprise some as unusual when, early in the volume, this gifted hermeneut makes the turn to art both as an analogy for religion and an element of religion. In drawing an analogy with religion, Tracy laments the fact that art (like religion) has become increasingly marginalized and privatized in contemporary society.[6] He even goes so far to suggest that where art is marginalized, religion will be privatized as well [13]. The underlying assumption is that art (like reli-

2. See, for example, Stephen Ross, ed., *Art and Its Significance: An Anthology of Aesthetic Theory*, 3rd ed. (Albany: State University of New York Press, 1994).

3. Alejandro García-Rivera, *The Community of the Beautiful: A Theological Aesthetics* (Collegeville, Minn.: The Liturgical Press, 1999) 9.

4. García-Rivera, *The Community of the Beautiful*, 11.

5. David Tracy, *The Analogical Imagination: Christian Theology and the Culture of Pluralism* (New York: Crossroad, 1981) 3. Numbers in brackets throughout this article are page references to this work.

6. Tracy, 6–14, believes that "society" encompasses three realms: (1) the technoeconomic realm, which is concerned with the organization and allocation of goods and services; (2) the realm of polity, concerned with the legitimate meaning of social justice and the use of power; and (3) the realm of culture, which he defines chiefly but not exclusively as art and religion.

gion and other aspects of culture) has the ability to disclose truth about our common human condition and thus is not simply a matter of private taste or consumption [12]. Rather, art and the other elements of culture are important and powerful resources *for raising value questions in the realm of polity* [13]. To illustrate this point, Tracy evokes the memory of Martin Luther King, who, "through his personal appropriation of the symbolic resources of his religious and cultural heritages, was able to articulate, and to express in action, otherwise unnoticed and untapped ethical resources for the societal struggle for social justice" [13]. In this same vein, if theologians are going to accept their public responsibilities to genuine public discourse for the good of society, the resources of culture (primarily art and religion) need be engaged.

Tracy returns to a discussion of art later in *The Analogical Imagination* when he considers the nature of a classic. His reflections on the classic emerge from a consideration of how systematic theologians interpret a living religious tradition. Tracy contends that systematic theologians, aware of their radical finitude and own historicity, risk a trust in a particular religious tradition. "They seek, therefore, to retrieve, interpret, translate, mediate the resources—the questions and answers, form and content, the subject matter—of the classic events of understanding of those fundamental questions embedded in the classic events, images, persons, rituals, texts and symbols of a tradition" [104]. According to Tracy, classics have a normative role in culture, and the experience of a classic remains a permanent feature of any human cultural experience. This permanence and normativity are undeniable because certain texts, events, images, rituals, symbols, and people consistently disclose compelling truth about human existence [108]. To explain the classic's capacity for such compelling disclosure, Tracy returns to a consideration of art, which becomes a central analogy for the classic.

An experience of "art-as-classic" for Tracy is an encounter with truth, knowledge, and reality. It is a shocking, surprising, challenging confrontation in which people are transformed, so that when they return to ordinary reality, they discover new sensibilities for the everyday [112]. Thus an artistic encounter is not the private act of a consumer, slaking some personal thirst for what pleases, entertains, or comforts. It is not an autonomous subject dispassionately considering some dispensable object.[7] Rather, the artistic encounter is life-arranging, deconstructive, reconstructive conversation. Tracy summarizes:

7. Useful here is Eric Havelock's chapter "Psyche or the Separation of the Knower from the Known," in his *Preface to Plato* (Cambridge: Harvard University Press, 1963) 197–214.

When anyone of us is caught unawares by a genuine work of art, we find ourselves in the grip of an event, a happening, a disclosure, a claim to truth which we cannot deny and can only eliminate by our later controlled reflection: it was only a play, merely the private expression of a private self, a new quality, an illusion, magic, unreal. But in the experience of art we lose our usual self-consciousness and finally encounter a rooted self—a self transformed into both new possibility and the actuality of rootedness by its willingness to play and be played by that transforming disclosure [114-115].[8]

The Turn to Language

While Tracy admits works of art, symbols, even people as potential classics, most of his own consideration of classics revolves around texts. While our focus is not on texts alone, his discussion of theological language in classic texts does provide a useful framework for considering broader aesthetical issues. In particular, Tracy notes that theological language—ordinarily different from the language of any foundational religious experience or its articulation—not only has particular purposes but also specific criteria to ensure its adequacy for reflecting upon and adequately interpreting the originating religious experience [408]. In Tracy's opinion, there are two types of language that achieve such adequacy: the analogical and the dialectical.

As he defines it, analogical language is that which attempts to order relationships by emphasizing "similarity-in-difference." This language ordering proceeds by considering and clarifying various relationships (e.g., between self, others, world, and God) in view of some primary analogue.

> In Christian systematics, the primary focal meaning will be the event of Jesus Christ. . . . That focal meaning as event will provide the primary analogue for the interpretation of the whole of reality. The event will provide the major clue to the similarities-in-difference awaiting explication among the realities God, self, other selves and world (society, history, nature) [408].

One of the great contributions of such language in theological discourse is its validation of human experience and speech as appropriate for seeking understanding of God. Thus we can speak of God as a

---

8. A similar point is made by George Steiner, who believes that the direct experience of aesthetic meaning, in particular the arts, infers the necessary possibility of God's presence. *Real Presences* (Chicago: The University of Chicago Press, 1989).

being or consider the Christ-event in terms of human relationships, without resorting to univocal language and reducing God or the death and resurrection of Jesus Christ to human realities.

Despite the great contribution of analogical language, however, Tracy readily admits that there is an unavoidable tension for the theologian employing such language. This tension arises because second-order speech is employed to explain and interpret a foundational event—such as the death and resurrection of Christ—which at its core must be recognized as ultimately incomprehensible. Tracy believes, however, that by remaining faithful "to the power of the uncanny negatives disclosed in the event"—by giving critical attention to the difference despite the similarity—the theologian can achieve faithful reflection on such a foundational event without depleting it of its mystery [409—410].

Tracy's second classical theological language *par excellence* is the dialectical. Whereas the analogical lifts up similarity while admitting radical difference, the dialectical for Tracy is about rupture, absolute paradox, and radical negation at the heart of theological language. This is theological language

> expressive of a negation of all human efforts to save oneself, the negation of all poisonous dreams of establishing any easy continuities between Christianity and culture, the negation of all claims to a deluded, self-propelling "progress" within society and culture, the negation of all aesthetic, ethical, and "pagan" religious possibilities. These negations in the proclamation must be reexpressed in any theological language that dares to claim hermeneutical fidelity to authentic Christian faith hearing the Word of Jesus Christ: a word disclosing the reality of the infinite, qualitative distinction between that God and this flawed, guilty, sinful, presumptuous, self-justifying self [415].

Such second-order language is essential if God is going to be allowed to be God and, for Christians, if the Christ-event is to be proclaimed with any integrity. It is language that undercuts any philosophical arrogance, religious delusion, or theological self-confidence. The dialectical is thus what Tracy calls the language of "prophetic suspicion," which in our own day has retrieved from the Christian tradition "the necessity of some confrontational, conflictual *no* to any complacent self, culture or society" [416—417].

While dialectical language is essential for the integrity of Christian theology, it is also problematic in its own way. Language that shatters all surety could shatter hope as well. Where does the dialectical allow for the validation of human experience in the religious event, the quest for order, the need for understanding? Interestingly enough, Tracy's examination of significant theologians predisposed to dialectical exposition reveals that these did not remain stalled in negation but developed alternate theological languages that, while remaining rooted in the power of negation, admitted continuities and ultimately turned to similarities-in-difference as well. The dialectical thus gave way to new analogical languages.[9]

While Tracy is careful in his exposition not to suggest any simplistic identification between either of these two classical theological languages and any single religious tradition, his analysis of Christian classics clearly reveals a Catholic propensity for the analogical and a Protestant propensity for the dialectical.[10] Thus it is Aquinas and Rahner whom he lifts up to exemplify the former, while Barth and Bultmann provide evidence for the latter. He himself sits in what he calls the "Catholic theological analogical tradition" and at the end of this analogically titled opus offers a proposal for "a Christian systematic Analogical Imagination" [421—429]. The classics of Catholic theology, among which Tracy's work need be numbered, give evidence of a strong preference for analogical language and analogical reasoning.

A Catholic Imagination and Spirituality

While Tracy gives significant attention to discussions of classics, language, and even art, he expends much less energy considering the pivotal issue of imagination. He explicitly addresses the topic of imagination only once, when discussing the production of a classic text. There he links imagination, and by extension the analogical imagination, to language.[11]

Tracy's analogical agenda has been taken up by a variety of authors.[12] Mary Catherine Hilkert, for example, has crafted a vision for

9. In considering Karl Barth's *Dogmatics*, for example, Tracy, 417, demonstrates that while negative dialectics endures, it does not prevail. Rather, what prevails is the radical "yes" that is the triumph of grace.

10. Previous to the publication of *The Analogical Imagination*, Tracy made this point in his presentation "The Catholic Analogical Imagination," in *Proceedings of the Catholic Theological Society of America*, ed. Luke Salm (New York: CTSA, 1977) 234–244.

11. " . . . imagination *is* the correlative intensification power which produces in language the meaning which the work expresses. A classic text is produced only when imagination at work, in a work, impels, drives, frees the creator to express the meaning—both the sense and the referent—of the work in the work" [128].

12. For an exploration of Tracy's work around the question of inculturation, see Stephen Bevans, "Protestant, Catholics and Inculturation: Similarities-in-Difference, Differences-in-Similarity," *Japan Christian Review* 1 (1996) 5–16.

preaching that draws on Tracy's work. Rather than "analogical," however, Hilkert speaks of a "sacramental imagination."[13] Hilkert makes this turn in her attempt to offer a distinctive Roman Catholic contribution to a theology of preaching. She believes that while Catholics have not significantly contributed to a theology of preaching, they can by relying on the resources of their sacramental imagination. She describes the sacramental imagination as one that

> emphasizes the presence of the God who is self-communicating love, the creation of human beings in the image of God . . . the mystery of the incarnation, grace of divinizing as well as forgiving, the mediating role of the church as sacrament of salvation in the world, and the "fore-taste" of the reign of God that is present in human community wherever God's reign of justice, peace, and love is fostered.[14]

Hilkert's volume offers three contributions that are important for our own enterprise. First, by focusing on a praxis like preaching rather than a classical text, she exemplifies in an accessible way how the "analogical" or "sacramental" imagination is a resource for ordinary ministers and not just theologians. Second, in counterdistinction to what might appear to be Tracy's preoccupation with texts, Hilkert underscores depth human experience as a central arena for analogical reflection. The mystery of human life thus becomes the place to discover the "God who often remains hidden."[15] Finally, her reinterpretation of "analogical" as "sacramental" and her parallel emphasis on symbol, ritual, and liturgy allow us to consider Tracy's insight at the heart of Roman Catholic practice and not simply at the heart of Roman Catholic thinking.

Hilkert, like Tracy before her, is careful not to define the sacramental imagination as an exclusive Roman Catholic prerogative and notes how her perspective is shared by representatives of the Orthodox, Anglican, Methodist, and Lutheran traditions.[16] At the same time, however, by making the sacramental imagination foundational for

13. Mary Catherine Hilkert, *Naming Grace* (New York: Continuum, 1997); this turn is reminiscent of earlier work by Richard McBrien, who suggests that the first and most central distinguishing Roman Catholic characteristic is sacramentality. Richard McBrien, *Catholicism*, 2 vols. (Minneapolis: Winston Press, 1980) 2:1180; also his "Roman Catholicism," in *The Encyclopedia of Religion*, ed. Mircea Eliade (New York: Macmillan, 1987) 12:429–445.

14. Hilkert, *Naming Grace*, 15.

15. Ibid., 50.

16. Ibid., 195, note 7.

developing a Roman Catholic contribution to a theology of preaching, she underscores that such an imagination is a defining Roman Catholic characteristic.

One further element from Hilkert's work deserves comment. Early in her volume she makes a temporary shift from the language of imagination to that of spirituality and, in view of Tracy's distinction between the analogical and dialectical, suggests that these might be understood as two distinct Christian spiritualities. While she leaves this concept undeveloped, it yet evokes a recognizable truth about the distinctive, almost contradictory ways that Christians have imaged salvation throughout the centuries. Already in the New Testament, entry into Christ's life is alternately viewed through the prisms of rebirth (e.g., John 3:3) and death (Rom 3:6). In the patristic period, the polarities of analogical and dialectical "spiritualities" are exemplified in the writings of Pseudo-Dionysius (late fifth, early sixth century) and Origen (d. ca. 254) respectively. During the medieval period, two institutional icons of such disparate spiritualities were Cluny (founded in 909) and Citeaux (founded in 1098).

Thus, as Hilkert notes, these strands cannot simply be identified as Protestant and Catholic, for both can be found in each tradition. On the other hand, in terms of the popular spiritualities embraced by ordinary Catholics over the centuries, it would be difficult to deny the strong propensity for the analogical/sacramental over the dialectical, for the spirituality of a Francis of Assisi (d. 1226) rather than that of Bernard of Clairvaux (d. 1153). In Roman Catholic classics, as well as in the enduring spiritualities of Roman Catholics, there clearly appears to be a stronger analogical than dialectical flow.[17]

The Empirical Evidence

For many years Andrew Greeley has attempted to demonstrate empirically what Tracy, Hilkert, and others have asserted theologically. Greeley, who once called himself a "sociologist of the religious imagination,"[18] was regularly publishing his sociological explorations of Tracy's insights in the 1980s. Helpful to our point is his 1991 report

---

17. "Flow" is a term employed in sociology, anthropology, and communication science to denote "a circulation of information that is patently visible yet hard to define." Robert Schreiter, *The New Catholicity* (Maryknoll, N.Y.: Orbis Books, 1997) 15.

18. Andrew Greeley, *The Catholic Myth: The Behavior and Beliefs of American Catholics* (New York: MacMillan, 1991) 35; already in 1981 he had published *The Religious Imagination* (New York: Sadlier).

on a study conducted in the spring of 1990 in the Archdiocese of Chicago concerned with asking, "Why do people want to be Catholic?" At the end of the study Greeley summarizes:

> How do the reasons for being Catholic relate to staying in the Church? In a multiple regression equation, two of the 13 [reasons] emerged as statistically significant: faith to pass on to children and the sacraments. The sacraments and a faith to pass on are not only two of the three most important reasons for being Catholic, but are also the strongest checks on leaving the church. Note that . . . substitutes can be found from other agencies for all the reasons for being Catholic except for sacraments, faith and an infallible pope. The pope is not a statistically significant correlate of staying in the church. A faith to pass on can be found in other religions, but the sacraments are uniquely Catholic.[19]

Independent collaborating evidence of this assertion is found in the recent study of young adult Catholics by Dean Hoge and William Dinges. When Catholics aged 20 to 39 were asked what elements are "essential to the faith," the number one response (65 percent of all respondents) was "believe that God is present in the sacraments."[20]

Over the next decade Greeley continued to publish a myriad of articles and monographs that repeatedly drove this point home. As he attempted to demonstrate empirically the existence of a decidedly analogical or sacramental imagination for Catholics, he also expanded the boundaries of his research into a broader consideration of metaphor, narrative, and the arts. For example, in his 1994 work *Religion as Poetry*, he turned to a consideration of narrative. Yet reliant on Tracy's basic insight, Greeley here explores the religious imagination through story and contends that religious stories (the "poetry" in his title, in contradistinction to the "prose" of doctrine), particularly as they are expressed in images of God, will predict (at what sociologists call low to moderate levels of correlation) the political, social, and familial stories of ordinary Catholics.[21] The bottom line here for Greeley seems to be summarized in his assertion, "Religion is story, story before it is anything else, story after it is everything else, story born from experience, coded in symbol, reinforced in the self, and shared with others to

19. Andrew Greeley, "Sacraments keep Catholics high on the church," *National Catholic Reporter* (12 April 1991) 12–13.

20. Dean Hoge, William Dinges, Mary Johnson, Juan Gonzalez, *Young Adult Catholics: Religion in the Culture of Choice,* as reported in *The Cara Report* 7:2 (Fall 2001) 9.

21. Andrew Greeley, *Religion as Poetry* (New Brunswick, N.J.: Transaction Publishers, 1994).

explain life and death."[22] Not surprisingly, for Greeley, the images of God in Catholic stories (God as mother-spouse-lover-friend) document the Catholic analogical imagination, distinguished from the God of Protestant storytelling (God as father-master-judge-king).

More recently Greeley has turned to a consideration of the Catholic imagination and the arts.[23] There he has found that Catholics, responding to the 1993 General Social Survey from the National Opinion Research Center,[24] were more involved in the fine arts than Protestants in the United States. He further suggested that among Catholics the link between "graceful" images[25] and regular churchgoing is strong. Finally, he argued that these findings suggest a distinctive and very powerful liturgical spirituality among Catholics, and if this liturgical imaging continues to survive, it will do so because it is rooted in the depths of the Catholic psyche, with its ability to see grace lurking everywhere.[26]

Greeley draws this artistic turn to summary in *The Catholic Imagination.*[27] Here he is less concerned with demonstrating the distinction between analogical and dialectic imaginations, and more concentrated on stressing the existence of a Catholic style of storytelling about God and life; a Catholic way of imagining God and human existence in architecture, music, and literature; and a Catholic approach to family, sexuality, and neighborhood. He does so by examining examples of high art produced by Catholics over the centuries—from Cologne Cathedral and Bernini's St. Teresa, and from the novels of Graham Green to Martin Scorsese's film *Mean Streets*—in attempts to show a correspondence between these artistic works

22. Ibid., 40.

23. See, for example, his "The Apologetics of Beauty," *America* 183:7 (2000) 8–14.

24. Affiliated with the University of Chicago, the National Opinion Research Center (NORC) is concerned with pursuing empirical research to serve a broadly conceived public interest. One of the main tools of this research has been the General Social Survey (GSS), administered twenty-three times since its initial fielding in 1972. The GSS has been a foundational source of data for Greeley in many of his assertions about the Catholic imagination. For more on NORC and GSS, see http://www.norc.uchicago.edu/.

25. Over the years Greeley has developed a "Grace Scale," which measures a respondent's image of God as (1) mother versus father, (2) lover versus judge, (3) spouse versus master, and (4) friend versus king. See his *Religion and Poetry* for a lengthy discussion of the development, rationale, and predictive power of this scale.

26. See his summary in "Catholics, Fine Arts and The Liturgical Imagination," *America* 174:17 (1996) 9–14.

27. Andrew Greeley, *The Catholic Imagination* (Berkeley: University of California Press, 2000).

and the sensibilities of ordinary Catholics. Such works of high art, for Greeley, reveal that Catholics have an "enchanted imagination." He explains, "There is a propensity among Catholics to take the objects and events and persons of ordinary life as hints of what God is like, in which God somehow lurks, even if . . . they are not completely self-conscious about these perceptions of enchantment."[28]

As Greeley spins out a dizzying array of minor theses, ecclesial critiques, and liturgical agenda in his avalanche of publications on the Catholic imagination, he provides sufficient diversion and passion to be dismissed by the casual or unduly prejudiced reader.[29] If, however, we remain focused on his fundamental and sustained thesis—that there exists a strong verifiable flow among Roman Catholics of an imagination (even spirituality) that can be characterized as analogical, sacramental, and enchanted—then both his argument and the impressive marshaling of empirical data to sustain it emerge as formidable. It is true that every social scientist is not persuaded by Greeley's claims, and he has been taken to task in various reviews for drawing conclusions that the data do not seem to sustain.[30] Overall, however, the social scientific community admits the need for reckoning with Greeley's theses on religious imagination. No less a figure than Robert Bellah, for example, has taken up Greeley's agenda and argued that it would be useful to "turn to a Catholic cultural tradition in America that has never been completely Protestantized . . . [and] to reconstitute our cultural code by giving much great salience to the sacramental life (Greeley uses the terms Catholic imagination and sacramental imagination interchangeably), and, in particular, to the Eucharist."[31]

Leadership in Aesthetic mode

Given the language of "sacramental" and "liturgical" imagination that emerged in the writings of Hilkert, Greeley, and others—as well as Bellah's proposal about the importance of the sacramental life and

28. Ibid., 18.

29. Few theologians, for example, have drawn on Greeley's insights in their own work. One exception is Regis Duffy, who extensively employs Greeley's work in his *An American Emmaus: Faith and Sacrament in the American Culture* (New York: Crossroad, 1995) e.g., 27.

30. See, for example, Daniel Johnson's review of *Religion as Poetry* in *Journal for the Scientific Study of Religion* 34 (1995) 393–394.

31. Robert Bellah, "Religion and the Shape of National Culture," *America* 181:3 (1999) 14; Johnson, as well (see previous footnote), admits that all have "benefited greatly" from Greeley's work on religious imagination.

Eucharist—it could seem that the aesthetic proposal at hand is leading us primarily or even exclusively to a consideration of *liturgical*
leadership. A closer examination of the sources at hand, however, reveals that the issue is much larger than liturgical presidency or worship as traditionally defined. Recall, for example, that Tracy's main
agenda in *The Analogical Imagination* is to present theology as *public
discourse.* His turn to art and analogical reasoning is in service of his
belief that the resources of culture are important and powerful resources for raising value questions in the area of polity or that realm
of society concerned with the legitimate meaning of social justice and
the use of power.[32] Thus his previously cited invocation of Martin
Luther King was offered precisely as an example of a gifted leader who
understood the power of the aesthetical and who centrally deployed
the cultural resources of music, rhetoric, public theater, and symbolic
display in the struggle for civil rights. One could rightly wonder how
much of an impact Dr. King might have had if his aesthetic sensitivities and skills had been less developed.

A powerful, and to many repulsive, example of such aesthetic leadership in another context is that exercised by the Nazi hierarchy in Germany through the 1930s. In a forthcoming article on "Liturgy and the
Holocaust," ethician John Pawlikowski examines the symbolic genius of
Nazi leadership as a way to underscore the importance of symbolic mediation for the good not just of a church but of a republic.[33] Rather than
relying on Tracy's analogical/dialectic paradigm, Pawlikowski draws on
Reinhold Niebuhr's distinction between the vitalistic and the rational.[34]
As Pawlikowski summarizes, "vitalistic" covers those areas of human
consciousness not controlled by the rational faculty, for example, feeling, memory, myth-making, and the sexual drive among others. While
many wanted to locate ethics primarily in people's rational capacity,

---

32. In a parallel vein, Pope John Paul II, in his millennium letter to artists, notes
that artists "render an exceptional social service in favor of the common good." Letter
of His Holiness Pope John Paul II to Artists (23 April 1999), no. 4.

33. John Pawlikowski, "Liturgy and the Holocaust: How Do We Worship in an Age
of Genocide," in a yet untitled volume, ed. Donald Dietrich (Syracuse University Press).
What follows on the Nazis as well as on Niebuhr is drawn from Pawlikowski.

34. See Reinhold Niebuhr, *The Nature and Destiny of Man*, vol. 1: *Human Nature*
(New York: Charles Scribner's Sons, 1964); Tracy generously draws upon Niebuhr in
The Analogical Imagination, especially for his ethical-political theological emphasis,
and cites volume 2 of *The Nature and Destiny of Man*. One wonders whether Tracy, so
well versed in Niebuhr, was also influenced by the vitalistic-rational polarity in shaping
his own analogical-dialectical frame.

Niebuhr stressed that authentic and effective human ethics required involving the vitalistic energies.

Pawlikowski illustrates Niebuhr's wisdom by discussing how "the regeneration of the vitalistic side of humanity . . . stood at the heart of the Nazi enterprise." Drawing upon the work of historians and Holocaust scholars, he notes, with special references to their "public liturgies," how perceptive Nazi leadership was in recognizing the influence of symbolism in human life. Pawlikowski concludes:

> One of the convictions that has continued to deepen with me . . . is that moral sensitivity remains an indispensable prelude to moral reasoning. We ethicists can provide the necessary clarifications of human response mandated by such sensitivity. Such clarifications are absolutely essential if religious experience is not to degenerate into religious fanaticism. But, as an ethicist, I cannot create the sensitivity itself. Mere appeals to reason, authority, and/or natural law will prove ineffective by themselves. Such sensitivity will reemerge only through a new awareness of God's intimate link with human kind, in suffering and joy, through symbolic experience. Nothing short of this will suffice in light of the Holocaust.[35]

Pawlikowski's analysis calls to mind the Lukan parable of the rich man and the wasteful steward about to be dismissed (Luke 16:1-8). In a pivotal line in that parable, the evangelist writes, "His master commended the dishonest manager because he had acted shrewdly; for the children of this age are more shrewd in dealing with their own generation than are the children of light" (16:8 NRSV). What have the daughters and sons of this age learned about aesthetic competency that Church leaders have yet to grasp? Have they learned that the poetic, analogical, vitalistic, broadly sacramental, and enchanted imagination is more potent than the prosaic, flat, doctrinal "church speak" to which so many ecclesial leaders often resort?

While the image of Nazi leadership may be so repulsive that it diminishes the argument, a similar point can be made by considering any number of great leaders throughout history. Alexander the Great (d. 323 B.C.E.), for example, was ultimately able to transform Western civilization because of his cultural prowess, providing political and cultural incentives to those who acquainted themselves with Greek language and culture. Constantine (d. 337 C.E.) understood the potency of cultural icons, to the point of reshaping his power base through

---

35. Pawlikowski, "Liturgy and the Holocaust."

the construction of the first truly Christian city. Pondering Charlemagne (d. 814) at Aachen, Suger at St.-Denis (d. 1151), Lorenzo de Medici (d. 1492) in Florence, and Joseph II (d. 1790) in Vienna, it becomes clear that effective leadership often presumes aesthetic competency and the ability to engage the cultural, artistic, and religious symbols of a culture. Sometimes leadership's aesthetic competency has more to do with the fine arts and is aligned with the tastes of the elite and powerful. Yet, no less a leader than Mahatma Gandhi (d. 1948) has demonstrated that even a simple spinning wheel or the loincloth and shawl of the lowest peasant can speak more loudly than the polished rhetoric of the British Empire. In our own day, few non-Catholics around the world remember the elocutions of Pope John Paul II. For many such people, however, the image of the Pope prostrating on a tarmac to kiss the soil of their country is seared in their collective memory. While the aesthetic mode, and its special sensitivity to cultural symbols and the fine or folk arts of a culture, is not the only viable mode of leadership, it is difficult to imagine that aesthetic competency, particularized by the frame of theological aesthetics and its concern with discovering "what moves the human heart to God," is not an essential mode of episcopal leadership.

Teaching, Sanctifying and Governing

While it is not feasible to provide any syllabus for episcopal aesthetic leadership here, it is possible to offer some suggestions of how such aesthetic competency could be exercised. Vatican II's Decree on the Pastoral Office of Bishops in the Church (*Christus Dominus*) highlights episcopal leadership under the triple rubric of teaching, sanctifying and governing. While these are certainly permeable categories, they are nonetheless useful and will provide us with a framework.

Teaching. Early in this essay we noted that if the aesthetic is admitted as part of episcopal ministry at all, it is ordinarily subsumed under the teaching ministry. The documentary evidence for this is *Christus Dominus*, which notes that bishops should teach, according to the doctrine of the Church, the great value of things, among which the arts are numbered.[36] Aesthetic competency in episcopal leadership, however, is not so much teaching *about* the arts as it is moving people to God *through* the arts and other cultural resources.

---

36. CD 12.

Broadly speaking, this is inviting bishops to be mystagogues, not in the liturgical sense of those who theologize out of the ritual, but mystagogues of the culture, capable of teaching symbolically in ways that lead to God by employing key cultural icons, symbols, and arts. While not a bishop, one outstanding example of such a cultural mystagogue was the Jesuit Matteo Ricci (d. 1610). Ricci's genius, in part, was his ability to read Chinese culture, recognize Confucianism (rather than Buddhism) as that which held the position of orthodoxy in the China of his day, plumb the Confucian classics, pen his own treatise in Confucian mode, and negotiate ritually between Confucianism and Catholicism.[37]

On the other side of the world, in this same era of exploration, another cultural mystagogue was plumbing the depths of an indigenous culture. This was Bartolomé de la Casas (d. 1576), whose experience of the Spanish oppression of the native peoples in the New World was both a source of personal conversion and the impetus for a lifelong journey into the lives of simple Indian folk.[38] De Casas, who eventually became the first bishop of Chiapas in Guatemala, was similar to Ricci in his attempt to reach and defend a community in faith through their cultural symbols. Yet, while Ricci was engaged with the literati who honored him with the title "Western Confucian scholar," de Casas was engaged with rustic, folk, and primitive customs, symbols, and arts. His monumental *Apologética historia sumaria* was an ethnographic encyclopedia of what many at the time would hardly consider a culture at all. Through it he strove to demonstrate that these indigenous people fully met the requirements laid down by Aristotle for the good life and were entitled to respect and freedom.

Although the teachings of Ricci and de Casas were broadly challenged, these were outstanding pedagogues in analogical mode whose aesthetic competency built bridges in the past that we sorely need today. The Roman Catholic Church in the U.S. today swells with believers from many Asian and Hispanic cultures. In order to build bridges to these communities, it is essential that ecclesial leadership be able to acknowledge, embrace, and employ the cultural resources of

37. See George Minamiki, *The Chinese Rites Controversy: From its Beginning to Modern Times* (Chicago: Loyola University Press, 1985).

38. While he does not give much attention to de Casas, García-Rivera, *The Community of the Beautiful*, 44–49, does discuss other missionaries in the New World and their ability, through symbolic aesthetics, to construct a tradition of intellectual inquiry into the nature of signs and symbols.

these communities. If the mystique of Our Lady of Guadalupe[39] or the treasures of the Confucian tradition are ignored, however, so is the authentic teaching ministry to the communities that embrace these cultural heritages proportionately impaired.

Sanctifying. In considering the episcopal ministry of sanctification, we turn from proposing that bishops be "mystagogues of culture" to a more traditional understanding of bishops as liturgical mystagogues. Largely under the influence of the Rite of Christian Initiation of Adults, mystagogy has come to be defined as a period of post-baptismal catechesis. Historical precedents that equate mystagogy with post-baptismal instruction can be found in the writings of Cyril of Jerusalem (d. 386?), Ambrose of Milan (d. 397) and others. There is evidence from other fourth-century mystagogues such as John Chrysostom (d. 407) and Theodore of Mopsuestia (d. 427), however, that indicates mystagogical catechesis *before* initiation.[40] These historical sources as well as contemporary reflection provide an important caution to the sometimes narrow instinct to define mystagogy essentially in terms of chronology. Authentic mystagogy is less a question of "when" than of "how." It is not so much a post-ritual or post-experience manner of formation as it is a way of entering into the mystery that respects both personal experience as well as the "event" nature of worship.[41]

In terms of our aesthetical agenda, "sanctifying" in analogical mode within the liturgical context is a decidedly mystagogical affair. It is inviting people into a graced relationship with God through Christ in the Spirit through the symbols, poetry, ritual actions, and music of worship. Because the bishop is the chief liturgist in his diocese and presides at pivotal liturgical events with the full range of ecclesial symbols and arts, he is in a privileged position both to sanctify in analogical mode and to model for others in the diocese how this is to be done.

From my perspective, presiding in aesthetic mode, however, is one of the great underdeveloped skills in the Catholic Church today. Many

39. See, for example, Virgilio Elizondo, "Our Lady of Guadalupe as a Cultural symbol," in *Liturgy and Cultural Traditions,* ed. Herman Power and David Schmidt (New York: Seabury Press, 1977) 25–33.

40. These sources are rehearsed in my "Musical Mystagogy: A Mystagogy of the Moment," *Pastoral Music* 25:6 (August–September 2001) 15–20.

41. It can be defined as a way of doing theology that (1) takes the whole of the ritual seriously, (2) gives parallel attention to the embodied experiences of the worshipers, (3) employs some poetic or evocative catalyst, (4) to elicit new meaning, (5) in a shared context, (6) for the sake of personal and ecclesial transformation. Ibid., 20.

preside *in* the liturgy but not always *of* the liturgy. A simple example: few are the presiders (episcopal or presbyteral) whose introductory comments at Sunday Eucharist ever acknowledge, much less take seriously, the opening song that immediately preceded. Yet most Roman Catholics are more versed in musical tunes and texts than in the Bible. The music we sing in worship gives form to the artistic, liturgical, sacramental imagination that so marks us. So do those other pivotal acts of anointing, blessing, processing, and incensing. Yet our presiders seem much more taken with prosaic commentary than poetic engagement. Some don't even feel compelled to join in singing the opening song or other worship music that spiritually sustains so many believers. This is symptomatic of leadership that has yet to be convinced of the power of the poetic and persuasion of the aesthetic.

Besides the aesthetic as a sanctifying mode within Roman Catholic worship, bishops increasingly are called to exercise their sanctifying role in both ecumenical and interfaith situations. In these situations heightened religious, social, and political sensitivities often render the aesthetical turn an especially important one. This is true, in part, because language characterized as prosaic, didactic, or dogmatic has traditionally been employed in Western Christianity for highlighting differences and delineating religious boundaries. Therefore, it is often more effective to enact ecumenicity in the aesthetic rather than prosaic mode. Some of the most memorable interfaith and ecumenical contributions of Pope John Paul II, for example, have been his prayer gestures. In May 2001 he became the first pope to enter a Muslim place of prayer, visiting the Omayyad Mosque in the old walled city at the heart of modern Damascus. The sight of the 80-year-old pontiff slipping off his shoes as required by tradition, entering the mosque, and walking side by side with Syria's top Muslim cleric remains seared in the memory. Few may recall the words of reconciliation spoken that day, yet the grace of ritual gesture and the sanctifying art of the poetic action linger.

Governing. Earlier we briefly touched upon the importance of aesthetical competency for a wide range of historical leaders, from Alexander the Great to Mahatma Gandhi. Such reflections were designed to underscore and illustrate a foundational issue for this essay borrowed from David Tracy, namely, that art and the other elements of culture are important and powerful resources for critiquing, affirming, and otherwise raising value questions in that realm of society concerned with social justice and the use of power. This is an ability bishops need to exercise both outside and inside the Church.

A contemporary example of an episcopal leader who excelled in this area was the late Cardinal Joseph Bernardin (d. 1996). At the time of his death, the 68-year-old cardinal was recognized as a clarion moral voice in U.S. society. His moral authority, recognized by civic and religious leaders alike, stemmed from an unusual combination of personal integrity, theological acuity, and a personal gracefulness that was at once persuasive and powerful. While he was a gifted behind-the-scenes negotiator, it is interesting that in recalling his life, it is often the symbolic moments and examples of leadership in aesthetic mode that are remembered. Virtually every obituary, for example, recalls his willingness to go to the White House and accept the Presidential Medal of Freedom from a president who supported partial-birth abortion. While roundly criticized by some, the ceremonial image of the frail cardinal standing with President Clinton, accepting the presidential medal while holding his moral ground—dignity untarnished—only served to enhance his ethical authority.

Examples abound of Cardinal Bernardin's ability to employ a whole range of cultural symbols in the exercise of his leadership in the civic realm, from ceremonies at the White House to visits to the cell of a death-row inmate. As for his religious leadership and ministry of governance *ad intra,* Cardinal Bernardin's ritual introduction to the clergy in the Archdiocese of Chicago stands as a paradigm. From all accounts, Bernardin was a collaborator who was assuming leadership in an archdiocese whose previous bishop was a legendary autocrat. In an unforgettable moment, the archbishop-designate signaled this seismic transition in leadership style and substance with a memorable aesthetic turn. On the night before he was to be installed as archbishop in 1982, Chicago's Holy Name Cathedral was filled with Chicago clergy who had been invited for Vespers. At the onset of that prayer, however, it was not the blare of trumpets or a blast from the organ that announced the arrival of the new archbishop; rather, it was Bernardin himself, carrying the paschal candle down the darkened nave, singing "Jesus Christ is the Light of the World," who not only ritually announced that a new era had begun but poetically inaugurated that new era.

Later in that service the aesthetic instinct was translated from ritual action to homiletic word. Shepherding in mystagogical mode, Bernardin closed his first homily to Chicago's legendarily independent clergy with these words:

As our lives and ministries are mingled together through the breaking of the Bread and the blessing of the Cup, I hope that long before my name falls from the Eucharistic Prayer in the silence of death you will know well who I am. You will know because we will work and play together, fast and pray together, mourn and rejoice together, despair and hope together, dispute and be reconciled together. You will know me as a friend, fellow priest, and bishop. You will know also that I love you. For I am Joseph, your brother![42]

I would contend that such shepherding in aesthetic mode was not only memorable but effective. Fourteen years later, when the archdiocesan clergy returned to Holy Name Cathedral to bid farewell to Cardinal Bernardin, it was clear that he had become their bishop not only in title but in commitment and affection. The grace that had marked his life came full circle, and a church—even a city—stood still one day for a final poetic adieu.

Conclusion

The intent of this essay has been to demonstrate both the usefulness of and necessity for Roman Catholic bishops to recognize and embrace an aesthetic mode of leadership. Toward that end we drew on the work of David Tracy to underscore the power of the aesthetical for shaping religion as well as the public good, to lay bare the power of the art, and to hypothesize about the Catholic imagination as analogical and artistically tuned. The work of Mary Catherine Hilkert both supported Tracy's basic insights and expanded them in terms of praxis, imagination, and spirituality. Andrew Greeley's sociological reflections were employed to give empirical support to these ministerial and theological reflections. Considering the power of the aesthetic mode of leadership outside the Church, finally, led to reflections on how this could be an appropriate prism for thinking about the key episcopal functions of teaching, sanctifying, and governing.

What is being promoted here is religious leadership that demonstrates clear symbolic competency[43] without any appearance of cultural elitism or aesthetic snobbery. This is not evangelization *for* the

---

42. *The Selected Works of Joseph Cardinal Bernardin*, vol. 1: *Homilies and Teaching Documents*, ed. Alphonse P. Spilly (Collegeville, Minn.: The Liturgical Press, 2000) 288.

43. I am indebted to Regis Duffy for this language; see his "Sacraments in General" in *Systematic Theology: Roman Catholic Perspectives*, ed. Francis Fiorenza and John Galvin (Minneapolis: Fortress Press, 1991) 207–208.

fine arts, but evangelization through the range of arts, crafts, poetry, and symbols that "moves people's hearts to God." The ability to exercise such leadership would, by definition, seem to eschew any narrow predisposition favoring one art form or the crafts of a single class, age, or culture over another.

While not specifically addressing Church leaders, Frank Burch Brown offers a helpful frame for thinking about aesthetic competency in this way when he speaks of "ecumenical taste" as a way to be both inclusive and discriminating, generous and exacting.

> The goal of ecumenical taste is not necessarily to enjoy, personally, the arts and worship styles favored by various other people and groups. . . . The great and more useful goal is to try to perceive for oneself what others are perceiving in forms of art and worship that one finds alien; to go on to enjoy their enjoyment (without necessarily liking what they enjoy); and eventually to appraise provisionally those more "alien" tastes in relation to the arts and worship styles one finds more congenial.[44]

The first important stage in exercising "ecumenical taste" clearly seems to be one of attending, listening, observing, and respecting rather than moving too quickly to aesthetic critique. James and Evelyn Whitehead stress the same point in their classic work on ministerial method, cautioning for the need to "suspend judgment" until sufficient "attending" and "asserting" have been achieved.[45] To be effective leaders in aesthetic mode, therefore, bishops have to be participant-observers of those cultural, poetic, and artistic symbols that move the hearts of the Catholic faithful and all people of good will.

If there is to be any aesthetical prejudice at all in our episcopal leaders, maybe it is for the beauty found in difference. Alejandro García-Rivera makes this a singular agenda in *The Community of the Beautiful*, when he defines his reflections as "a search for a theology that does justice to the authenticity and originality of the Latin Church of the Americas found in the signs and symbols of its popular religion yet also discloses which of these signs and symbols are transformative and redemptive."[46] As he brings his aesthetic reflections to a close, García-Rivera turns to a principle, embedded in the *Magnifi-*

44. Frank Burch Brown, *Good Taste, Bad Taste, and Christian Taste: Aesthetics in Religious Life* (Oxford: University Press, 2000) 192–193.

45. James and Evelyn Whitehead, *Method in Ministry*, rev. ed. (Kansas City: Sheed & Ward, 1995), esp. 13–17.

46. García-Rivera, *The Community of the Beautiful*, 61.

cat, of "lifting up the lowly." In this principle the experience of divine Beauty is wed to a vision of justice.[47] This is not beauty for beauty's sake, but beauty that moves the human heart to God by embracing the other, particularly the other who dialectically reflects God's difference from the world in their own difference from me.

Nathan Mitchell makes the point more bluntly. He writes, "Secretly, many of us believe that God loves the poor, but hates their art. Surely, we suspect, God prefers Mozart to Randy Travis."[48] The leadership challenge in aesthetic mode for most U.S. bishops will probably not be in teaching or sanctifying or governing through Mozartian symbol, but in establishing common ground with that larger number of Americans whose hearts are moved to God and one another through Randy Travis. The pilgrimage into the poetic, therefore, requires not only a commitment to lead others analogically but also a willingness to be self-transformed in the crucible of another's art. It is certainly a great deal to ask of church leaders, but the People of God deserve no less.

47. Ibid., 194.
48. Nathan Mitchell, "Amen Corner," *Worship* 70:3 (1996) 258.

Epilogue

"And a Little Child Shall Lead Them"

David A. Stosur

The wolf shall live with the lamb,
  the leopard shall lie down with the kid,
the calf and the lion and the fatling together,
  and a little child shall lead them (Isa 11:6).[1]

At that time the disciples came to Jesus and asked, "Who is the greatest in the kingdom of heaven?" He called a child, whom he put among them, and said, "Truly I tell you, unless you change and become like little children, you will never enter the kingdom of heaven. Whoever becomes humble like this child is the greatest in the kingdom of heaven. Whoever welcomes one such child in my name welcomes me. If any of you put a stumbling block before one of these little ones who believe in me, it would be better for you if a great millstone were fastened around your neck and you were drowned in the depth of the sea. Woe to the world because of stumbling blocks! . . . Take care that you do not despise one of these little ones; for, I tell you, their angels continually see the face of my Father in heaven" (Matt 18:1-7, 10).

In the wake of the terrorist attacks on September 11, 2001, and in the midst of the public attention since early 2002 drawn to the scandal of the sexual abuse of children by Roman Catholic clergy in the United States and elsewhere, it seems imperative that a collection of essays on the contemporary Roman Catholic episcopate include some remarks on how these events are coming to shape the status and role of the bishop

---

1. All quotations from Scripture are from the New Revised Standard Version (NRSV).

today.[2] Because the preceding essays were written, for all practical purposes, prior to these occurrences, and because we are still living so very much in their aftermath, I offer in this Epilogue a brief proposal for a future theological direction in consideration of the episcopate. The question I wish to pose is this: What light might be shed on the contemporary episcopacy by a thoroughgoing theology of childhood that honors and values the place of the child in the Church and the role of children as a genuine theological, pastoral, and global human resource?[3]

2. "Status" and "role" are chosen here as terms that attempt to remain neutral with respect to the present debate over the "ontological" versus the "functional" views of priesthood (and therefore of the fullness of priesthood, the episcopate) held in some theological quarters. One who holds an extreme "ontologistic" view might claim that the status of the bishop "in reality" remains unchanged by such earthly events. Statements like the following might be taken in support of such a view: "Apostolic succession is not only physical and linked to time; it is also ontological and spiritual, because of the grace of episcopal ordination," and "Because of his continual union with the *person of Christ*, the true image of the Father and manifestation of his presence and mercy, the Bishop, as head and spouse of the Church entrusted to him, also becomes the living sign of Jesus Christ through the grace of the sacrament. . . . the Bishop receives at his ordination the fullness of the *anointing of the Holy Spirit* who descended on the disciples at Pentecost, the Spirit of the High Priest who interiorly equips him, configuring him to Christ, so that he can be the living continuation of his mystery for the sake of his Mystical Body." Synod of Bishops, Tenth Ordinary General Assembly, *The Bishop: Servant of the Gospel of Jesus Christ for the Hope of the World—Instrumentum Laboris* (Vatican City: General Secretariat of the Synod of Bishops and Libreria Editrice Vaticana, 2001), nos. 38 and 40, respectively; available from http://www.vatican.va/roman_curia/synod/documents/rc_synod_doc_20010601_instrumentum-laboris_en.html; Internet; accessed 23 October 2002.

I would argue that any viable communion ecclesiology precludes the pitting of ontology against function, or even the attempt to make ontology prior to function. Put differently, a relational ontology, that is, one that understands the category of relation as intrinsic rather than extrinsic to the fundamentally real (and hence to identity), regards functional relations as essential. One *is*, always to some extent, what one *does*, and vice versa. See John Macmurray, *Persons in Relation* (London: Faber and Faber, 1961), and Harold H. Oliver, *A Relational Metaphysic*, Studies in Philosophy and Religion 4 (The Hague: Martinus Nijhoff Publishers, 1981).

3. On the theology of childhood, see the very fine collection of historically arranged essays in Marcia J. Bunge, ed., *The Child in Christian Thought* (Grand Rapids, Mich., and Cambridge, U.K.: Wm. B. Eerdmans, 2001). While the essays dealing with pre-Reformation theologians (chs. 1–4), the essay by Clarissa W. Atkinson on seventeenth-century missionaries to New France (ch. 8), and in particular the essay by Mary Ann Hinsdale discussing Karl Rahner's reflections on childhood (ch. 16) may have the most direct relevance to the Roman Catholic context, reflections on childhood from theologians of Christian traditions beyond Roman Catholicism should not be overlooked, given that the source of intimate understanding of children for these traditions is the lived experience of parenthood by so many of its ministers—a source generally unavailable to Roman Catholic priests and bishops (who until recent generations have represented, and to a large extent still do represent, the primary pool from which Roman Catholic theologians have been drawn).

The quotations from Isaiah and Matthew above are chosen to suggest some lines of thinking about the post-September 11th and the present abuse-crisis contexts in which the bishop of today finds himself. It goes without saying that these passages cast judgment on both of the tragedies that these contemporary circumstances represent. The contrast of 9-11's terror and ensuing war with Isaiah 11's prophetic and eschatological depiction of peace could hardly be more manifest. What is remarkable, perhaps, is the idea that the vision of peace to which the whole of creation is called is described as coming through the leadership of a little child. Can the episcopate learn something by following the child's lead? The contrast in Matthew 18 of the true greatness of a child's humility with the woefulness of those who would despise and abuse the little ones could not be clearer. What is remarkable, perhaps, is the idea that in offering genuine hospitality to the child one welcomes Christ himself.[4] Can the episcopate learn something about authentic leadership by hospitably opening itself to the true humanity revealed in the humbleness of a child?[5]

The line of thought I am suggesting runs like this. Clergy sexual abuse of children, along with the deplorable response of many bishops in shuffling offenders from parish to parish, is at the far negative end of a spectrum representing clerical valuation of children in the Church, with the projected positive end exemplified in Gospel depictions of Jesus welcoming, blessing and raising up children as examples of humility,

---

4. The linguistic and conceptual resonance with the judgment passage in Matthew (25:31-46) should not be overlooked: "And the king will answer them, 'Truly I tell you, just as you did it to the least of these who are members of my family, you did it to me'" (v. 40). One could make the claim that the children ("little ones," *tōn mikrōn*) in Matthew 18:10 is a preeminent example of "the least" (*tōn elachistōn*, the superlative of *mikrōn*) in Matthew 25:40. In both chapters 18 and 25, it is not only the ethical injunction to provide hospitality and care for the "little ones" but also the fact that these little ones represent Jesus himself that is so striking. Cross-references between these chapters are made, for example, in Robert H. Gundry, *Matthew: A Commentary on His Literary and Theological Art* (Grand Rapids, Mich.: Wm. B. Eerdmans, 1982) 361 and 514; in John R. Donahue, "The 'Parable' of the Sheep and the Goats: A Challenge to Christian Ethics," *Theological Studies* 47 (1986) 3–31, at 25; and in Daniel J. Harrington, *The Gospel of Matthew*, Sacra Pagina 1 (Collegeville, Minn.: The Liturgical Press, 1991) 264.

5. Apropos of a consideration of authentic hospitality is Rosemary Luling Haughton's analysis of the distinction between *charity* (in the contemporary socioeconomic rather than the theological sense of the term), which "assumes that structures need no change but only modification," and *hospitality*, which "proposes an entirely different political and moral structure for human living." *Images for Change: The Transformation of Society* (New York/Mahwah, N.J.: Paulist Press, 1997) 133.

dependence and trust.[6] Exactly where along this spectrum bishops' average estimation of children presently falls is certainly a point for debate. As a liturgical theologian, seminary dean, and parent of two young children, however, I would judge that the location is regrettably not far enough on the positive side. Bishops on the whole do not spend much time relating to children and consequently display little understanding of them and lack of attention to their pastoral needs. Granted, a similar charge may be leveled at contemporary society in general. In order to be *leaders* of the Church, however, which claims *to offer society an example* of how to seek the way of peace (contra 9-11 terrorism and post–9-11 warmongering), bishops must develop their leadership in ways that honor and value children (and other "least ones") as spiritual models in whom Christ himself is represented. So an important issue becomes just how and where such valuing of children might take place.

The following reflections regarding the need for greater episcopal care for and attention to children are offered in terms of the threefold office of the episcopate: teaching, sanctifying, and governing, reflected in the threefold christic functions of prophet, priest, and king (along with "shepherd"). Under each of the three aspects I consider an example of how episcopal leadership has given children short shrift, and propose that a deeper appreciation on the part of bishops for children's value in and for the Church may strengthen the episcopate. Since the liturgical area is where I am the surest, I begin there.

Sanctifying: The Priestly Function

> Christ, indeed, always truly associates the church with himself in this great work in which God is perfectly glorified and men and women are sanctified. The church is his beloved bride who calls to its Lord, and through him offers worship to the eternal Father.
>
> The liturgy, then, is rightly seen as an exercise of the priestly office of Jesus Christ. In the liturgy the sanctification of women and men is given expression in symbols perceptible by the senses and is carried out in ways appropriate to each of them. In it, complete and definitive public worship is performed by the mystical body of Jesus Christ, that is, by the Head and his members.
>
> From this it follows that every liturgical celebration, because it is an action of Christ the priest and of his body, which is the church, is a preeminently sacred action (SC 7).

6. See Judith M. Gundry-Volf, "The Least and the Greatest: Children in the New Testament," in Bunge, ed., *The Child in Christian Thought,* 29–60.

It is very much the wish of the church that *all* the faithful should be led to take that full, conscious, and active part in liturgical celebrations which is demanded by the very nature of the liturgy, and to which the Christian people, "a chosen race, a royal priesthood, a holy nation, a redeemed people" (1 Pet 2:9; see 2:4-5) have a right and to which they are bound by reason of their *Baptism.*

In the restoration and development of the sacred liturgy the full and active participation by all the people is the paramount concern, for it is the primary, indispensable source from which the faithful are to derive the true Christian spirit (SC 14, emphasis added).

An essential area in which bishops could lead the Church toward holding children in higher esteem is that of a more profound respect for children's baptismal identity and dignity. Many bishops themselves may be unaware of some significant details in the historical "dissolution" of the rites of Christian initiation that led, in many cases accidentally, to the separation and re-sequencing of initiatory rituals into separate (and in the popular view, *disparate*) sacraments in the Western Church. One thinks of such developments as withholding the eucharistic bread from infants out of fear of their spitting up consecrated particles, leaving them only with wine—until withholding the cup from the laity as a whole ended young children's reception of Communion altogether; or of our modern presupposition that confirmation primarily reflects the teenager's free acceptance of the faith given to her at baptism, as opposed to the actual origins of the separation having to do rather with the bishop's availability, in a geographically expanding Christendom, to confirm the *presbyter's* baptizing of the infant.[7]

The typical present pattern of initiation of very young children follows the sequence: infant baptism; second-grade first Communion, *preceded* by first reconciliation (now part of the "initiatory" sequence); and confirmation sometime between pre- and late adolescence. From

7. See Nathan D. Mitchell, "Dissolution of the Rite of Christian Initiation," in The Murphy Center for Liturgical Research, *Made, Not Born: Perspectives on Christian Initiation and the Catechumenate* (Notre Dame, Ind., and London: Notre Dame University Press, 1976). For an extended and well-documented discussion of developments throughout Christian history in the sequence and age of reception of the sacraments of initiation, see Paul Turner, *The Ages of Initiation: The First Two Christian Millennia* (Collegeville, Minn.: The Liturgical Press, 2000). For an application of Karl Rahner's theological reflections on childhood ["Ideas for a Theology of Childhood," *Theological Investigations*, vol. 8, trans. David Bourke (London: Darton, Longman & Todd, and New York: Herder and Herder, 1971) 33–50] to post-Vatican II initiatory practices with children, see Nathan Mitchell, "The Once and Future Child: Towards a Theology of Childhood," *The Living Light* 12 (1975) 423–437.

the perspective of a child, and of the Rite of Christian Initiation of Adults, children are "partially" initiated as babies, then immediately excommunicated (presumably for not being old enough to understand the grace of God in the Eucharist—as if adults can truly comprehend this mystery!), then reconciled to the Church in order to be "made worthy" for Communion (just what understanding of the "grace" of Eucharist is being presented and appropriated?). Eventually, some years later, the bishop himself (or his delegate) is personally involved, celebrating with teenagers the ostensible "completion" of initiation. (Theologically, of course, Eucharist is the completion and ongoing, "repeatable" part of initiation.)

The possibility of bringing theological coherence to these sacraments is further complicated by the pastoral need for catechetical preparation and the varying local "traditions" of age requirements and corresponding catechetical programming. Few bishops, pastors or religious educators are willing publicly to admit that holding off on sacraments until a later age is actually viewed rather pragmatically, as a major motivation for children and their parents to stay involved and receive catechesis in the Church for as long as possible.

But what if bishops took seriously the statement in *Sacrosanctum Concilium* 14 that "*all* the faithful should be led to take that full, conscious, and active part in liturgical celebrations which is demanded by the very nature of the liturgy, and to which the Christian people . . . have a right and to which they are bound by reason of their *Baptism*"? Imagine the message bishops would be sending about both the value of our children and the value of baptism if, following the continuous practice of the Eastern Churches and like many denominations in the West, full initiation of infants and children, with regular and frequent Communion even of these "least ones," were restored in the Roman Catholic Church. Imagine the potential benefit to the quality of catechesis in general and of liturgical and sacramental catechesis in particular if bishops, pastors, and religious educators could catechize from the experience of frequent eucharistic reception as something that has already penetrated to the bone in a child's most formative years. Imagine how the liturgy as "an exercise of the priestly office of Jesus Christ" (SC 7) can be enhanced and deepened for all the faithful by full inclusion of those in whom we welcome Christ himself *(in persona Christi)* and whose "angels continually see the face of [his] Father in heaven."

Teaching: The Prophetic Function

> The blind and the lame came to him in the temple, and he cured them. But when the chief priests and the scribes saw the amazing things that he did, and heard the children crying out in the temple, "Hosanna to the Son of David," they became angry and said to him, "Do you hear what these are saying?" Jesus said to them, "Yes, have you never read, 'Out of the mouths of infants and nursing babies you have prepared praise for yourself'?" (Matt 21:14-16).

The section of the *instrumentum laboris* of the 2001 Synod of Bishops dedicated to the teaching and preaching function of the bishop begins by focusing on the uniqueness of the bishop's magisterial role and mentions the need for bishops to engage in collaborative dialogue with theologians and with all the faithful. Children and parents are mentioned in no. 105:

> The Bishops ensure that the authentic Catholic faith is transmitted to parents so that they, in turn, can pass it on to their children. Teachers and educators at all levels also assist in this process. The laity bear witness to that purity of faith which Bishops take pains to maintain. It is important that each Bishop endeavor to provide the laity with the means for a suitable formation through centers set up for this purpose.

Not surprisingly, children are seen in this Roman document as the recipients, through the medium of parents and others, of the bishops' teaching, in a transmission of faith that is one-directional. There is no possibility envisioned that the bishops might learn something of the faith *from* children. What might go unnoticed, however, especially in light of such section titles as "Dialogue and Collaboration with Theologians and the Faithful," is the fact that bishops are not depicted as having anything to learn about faith from *anyone*.[8] The only reference even to the possibility that a bishop actually has something to learn at all is in no. 107, which seems to say that while lack of knowledge may be an impediment to teaching "in the temporal order," the bishop's authority is in another realm and is not based on such knowledge:

> Called to proclaim salvation in Jesus Christ, the Bishop in his preaching is a sign of certainty of the faith for the People of God. If he, like the

---

8. No. 106 speaks of the bishops giving support and encouragement to theologians, who, along with "the magisterium of Pastors . . . have the same goal of conserving the People of God in truth." As for dialogue with the faithful, this is a means by which bishops can "[come] to know how to recognize and appreciate their [i.e., the faithful's] faith, to strengthen it, to free it from anything superficial and to give it proper doctrinal content."

Church, does not always have at hand the solution to people's problems, nevertheless, he is the minister of the splendor of the one truth which is capable of illuminating the path to follow.[9] Even though he does not possess specialized knowledge in promoting the temporal order, the Bishop, in exercising his teaching office and educating in the faith the persons and communities entrusted to him, prepares the faithful, nonetheless, through solutions which the Bishops have the responsibility to offer in keeping with their respective abilities.

This "top-down" depiction of the teaching office of the bishop resonates strikingly with what Paulo Freire calls the "banking concept of education," wherein education is considered "an act of depositing, in which the students are the depositories and the teacher is the depositor. Instead of communicating, the teacher issues communiqués and makes deposits which the students patiently receive, memorize, and repeat."[10] Freire lists the following "attitudes and practices" of this concept:

a) the teacher teaches and the students are taught;

b) the teacher knows everything and the students know nothing;

c) the teacher thinks and the students are thought about;

d) the teacher talks and the students listen—meekly;

e) the teacher disciplines and the students are disciplined;

f) the teacher chooses and enforces his choice, and the students comply;

g) the teacher acts and the students have the illusion of acting through the action of the teacher;

h) the teacher chooses the program content, and the students (who were not consulted) adapt to it;

i) the teacher confuses the authority of knowledge with his own professional authority, which he sets in opposition to the freedom of the students;

j) the teacher is the Subject of the learning process, while the pupils are mere objects.[11]

Insofar as the view of the bishops' teaching found in the *instrumentorum laboris* is indeed uni-directional, the question arises as to whether its understanding of education in the faith is too securely

---

9. The document here cites, in no. 158, the Congregation for the Doctrine of the Faith, Instruction on the Vocation of Church Theologians *Donum veritatis* (24 May 1990) no. 21: *AAS* 82 (1990) 1559.

10. Paolo Freire, *Pedagogy of the Oppressed*, trans. Myra Bergman Ramos (New York: Continuum, 1990) 58.

11. Ibid., 59.

locked into the "banking" concept (one need only think of the phrase *depositum fidei*, "deposit of faith").[12]

To the extent that the catechetical image needs to move from securities to exchange, Judith Gundry-Volf, commenting on Matthew 21:14-16, observes:

> In the gospel tradition, children are not mere ignoramuses in terms of spiritual insight. They know Jesus' true identity. They praise him as the Son of David. They have this knowledge from God and not from themselves, and because they do, they are living manifestos that God is the source of all true knowledge about Christ. Jesus' affirmation of the children's praise of him in this pericope is thus an affirmation that children who 'know nothing' can also 'know divine secrets' and believe in him.[13]

It is children's lively relationship with God so simply assumed ("their angels continually see the face of my Father in heaven") and so readily proclaimed that allows the little ones to teach the adults—the religious leaders in particular—that Jesus is the Christ. The doxological aspect of this pericope reinforces the previous point about children's priestly role: to welcome children is to welcome Christ himself. To glorify God in Christ is an expression of gratitude and joy for God's first making us holy, and children's nearness to God and readiness to praise him offer a mystagogical path often experienced but less often acknowledged by parents and rarely experienced by Roman Catholic clergy.[14]

On the contrary, one detects an unspoken denial of children's ability to offer anything to the assembly gathered to hear the Word in practices like the dismissal of children for a separate Liturgy of the

12. In her article "'Infinite Openness to the Infinite': Karl Rahner's Contribution to Catholic Thought on the Child," in Bunge, ed., *The Child in Christian Thought*, 406–445, Mary Ann Hinsdale offers the example of one bishop who understood eighty years ago how counterproductive the banking concept of education was for catechesis: "In France, Bishop Ladrieux, the bishop of Dijon, wrote a pastoral letter in 1922 that became a kind of manifesto for catechetical renewal there. He observed wryly that 'instead of going in directly by the open doors of the child's imagination and sense perception, we waste our time knocking on the still bolted doors of his understanding and his judgment'" [434, citing in note 95 P. Ranwez, as cited in *Shaping the Christian Message: Essays in Religious Education*, ed. Gerard S. Sloyan (Glen Rock, N.J.: Paulist Press, 1963) 120].

13. Gundry-Volf, "The Least and the Greatest," 47–48. See the prayer of Jesus in Matthew 11:25ff.: "I thank you, Father, Lord of heaven and earth, because you have hidden these things from the wise and intelligent and have revealed them to infants . . . ."

14. See the chapters on the liturgy's "playfulness" and "seriousness" in Romano Guardini's dated (1918, in the original German edition) but still inspiring classic *The Spirit of the Liturgy* (London: Sheed & Ward, 1930; repr. New York: Crossroad, 1998) 61–84.

Word "at their own level,"[15] a practice gaining in popularity and thus far going so unchecked by bishops as to appear to have their endorsement. Here the prevailing attitude of liturgical preaching buys into the "banking" concept—children being too young to open an account, or at best permitted only to receive small change. Imagine if we were to take seriously Jesus' injunction that "unless you change and become like children, you will never enter the kingdom of heaven" (Matt 18:3). Not only would their value as models for the assembly be such that we wouldn't want them to leave, but preachers would look to children as mystagogues whose natural love for God and unbridled recognition of Christ could guide their own teaching and preaching.

Governing: The Kingly (or "Shepherding") Function

> People were bringing little children to him in order that he might touch them; and the disciples spoke sternly to them. But when Jesus saw this, he was indignant and said to them, "Let the little children come to me; do not stop them; for it is to such as these that the kingdom of God belongs. Truly I tell you, whoever does not receive the kingdom of God as a little child will never enter it." And he took them up in his arms, laid his hands on them, and blessed them (Mark 10:13-16).

This third office of the bishop is perhaps the most difficult to view from the perspective of the child. This is partly due to the fact that the metaphor of "shepherd" is utilized not only for this third function of the episcopal office but also for the unity of the three diverse functions, and to the fact that prior to Vatican II the typical distinction was not threefold (sanctifying, teaching, and governing) but twofold (power of orders and power of jurisdiction), as David Coffey has pointed out.[16] This complicated state of affairs is a useful reminder of the metaphorical nature of this language, not only in terms of the limit that the de-

---

15. For more extended critiques of the practice of separate children's Liturgy of the Word, see my articles "'Children Go'? Children's Liturgy of the Word and the Sunday Assembly," in *Prayer and Worship Newsletter* [Archdiocese of Milwaukee] (Summer 1997) 1–3; reprinted in *Emmanuel* 105/5 (June 1999) 276–281, and in *AIM: Liturgy Resources* 28/3 (Fall 1999) 20–22, and "Children at Table, Part I: The Table of the Word," in *TLC: Today's Liturgy with Children* (Winter 2002) 3–4. It is worth noting that the Directory for Masses with Children (no. 17; quoted also in the Introduction to the Lectionary for Masses with Children, no. 7), understands this practice to be occasional and conditional: "*Sometimes*, moreover, *if* the place itself and the nature of the community permit, it will be appropriate to celebrate the liturgy of the word, including a homily, with the children in a separate, but not too distant, room" (emphasis added).

16. See pp. 5–6 above.

piction "priest, prophet, and king" has for positively describing the office of bishop, but even more in terms of the primary christological referent and therefore only secondary application to the Church as a whole and to the episcopate in particular: Jesus the Christ, *the* Good Shepherd, is the *one* true priest, the *one* true prophet, and the *one* true king, who ushers in a new age that makes the former understanding of these roles obsolete and any subsequent designation of these functions to anyone else radically relative.[17]

It comes as no surprise that children are not given governing roles in the Church,[18] as they are not given such roles in any social institution (with a few exceptions like grade school student council representative or sports team captain, which nonetheless remain under adult control and supervision). But the sociological fact that children are not given powers of jurisdiction is precisely what makes Jesus' statement about the reign of God so radical: the kingdom *belongs* to them. Anyone claiming to share in Christ's kingship—a sharing that is *reception* and *not control of a portion* of the kingdom—cannot even enter unless he or she receives it as a little child. This reign is an eschatological one, better reflected in the openness of a child than in the power of a ruler.

The eschatological nature of this true "kingship"—what makes the baptized adult or child a member of the "royal priesthood" (1 Pet 2:9)—resonates in particular with children. Nathan Mitchell, taking up Karl Rahner's thoughts on the significance of childhood, puts it this way:

> [C]hildhood is a kind of sacramental mystery whose meaning is fully explored only when as adults we meet once again the childhood that springs freshly recreated from the hands of the God who is our future. Children are part of the baptismal community not because they are potential adults who will (we hope) "keep the church running" in the decades ahead. No. Children are introduced into the baptismal community because they reveal what that community's ultimate destiny and goal is. Understood in this way the baptism of children is neither a concession to human sentiment nor a concession to Augustine's fears about the dismal fate of those who die unbaptized. Children are baptized because in them the church meets its future—future in the sense of openness, expectation and readiness

---

17. See Robert Taft, "Toward a Theology of the Christian Feast," in *Beyond East and West: Problems in Liturgical Understanding* (Washington: Pastoral Press, 1984) 1–13.

18. For an overview of another aspect of governance concerning children, see Michael Smith Foster, "The Promotion of the Canonical Rights of Children," in *Proceedings of the Canon Law Society of America* 59 (1997) 163–202.

to surrender to the God who called us before we were born. That is the future Christians aim for, the future that meets us whenever, as adults, we hand ourselves over unconditionally in love and faith to the mystery of God.[19]

Whether the governing function of the bishop is related to the image of "king" or "shepherd," then, it is the eschatological reality, manifested in the span of a human life that begins in childhood and recapitulates childhood as its final destiny, which is essentially signified. The governing function of the bishop is to shepherd on the model of the Good Shepherd, who holds up the little child as the one who can shepherd us to the place where the wolf shall live with the lamb— the paradigm of eschatological governance.

Conclusion

David Coffey's essay that opens this collection pointed out that although priesthood, prophethood, and kingship "are distinct at the level of function, any one of them can be selected for investment with a deeper, unifying meaning at the level of office. . . . [T]here is nothing absolute about this: it may be done equally with any of the three to give the desired emphasis."[20] From the perspective of a theology of childhood, the prophetic function, with its eschatological orientation, "governs" the priestly and kingly functions: Christian hierarchy ("rule of priests") is so derivative of Christian monarchy ("rule of one," i.e., of Christ) that any ordinary sense of hierarchy or monarchy is overturned. All prophethood, all priesthood, and all kingship are related to and derived from Christ himself. In his Body, the Church, leadership is humble leadership, leadership in the way of peace, leadership in service to the "least ones." Parenthood (in the full, not merely biological, sense) is the primary way in which adults have ready and ongoing engagement with the world of children, and perhaps some day Roman Catholic bishops will be given access to this world as fathers (and mothers!) of their own children. All adults, however, carry the *anamnesis* of childhood throughout their lives. In the words of Nathan Mitchell, mature adulthood depends on our ability "to meet and affirm our childhood as not only 'past history' but also 'present experience' and 'future becoming' . . . allowing childhood to be released in us not as a fond or bitter mem-

19. Mitchell, "The Once and Future Child," 432.
20. See p. 8 above.

ory but as a facet of what we are and hope to become."[21] Members of the episcopate, in concert with parents and other adults, must become hospitable to the presence of Christ that children can mediate, to the humble lessons that children can teach, and to the leadership into the peaceable kingdom that children can provide. If bishops are to lead the Church, they owe no less than this to victims of abuse and to victims of terror and war—in the end, to all God's children.

21. Mitchell, "The Once and Future Child," 427.